Gravity's Rainbow, Domination, and Freedom

EST. 75 1938
YEARS
THE UNIVERSITY OF GEORGIA PRESS 2013

$30.45

Gravity's Rainbow, Domination, and Freedom

Luc Herman and Steven Weisenburger

THE UNIVERSITY OF GEORGIA PRESS

Athens and London

© 2013 by the University of Georgia Press
Athens, Georgia 30602
www.ugapress.org
All rights reserved
Set in Sabon and Futura by Graphic Composition, Inc.
Printed and bound by Thomson-Shore
The paper in this book meets the guidelines for
permanence and durability of the Committee on
Production Guidelines for Book Longevity of the
Council on Library Resources.

Printed in the United States of America
17 16 15 14 13 P 5 4 3 2 1

Library of Congress Cataloging-in-Publication Data

Herman, Luc.
Gravity's Rainbow, domination, and freedom / Luc Herman and
Steven Weisenburger.
      pages cm
Includes bibliographical references and index.
ISBN 978-0-8203-3508-7 (hardcover : alk. paper) —
ISBN 0-8203-3508-8 (hardcover : alk. paper) —
ISBN 978-0-8203-4595-6 (pbk. : alk. paper) —
ISBN 0-8203-4595-4 (pbk. : alk. paper)
      1. Pynchon, Thomas. Gravity's rainbow. I. Weisenburger, Steven. II. Title.
PS3566.Y55G73455 2013
813'.54—dc23   2013015147

British Library Cataloging-in-Publication Data available

Contents

Acknowledgments

The concept and argument for this book took shape during our joint 2009 fellowship at the Flemish Academic Centre for Science and the Arts in Brussels. Without the center's generous support and collegial environment, no amount of transatlantic emailing or Skype calling would have gotten us here. At the center, Marc Demay, Inez Dua, and Chris Brossé provided thoughtful and kind encouragement and assistance—and daily coffee! Also in Brussels, at the Royal Library's Center for American Studies, Myriam Lodeweyckx provided access to and guidance through the center's holdings. Southern Methodist University provided a research leave, enabling Steve's residency at the Royal Academy, while the Jacob and Frances Mossiker Trust funded his travel to Europe and to American special collections libraries, without which we also would not have gotten the book done.

At the University of Texas, librarians at the Harry Ransom Center assisted our research in the Thomas Pynchon Collection and in their archived sixties-era underground press materials. Sue Hodson, curator at the Huntington Library in San Marino, California, assisted us during several visits for work with the Stephen Michael Tomaske Collection of Pynchon-related materials; Luc, in particular, is grateful for the Huntington fellowship that enabled his stay in April 2011. Staff at the University of California's Bancroft Library assisted our research in their archive of sixties-era small press and free speech movement materials.

Portions of this book were adapted from previously published essays in *Texas Studies in Literature and Language* (34.1, 1992), *Pynchon Notes* (34–35, 1994; and 56–57, 2009); and *Revista di Studi Anglo-Americani* 8.10 (1994), and from the commemorative collection *Sans Everything* (2004). Other portions were field-tested before savvy audiences at the University of Antwerp and at International Pynchon Week conferences, and we are grateful for their questions and suggestions.

Editor Nancy Grayson of the University of Georgia Press helped get this book under contract in 2009, then waited patiently until we delivered the manuscript three years later—as she stood on the threshold of retirement. We owe Nancy great thanks, and trust that her travels are going splendidly. For their expert peer reviews of our manuscript, we are especially grateful to

David Cowart and John Krafft, who provided detailed suggestions and useful critiques. John, for decades the dean of Pynchon studies, provided what may well be the greatest epic in the history of readers' reports—closely incisive and expansive in its corrections and critique—and David, also a long-time Pynchon and contemporary literature scholar, offered useful advice that helped us sharpen the book's argument at key points. Many thanks to both. We are also very grateful for the help of photographer Debora Hunter, who assisted with several of our images.

Gravity's Rainbow, Domination, and Freedom

Rue Rossini in Nice, France. Photo by Steven Weisenburger, 2012.

"What's Free?" (An Introduction)

His first free morning. He *doesn't* have to go back. Free? What's free?
— *Gravity's Rainbow*

When our main character ponders liberty one-third of the way into Thomas
Pynchon's great novel, Tyrone Slothrop doesn't ask *who* is free or *what* freedom is. Rather, he asks himself: What does the word "free" *mean*? He asks:
Does any thing, any being under the sun, exist any more in a "free" condition? At that moment in a rented room on the Rue Rossini in Nice, he is an
absent-without-leave American lieutenant, fleeing superiors who have employed and manipulated his mind and body in uniquely dominating ways.
Outside his room, the world war still ravages Europe in early 1945; if captured, he could lose his liberty or his life for desertion. Slothrop therefore has
profoundly compelling reasons to ask his questions. But in the next sentence
he "falls asleep." Our antihero characteristically lapses into the deadly sin of
sloth specified in his patronymic. Deadly because the act of being careless or
indifferent, what the church names *acedia*, severs access to whatever grace it
is, God's or Nature's, that is presently giving Slothrop access to a new life
and an appreciation of his free will, the issue attending seemingly every point
in his life's trajectory so far, and the issue which he abandons to sleep.[1]

In the snarled plot of *Gravity's Rainbow*, Slothrop has just fled Monaco
and Allied intelligence officers who, having contrived his Hollywood-style
"cute meet" and libidinous captivity with a lovely Dutch woman in their control, then cut off his easy escape by stealing Slothrop's uniform and identity
papers.[2] They launch him on a months-long crash course covering every shred
of paper Allied intelligence has gathered on Germany's v-2 rocket program.
Managing Slothrop's libido and his study is the Dutch woman, Katje Borgesius. She puts before Slothrop files on subfields such as liquid fuels and propul-
sion chambers and problems in the ballistics and guidance of supersonic missiles, as well as the complexities of governmental and corporate research and
development efforts. While working through this makeshift archive, Slothrop
stumbles upon a personal tie-in to a unique polymer sheeting, or skin, apparently developed for some mysterious version of the rocket and linked to
a polymath scientist, Professor Jamf, who had previously tested this tactilely

pleasing stuff to condition experimentally baby Tyrone's erectile reflex in a psych-lab experiment. Still worse, in exchange for such grossly unethical uses of a human subject, Jamf's lab had compensated the child's father, Broderick Slothrop (later dubbed "Pernicious Pop"), with a contract ensuring that Harvard University would give a free ride to "Infant Tyrone." Reading the documentary evidence at age twenty-seven in 1945, Slothrop recognizes that all he has experienced in his life as exercises of free will may in fact have been subject to apparatuses of surveillance, manipulation, and domination and, furthermore, that this chain presently binding his deepest memories—not indeed to pleasure but to fear and trauma—might also account for a recent and most uncanny symptomatology that had put him squarely on Their radars. Those v-2 rockets that began raining down on greater London in September 1944 seemed to strike the very sites where the lusty lieutenant had previously recorded his every sexual conquest of young Englishwomen, assigning to each her own colored star, pasted on a city map tacked to a beaverboard wall in the bureaucratic warren where Slothrop worked. Was the map accurate or a figment of his imagination? No matter: for military authorities and managers, soon made aware of the mystery, interpret each blast as another node in a serial unfolding of coitus and dying so consistent as to defy statisticians' probabilistic analyses and to beg instead for deterministic reasoning, for a causal order, or plotting, to explain the enigma—and to rationalize the enigma-within-the-enigma: for those authorities also conceived the apparent reversal or negation of cause and effect manifested on Slothrop's map as a phenomenon mimicked, or mocked, by how the v-2 travels faster than sound, its "screaming" uncannily *following* its deadly blast—an aural paradox known only to the surviving neighbors of the already ghostly dead.

The problem then is how to read (or naturalize) these "ultraparadoxical" phenomena. For example, was it antiwar partisans tasked by their bureaucratic hierarchy to investigate the enigma of Slothrop's sexual member who decided in the early stage of forming their resistance movement (the "Counterforce") to enable his flight from Monaco, thus enlisting the lieutenant and ironically casting him as the cautionary icon of novel, inhuman uses of human beings developing in late modernity? Or, alternately, might his "escape" have been plotted by a high-level managerial elite known colloquially in the novel as They, who may have sussed out the conspiracy to liberate Slothrop and either conspired on their own to make him run, or merely put surveillance on the nascent Counterforce that enabled his quasi-escape, the better thoroughly to track where this American's "Penis He Thought Was His Own" might, like a dowsing rod, take both him and the Counterforce around postwar Europe, perhaps locating for that elite's global military-industrial networks yet unknown but potentially applicable knowledge related to intercontinental ballistic missiles They will soon be mating to nuclear warheads, birthing the Cold War? In any case, They absolutely must track Slothrop's adventures. The American is so deeply yet naïvely connected to forces dedicated to integrating and controlling devices and bodies that the odds are he will scuffle his way into something valuable.

Such are the gnarly, many-faceted, forthrightly paranoid plots within plots within plots of *Gravity's Rainbow*. One of the novel's great ironies, however, is that Slothrop does *not* scuffle his way into anything finally important to Them. The arc of his story describes no great movement from enigma to answer; between those two poles the narration instead diddles tirelessly in *la comédie humaine*. Thus the novel composes, in Tony Tanner's words, "an exemplary experience in modern reading" because it keeps us amid "confusion."[3] We—Luc and Steve—understand the act of reading this novel as "confusion" in every sense: discomfort, blending, babel, argument, civil disorder, overthrow, and ruin. We know the ways critics have attempted to sort, coordinate, and stack elements and substructures of this narrative using the means of close reading and recent narrative theory. We've also reckoned with poststructuralist ways of unpacking or deconstructing the text that disclose instabilities inherent to its writing, and that are anticipated in the novel's figurations.[4] Making our own contributions to such enterprises over the years has brought us individually, then jointly, to realize the need for studies of this novel's "confusion" in terms of its major concerns—domination and freedom.

Hence this collaborative book. The two of us certainly delight in this novel's laugh-out-loud absurdities, elaborate jokes and hoaxes, slapstick humor, comical ditties, and quite outrageous (at times, gut-wrenching) sexual and political fantasies that would not have made it past editors, censors, police, or judges had Pynchon completed his manuscript fifteen or twenty years earlier than he did. We are mindful of the powers of play in Pynchon's dialogue of domination and freedom in *Gravity's Rainbow*. He produced some of the most outrageous and daring scenes of satirical representation known in twentieth-century fiction. And, as with all great satire, he could be deadly serious.

That dialogue of domination and freedom, satire and seriousness, consistently shaped Pynchon's work, beginning with the first published stories in 1959. And *Gravity's Rainbow* remains his master text. Four decades after its publication, the novel's enduring significance stands as a fact; it's the book that made "Pynchonian" a meaningful adjective and that defined—along with Toni Morrison's *Beloved* (1987)—a period in American literary history. In these chapters we argue that *Gravity's Rainbow*'s enduring significance arises from the ways that Pynchon's art turned the history of Nazi rocket craft into an imaginative critique of modernity's twin illiberal legacies: total war and totalitarian domination. The questions he asks about "the chances for freedom" in the age of late capitalism press as forcefully as ever on our ordinary lives.

We think those questions need to be better situated against the variably

defined "Long Sixties."[5] That epoch of American and global rights and resistance movements opened in the mid-fifties with the U.S. Supreme Court's
school desegregation ruling (1954), the 1956 Suez crisis, the bloody repression of anti-Soviet resistance in Hungary, and the defense of Allen Ginsberg's
"Howl" against obscenity charges. The epoch's early years also brought the
first stirrings of U.S. civil rights and antiwar activism; indeed, from Alge-
ria to Alabama and around the globe, the Long Sixties was an era of liberation and peace struggles. It closed in the mid-seventies with the release of
Gravity's Rainbow (February 1973), President Richard Nixon's impeachment
and resignation (1973–74), the collapse of U.S. military–backed regimes in
Southeast Asia (1975), and the unraveling of American antiwar and rights
movements, sidelining dissident and antiauthoritarian voices and presaging
the Reagan eighties. Moments and crises from that epoch also mark the historical settings and historicize the struggles of characters in two other Pynchon novels: *Vineland* (1990) and *Inherent Vice* (2009).

The historical present of *Gravity's Rainbow* is a nine-month stretch from
December 1944 to September 1945, with numerous elegantly scripted flash-
backs reaching into the seventeenth century and, at novel's end, a startling
leap forward to circa 1972. The novel makes no representation of the Long
Sixties. Yet that's when it was written. That epoch's radical contributions
to social theory and freedom of expression, its debates over a U.S. military-
industrial complex and over government secrecy and colonialist wars carried
on in the names of anti-Communism and liberation, its arguments over government manipulation of information (the 1964 Gulf of Tonkin incident, the
1971 Pentagon Papers incident), over civil rights in general and desegregation
in particular, are vital contexts for understanding *Gravity's Rainbow*. Pynchon
scholars have given only limited attention, we will argue, to Long Sixties polemical books by neo-Freudian thinkers like Erich Fromm, Herbert Marcuse,
and Norman O. Brown, in addition to the work of Hannah Arendt.[6] Regarding
the forms of domination and freedom, these works can be seen to frame the
novel's thematic terms and narrative outcomes in vital ways.

Equally significant are the ways Pynchon's narrative liberties—his artistic
uses of language formerly prosecuted for violating state and municipal laws
barring obscene, pornographic, or libelous expression—owe a great but untold debt to socially engaged writers and performers, free speech movement
activists, and committed underground press people. The *Gravity's Rainbow*
we know simply would not exist were it not for the persistently disruptive artistic expressions, courtroom defenses, and antics—not always triumphal—
of artists like poet Allen Ginsberg, novelist William Burroughs, comedian
Lenny Bruce, and poet-publisher-rock-singer Ed Sanders. Sanders, for example, secretively distributed from his New York apartment in the East Village thirteen issues of a mimeographed and hand-stapled 'zine, *Fuck You: A*

Magazine of the Arts, which appeared in irregular and limited runs (now exceedingly rare), each blazoning his motto—"Total Assault on the Culture." Like many other writer-activists, he spent a portion of his time and money defending his rights to free speech, assembly, and privacy against local and federal surveillance, searches, seizures, and court actions. Bruce, Burroughs, Sanders, and at times (particularly in "Howl") Ginsberg all mined veins of subversive satire, and the era they helped define is an understudied yet vital cultural-historical context for reading Pynchon's novel.

We think that recovering such neglected and forgotten contexts recasts one's sense of Pynchon's humor in *Gravity's Rainbow*. It's been far too easy for readers to lay those practices aside as just zany—a stoner's whimsy. At times, that is so. The prevailing mode of humor in *Gravity's Rainbow* turns, however, into a sharp and consistent social and political critique of the "military-industrial complex" President Dwight Eisenhower warned about in his January 1961 "Farewell Speech to the Nation." The novel mixes sex, drugs, and rocketry to develop a satirical fable fired back at the West's abiding, deathly legacy: perpetual war, and its creation of masses who if not actually dead are nonetheless socially dead, without rights and at times bluntly but more often subtly dominated by forms of soft power, a condition some characters in the novel have been persuaded perversely to desire.[7]

In Pynchon's storyworld the task of inculcating such desires goes to modern mass media—print, radio, and cinema. Their work is to make repression bearable, to present the simulacra of a tolerant, egalitarian society of free or even, when called to it, heroically free individuals, despite how alternate facts define a social order wholly committed to sustaining and spreading existing hierarchy and domination. Media *seem* to reify people's fantasies while merely peddling "mindless pleasures," the novel's working title as it went into production at Viking in late 1972.[8] Refashioned for purposes of narrative critique, mindless pleasures track through the novel from beginning to end, though some readers (particularly those unused to satire this dark) may scarcely realize their workings in scenes of (apparently just) whimsical fantasy.

In these introductory pages, we wedge a way into Pynchon's dense and difficult work by taking up some of those most off-the-wall—and therefore too easily dismissed and unstudied—scenes. We then work on the narrative's mainline—the rocketry, Slothrop's strange sojourn, and so forth—in the following three parts. Here, it will be useful to explore how the dialogue of domination and freedom operates in several of the novel's least likely moments, scenes of outlandish satirical fantasia too easily read as mere play, stoned mind-tripping, or pointless diversion. There may well be mind-tripping, but it is not pointless.

Our first instance is literally the way into *Gravity's Rainbow*—the novel's opening episodes. They introduce both the rocket and British captain Geoffrey "Pirate" Prentice, who one December morning sights an incoming missile's contrail lit up by the winter sun rising over the North Sea. These pages also figure both the v-2's auditory paradox, a sign of death, and Pirate's luscious, homegrown, rooftop hothouse bananas, which he transforms into luxurious breakfast *frappés* and *glacées* dished to housemates with bonhomie and art, each plate a sign of abundant life and proof that while "it is not often Death is told so clearly to fuck off," nonetheless it may be done, using imaginative powers like Pirate's. So the banana breakfast sets out a romantic view of free-spirited imagination and individual enterprise: how they persist and prevail even in civilization's darkest times.[9]

Gravity's Rainbow is, however, a post-romantic book, as the closing pages of episode 2 make clear. It turns out Captain Prentice's most vital work for "the Firm," beyond even his derring-do as a behind-enemy-lines "commando," spiriting spies in and out of places like war-torn Holland, involves the government's use of the man's unique powers as a "fantasist-surrogate." To explain: since all waking or sleeping moments of "mentally healthy leaders and other historical figures are indispensable" to the war effort, Pirate's duty is to have their mentally unhealthy fantasies *for* them. He relieves leaders of "running their exhausting little daydreams," deflects the "oncome of thoughts the doctors feel are inappropriate," assumes their mortal fears on the one hand and on the other will even "get their erections for them," thus extracting both Thanatos and Eros from their psyches and keeping the dear leaders in a semblance of balance.[10] So it was, we're told, that during the years before World War II he took on the grotesque nightmare of Lord Blatherard Osmo, chief of the "Novi Pazar desk at the Foreign Office" yet terrorized in his dreams by "*a giant Adenoid*. At least as big as St. Paul's [Cathedral]," "growing hour by hour" as, with the sound of "a stupendous *nose* sucking in snot," the adenoid "*assimilated*" each team sent to attack it with poisons, "deadly gas," electric jolts, bomb blasts. For two and a half long years Lord Osmo's nightmare burdened Prentice's mind. What finally pacifies the giant adenoid and saves the empire, or at least the London metropole, only piles more absurdity on what is already absurdly weird: someone trowels into the giant protoplasm great doses of "the new wonderdrug cocaine."[11]

What to make of the novel's fantasist-surrogate mind-trip? Of course it's a comically absurd pastiche of numerous 1950s monster movies in which new, anxiety-inducing science (typically, atomic testing) mutates small creatures—ants in *Them!* (1954), spiders in *Tarantula* (1955), even a bizarre mollusk in *The Monster That Challenged the World* (1957)—into city-wrecking, humanity-ending giants. Alternately, rocket science in the form of a spaceship returns to earth some alien protoplasm—*The Thing from Another World* (1951) or *The Blob* (1958)—which poses world-ending threats from which only an all-wise, benignly heroic science has the power to save humanity—the obvious ideological content of the "mindless pleasures." Their message: Not to worry, people! Good science will always trump evil science. Equally clear are the ways the adenoid episode figures Pirate the "fantasist-surrogate" as a stand-in for the writer-fantasist. Our novelist will have, perhaps exorcise, our unconscious nightmares for us—if we wish.[12] So this multifaceted trope—comical, critical, metafictional—not only signals to readers still standing in the novel's foyer that they will at times need to set aside expectations for a storytelling art working in strict obedience to the conventions of fictional realism, including the causal plotting that upholds the fiction of a strictly deterministic world of reason and science. It also puts at stake one's willingness to cede control of (a part of) one's mind to another. For let us not neglect Prentice and Osmo: figures of the colonized mind, of demands to submit one's fantasy life to the service of state power, so of one's mind as another's tool. This form of domination surely explains why Pirate becomes a founding Counterforce member, finally living out the extralegal political economy signed by his nickname. That is, unless we reflect on the pirate as yet another romanticized, vacuous identity hyped in popular media, in children's tales for example.

Though a relatively minor character among the novel's myriad, Prentice plays a recurrent and significant role. Gossamer threads apparently tie him to key subplots. Or are the ties only happenstance? That morning v-2, we learn in episode 4, had despite all the violence of its supersonic crash into a London suburb miraculously delivered to commando Prentice a message sent by Katje Borgesius, who is across the North Sea in Holland where she's been planted as a spy inside a missile battery whose officer is Major Weissmann (aka Dominus Blicero). She penned the note using "Kryptosam," an invisible ink devised in the lab of our ubiquitous mad scientist Dr. Jamf. This ink has the bizarre quality that it becomes visible only with the application of seminal fluid. And this quirk required Katje, as the sender, to include "a proper stimulus" which itself required, in Jamf's words, her "thorough knowledge of the addressee's [here, Pirate's] psychosexual profile," a plausible knowledge because agent Prentice is her control officer, and they've either been intimate or his desires have been placed under some higher control that logged his "psychosexual profile" and made it available to her, either case suggesting in still further detail the extent to which the man's mind and desires have been colonized for state usage.[13] It suggests, as well, how Prentice appears to exist with only a few degrees of separation vis-à-vis Slothrop and the operant conditioning of his erectile response in Jamf's lab, in 1920. Indeed all of them (Prentice, Slothrop, Jamf, Katje) seem to exist in some ultimately meaningful relation to the greater discipline of behaviorist science the novel holds up—chiefly in the figure of Edward Pointsman—as a model of determinist thought and practice serving the ultimate domination of nature and man. Do they tie together in some elaborate plot with a far reach and deep history? Do these early episodes point toward a vast conspiracy, or just happenstance? The questions remain undecidable, for (in what may be a political turn) we will never acquire the total information or affirmative statement needed to untie the knots. What we *can* assert is that Prentice is radically unfree. Also, that his condition is typical.

Pynchon's divertimento with the giant adenoid is the first of many. Its mode of over-the-top pastiche, its mock serious treatment of foreign policy crises, its elaborate setup for the joke's kicker—those hods full of cocaine—establish a free-form comedy that saves the greater story from an otherwise relentless gloom. Reading our way down such detours, the laughter feels good, even just. They narratively divert or at least forestall catastrophe, held in freeze-frame at the novel's close. But even though they are structured as tales-within-tales, often developing flashbacks-within-flashbacks that reverse the temporal flow, thus serving as narrative means for telling "death to fuck off" (as Scheherazade showed storytellers, ages ago), these detours nonetheless move Pynchon's story forward. They fuel reading with the energies of unbounded, liberated play, appetite, and desire. They flout the law, beginning with the ways they upend conventions of narrative fiction and historiography. They defy formerly accepted community standards for what kinds of sexual content may be expressible and representable in print and onscreen. In their comedy and subversive mode of satire they may even embrace an ethics of anarchy.

On that note, consider next "The Story of Byron the Bulb," early in part 4. Byron is a light bulb manufactured at Osram AG, a Munich-based subsidiary of the Siemens electronics firm and the world's second-largest incandescent lighting manufacturer of the interwar years. Actually, he (yes, bulbs are gendered) was first assigned for manufacture (yes, bulbs are predestined) by the management at the Tungsram firm in Budapest. Yet just before leaving "Bulb Baby Heaven"—a kind of Platonic metaworld where he was pure potentiality and idea, although "BBH" is more like a virtual warehouse, dingy, with roaches that react like Pavlov's dogs when the virtual lights go on—Byron was "reassigned at the last minute" to Munich. Like all bulbs he possesses a soul, *Seele* being (our narrator explains) the German word for the tungsten filament, a double entendre we might read as sparking this digression in the first place. In any event Byron's *Seele* was that of an anarchist revolutionary even in bulb baby heaven. There he whiled away his (virtual) time plotting to "organize all the Bulbs," make them "hep to the Strobing Tactic," then deploy it against their human owners by first triggering a cataclysmic "epileptic fit" that would leave "humans thrashing around 20 million rooms like fish on the beaches," which would be followed by a strike force of select kamikaze bulbs self-exploding in the desk lamps of world leaders, "all of them, right in the face with one coordinated blast."[14]

But when he's translated from virtual to actual bulb life, Byron undergoes "a rude awakening." It turns out the light-bulb elites run a preexisting organization all their own, a worldwide "international light-bulb cartel, headquartered in Switzerland," named Phoebus.[15] This cartel allocates raw materials like tungsten to the manufacturers, fixes prices globally (it really did), and even sets the bulbs' operational life spans in order to ensure regular turnover of stock (actually, it didn't). Byron is thus born into "a state of general repression" which is further enabled by the ways electrical grids give the cartel powers of surveillance and regulation over every individual bulb. So it is an ideally regulated market, if totally unfree, not just for the bulbs but also for their human purchasers. Yet even Phoebus cannot control probabilities. The cartel does not know it has manufactured a statistically possible yet vanishingly unlikely anomaly, for "Byron is immortal." Out on the grid "he starts to learn about the transience of others," realizes love and loss, accepts his gift of immortality, becomes the "Permanent Old-Timer," and practices a yogic silence as cartel operatives check his filament at regular intervals. At one thousand hours the CIA (Committee on Incandescent Anomalies) "sends a hit man," foiled when a "street urchin" steals Byron, who commences an odyssey translating him to one European city after another, "screwed into mother (*Mutter*) after mother, as the female threads of German sockets are known." So our Oedipal bulb-hero learns to hide, burning at lesser frequencies in order to evade detection on the electrical grid (yes, the light-bulb elites have ordered up a technology to do that). The longer he lives, the more Byron realizes the geopolitical extent and power of the greater network he is in every sense *screwed* into, including price-fixing to benefit select companies like GE and Krupp, each vital to their nation's military-industrial capability but cooperating via agreements sustained even after war breaks out in September 1939. By then immortal Byron has become a legend, an icon of anti-cartel attitude to every mortal bulb on the grid, a threat to Phoebus operatives who relentlessly hunt him. The irony is that even as Byron learns more about the cartelization of seemingly everything everywhere, the more he realizes his actual chances of mounting resistance are "as impotent as before." Even though "the Grid is wide open," its very openness enables unlimited surveillance. "He is condemned to go on forever, knowing the truth and powerless to change anything." And the final irony is that Byron "will find himself, poor perverse bulb, enjoying it."

Such is Byron's story. Crazily off-the-wall and built from hijinks as silly as any other narrative detour in *Gravity's Rainbow*, at least it offers readers a straight-line chronology: from Byron's revolutionary idealism in bulb baby heaven to the "perverse" solipsism of eternally pleasuring in his own "anger and frustration," like an epigone of *The Waste Land*'s thousand-year-old glass-bottled Cumaean Sibyl, who knows men's dismal fates. This tale, however, lacks the narrative completeness of the giant adenoid riff, in which Pirate mock heroically defeats the monster and saves the British empire. It ends instead on a note of ongoing post-heroic angst. Here the ideal or myth of anarchistic popular resistance is already through: no more King Ludd, folks. Byron's story represents that potential as having been captured decades before September 1939, in the networks of corporate sovereignties exerting their dominion sometimes in concert with nations but oftener in fidelity to larger global markets from which, it seems, there is no longer any turning back, especially after 1945. War has geographically and politically disrupted and redrawn the maps of European nations. Yet it has left global corporations intact, capitalized and government-supported as never before, especially the booming U.S. corporations—unscathed by battle and uniquely blessed with legal personhood.

The narration in *Gravity's Rainbow* might be read as hesitating between the mock heroism of Pirate Prentice and the Counterforce he helps to spawn, and (what is nearly the same thing) between the post-heroism of Byron the Bulb and the perverse, solipsistic alienation for which he stands. Both modes may be seen as ways of having one's free individualism, and eating it too. We will save the wider ramifications of that thematic crux for later in this book. But before leaving Byron we pause over his story's further teachings, which will be applicable as we move on. First is its frame: somewhere in the central German Free State of Thuringia, in July 1945, inside an Eighty-Ninth Division U.S. Army tent, Byron is the bulb suspended above a colonel getting a haircut from amphetamine addict Eddie Pensiero, a "connoisseur" of his own barely controllable dope tremors, while in a corner sits his sidekick, Private McGonigle, "hand-pedaling the twin generator cranks" to provide electricity to illuminate Byron, who is, in other words, off the grid, uncommonly free. There are hints Eddie is into an angry amphetamine jag, leaning into murderous rage. There's also a long digression about decisive, epochal moments, narrated by Mr. Information, a humorous parody of a long-running (1951–65) TV science program for American kids, *Mr. Wizard*. In each half-hour segment Don Herbert, dressed even on Saturdays in a white shirt, tie, slacks, and wing tips, demonstrated a science concept to quizzical and amazed neighborhood kids.[16] Here, Mr. Information explains time as moments in the control of higher powers, a railroad "pointsman," say, who "throws the lever that changes the points," sending one down the tracks either to "Pain City" or to "Happyville." Our colonel from Kenosha seems bound for Pain. But just then the text veers into the nine-page "Story of Byron the Bulb." On returning, the narrator remarks: "There is no need to bring in blood or violence here," a curious demurrer as the episode's final paragraph leaves us with Eddie, shaking, feeling "the down, mortal blues" while "holding the scissors in a way barbers aren't supposed to"—just over the colonel's exposed jugular vein. At which point the episode concludes—with an em dash, as if the film has broken, the projector jammed, just as we anticipate the climax. So: Is Byron, disconnected from "the grid" while also, as the narration suggests, synced in to the wavelength of Eddie's dope-addled tremors, about to use Pensiero, sparking in this sad-sack private the kind of murderous anarchistic strike Byron had dreamed of back in "ввн"? Or does mere happenstance define the moment? The plain textual fact is that the episode's signifying activity ends in the white space following the em dash.[17]

The final narrative segment of *Gravity's Rainbow*, titled "Descent," reprises that narrative figure of stopping, or incompletion: the "film has broken" (or a projector bulb has burned out), leaving a "bright angel of death"—a rocket—poised (like those scissors) right above our theater, circa 1972, and we're invited to join in a sing-along, which is once more broken off by an em dash: "Now everybody—" So there's a tight figural link between the Byron divertimento and the novel's close. And there's more, if we wish. The narrator's parting glance at Byron, a sentient being "condemned to go on forever, knowing the truth and powerless to change anything," might as concisely apply to our scuffling schlemiel, Slothrop. And still more: for just as a drugged Slothrop fantasizes a desperate, life-saving escape down a toilet in Boston's Roseland Ballroom, so Byron, in a moment accented by similarly bizarre psychosexual elements, plops down a Hamburg toilet, washes out the Elbe River and "over the North Sea, till he reaches Helgoland," luckily escaping the Phoebus cartel terminators. We might easily go on this way, mapping scenes, characters, and plot structures (even punctuation!), thus to develop a unified reading—as we also supposed, in considering the giant adenoid—in which this or that part may be taken as a synecdoche of the whole narration, as if any narration can be whole rather than fissured by signifying itself, by the indeterminacy inherent to the signifier-signified relation. Were we to accept that as-if proposition, we might make all the tight interpretive moves formalist New Critics once taught students (like Pynchon, at Cornell in the mid-fifties), thereby seeming to close the interpretive circle and terminate reading—of *Gravity's Rainbow*, at least.[18]

Except that the narration has already second-guessed such moves and mocked the interpretive effort to "go on blundering inside our front-brain faith in Kute Korrespondences." Note the playful spelling: that Germanic *K* for the *C* that became a commonplace in sixties-era critiques of fascist elements in U.S. politics, society, and culture (evoked every time leftists dubbed the country "Amerika") and here signaling our narrator's mistrust of totalizing interpretation. Relatedly, in his 1981 study of irony in emerging postmodern fictions Alan Wilde marked the ways contemporary writers were turning away from an irony of form, of structural juxtaposition (or "Kute Korrespondences") deployed to stabilize hierarchical values and discernment by negating one term in the juxtaposition. Instead, Wilde argued, contemporary writers had worked out an irony of attitude, a willingness to leave writing open to potentially ceaseless composition, decomposition, and recomposition, an aesthetic practice that meant abandoning hierarchy and closure for a willingness to leave discernment open, suspended between opposing terms.[19] Wilde's book scants the politics of irony, its commitments to logics and powers of subversion and liberation in historical struggle. *Gravity's Rainbow* does not. Moreover, the novel understands struggle as fundamentally ceaseless, necessarily without an end point, because obedience to the ending (whose? why?) shackles action and thought to deterministic processes, to unfreedom. We can see this narrative commitment in the ways Pynchon (our Mr. Information?) worked up his detailing on the Phoebus cartel. The price-fixing, resource allotments, and global agreements, everything other than the Committee on Incandescent Anomalies, was sourced from economic histories similar to those he consulted on related cartels—in petrochemicals, dyes, plastics, electronics, and armaments. As with those sources, in the Phoebus history Pynchon zeroes in on evidence of organized control and dominion that plainly confutes the story of "free market" capitalism and that story's vise grip on "free world" political discussion. Translating the historical archive's abundance into art, into one of his novel's most eccentric fabulations, Pynchon casts Byron's tale in a familiar mode: the suspense-melodrama, a form conventionally purposed around its surprise, and just, ending. Not delivering that denouement is both an aesthetic and a political decision.

Refusing endings is consistent aesthetically and politically with the compositional process of superaddition. One of the novel's various narrative voices relates, for example, how the Soviets imposed a new alphabet on the Kazakh people, this in a passage that self-referentially analogizes writing to the manufacture of polymer plastics: "How alphabetic is the nature of molecules . . . our letters, our words: they too can be modulated, broken, recoupled, redefined, co-polymerized one to the other." Soon Kazakh subversives begin using this novel script "in a political way," putting up "the first Central Asian fuck you signs, the first kill-the-police-commissioner signs (and somebody does! this alphabet is really something!)." But if writing, novel writing especially, proceeds like polymerization in a logic of ceaseless composition, decomposition, and recomposition, then how does one ever get the book between covers? One answer to the dilemma is to utilize mere stopping, or random scission, rather than ending in the narrative sense of denouement and closure. We think this is what Pynchon signifies with the em dash, a mark conventionally followed by more discourse. He uses it to stop the episode framing the Byron yarn, and again (after concluding numerous related instances) as the novel's very last inscription. Also consistent with this rhetoric of open, suspended irony is how the novel's temporal structure is that of an unclosed circle, as one of us has argued elsewhere.[20]

Certainly the ceaseless, ever-morphing needs of a corporatized military-industrial management and production regime also shadow this great novel from beginning to end—an alternate mimetic reason for the rhetoric of superaddition. Throughout, Pynchon's tireless emphasis on the welfare of products, corporations, and managers explains why, as Khachig Tölölyan observes, *Gravity's Rainbow* is a war novel without the conventional blood-and-guts representations.[21] The book is radically unlike those by former GIS-turned-novelists: Norman Mailer's realist novel *The Naked and the Dead* (1948), or Joseph Heller's bitterly satirical (and nonsuspensive) *Catch-22* (1961), or even Kurt Vonnegut's humorously satirical (and somewhat suspensive) *Slaughterhouse-Five* (1969).[22] Pynchon is a fifties navy veteran, and he did yeoman's labor in the military-industrial complex, at Boeing, as a technical writer on intercontinental ballistic missiles in the company's "pilotless aircraft" division. His interest is in the particular ways that, as his narrator puts it, in "this latest War" the "real and only fucking" and killing are "done on paper." And there are moments when his narrative critique presses beyond the corporate form to argue: the postwar political economy will perpetuate the new, transnational wartime economy and its "crises of allocation and priority, not among firms—it was only staged to look that way—but among different Technologies, Plastics, Electronics, Aircraft," whose "needs are understood only by the ruling elite." Accordingly, products themselves (such as rockets) have achieved a kind of second nature, have transformed in other words into pseudo-beings, autotelic in their demands though dependent on corporate and governmental institutions and individuals, "the ruling elite" who understand how to serve those needs by managing flows of raw material, capital, and distribution. The novel consistently represents that elite and its next lower class of subordinates, "experts" like Edward Pointsman, as understanding very well how the war was their boon, how, in other words, a sustained state of globalized national emergency empowered them to route funding their (or rather, their project's) way. Thus, vampire-like, those whom the novel names the "elect" may always cry: "'Money be damned, the very life of [insert name of Nation] is at stake,' but meaning, most likely, *dawn is here, I need my night's blood, my funding, my funding, ahh, more, more.*" As far as the novel's vampire-like managerial class is concerned, the rocket is running things. This is why several reviewers supposed that since *Gravity's Rainbow* seemed to lack a conventional protagonist, Slothrop inexplicably vanishing from the story three-fourths of the way through, the rocket was best suited to that role.[23]

Gravity's Rainbow presents German efforts to design and operate the V-2, and how those efforts were part of a process that cartelized and governmentalized industrial production, as a model stage in the global transition to late capitalism. On that, readers seem to universally agree. Yet how does this representation serve the efforts of sixties-era critical satire? We aren't persuaded by claims the novel aligns itself with ("sutures" itself to) sixties countercultural efforts merely to escape from "technocratic life" through forms of libidinal, spontaneous, and nondiscursive expression.[24] We think that view oversimplifies the sixties and *Gravity's Rainbow*. It scants the efforts of the radical social theorists Pynchon was reading. In particular, we think such a view mistakes the novel's exercises of "mindless pleasures" as means to liberation, because sixties-era debates informing Pynchon's writing stress, instead, how those means are tokens of an escapism that only enables more supple modes of repression.[25] In our view, Pynchon's novel represents the gridded, networked dominion that emerged from the crucible of war as already foreclosing not just prospects for "escape," but more fundamentally prospects for freedom per se. We therefore read the novel as playing devil's advocate—the advertisement on a shingle hanging over a dilapidated "corrugated shack" occupying an unspecified circle in a satirical version of Dante's hell. The shack's resident is a Jesuit priest, Father Rapier. Rather like him, we think *Gravity's Rainbow* intends to cut through decades of accumulated bullshit[26] (chiefly about the romance of techno-scientific discovery) in order to ask if, now that "the technical means of control have reached a certain size, a certain degree of *being connected* one to another, the chances for freedom are over for good. The word has ceased to have meaning." At the prospect of freedom's unmeaning, Slothrop "falls asleep."[27] The novel in our hands would rather not.

The Western and especially the Anglo American tradition of philosophical and jurisprudential thought commencing in 1698 with John Locke's *Two Treatises of Government* analyzes freedom in two interrelated aspects. *Negative liberty* is primary, understood as ontological, a matter of self-evident natural law. It defines each individual as innately dignified and possessing, within a private domain where he exists as his own master and sovereign, rights contractually guaranteed by the state and specifying how he cannot be coerced or controlled by others or by the state. Negative liberty is *freedom from*: from restraints or takings, incursions or dominations by superiors or government. *Positive liberty* is a second-order concept, a matter of manmade law extending from and dependent on the first while also being granted and governed by the state, which ensures the universal rights of individuals to seek full selfhood in the public sphere by engaging in civic and political life. It defines *freedom to*: to speak one's mind and to league with like-minded others. Two common but problematic assertions follow from this twofold analysis. First is the claim that unshackled individuality enables the advance of community toward Enlightenment goals for a perfected social order. The second and related claim is that eliminating or at least ameliorating conflict between groups of individuals will normalize, rationalize, and thus optimize socioeconomic progress toward Enlightenment ideals. Enlightenment *practice*, however, diminished or denied lower-class people's, bondservants', and slaves' access to those freedoms. For those groups, whenever their dissent and resistance coalesced during the age of revolutions, state power brought down upon them the sword of oppression and rightslessness, and Enlightenment idealism unmasked itself. A state's lofty, universalized claims were revealed as convenient legal fictions, stories that established powers promulgated in order to legitimize domination and stifle dissent. Those negative and positive liberties didn't look so inherent and universal, after all.[28]

About the other key word in this book's title: The term "domination" may not appear quite so often in *Gravity's Rainbow* as "control," or the equally ubiquitous "slavery," or other represented practices of manipulation, repression, coercion, and outright violence, whether practiced by individuals, institutions, or sovereign powers. Scenes of masochistic dominance and submission, of master-slave pairs and relations, do appear throughout this novel. Typically Pynchon narrates them in a mode of deceptively alluring comical hijinks—in the novel's songs and movie scenes, for example. Still, as a way to cut through the political culture of bullshit attending those moments, Pynchon also gives us the corporatized and militarized Nazi rocketman Weissmann, his novel's consummate figure of state-sponsored domination and death, as signified in the captain's nickname, Dominus Blicero. Thus we understand "domination" in this capacious sense, encompassing a full range of practices—from verbal and symbolic degradation and stigmatization of a group, to bureaucratic and state-organized repression and coercion of a citizenry, to mental and physical trauma inflicted on individuals and whole populations—as posing the greatest threat to the "chances for freedom" in Pynchon's storyworld and, arguably, the readers' world as well. It's the term used in the works of Erich Fromm, Hannah Arendt, and Herbert Marcuse, whose influences on the novel we will show. "Domination" is also the term of choice among contemporary thinkers, such as Pierre Bourdieu (writing about masculine domination) and Giorgio Agamben (writing about concentration camps), whose work informs our approach to Pynchon's great historical novel.[29]

Domination is freedom's antonym, defining what threatens the supposedly inherent rights upheld in liberal thought and practice. American debates over freedom have, for generations, struggled over meanings, at times reaching a fever pitch—in the *Federalist Papers* debate over the dangers of political parties and mobocracy, in Ralph Waldo Emerson's and Henry David Thoreau's deep mistrust of groups and especially the state, and in sixties-era struggles for expressive freedom, an end to segregation, and an end to war's entrenched presence. During and after the sixties, critiques of the liberal tradition in

Western thought increasingly zeroed in on the ways thinkers hadn't needed to theorize freedom as self-mastery until the seventeenth century, when Europe rapidly expanded masters' powers in the transatlantic slave trade.[30] This work shows how Locke's lucrative stakehold in two companies engaged in slave trading, in addition to his collaborative work on the 1669 *Fundamental Constitutions of Carolina*, which legalized white serfdom and African slavery, quite literally colored his defense of slavery in the Second Treatise. Scholars have further shown how Locke's own profit taking emblematizes the ways modern political liberalism has always been implicated in and complicit with the expansion of markets profiting from slavery even as those markets expanded the new, non-aristocratic class of mercantilists, their freedoms secured by the social contract.[31]

We can see Pynchon realizing and deploying this critique of liberalism's freedom-domination dyad throughout *Gravity's Rainbow*. It surfaces most obviously in the novel's treatments of ethno-racial differences, particularly the Herero refugees and concentration camp laborers. Yet that dyad also surfaces in representations of Pavlovian behavioral conditioning, and Pointsman's sexual fantasies, as modes of mind control; Blicero's sexual enslavement of Katje and Gottfried, imagined as "wanting it"; Pirate Prentice's "permanently enslaved" mind, represented as the depressing legacy of his forced labor as "fantasist-surrogate"; rocket technician Franz Pökler's slavish desire always "to be at someone's command"; and even the rocket's enslavement to gravity, which betrays its "drive toward—is it freedom?"[32] Here, then, is the dilemma troubling this novel's characters, just as it troubled sixties dissidents. One must either struggle to expand freedom in communitarian resistance to the total state, though its agents will not only co-opt one's exercise of positive liberty, they will also use all of its powers, soft and hard, to make domination desirable. Or, content oneself with promises of negative liberty, but in an atomized and alienated individualism.

From the autumn of 1962 through mid-1965 Thomas Pynchon was on the move and writing. His letters to Cornell friends Kirk and Faith Sale track those years of sojourning. Leaving an apartment in Seattle's University District, home base until he resigned from the Boeing job, he traveled first to Mexico City (in November 1962), then Guanajuato, Mexico (by early 1963, when his first novel, *V.*, was published), and back to Mexico City (that summer). That August he was in the San Francisco area for the wedding of Cornell schoolmate and poet-novelist Richard Fariña to Mimi Baez (younger sister of folksinger Joan), during which time he also sought admission to the mathematics program at the University of California, Berkeley (they declined). He returned to Mexico City (by early 1964) and left (by late 1964) for Houston and the home of Boeing friends, and then (in mid-1965) he moved to Los Angeles as he brought *The Crying of Lot 49* into print. The Sales too were on the move—from New York to Africa. Kirk, a sometime journalist for the leftist magazine *New Leader* and the *New York Times Magazine*, was off to a sponsored lecturing position in European and African history at the University of Ghana; Faith had put on hold her career as a fiction editor, including a stint at J. B. Lippincott, where she worked on the typescript of *V.* From Pynchon's half of their correspondence we can tell that it was punctuated by long hiatuses as letters sought their mobile addressees, and that in the spring and summer of 1963 Pynchon began struggling against a writer's block which no amount of geographical change or temporal discipline (in the form of self-imposed deadlines) was enabling him to break through.[33]

The blockage seems to have involved two general issues. The first, described in a June 29, 1963, letter, was that he had begun to doubt his powers as a novelist, or, what amounted to the same thing, to doubt his temperamental suitability for writing what people understood "The Novel" to be. In a prior letter, Faith Sale had evidently commented to him that *V.*—fine as it might be—lacked a measure of suspense, what she'd named a quality of "can't-put-it-downness" that hooks readers on something "other than sheer interest in the next tour de force" chapter. Pynchon granted her point, agreed suspense is "basic to good novel writing," expressed his desire to write such a "traditional realistic kind" of novel, but insisted that until he did so it was no use calling him a novelist, though he might be defined as a competent "surrealist, pornographer, word engineer, maybe." The letter also expressed a commitment to "going out and gathering information," a process Pynchon regarded as foundation-building work for any fiction or nonfiction writing— and one he would comfortably self-parody ten years later in the riffs on Mr. Wizard/Mr. Information.

By 1973, the identity crisis had long passed. Concern that his narrative technique was keeping readers engaged merely by making them anticipate "the next tour de force" episode had clearly given way to a recognition that such tours, or detours, are precisely what picaresque satires had accomplished for centuries. As our own reading of the giant adenoid scene and Byron the Bulb's story argue, *Gravity's Rainbow* is the work of a writer delighting in the ways his late modern revisions of satirical practice depend on the very "elements" he once seemed ready to disavow. Among them, as we will further explore in what follows, are indeed the alluring yet disruptive powers of absurdly humorous surrealist representation, the salacious but disturbing energies of mock pornographic parodies, and the practices of the "word engineer" who satirizes the dullness of actual engineers while realizing how his writing's engine fuels itself by disrupting conventions of realist fiction and proceeding, as we've indicated, by a logic of superaddition. Indeed, why not? If one's combined aesthetic and political program is to unchain experience from determinist logics, from the global trajectory toward death that the rocket emblematizes, then it would be vital to resist putting one's narrative practice on autopilot. Freeing writing from the cause-and-effect poetics that define the realist novel and enable the easy gratifications or "mindless pleasures" of suspense and empathy might thus become a means for attempting resistance to apparatuses dedicated to control and domination, and perhaps even for rethinking realism.[34]

Pynchon indicates the second source of his 1963–64 blockage in a letter of March 27, 1964, datelined from Mexico City. Answering the Sales' inquiry about what he's writing, Pynchon answers: "Same old shit as last time, plus one more, making four." He means four fictional projects. One was *The Crying of Lot 49*, an "optionbreaker" to complete his contractual obligation with Lippincott. A second was probably "The Secret Integration," a story published in the December 1964 *Saturday Evening Post*. The third most likely consisted of early work on what became *Gravity's Rainbow*, the context for remarks in his June 29, 1963, letter about "the rocket" as the symbolic vehicle of the times: evil when it carries a nuclear warhead, good when it carries men to places that, ironically, cannot sustain human life (words echoed a decade later in *Gravity's Rainbow*: "a good Rocket to take us to the Stars, an evil Rocket for the World's suicide"). Pynchon's fourth project is anyone's guess. It might well have been another of his discarded texts, or early sketches that wound up in *Mason & Dixon* (1997).[35]

At any rate the issue—really, a writer's boon—seems to have been the fecundity of imaginative material and historical information then claiming this writer's attention. His lengthy letters from 1962–64 reveal a young artist flush with early success and broadly concerned not only with technical problems of fiction writing but also with U.S. and global history in addition to then-contemporary freedom struggles in the United States, Mexico, South America, and Africa. Focusing this abundantly free mind but without formally constraining it was the issue Pynchon was working through in the early and mid-sixties. *Gravity's Rainbow* invites readers into a related challenge. We think that focusing on this novel's dialogics of domination and freedom, a process of form and content that the novel itself opens but refuses to close, and that is both of and beyond its moment in the Long Sixties, is a critically powerful yet untried way into and around Pynchon's pages.

Whether *Gravity's Rainbow* winds its way out of its own labyrinth is the question for our book. We understand it as equally and profoundly a question of history and politics, and of content and form. As we wrote, dialogued, and argued this book's chapters into final shape, we realized a much darker and more cynical (but not despairing) *Gravity's Rainbow* than most of Pynchon's readers, and we ourselves, have been willing to see. By novel's end, the forces of domination are a split second away from ultimate triumph.

ONE

NOVEL AND DECADE

Trial cover art for *Gravity's Rainbow*; an earlier iteration bore the title "Mindless Pleasures."

History professor Theodore Roszak's bestselling 1969 book *The Making of a Counter Culture* put the project of sixties radicals in a concise formula: "change the prevailing mode of consciousness and you change the world."[1] The formula's implicit dilemma was equally clear: How could a cultural movement accomplish world-changing political work without also becoming "political"? Roszak's scare-quoted "political" referred to an American financial, technocratic, and governmental apparatus with global reach, its grip sustained by a machine politics and a power elite controlling not just electoral processes but what and who counted as political subjects. Those powers had no incentive to cede control or change course on issues vital to New Left activists: the civil rights struggles of African Americans and, increasingly, all people of color and women; antiwar struggles that initially gathered against nuclear armaments and then galvanized against the Vietnam War; and anti-imperialism, the issue uniting freedom and peace struggles against human rights abuses, poverty, and environmental degradation at home and abroad. But still, how would the metaphysical and cultural work of consciousness changing address the material realities of those struggles? Was not the *cultural* inherently *political*?

Roszak's book stated some of the core contradictions and weaknesses in New Left activism. The movement neither offered nor made durable changes in the American political system; if anything, it more deeply entrenched a conservatism soundly defeated in the 1964 election but resurgent four years later with Richard Nixon's election. Nonetheless, as Michael Kazin argues, movement activists did lay out a powerful critique of everyday life in the age of late capitalism, and thus greatly expanded the concepts and boundaries of identities, personal freedoms, self-expression, and moral good in the Cold War era. These challenges and changes have defined the movement's legacy— still embattled, still unfolding.[2] Kazin sees one measure of the movement's lasting impact in the extent to which American political parties and groups still fight for the high ground on issues such as women's reproductive freedom, marriage rights, the size and tasks of government, and climate change. He also concludes that the Long Sixties rediscovered a "brash, ultra-romantic universalism" absent from American liberal activism since the 1840s–1850s antislavery movement.[3]

In this part of our book on domination and freedom in *Gravity's Rainbow* we consider Pynchon's novel as a narrative both *of* and *about* its time—illuminating the romantic allure of cultural-political struggle in the Long Sixties and the gritty realities of nuclear crises and a seemingly ceaseless Southeast Asian war.[4] We aren't interested in teasing out Pynchon's political identifications or his fictionalization of particular sixties events and people. Neither do we mainly intend to study how Pynchon's narrative judges the "assets and liabilities" of sixties counterculture.[5] Our work does rummage up a few new sources and reference points, and does call us to think about postmortems of the Long Sixties, Pynchon's included. Mainly, however, we focus on this writer's two great gifts. First is Pynchon's ability to make art—to write historical fiction—that explores contemporary life and dilemmas through a vision of the recent past. Nothing new there, as students of Cooper, Twain, Dos Passos, Faulkner, and Morrison well know. Second is Pynchon's amazingly deft hand and sharp ear for literary satire. Nothing new there, either: think Rabelais, Swift, Melville, Twain, and West. Long Sixties thinkers and artists took on the unique dilemmas and existential threats of the Cold War: the ghastly prospect of nuclear nations launching their missiles, which created a sustained climate of national emergency and new threats to civil liberties, including the sense among old guard segregationists that Cold War crises trumped African Americans' cries for equality and justice. Long Sixties writers addressed that paranoid new world with a politically engaged, deeply challenging satirical mode that did its best work using age-old material: the unruly, desiring human body understood as both the origin and the bête noire of the body politic. Their pop cultural and literary satires mixed social and political critique with proudly, perversely pornographic and obscene expression. Writers, editors, and books were hauled into courts, where lawyers persuaded judges that for all their supposed "filth," works such as *Howl* or *Naked Lunch* did offer "redeeming social value," so that they amounted to lawfully protected free speech. In terms of what might be said and shown, read and seen, this was a time like no other.

Gravity's Rainbow is the towering achievement of that time. Our specific focus is on the ways Pynchon evokes both the changing means for state power to condition and control subjects, and also the "chances of freedom" still recognizable and *usable* in a technocratic state capable of legitimizing practically anything in the name of self-preservation in a nuclear world. To work those lines of inquiry we do two things here. First, we take up the writings of neo-Freudians who shaped Long Sixties thinking about some core historical and cultural problems—fascism, patriarchy, and modes of soft power—clearly manifested in *Gravity's Rainbow* but lacking thorough examination for some time now. Second, we situate Pynchon's novel in the history of sixties-era print culture, including the formerly banned works and expressive practices of now-canonical writers as well as the vast, outrageously sexual and satirical, overtly anarchist and revolutionary work of underground publications which, if ink were blood, really were the organs that circulated the images and ideas that kept alive the movement's dreams of consciousness raising and freedom. We show how Pynchon's signature narrative practices, many of his most stunning representations, need to be seen in relation to underground press practices whose logic, their expressed raison d'être, also owed much to the work of neo-Freudian, radical Left, and anarchist thinkers and activists.

CHAPTER 1

Fromm and the Neo-Freudian Library

Alongside the work of Norman O. Brown and Herbert Marcuse, Erich Fromm's *Escape from Freedom* (1941, reissued in 1961, 1964, and 1969) rounds out the neo-Freudian library we want to assume Pynchon read. Their books were common reading for Old Left, New Left, and countercultural thinkers, activists, and anarchists, as Theodore Roszak pointed out in his 1969 book. Fromm, Marcuse, and Brown supplied differently nuanced and provocative templates for concretely analyzing contemporary phenomena in psychological, cultural, and historical contexts. Pynchon used them, and if this casts him as a conventional historical novelist then let us also recall how often his historical imagination runs wild in *Gravity's Rainbow*, as his characters—caricatures, ciphers, and clichés as they may well seem—enact extreme and at times grotesquely violent desires. Some, including even the realistically drawn figures such as Roger Mexico and Jessica Swanlake, may rather self-consciously enact movie scripts yet still realize strong individual agency, desires, and needs that round them out.

Fromm and Marcuse are thinkers who keep their feet on the ground, rejecting the pitfalls of Freudian universality, a more promising approach as Pynchon sought to diagnose the nitty-gritty of late modern conflicts from a long-range historical view. Brown, on the other hand, provides a universal recipe for an unfettered, happy humanity: desires freed from repression and romping in erotic green fields of polymorphous perversity. His major works, *Life against Death: The Psychoanalytical Meaning of History* (1959) and *Love's Body* (1966), find their way into *Gravity's Rainbow* partly by direct allusion, partly by inference, in both cases referencing (at times indicting) the decade's libidinous radicalism in ways that need fresh critical understanding.

One path into this archive involves how Pynchon's narrative connects American Puritanism and German Nazism. It begins in 1630, with dissident Puritans migrating in their little armada from England to the Massachusetts Bay Colony, there to build a deeply religious and hard-working community, a new Jerusalem, or "city on a hill," beaconing redemptive hope for humanity. Pynchon's own ancestor William (founder of Roxbury and Springfield, Massachusetts) typified those emigrants whom Alexis de Tocqueville identified, in his *Democracy in America* (2 vols., 1835, 1840), as *the* forebears of

American democracy—dissidents and freethinkers, with issues. In *Gravity's Rainbow*, Slothrop's family line parodies Pynchon's. It is his way to investigate Tocqueville's creation myth and especially to probe the Puritan impact on American attitudes toward capitalism and business. At the Casino Hermann Goering, Slothrop imagines the numerous "word-smitten Puritans dangling off of [his] family tree," and figures his lineage might explain why They have sent a British philologist (Sir Stephen Dodson-Truck) to tease out the centuries-old etymological roots of technological terms used in German rocketry. Slothrop thinks that, along with "shit" and "money," it was "the Word"—the power in biblical language and Puritan eschatology—which had "claimed the Slothrops," beginning with ancestor William, imagined as "vomiting a good part of 1630 away over the side of that *Arbella*," the emigrants' flagship. A nonconformist, William musters the courage to leave Boston's confines and trade with Indians, then starts a pig operation with his son. He learns to love the animals' "nobility and personal freedom, their gift for finding comfort in the mud on a hot day—pigs out on the road, in company together, were everything Boston wasn't."[1] Soon he begins subverting the Puritan doctrine of predestination by arguing "holiness" for the preterite, "the many God passes over when he chooses a few for salvation"; and for his heretical writings on this theme William is compelled back to England. Pynchon's America goes on without him, though his antiestablishment attitudes and opinions still seem to infect his youngest American descendant, Tyrone. Both Slothrops manifest an urgent psychological need to question authority, yet Puritan thought and discipline remain latent in Tyrone. Inspecting the London v-2 ruins early in the novel, for instance, he "hangs at the bottom of his blood's avalanche, 300 years of western swamp-Yankees, and can't manage but some nervous truce with their Providence."[2] Later, when shaken down in Berlin, he calls for help—"Providence, hey *Providence*, what'd you do, step out for a beer or something?"—whereupon his lost boots miraculously reappear.[3] A sign of grace? Perhaps, though Pynchon's storyworld is self-evidently secular, godless yet spiritual. Why then does the narrative insist on the persistence of a religious framework?

Some critics explain Pynchon's take on Protestantism by way of Max Weber's *The Protestant Ethic and the Spirit of Capitalism* (1905, English translation 1930).[4] Weber's study traces how Protestant ethics and ideas influenced capitalism's development in the West; and one way they did so, referenced three different times in the novel, involves Weber's concept that secular capitalism rationalized the charismatic qualities of earlier Christian belief and practice.[5] So Weber was definitely a source, but Erich Fromm's *Escape from Freedom*, which provides a psychological analysis of Protestantism, capitalism, and the rise of Nazism, was surely more important. Fromm reads Nazi ideology and politics as symptomatic of "modern man's" various efforts to solve problems resulting from a lack of traditional authority, first experienced as the Middle Ages ended and then more decisively as Protestantism and capitalism spread during the seventeenth century. As it happens, psychoanalyst Fromm was partly inspired by sociologist Weber, yet Fromm's jump-cut reading of history provides such a fitting model for Pynchon's combination of America and Germany that critics working on *Gravity's Rainbow* can no longer overlook this important book.

Fromm is a traditional thinker on liberty in the sense that he relies on the distinction between negative and positive freedom. In the course of history man "has become free from the external bonds that would prevent him from doing and thinking as he sees fit," but this has created many difficulties.[6] Doubts about identity, the meaning of life, and morality compel the individual to retreat from this newfound freedom into old forms of bondage. Judging from a chapter on freedom and democracy near the book's end, Fromm seems to believe that this process is avoidable and that there really is "a state of positive freedom in which the individual exists as an independent self and yet is not isolated but united with the world, with other men, and nature." Positive freedom "consists in the spontaneous activity of the total, integrated personality," yet Fromm recognizes that spontaneity remains notoriously difficult to describe. Artists and small children express themselves spontaneously, and "most of us can observe at least moments of our own spontaneity." Vague though it may be, Fromm's idea of play and art as "spontaneous," as nonteleological and nondeterministic, does lead into a theory of democracy. The two foremost "component" factors driving spontaneous activity are love and work, because they entail embracing the world without giving up the individual self. He means, when love and work aren't geared to success, or any telos; for in good work and proper love, "what matters is the activity as such, the process and not the result." Positive freedom therefore affirms the individual's uniqueness but without leading to competitive conflicts between people: "Their relationship is one of solidarity, not one of domination-submission."[7] In positive freedom there is no higher power than uniquely developed persons. Two risks ensue, but they can be overcome. First, genuine ideals will avoid the risk of selfish egotism and will enhance the happiness of all. Second, rational authority will reduce the risk of anarchy, and since real democracy nourishes such authority it will not threaten the individual happiness growing from human spontaneity.

Writing in the late 1930s as Nazism triumphed and war broke out, Fromm adds that democracy will only survive if positive freedom, the "realization of the individualism that has been the ideological aim of modern thought since the Renaissance," wins the day.[8] The rest of his book accepts the grim likelihood that this vital victory is a pipe dream. As Fromm tells the story, modern man represents the apex of negative freedom's growth since the Middle Ages ended. The problem facing modern society is that various disorders afflict positive liberty, and Fromm diagnoses them as failures to harmonize individualism and communalism, failures he regards as symptomatic of Protestantism. We think this is what brought Fromm's book to Pynchon's desk, for Protestantism, evoked throughout *Gravity's Rainbow* as a culprit religion, also appears in *Escape from Freedom* as the mother of all problems. In Pynchon's novel even a special Puritan like William Slothrop cannot thwart Protestantism's powers in the New World. Maybe his pigs, each basking in its own sun but still "in company together," enjoyed something like Fromm's positive freedom. Yet William's thinking that swine might teach his fellow Puritans life lessons was surely, and comically, doomed. Indeed, rather like Fromm, Tyrone Slothrop wonders if, with "all the fences down" at the war's end, "there might be a route back" to "the fork in the road America never took," an alternative to Puritanism that William had glimpsed in his pigs, a new path without "a single set of coordinates from which to proceed, without elect, without preterite, without even nationality to fuck it up." Yet it turns out this potential for anarchistic erasure of map coordinates is little more than a pleasant illusion that keeps Slothrop going. For a long stretch in part 3 he wears a pig suit, is even taken as the mythical Teutonic pig hero, Plechazunga. Moreover, he seems to have forgotten that William's pigs living "in company together" were actually slaughterhouse bound.[9] The devil's always in such details. Thus while Counterforce characters may wish to see Slothrop on a journey ending with his wise and just sociopolitical exit or dropping out, readers already have reason to regard such a course as his defiant yet failed "escape from freedom." His relevance as the Counterforce mascot rests on that kind of conflicted textual evidence.

The task of social psychology, as Fromm sees it, is "to understand [the] process of man's creation in history."[10] Contrary to Freud, he holds that the psychological forces determining history are themselves socially conditioned. Self-preservation is a need under all circumstances, but strivings and traits such as "love, destructiveness, sadism, the tendency to submit, the lust for power, detachment, the desire for self-aggrandizement, the passion for thrift, the enjoyment of sensual pleasure, and the fear of sensuality" can vary greatly between regions and periods, since they develop in childhood "according to the whole mood of life" to which people are acculturated.[11] Fromm sees a parallel between the growth of an individual and that of society at large. Every child "becomes more free to develop and express its own individual self unhampered by those ties which were limiting it." Still, that developmental and expressive freedom is perilous, for such a person also "becomes more free *from* a world which gave it security and reassurance." This dynamic of freedom and fear, individual growth and destructive anxiety, is inherent to modernity and always conflicted, a source of various psychological cruxes Fromm locates in social history, which began when man managed to overcome the "instinctual determination of his actions" in realizing negative liberty. Throughout subsequent history, then, positive liberty went begging because economic, social, and political conditions thwarted its realization and consigned humanity to feeling freedom as an insufferable burden. Indeed Fromm sees the Reformation era and the age of European fascism as resembling each other, because Protestantism and Nazism both manifest an ideological "emphasis on the wickedness of human nature, the insignificance and powerlessness of the individual, and the necessity for the individual to subordinate himself to a power outside of himself."[12] *Gravity's Rainbow* is populated wall-to-wall with characters desiring—often masochistically—precisely this subjection Fromm analyzes. His way of narrativizing history also jibes with Pynchon's, who figures Puritanism and Nazism as essential to a polity that keeps Them in charge of distressed individuals, who do not know where else to turn. In this context even Slothrop's getting off the grid may seem a necessary act of self-rescue; perhaps that's why Counterforce folks want to mythologize him for doing so.

How exactly does *Escape from Freedom* plot history? Medieval society offered little individual freedom and hardly any social mobility. People were identical with their role in society, with the church providing people security, belonging, and spiritual alleviation of their suffering, without preventing self-expression in their work and emotional life. Judging from how Fromm presents the period and from his later descriptions of the democratic society to which he thinks we should still aspire, one might believe he saw the Middle Ages as a time when people nearly realized positive freedom. Yet "the individual," so central to Fromm's view of contemporary experience, didn't exist yet. S/he is a byproduct of changes during the late Middle Ages when centralization diminished and capital, individual economic initiative, and competition redefined psychological and social life. Fromm first turns to Jacob Burckhardt's work on the Renaissance in Italy to portray the experience of wealthy "nobles and burghers," who were "more free, but . . . also more alone."[13] They operated independently, but also had to control the masses and deal with competitors. Egocentricity crept in, and the growing craving for status and fame compensated for the new doubts and fears. While the Italian Renaissance brought decisive changes only to a small group of rich people, the Reformation in Central and Western Europe affected the middle and lower classes and the peasants. Here Fromm's argument borrows from Max Weber and other scholars, such as Werner Sombart and Richard Tawney, who wrote on late medieval and Renaissance economic history. In medieval society, economic interests were secondary to the search for salvation, and they were ruled by a strict morality. By the fifteenth century, capital's rise led to monopolies, pushing to the brink some guild members, journeymen, and small merchants. Industry and agriculture also saw a growing division between rich and poor. Fromm's adaptation of this accepted historical narrative returns again and again to a division essential to Pynchon's storyworld: a small minority of capitalists and power brokers dominate the middle and lower classes. The system does not change because it cannily produces new guises of individualism for workers to try on, a virtual wage in exchange for their impassivity, for remaining true to their condition, for better or worse. Social change and class mobility thus become phantasms while the law of perpetually accelerating economic and technological growth rules.

Fromm argues that Lutheranism and Calvinism appealed to dominated groups because "they gave expression to a new feeling of freedom and independence as well as to the feeling of powerlessness and anxiety by which members [of these groups] were pervaded." The two Protestant religions managed this tension by activating radical psychological mechanisms that do their job by sustaining a condition of panic. Luther emphasizes the moral depravity of human nature, so that "only if man humiliates himself and demolishes his individual will and pride will God's grace descend upon him." Faith alone guarantees salvation, and faith in action requires losing, abjecting the self before God's power. For Fromm this religious axiom expresses the strong need for certainty in an era of persistent individual doubt. Yet this need was not equally strong in all classes. The lower classes initially found hope in Luther because he focused on the Gospels, whose message should have aided their quest for justice and equality, though Luther disavowed their struggles against the new social order. Wedged between poverty and riches, the rising middle class remained essentially insecure after the feudal system broke down and therefore flocked to Lutheran theology, which mirrored their situation at the same time it provided them a foolproof solution: complete submission to God instead of the church. This submission became so central to post-medieval society that it "paved the way for a development in which man not only was to obey secular authorities but had to subordinate his life to the ends of economic achievements."[14] Marcuse's analysis, perhaps indebted to Fromm's, identifies the same ideological controls operating in advanced industrial society.

Fromm sees Calvin's theology also appealing to the middle class, and for the same reasons, though he identifies two differences with Lutheranism vital to our understanding of the Calvinist/Puritan presence in *Gravity's Rainbow*. Calvin's doctrine of predestination holds that individuals are destined for grace, or damnation, even before birth. People thus created unequally would have no reason to exert will and effort; moreover they'd be disabled by doubts as to their fate, elect or preterite. Calvinists answered this problem by preaching the conviction that their religious community "belonged to the chosen ones." The other difference between Calvinism and Lutheranism connects directly with Weber's understanding of capitalism, which at first sight contradicts predestination. Calvinists disagreed because much more so than in Lutheranism their teachings emphasized effort and virtue. An individual cannot change his fate, but "the very fact that he can make the effort is one sign of his belonging to the saved." Now, palpable results of effort such as an individual's success and financial gain evidenced salvation as one of the elect. Indeed Calvinism's most important means for helping individuals to overcome doubt and a sense of powerlessness as to their meager ration of negative freedom was that relentless activity and striving promised salvation, their ultimate wage. In post-medieval society, then, people worked "not so much by external pressure but by an internal compulsion."[15] Their fidelity to work became an internal control mechanism guiding people's trajectory from birth to death.

Fromm further emphasizes how Luther and Calvin also appealed to middle-class envy of and quiet hostility toward wealthy and powerful capitalists, while offering no such lure to the lower class. Calvin's despotic God gave the middle class a perfect projection of their own anxiety and anger, which also found expression in a moral indignation toward all others. In this connection Fromm references the paranoia of Calvin's Geneva regime, an attitude Pynchon highlights in Puritanism. Slothrop, for example, manifests "a Puritan reflex of seeking other orders behind the visible, also known as paranoia," and in Puritanism, the orders behind the visible are divine: "Data behind which always, nearer or farther, was the numinous certainty of God." For Slothrop, who still uses Puritan thought to rationalize his secular world, God has been replaced by Them. As John Krafft puts it, "the attributes of the Elect and the vastness and intricacy of *Their* order are such that They seem to take on qualities once ascribed to God, to have a power and extent explicable only in supernatural terms." For the longest time, then, Slothrop's paranoia remains "operational" because it enables him to sustain his quest for self-discovery, which might be seen as ending in a disappearing act that defies Them.[16] Or, does it ultimately submit to Them, just as middle-class men effaced themselves before Puritanism's authoritarian God? If we readers cannot say one or the other, we certainly realize They may be Slothrop's projection, a God surrogate explaining his inner compulsion to uncover his past conditioning, to reckon how he connects with the rocket, and thus to learn who he is, with all the agitated travails of his search. They cater to his individuality while keeping it in check. At the same time, They even allow his direct hostility toward Them, whereas to Fromm the Calvinists' hostile God only served as a partial deflector of middle-class hatred.

In Fromm's analysis Nazism's appeal does not differ all that much from that of Protestantism. He points to "a state of inner tiredness and resignation" to explain why the German working class and the bourgeoisie (liberal and Catholic) readily submitted themselves to the Nazi regime. By 1930 the post–World War I dream of socialism lay shattered, and thanks to Hitler's impact as a popular leader, Germans who had other political convictions still accepted Nazism (misleadingly called National Socialism) because it channeled their anger toward foreign nations. Even more receptive to Nazi ideology than the working class and the bourgeoisie were the "lower strata of the middle class." They projected their social inferiority onto the national inferiority resulting from the 1918 defeat. So devoted were they to the cause that Hitler could easily reduce their socioeconomic status in order to bolster German industrial and economic interests, a support *Gravity's Rainbow* figures in the (historical) Jewish politician Walther Rathenau, the "prophet and architect of the cartelized state," whose mistake was to buck the socialist tide during the Weimar regime. According to Fromm, Hitler and the Nazi system effectively managed Germany's middle and working classes because their grip was an authoritarian fist, and as such it "made a powerful appeal to those parts of the population which were—more or less—of the same character structure." This wide-ranging thesis joins hands with Fromm's argument that Nazi Germany's authoritarian character generally combined sadism and masochism, "the craving for power over men and the longing for submission to an overwhelmingly strong outside power."[17] Both strivings supposedly compensated the individual agonized by feelings of solitude and helplessness.

Some of Pynchon's German characters seem to frankly narrativize aspects of Fromm's analysis. Chemical engineer Franz Pökler realizes only belatedly that he has freely submitted to a dangerous ideology. Struggling with "the burden of his poor Berlin self," he willingly abandons that version to the V-2 project, seen as the literal vehicle of Nazi revenge to restore Germany's, and thus his, greatness. Naming that abandonment as a "fear of extinction," Pökler gives in to the rocket "beckoning him in" because maybe in "this extinction he could be free of his loneliness and his failure." For a time Pökler imagines himself dithering between two equally compelling possibilities: on the one hand, "personal identity," which would enable him to resist the rocket's lure and achieve positive freedom in Fromm's sense; on the other hand, "impersonal salvation" in total subjection to Nazi authority as embodied in Major Weissmann, the senior SS man assigned to the V-2 project. Actually he's long been under Weissmann's control. Pökler well knows but cannot consciously admit that Weissmann has employed girls to impersonate his daughter, Ilse, for annual Peenemünde visits. Those ultimately selfish moral ditherings turn out to be remnants of an individual self the system has not bothered wholly to eradicate. There really is no need to, because vacuous doubting is the strongest reaction the engineer can muster. Pökler's masochism already fits Fromm's authoritarian profile and its complementary sadistic side.

The long chapter devoted to Pökler's perspective on the rocket opens with a memory of him whipping a sexual partner (a figure who melds actress Margherita Erdmann, whom he has just seen in a movie, with his wife, Leni), "fucking her into some submission" and perhaps conceiving their daughter, Ilse. Years later in Peenemünde he again manifests that power craving in a fantasy featuring "hours of amazing incest" with a girl he partly wants to be his long-lost daughter while partly fearing she is a well-scripted imposter in Weissmann's employ. This fantasy begins with Franz hitting the girl "upside the head with his open hand," then indulging in "hours" of incestuous and pedophilic desires. Even when thinking They have provided this diversion as a way to control his labors, "his first feeling [is] pride" for the way he has made himself important to the system.[18] That's how its compensations are supposed to operate. As we'll see, this dithering continues for six more years, Pökler's grotesquely pathetic illusions of grandeur reinforcing his bondage to rocket work and the sadness, or despair, Pynchon wrings from this man's loss of self.

As "Captain Blicero" (either an error, or he's been demoted in rank) Weissmann enacts his own sadomasochistic fantasia with Katje Borgesius and the teenage Gottfried in The Hague. Katje's perspective frames this episode (number 14 in part 1), as she first remembers in gruesome detail the "Oven" game Blicero directed, an erotic version of the Hansel and Gretel tale with himself as the witch, "in highest drag." His mock labia and clitoris are made of synthetic rubber and a new polyvinyl chloride, and "tiny blades of stainless steel bristle from lifelike pink humidity, hundreds of them, against which Katje, kneeling, is obliged to cut her lips and tongue, and then kiss blood abstracts across the golden ungessoed back of her 'brother' Gottfried." Blicero having set all the rules, he shouts commands and humiliates the fairytale children in round upon round of the *Hexeszüchtigung*, or witch's whipping, meted out by the witch himself, in a stunningly parodic reversal illustrating just how tightly sadism and masochism bind this threesome to a bloody mockery of human communion in positive liberty. Blicero's consciousness also comes to the fore in this episode. He needs "the straps and whips leathern" and especially the various forms of pain he inflicts: "in all the winter these are sure, can be depended on." At the same time "he doesn't even know the Witch, can't understand the hunger that defines him/her." Just like Franz Pökler, Blicero mildly questions his own behavior when he is already very far gone, believing that "his Destiny is the Oven." Glimpses of Gottfried's thinking indicate that he too is well conditioned for this grotesque erotic constellation. He is only slightly embarrassed that he enjoys all the trappings of domination so much, from the captain degrading him as "bitch" to the officer's penis forced down his throat. Remarkably, Katje plays the empty cipher in the oven game. To her it's merely another assignment as a secret agent of "The Firm" back in London; and after Pirate Prentice finally extricates Katje "she avoids all mention of the house in the forest," so well conditioned is she to repression's work. Except that a page later Pynchon turns the screw: Katje recalls how her seventeenth-century Protestant ancestor Frans van der Groov helped to systematically exterminate the dodoes of Mauritius.[19] This family story historicizes and tacitly judges the meanings of the oven game she's played with Blicero and Gottfried. It makes clear that sadomasochism is one outcome of fascist authoritarian society, as Fromm explained. Extermination is of course another, suggested by those doomed dodoes.

Pynchon does not just expose sadomasochism as an illustration of the individual's pitiful state under Nazism (or any system They control). In one of the surreal episodes near the novel's end, Miklos Thanatz, Margherita Erdmann's husband and no stranger to sex combined with pain, playfully suggests that "a little S and M never hurt anybody."[20] The moment references Freud, and a complicated discussion among neo-Freudians, summarized partly in Fromm. Thanatz explains that the state would disappear if sadomasochism were practiced generally within families. "Because submission and dominance are resources [the state] needs for its very survival," the state cannot cede control of those means to nonstate actors. Whereas Fromm emphasizes how the system lures the individual back from the threshold of a freedom s/he cannot bear, Thanatz insists that the system exerts power over individuals by disallowing a specific mode of sexuality the state alone must control.[21] Fromm's individual can hardly recover; in contrast Thanatz holds out the prospect that one may employ what's forbidden to gain release from the system's control.

If anything, this "sado-anarchism" clearly discloses a Pynchon innovating, riffing on Fromm's theses, and probably also a Pynchon well aware of sixties anarchist projects for releasing and enacting prohibited desires as a means to counter and even defeat the system. The same logic may lie behind another, still more complicated and outrageous instance in *Gravity's Rainbow*. In episode 4 of part 2, Brigadier Pudding, the aged general given responsibility for the White Visitation, plays out an elaborate script requiring him to eat Katje's feces, certainly the most gut-wrenching of all the novel's scenes of paraphilia, though its representational elements and meanings might dovetail with the same subversive program Thanatz proposes. We will see.

CHAPTER 2

Marcuse: (No) Chances for Freedom in Advanced Industrial Society

Herbert Marcuse regards *Escape from Freedom* as the last book Fromm wrote before he sadly "regressed" from "revisionist psychoanalysis toward pre-Freudian consciousness psychology."[1] In an earlier essay for *Dissent*, later the epilogue of his own "philosophical inquiry into Freud," *Eros and Civilization* (1955), Marcuse scolds Fromm's later work for promoting classical values such as "inner strength . . . which can be practiced even in chains and which Fromm himself . . . denounced in his analysis of the Reformation [in *Escape from Freedom*]." With Fromm's regressive turn "the social issues become primarily spiritual issues, and their solution becomes a moral task."[2] Marcuse despises this development for being untrue to the Freud who, he argues, showed in *Civilization and Its Discontents* (1930) that the instinctual freedom humans covet differs from what a repressive society names freedom and happiness. To Marcuse, the Fromm of books such as *Man for Himself* (1947), *Psychoanalysis and Religion* (1950), and even *The Sane Society* (1955) was settling for a reinforced status quo under the hypocritical guise of a "non-conformist humanism."[3] While part of this acid polemic may derive at once from Freud's relative incoherence on the topic of civilization and from Marcuse's and Fromm's competing desires to claim first chair in American sociopsychological criticism, their exchange already indicates why Marcuse would become a major sixties "intellectual celebrity."[4] He managed to cast himself as the *true* nonconformist, largely by combining a piercing analysis of repression in late capitalism with what many saw as a revolutionary program. Perhaps holding out a chance for unrecuperated art to express the free imagination—an opening to which we will return because of its evident importance for the status of *Gravity's Rainbow*—Marcuse mainly found the possibility for real opposition to the system in people who live outside it: "The fact that [the outcasts and outsiders, the exploited and persecuted of other races and other colors, the unemployed and the unemployable] start refusing to play the game may be the fact which marks the beginning of the end of a period."[5] Marcuse's enthusiastic endorsement of such a great refusal at the end of *One-Dimensional Man* (1964) made him popular with those wanting radical change. If that explains why Slothrop finally goes off the grid, it would seem a first step into radical activism.

In two important, overlapping essays Molly Hite has broken fresh ground in Pynchon studies, showing not only how *Gravity's Rainbow* "picks up specific motifs" such as Orpheus and the figure of the rainbow arc from *Eros and Civilization*, but also how Pynchon's narrative borrows from Marcuse its parallel between the World War II period and the Long Sixties epoch. In this respect the difference between Marcuse's warning to his readers and Fromm's suggestions about the sixties in his second (1965) foreword to *Escape from Freedom* perhaps amounts to not a contradiction but a matter of degree. While Fromm acknowledges that the nuclear arms race only amped up the tendency to escape from freedom, he also sees "hopeful signs" in the cybernetic revolution, the population explosion, the vanquishing of European dictatorships, and, in the United States, "important steps" toward "the political and social liberation of the Negroes." Marcuse makes a much more pessimistic assessment, not least because his diagnosis is more comprehensive. He argues that advanced industrial society has created numerous possibilities for shallow pleasure and happiness, mindless pleasures (we might add) which he famously gathered under the label "the leisure society." Its endless attractions, events, and spectacles, however, require a constant focus on productivity and therefore lead to the individual's increasing repression. Hite explains that Marcuse particularizes Freud's historical account by suggesting that "the performance principle, an impetus to detach from and dominate the natural order," typifies Western industrial society where work is generally done in alienation, labor time is "painful time," and an entertainment industry controls even the vital element of leisure. Hite poses as an alternative the novel's remnant of African Hereros, whom she sees as an adaptive and still surviving tribal culture.[6] We find them represented as so psychically colonized and corrupted by Western military industrialism—in fact so near annihilation's brink that some Hereros desire and promote suicide—as to doubt such a claim.

The growing impact of the performance principle is what makes repression more and more necessary. Late capitalism is finally capable of satisfying most basic human needs, but has passed a tipping point. The denial of pleasure Freud described as a requirement for civilization has become so total that its only compensation is in more domination of nature and more consumer goods requiring still more technology—a vicious spiral most people do not even realize it might be wise to quit, no matter how much it threatens human survival. Indeed the death drive, or Thanatos, as Freud described it in *Beyond the Pleasure Principle* (1920), the opposite of the life-giving sexual drive, or Eros, could become so dominant as a result of delayed gratification that the already precarious balance between the two vanishes irrevocably. And since swift technological progress defines the leisure society—to Marcuse, a truly contradictory outcome of productivity—the performance regime in Western industrial society deterministically trends toward total annihilation, with nuclear winter its popularly imagined ending.

Pynchon buys into this script, but how earnestly he buys in depends on one's reading of his novel's ending. There the v-2 rocket, seen as the technological climax of German aerospace supremacy through 1944–45, morphs into a nuclear missile, *the* icon of Cold War paranoia, descending on the (fictional) Orpheus movie theater in Los Angeles. Given the closing pages' jump-cut technique, that rocket is either manned or ghosted by the German boy Gottfried, or "God's Peace." Readers may thus ponder the ending in two contexts. First, the moon race triumph in July 1969, led by a NASA team under the direction of former Nazi rocketeer Wernher von Braun (who could make up such stuff?). Second, that famous closing shot in Stanley Kubrick's *Dr. Strangelove* (1964), as cowboy-hat-waving Major Kong rides a nuclear bomb down into a Russian city as if he were astride a bucking bronco. (To which associations we also add: during the war a v-2 really did come down, with horrific results, on a movie theater in Antwerp.)[7]

In the performance principle's relentless logic, stagnation equals regression. Constant transcendence or progress, even though "bound up with intensified unfreedom," becomes the norm that Marcuse draws as an ascending curve. Pynchon's central figure of the rocket's arc in *Gravity's Rainbow*, Hite beautifully shows, thus draws amplified meaning from *Eros and Civilization*: "The Rocket rises under human guidance and in response to a humanly defined demand to mount above natural processes, but ultimately it is 'betrayed to Gravity' and descends uncontrolled and unguided." The performance principle literally yields to the death drive. Hite argues that for Pynchon it need not do so because the novel does offer glimpses of redemptive technology, again through the Hereros, who are assembling their own missile, numbered 00001. As Enzian moves across the Zone with scavenged subassemblies for that missile, the narrator suggests, "the Rocket has to be many things." These include (at least) the duality of some "Rocket-Manichaeans" who see a "good Rocket to take us to the stars" (Enzian's?) and others who have "an evil Rocket for the World's suicide" (Blicero's?). Actually the good one probably exists only in some readers' minds. The narration never discloses its fate, while the book's ending merely puts its deadly counterpart, Blicero's morphed 00000, on pause.[8] About Cold War annihilation, Pynchon is every bit as pessimistic as Marcuse.

There are further psychoanalytical signpostings in Pynchon's narrative, and all readings of them must take up a well-known passage about the "Oedipal situation in the Zone." There Hite, for example, finds Pynchon's narrator mourning the "attenuated oedipal sexuality" that results from the replacement, smartly signaled in Marcuse, of the Oedipal father by the system. In a society whose operational principle is an overall repression, as in Germany circa 1930–45 or America in the Long Sixties, the nameless administrators, or They, have taken over. In a practical move They have also enlisted mothers, "masculinized to old worn moneybags of no sexual interest to anyone." No need any more for an Oedipal conflict! As Leni Pökler understands much earlier in the novel, "Mothers work for *Them!* They're the policemen of the soul." They even, as Otto Gnahb later explains to his girl, convene "giant conventions, and exchange information" about ways to better dominate children—an actual "Mother conspiracy" (as if there weren't enough conspiracies to track). Fathers in this novel rarely assert such power, and always only perversely. Hite draws a bead on Weissmann/Blicero, "a figure of the archaic father who wields murderous power"; and in her reading he's a much more complicated character than Fromm's sadomasochist whose authoritative position is his escape from freedom. Weissmann's paternal identity as a "Rilkean hero climbing toward his Lament" is already voiced during his sadomasochistic orgy with Katje and Gottfried in The Hague. Hite directs our attention instead to memories Blicero recalled, late in the war, then related by his friend Thanatz. With a friend so named as to blazon his Freudian allegiances to Thanatos, the humorous pastiche in this testimony should put us on guard. In any event when the narrator (or the ss man himself, it's hard to tell) addresses Thanatz, the relevant motif becomes Blicero's wish to murder Gottfried, "his metaphoric child." The voice asks: "Haven't you wanted to murder a child you loved, joyfully kill something so helpless and innocent? . . . The cry that breaks in your chest *then*, the sudden, solid arrival of loss, loss forever, the irreversible end of love . . . no denying what you finally are." An Oedipalized obsessive, for starters, this Blicero or his ventriloquized voice is represented as so far gone into infanticidal manias as to stand utterly outside the order of things, *contra naturam*, a monster. And is it, as such, perversely *free*? Here readers confront a dialogue that is incredibly ambiguous in its thematics as well as in the matter of who speaks. One can easily tell how it casts Blicero as Herr Death Drive, the voracious and violent patriarch the novel may seem to have stood upon Marcuse's shoulders. Hite, for example, regards Blicero as a force of desire that might oppose "the impersonal power structure."[9] Is Pynchon *that* serious about all this? Does Blicero become one who escapes organized, efficient society for a reign of mythic Titans, "reminders of an abandoned human possibility that might be reclaimed"? Hite even dares to associate this potential with the book's "mindless pleasures."[10]

There are other pertinent signals. In a concluding section titled "Weissmann's Tarot," the narration sums up the man's divinatory reading with this advice: "If you're wondering where he's gone, look among the successful academics, the Presidential advisers, the token intellectuals who sit on boards of directors. He is almost surely there. Look high, not low."[11] Blicero's free in America, perhaps; and if so, then seek him in the boardrooms or the control stations at NASA, for instance, where (circa 1970) von Braun and others of his Peenemünde crew were working. In this passage we find something quite different in tone and logic than that earlier grotesque and quite ambiguous pastiche structured around Thanatz and the theme of child murder. Here we find a clear, vigorous moral satire fingering guilt while also pointing out an unfathomable ethical abyss: Nazi mass murderers? Free, reunited with wives, and richly rewarded for helping the American space program beat those evil Russians to the moon? Good, apolitical technicians and bureaucrats, disciplined to their work. *Jawohl, mein Herr!*

If Pynchon were so dead serious about that Thanatz dialogue, as some readers wish him to be, then how would "mindless pleasures" come into play? That phrase first appears in the novel when the "Anglo-American team of Harvey Speed and Floyd Perdoo" quickly give up on their detective-style investigation of Slothrop's sex adventures and begin passing "whole afternoons sitting out in restaurant gardens dawdling over chrysanthemum salads and mutton casseroles."[12] Even when the phrase returns much later, in the section titled "The Low-Frequency Listener," our narrator doesn't use it in relation to any compelling issue: "No one Slothrop has listened to is clear who's trying whom [in Nuremberg] for what, but remember that these are mostly brains ravaged by antisocial and mindless pleasures."[13] "Ravaged" could be ironic, or only just darkly humorous in calling to mind that from any *normal* ethical or juridical view of things, von Braun also should have been a war crimes defendant sitting in the dock of a Nuremberg courtroom. We don't see how these "mindless pleasures" point the way back to some "abandoned human possibility." More likely they're a target of the novel's satirical critique.

This qualification does not have to mean that numerous critics (Hite included) have been mistaken about "mindless pleasures" as a general name for Pynchon's interest in alternative modes of consciousness: drink, dope, sex, fantasy, English candies, mystic visions, tarot readings, music (Rossini's perhaps, or Charlie Parker's), banana breakfasts, séances, harmonica and kazoo playing, the consciousness of rocks or trees. Pynchon's, or perhaps the Viking editors', extraction of that phrase for the book title, although scotched, surely indexed some shared sense of thematic relevance. An early trial cover put the title "Mindless Pleasures" over a cleverly stylized version of the Tower, a key card in Weissmann/Blicero's tarot reading. A second trial cover, also scotched, put "Gravity's Rainbow" over the same image. The Tower gathers several interpretations, most notably (says our narrator) that of "a Gnostic or Cathar symbol for the Church of Rome, and this is generalized to mean any system which cannot tolerate heresy: a system which, by its nature, must sooner or later fall. We know by now that it is also the Rocket."[14] The notion of tolerance and intolerance is catchy and may also link to Marcuse on repression (more on that momentarily). One reading of this cover would be that mindless pleasures bring down the system, are anathema to it. The common gloss of "mindless" is that it refers to the contrary of normativity, or not a mentality conditioned or "defined within rigid societal parameters" (Hite again).[15] This contrariness presumes a hierarchy, an established order elevated above a variety of upstart alternatives, many of them popular, carnivalesque, of the body. And the arts are among them, as our listing indicates.

In *Eros and Civilization* Marcuse adapts Coleridge's definition of the primary imagination (which leads to an experience of authentic reality) and, following Freud, offers as a synonym "phantasy," what Hite names "the activity of dreams and those daytime dreamers, artists."[16] Yet Marcuse also associates art with primary narcissism, that stage in child development "which is more than autoeroticism; it engulfs the 'environment,' integrating the narcissistic ego with the objective world." In a crucial passage Marcuse lets Adorno describe art's function: "Under the rule of the performance principle, art opposes to institutionalized repression the 'image of man as a free subject; but in a state of unfreedom art can sustain the image of freedom only in the negation of unfreedom.'"[17] Freedom appears in the form of subversion—an instance of the great refusal that might lead back to the bliss of primary narcissism but that might also be recuperated in the system, as we will see.

Some *Gravity's Rainbow* critics make strong claims for the subversive power of sex, instead of art. Hite, for example, promotes Pynchon's scenes of perversion or paraphilia (e.g., sadism, masochism, coprophagia) as Marcusian nonreproductive sexualities used "as an expression of phantasy" thrown against the system. Thanatz's sado-anarchism captures exactly that sense as well, particularly if its spread in families would make the state "wither away."[18] And finally the most compelling evidence for Marcuse's influence on *Gravity's Rainbow* is that, in Hite's phrasing, he "aligns nonnormative sexual desires and behaviors with the mythic figures of Narcissus and Orpheus."[19] Kathryn Hume has also shown that the Orpheus myth provides a script for reading Slothrop's fantasy dive down Boston's Roseland Ballroom toilet into an underworld, a foreglimpse of Slothrop's apparent "scattering" near the novel's end. The case for Marcuse's relevance rests, for Hite, on the potential for "Slothrop's sexual diffusion" to link with his "Orphic tendency toward polymorphous perversity."[20] Whether this makes the character a tough survivor and an Orphic counterculture warrior remains unclear. Yet by some kind of miracle, anarchist or not, Slothrop does recover his long-lost mouth harp.[21] And whether he's polymorphously perverse or not, the novel's use of Freud's famous phrase naming the infant's nonphallic, all-body sexuality in a passage about classical music does constellate Freud, Marcuse, Norman O. Brown, and the powers, subversive or not, of art. Finally, though, nothing in the criticism has persuaded us to read Slothrop as a political dissident or war resister.

One more foray into Marcuse and the Orpheus myth: In *Eros and Civilization* the images of Narcissus and Orpheus "recall the experience of a world that is not to be mastered and controlled but to be liberated—a freedom that will release the powers of Eros now bound in the repressed and petrified forms of man and nature." Marcuse quotes Horace's *Art of Poetry* to show that the harp player Orpheus is the poet who works against repression. Orpheus as poet-artist thus figures potentials for evading the system and battling it, which sixties radicals understood as a matter for regular practice. At every march against the Vietnam War and every countercultural powwow— the November 1965 antiwar march on Washington, the San Francisco Human Be-In of January 1967, the 1969 Woodstock Festival, and the March Against Death in November of that year—political speakers took the stage alongside poets Allen Ginsberg, Robert Lowell, Lenore Kandel, Amiri Baraka, William Merwin, Galway Kinnell, Gary Snyder, and many others. No one knows how many times Ginsberg recited "Howl" or "America" at antiwar demonstrations. Marcuse had foretold poetry's subversive powers in *Eros and Civilization*, and the realization of that prediction in sixties activism further burnished his star as a prophet of the revolution. Actually, though, *Eros and Civilization* also cautions that Orpheus-like figures model the release of new, transformative libidinous potentials as "the isolated deed of unique individuals"; and as such, their release always unfolds under the sign of Thanatos, death. The only way for the Orphic and Narcissist sublimation of libidinal energy really to avoid the cul-de-sac of mortality, Marcuse argues, is to make it "a supra-individual process on common ground."[22]

Subversive art must therefore sustain communal life by correcting errant sociocultural processes and adding to positive liberty. That said, how can we valorize Slothrop as Orpheus? He surely does become a Counterforce hero, but we cannot see how that role differs from mere celebrity status. Neither Slothrop nor the Counterforce stages any effective opposition to the system, unless we count a disrupted Krupp dinner party. Marcuse's work cautions readers about the problem of mounting a real liberation struggle, warning that revolutions are defeated within themselves.[23] Hite concludes her essay on *Gravity's Rainbow* with a caution that "the *writing* of resistance is also fatally compromised," and she reads Pynchon's novel as self-reflexively aware of that limit.[24] When a Counterforce "Spokesman" grants an interview to the *Wall Street Journal*, the interviewee, in bracketed sections, inserts a kind of meta-commentary on himself, sixties dissidents, and the *Journal*'s editors, branded as "Typhoid Marys," who infected him and the movement with their deadly, capitalist virus and ended what he nostalgically names "the years of grease and passage, 1966 and 1971."[25] Those dates mark the period of the countercultural New Left's apogee and the beginning of its descent. They also mark the period when Pynchon was writing *Gravity's Rainbow*.

The parallel, which hardly seems coincidental, might tempt one to identify that "Spokesman" with the narrator-author, thus to valorize this novel on Marcusean terms: as experimental art whose subversion endures and matters because it manifests fantasy and "becomes surrealistic and atonal."[26] Hite concludes that the writing cannily admits complicity as a way to deny, or one could say to transcend or sublate, the charges of acting in complicity with the system.

This seems a nifty way to snatch artistic triumph from the jaws of political defeat. But before nodding assent to such an upbeat reading of *Gravity's Rainbow* one ought to recall Marcuse's requirement that subversive artwork must be communally sustainable and have social utility. This again is the positive freedom in a liberation struggle that Fromm sees as its acid test. So it is for all critical analyses of Long Sixties activism, and this helps to frame analyses of what Pynchon's historical novel finds. We position that inquiry by making one more sojourn in sixties intellectual history: through Marcuse's critique of Brown, then into the ways these things inflect a reading of polymorphous perversity in *Gravity's Rainbow*.

CHAPTER 3

Brown's Polymorphous Perversity and Marcuse's Repressive Tolerance

In early 1967 Herbert Marcuse and Norman O. Brown squared off on the pages of *Commentary* magazine.[1] By then they were the New Left's brightest intellectual stars. Since 1945 the magazine had been publishing their kind of work: essays and reviews from Old Left but anti-Communist writers like Irving Howe, Hannah Arendt, and Daniel Bell—work with historical and philosophical heft. *Commentary* was still months away from initiating its hard-right turn under the editorship of Norman Podhoretz, though he was already chastising New Left leaders for their drugs, their disheveled, dissolute ways, their disrespect for conventional political organizing, and most of all their sympathy for the devil—namely, Communist-backed anticolonial revolutions. Soon Podhoretz's displeasure would turn to disgust, when New Left leaders criticized the Israeli occupation of Gaza, Sinai, and Old Jerusalem following the June 1967 Six-Day War. Thus in its way and at that moment, the Marcuse-Brown dustup amounted to a crucial turf battle.

Marcuse went first, with a sharply critical review of Brown's latest book, *Love's Body* (1966). Reproaching Brown for seeking to "mystify the possibilities of liberation" from America's racist and repressive system, Marcuse argues that the book's seemingly progressive plan to apply psychoanalysis to "the final liberation of the repressed content" actually amounts to a dangerously regressive turn. Glorifying and prioritizing the unconscious would hardly solve anything, Marcuse contends, and not least because that would deny the very real facts of repression that minorities and dissidents face daily. He quite agrees with Brown that representative government has created mere illusions of "life, freedom, fulfillment" to satisfy legitimate pleas for truer, freer selfhood, thus easing one's translation into "the subject of voluntary servitude in production and consumption, the subject of free enterprise and free election of masters." This mode of soft power being the way domination works in Cold War America, Marcuse flatly refuses any answer that avoids a rational critique of that regime's stark reality: "The roots of repression are and remain real roots: consequently, their eradication remains a real and rational job." What use in that political struggle to improve lives is Brown's program to restore a mythical, Edenic "total unity" as it existed, in the Judeo-Christian parlance of *Love's Body*, before the Fall? Marcuse criticizes the universalism of that program, dismisses its dream of original unity as a "negation of all freedom" because too absolute, and insists that without rational reflection on and analysis of particular conditions, human understanding would fail to constitute a polity offering real freedom equally to all. Still worse is how Brown's book itself testifies to the limitations of his proposals. Marcuse recognizes that it seeks a new medium to capture a deeper truth, but despairs that this "new language" inevitably "looks for support in the old."

Answering Marcuse, Brown first figures the two of them as brothers quarreling over "which of them is the *real* 'revolutionary.'" Then he insists again on his book's main message: "the real fight is not the political fight" because "poetry, art, imagination, the creator spirit is life itself; the real revolutionary power to change the world; and to change the human body." So he does draw a sharp line between them. As Marcuse understood, Brown has committed his work to releasing repressed psychic content, realizing personally and socially its symbolic, universal, and eternal power to recoup a fallen human world by restoring its free, erotic body. He is the new cultural revolutionary, his field of action the mind's repressed fantasias, some of which would need to be disabled, the rest liberated in the arts. Marcuse, he holds, is the old-style political revolutionary committed to dismantling the system by rationally identifying, then disabling its soft machineries of control over bodies and minds.

This fraternal rift was already playing out nationally in the loosely framed movement. Historians Michael Kazin and David Chalmers both point out that between 1965 and 1967 a sharp divide opened. On one side were civil rights and sds leaders committed to organizing, to living the idea of participatory democracy and taking it into the streets as well as into legislative halls and legal chambers. On the other were the cultural dissidents who eschewed organization and built no durable membership, much less strong working affiliations and programs, but did lay out a powerful critique of how the military-industrial complex now dominated everyday life, so that activism needed to concentrate on expanded concepts of individual freedom, self-expression, and identity. Roszak's *Making of a Counter Culture* attended to that split and gave this other side their name. It also asked how the countercultural Left could achieve political change without being "political," as the New Left urged.

Brown's quarreling brothers metaphor aptly identified the movement's late sixties split into New Left and countercultural Left groups. It also put at stake the status of art. Marcuse would not categorically dismiss *all* art as mystification, but he did dismiss Brown's universalized claim for art as an engine for real political work. So what kind of artwork is *Gravity's Rainbow*? A text striving for Marcuse's rational revolution or indulging in Brown's revolutionary "creator spirit"? Or one that poses radical challenges on terms that both thinkers advocate? Our answers, while hardly definitive, are embedded in the philosophical and artistic divisions that defined the Long Sixties.

A few years after *Gravity's Rainbow* was published, critic Lawrence Wolfley argued for "Pynchon's pervasive indebtedness to the school of psychoanalytic culture criticism," best represented by Brown rather than Marcuse or Fromm. At the outset he confidently declared that Pynchon's "spirit of experimentation" was "liberating" the novel as a genre, restoring "its original concerns with social responsibility and the human comedy."[2] He also regarded Pynchon's novel as a Long Sixties work framed by Cold War anxieties, indeed attentive to "the deepest fears of the fifties intellectual" as found in Brown's *Life against Death* (1959). That book's argument is this: man's repression of unconscious desires having plunged him into an abyss of complexity even as man's rational consciousness has elevated him to a level of techno-scientific expertise where anything is possible, including nuclear annihilation, something has to give. Fail to analyze the bomb as a manifestation of latent fantasies and drives that together must be defused, and the game's over. Civilization's never-ending process of sublimation has brought humanity to a crisis where the "organic unity with nature experienced by every other animal" has vanished. History's storyline is thus the persistence of human error: a sorry record of misrecognized yet real desires. Brown sees two endings. Humanity will either commit "racial suicide," or people will learn to banish repression from daily life, restart a new/old erotic way of living freed from guilt and alienated consciousness, and become happy.

Let us back away from all these texts for a moment. Anyone trained in literary analysis might notice a certain preoccupation with endings: human history's unthinkable yet necessarily thinkable end, motivating Brown's thinkable and happy but historically untried ending of a proper psychoanalytical process, perhaps motivating Pynchon's ending for *Gravity's Rainbow*, which thinks the unthinkable but having approached it then pushes the pause button. And, finally, perhaps it is motivating critic Wolfley's will to close his own analysis of Pynchon's novel, including its end, by making this thinkably unthinkable stuff end on a certain note. Namely, tragic catastrophe. Wolfley concludes that Pynchon shares with Brown a longing for the bomb and racial suicide. In other words, like all of us these two writers yield finally to the death drive, the telos to end all teleology. To get there, Wolfley needs to read the novel's penultimate scene—the April 1945 launching of Rocket 00000, before the jump-cut to the Orpheus Theater circa 1972—as the opposite of a dystopian warning. His Pynchon empathizes with Blicero's desire to "leave this cycle of infection and death" by way of apocalyptic destruction. This ending is the culmination of prior interpretive moves inspired by the critic's wish to define a tight influence: Brown-to-Pynchon. For example: Wolfley reads "Gravity" as the "ultimate metaphor" for the generally manifested "human repression" that he takes as Pynchon's grand theme, via Brown's *Life against Death*, whose argument needs (desires) the specter of nuclear holocaust (off on the horizon) to move readers into revolutionary action (here and now). That argument scants some obvious interpretive problems. For instance, what is the referent of that deictic pronoun in Blicero's stated desire to "leave *this* cycle of infection and death"? Does the word "*this*" index the man's feverish sadomasochism with Gottfried, his rocket battery and its scorched natural setting, Germany and the vast trauma it visited on Europe, or the global catastrophe whose name is fascism? And why presume his leaving means death? For that matter, to what actual or virtual place will that "leave" translate him? Recall the omniscient narrator's reading of the man's tarot and advising readers that Blicero left Germany for someplace like America. If anything, this confluence of three texts—psychoanalytical (Brown's), fictional (Pynchon's), and critical (Wolfley's)—offers readers a cautionary tale. However we read the novel's ending, we should remember that it concludes a fiction which repeatedly evokes deeply held pragmatic, ideological, and philosophical misgivings about the dangers in Western deterministic thought, and particularly the teleological assumptions, often downright deadly, wrapped up in that way of knowing the world: in reverse, from a fantasy of its ending.

A different reading of Pynchon's ending might run like this: The closing representation in the Orpheus Theater refuses to exalt nuclear winter. Even if we wish to read it under the sign of gallows humor, the scene concentrates instead on human resources of solidarity in times of grave danger. The filmgoers cannot know they've been spared just in time, the rocket having been paused in a freeze-frame just above the theater's rooftop, though if we understand them as simulacra of real people then we might well agree that they should have known and had an ethical responsibility to thwart a process that would bring a world-ending missile overhead. Yet readers are given to know nothing more about their characters than that they watch movies and sing, though on the downside we see also that they are *conditioned* to follow a bouncing ball over the onscreen lyric. That bodes ill; but still, it's a long-lost William Pynchon hymn! It has made, like Slothrop's mouth harp, a marvelous journey to return here. Their singing highlights the enduring hopes of even these preterite souls to return to some prior state, and this after the narrator advises there is still time for us to touch each other or only ourselves, even at this late stage in the game of their perdition.

This preterite communion and intimate touching return us to Brown's hope that in liberating people from repression humanity may save itself from annihilation. Drawing on *Life against Death*, Wolfley summarizes the core problematic: "the reason social amelioration is impossible is that the slaves love their chains." Domination persists when subjects are conditioned to repress their deepest desires and yearnings, especially for a freedom they are conditioned to see as perilous, as Fromm reminds us. Indeed Brown agrees with Fromm that Calvinism not only reinforced that mentality, it also disrupted the previously stabilized dialectic of Eros and Thanatos celebrated in Freud's work. Beginning in the seventeenth century, Calvinism and capitalism consigned Western humanity to "a pure culture of the death instinct."[3] This is a strong thesis, and there is no reason to doubt it influenced Pynchon's imaginative work, as Wolfley and others show. Actually, though, an equally trenchant statement of the same idea about willing slaves had appeared in earlier work that was much more seriously discussed in New Left intellectual circles than Brown's 1959 popular book, and was also a cornerstone text for the countercultural Left: the work of Afro-Caribbean psychiatrist and revolutionary Frantz Fanon, whose theses on the function of repression in "the colonized mind" drove his two major works, *Black Skin, White Masks* (1952, translated 1967) and *The Wretched of the Earth* (1961, translated 1965). To these books one must add Tunisian writer Albert Memmi's *The Colonizer and the Colonized* (1957, translated 1967). These were the texts that schooled the movement's committed and militant activists, especially Black Panther writers Eldridge Cleaver and Huey Newton.

All of these works apply politically the elements of Freud's analysis, most concisely stated in "The Uncanny" (1919), that confronting *unheimlich* material (literally, that which is "un-home-like") will send the subject back into the safety of what is *heimlich*, or familiar. In Freud, the uncanny induces anxiety and fear precisely to the degree it constitutes an experiential manifestation, or return, of unconscious and usually repressed erotic impulses. The safely Oedipalized consciousness disarms anxiety arising from repressed infantile trauma by sublimating it. This is also a function (Freud argues, using E. T. A. Hoffmann's 1817 tale, "The Sandman") of art's transformative, symbolic powers. Yet the most *unheimlich* material, particularly those Oedipal anxieties gathering around "the castration complex," just will not stay down, as great literary art—Hoffmann's tale or Shakespeare's *Hamlet*—repeatedly teaches. In a trice, then, the return of the repressed brings on a deadly horror show. Hence those bodies strewn across the stage at *Hamlet*'s end, and the need for a ruler named Fortinbras, or Strong-in-Arms. And thus, for the subjects of any political system grounded in domination, especially racialized colonialism, the prospect of confronting the master or Big Daddy with one's demands for freedom, equality, and justice calls up precisely that fear of castration, the *unheimlich* master plot and key cog in the mechanism by which a patriarchal dominion conditions subjects to desire the very *heimlich* qualities of their domination.

What to do? These books, and Fanon's most persuasively, insist that a major function of revolutionary practice must be to make manifest the un-home-like energies, structures, symbolic complexes, and plots of the colonial system. The most acute of these post-Freudian thinkers (Marcuse included) understood that one way the system maintains its colonial hold on people's minds is by sustaining the fiction of a wall between private and public experiences. Granting patriarchal authority the privacy of its *heimlich* castle helps to bulwark Big Daddy's authority against interrogation. Also, it proscribes and represses certain things as unspeakable, polices supposedly "perverse" sexualities (especially those ignoring the penis), and regulates identities in their hierarchical array. Desublimating these complexes of power and domination by staging "the return of the repressed"—in other words, provoking authority to make its inner workings visible, recognizable, thus superable— summarizes the theory behind a good deal of sixties-era revolutionary praxis. Allen Ginsberg's *Howl* and William Burroughs's *Naked Lunch* gave early examples of what to do, in literature. The period's many sit-ins, teach-ins, be-ins, street theater events, and mocking provocations of police—such as public dope smoking, nudity, and sex—were attempts (trivial, some of them) at further means. While they were moments in a politics of liberation, they weren't conceived as interlinked, much less sequenced as progressive elements in a plot or determined movement toward an already defined social order. They were answers to the questions posed when the novel's narrative voice wonders: "Will Postwar be nothing but 'events,' newly created one moment to the next? No links? Is it the end of history?"[4]

Does *Gravity's Rainbow* present the abolition of repression? Critics who have read the novel alongside the neo-Freudian archive tend to think so, pointing for example to Thanatz's remarks about sadomasochism, or Brigadier Pudding's coprophagia, or various scenes that satirically mock father-figure authorities. Wolfley is typical in finding the novel's represented sexualities unhealthy, and nearly all enchained some way or another, though he does think Slothrop's "childlike animality" manifests a kind of polymorphous perversity that coexists with his deeply repressed side and at least gives the character chances to overcome the repression of his patriarchal sexuality. Wolfley also recovers, without remarking on it, the source text for one of the novel's most hilarious songs about Slothrop, "The Penis He Thought Was His Own." It is from a passage in Brown: "In genital organization we identify with the penis; but the penis we are is not our own, but daddy's."[5] In any case we think there's no need to hope, as Wolfley and others after him are wont to do, for a Tyrone Slothrop finally resolving the duality of his characterization. According to that reading, by the time he disappears Slothrop has recovered the repressed memory of his conditioning as Infant Tyrone. He has reckoned with the specter of Pernicious Pop and realized enough polymorphously perverse sexuality that he's achieved a measure of de-Oedipalized mentality.[6] He's become a legend to the Counterforce. Which accomplishes what? Arguably nothing: so there are reasons to doubt that romanticized reading, and to see why we take one more dip into Marcuse.

Critics who read *Gravity's Rainbow* against post-Freudian thought have tended to work with a too-limited library, neglecting two important Marcuse texts from the mid-sixties: *One-Dimensional Man* and the 1965 essay "Repressive Tolerance." At the end of *One-Dimensional Man*, Marcuse doubts the liberating powers of desublimated "phantasy" that he lauded in *Eros and Civilization*. Since then, imagination has abdicated to "scientific and empirical Reason." Looking to imaginative writers like Samuel Beckett and Rolf Hochhuth, he thinks fiction may represent "values alien to [the social] requirements" of the techno-scientific order.[7] Yet he also wonders if they instead constitute an exception that proves the rule of repression, keeping the flame of fantasy alive, as it were, but nothing more. As later in his review of Brown, so in *One-Dimensional Man* he insists on reasoned political action: "To liberate the imagination so that it can be given all its means of expression presupposes the repression of much that is now free and that perpetuates a repressive society. And such a reversal is not a matter of psychology or ethics but of politics."[8] Marcuse wonders if artists and especially writers who are "outcasts and outsiders," refusing the system, have a specially empowered role to play in subverting or even revolutionizing repressive society. And how about the self-outcast Pynchon, and such a deliberately outrageous book as *Gravity's Rainbow*? We might make the case for him as an insider, a publishing industry star in complicity with the system (comparable to that bracketed Counterforce "Spokesman" in his *Wall Street Journal* interview), than the more easily made case for him as a wacky maverick known publicly only by his voice: on two 2004 episodes of *The Simpsons* and dubbed over a 2009 promotional video for *Inherent Vice*. We don't know enough about him. And the insider-outsider distinction may not matter. As Toon Staes reminds us, even in *One-Dimensional Man* Marcuse considered "the liberating tendencies *within* the established society."[9]

One wouldn't think so, from a first reading of "Repressive Tolerance." The essay's title named a new idea: that power neutralizes subversion by seeming to accommodate revolutionary ideas, indeed by seeming to equitably regulate partisan differences within the polity. Repressive tolerance puts on the guise of true open-mindedness, allowing claims made from both the Right and the Left, including calls for aggression or for peace, demands for maintaining racist and colonialist orders or for civil rights and justice. It puts on that guise of neutrality or blindfolded tolerance precisely because it is wholly committed to sustaining the "already established machinery" which has vitiated individual freedom in the first place, the machinery of militarism, neocolonial aggression abroad, and police repression of racial disorder at home.

If called on to justify that guise, leadership points out the never-ending state of emergency, the threat of nuclear annihilation, as the new and transcendent normality. "The whole post-fascist period is one of clear and present danger," Marcuse concludes.

He also concludes—and here is his essay's payoff—that the repressively tolerant political regime actually encourages subversive *cultural* activity. Subversive expression "in an immediacy" of cultural production is a cheap price to pay for denying individuals "real self-liberation . . . in the political" sphere. Therefore the system

> encourages non-conformity and letting-go in ways which leave the real engines of repression in the society intact, which even strengthen these engines by substituting the satisfactions of private and personal rebellion for a more than private and personal, and therefore more authentic opposition. The desublimation involved in this sort of actualization is itself repressive inasmuch as it weakens the necessity and the power of the intellect, the catalytic force of that unhappy consciousness which does not revel in the archetypal personal release of frustration—hopeless resurgence of the Id which will sooner or later succumb to the omnipresent rationality of the administered world.[10]

In this passage Marcuse all but defines countercultural leisure, activism, revelries, mysticism, and artistic productivity as "mindless pleasures." He critiques them as an always-already co-opted subversion, counterrevolutionary in effect if not in spirit. Moreover, he composed this critique in 1967, a good two years before the countercultural Left fully emerged, and before Roszak named it as such.

It was a deeply pessimistic foretelling. "With the concentration of economic and political power and the integration of opposites in a society which uses technology as an instrument of domination," Marcuse believed, "effective dissent is blocked where it could freely emerge." In the media, meaning has been fully stabilized. "Other words can be spoken and heard, other ideas can be expressed," but they are immediately recuperated "in terms of the public language." (The imagined "Newspeak" of Orwell's novel *1984* fully realized, in short.) As for the role of educators, public intellectuals, and writers like himself, Marcuse looks around and finds that "repression invades the academic enterprise itself."[11] He does not explicitly discuss literature or art, but they are implied throughout his discussion of cultural production.

What about Pynchon, then, and *Gravity's Rainbow*? Scholars having so little biographical material about him, including for the second half of the sixties, are prone to grab the little there is and try to make much of it. One example: his celebrated introduction to the story collection *Slow Learner*, though it is a treacherous text when it comes to establishing Pynchon's narrative poetics, much less his worldly commitments.[12] We know, also, that Pynchon allowed his name to be used, among other signatories, in an advertisement opposing the Vietnam War in *Ramparts* magazine and the *New York Review of Books*, a move that landed all of them—his literary agent Candida Donadio, his friends Kirk and Faith Sale and Jules Siegel, and writers and editors such as Ed Sanders, Allen Ginsberg, Paul Krassner, and Kurt Vonnegut—on the FBI watch list or "Security Index."[13] We have his novels set in the sixties, especially *Vineland* and *Inherent Vice*, the latter with its notable epigraph from the radical Situationists who provided provocative slogans for the May 1968 Paris student uprising and general strike. But what to make of these bits? Our approach here is to read the novel in context with relevant intellectual and cultural history. When the novel's narrator reminds us how "the Man" operates "a branch office in each of our brains," we get the humor of it at the same time we recognize it as a common locution.[14] Using street speech to address antiracist and antiwar activists, it also shares a concept, and critique, of post-fascist domination ("the Man") operating as a persistent exercise of soft power, of repressive tolerance and its ways of colonizing (opening "a branch office in") one's mind. This was definitely *not* paranoia, in the common sense. Rather, Pynchon enunciated a way of thinking cynically about signifying activity in the age of late modern media, especially about the politics and the political means of disrupting the normally smooth operations of "mindless pleasures." And speech freedoms were critical in that effort.

CHAPTER 4

Total Assault on the Culture

In 1966 municipal and federal law enforcement officers raided the Atlanta home of Robert Eli Stanley, a suspected bookmaker for a "mafia-style" gambling operation. Their search uncovered no "wagering paraphernalia or records" but did reveal, in a desk drawer, three reels of eight-millimeter film which, when officers spooled them up on a projector stored elsewhere in the suspect's home, turned out to be quite sexually explicit. They arrested Stanley on a 1963 Georgia statute criminalizing the possession of obscene material. A jury convicted him, the county judge trying his case sentenced Stanley to a year in the state penitentiary, and Georgia Supreme Court justices denied his appeal. During that appeal Stanley's attorney argued that even if the films depicted (as the trial judge had put it) "incredible smut," they nonetheless hadn't been named in the warrant and so were illegally seized, and were further shielded from prosecution because Stanley had the First Amendment right to read or view whatever he wished in the privacy of his home. Stanley's appeal went to the U.S. Supreme Court, whose justices unanimously overturned the Georgia ruling in April 1969, three years after his arrest.[1]

The judicial record is unclear just how extravagant were the legally actionable sex scenes in the film with which Robert Stanley pleasured himself. We can safely guess those scenes fell short of the orgy Pynchon depicts on the good ship *Anubis*, somewhere on the Oder River north of Berlin, in episode 14 of part 3 of *Gravity's Rainbow*. As a thought experiment, we like to imagine Pynchon wrote the scene as Stanley's obscenity trial—among others like it—went forward. This scene no more offends conventional morality than numerous other outrageous ones in *Gravity's Rainbow*. It makes a good study, however, because of how the episode seems so determined to script various sexual modes, such as vaginal and anal penetration, fellatio, cunnilingus, and anilingus linking various hetero- and homosexual pairs, while also including a wide array of paraphilias, such as voyeurism, frotteurism (rubbing), sadomasochism, pedophilia, and fetishism. This catalog could have been lifted straight from Richard von Krafft-Ebing's 1886 classic, *Psychopathia Sexualis*, mentioned earlier in the novel.[2]

The action begins with Margherita Erdmann sadomasochistically disciplining daughter Bianca as the gathered crowd gapes voyeuristically, everyone finding "the medium of touch," groping one another, then collapsing in a range of positions linking everyone in a great daisy chain, all of it explicitly described. It ends with our narrator concluding, as if from a participant's view, that "it *feels*, at least, like everybody came together." Along the way the narrator also remarks on the number of nationalities represented (German, French, Wend, Yugoslav, Swiss, Russian, Austrian, Dutch, and American), the range of class affiliations (waiters to bankers), and the different racial types, including a "mulatto girl" who gropes Slothrop. So here we have the demos in all its desublimated, polymorphously perverse glory. Yet the people are, also, in the full grip of repressive tolerance, of mindless pleasures managed, it seems, by representatives of the power elite who evidently own and captain this ship, clearly depicted in the clutches of Thanatos, for Anubis was the Egyptian god protecting dead souls on their journey to the afterlife. Again, the devil is always in such details. And good for Slothrop, then, when (in episode 18) he utters "just a meek tearful *oh fuck*" when, during a storm, something or someone has tossed him from the *Anubis* into the waters, where he's soon saved, pulled like a fish, or Melville's Ishmael, into a passing boat. This is one way of reading the orgy scene's narrative logic, which satirizes overt and covert modes of domination, and Slothrop's fortunate extrication from what might seem alluring but is cast as, in every sense, a bad trip. Another would be to look not at the events but at the language, as a deliberately scripted, in-your-face challenge to existing obscenity and pornography laws, a resistance to governmental dominion over speech.

Today the case known as *Stanley v. Georgia* gets relatively little attention. Ostensibly turning on the issue of *possession* rather than *expression*, *Stanley* has seemed peripheral to the more important Long Sixties narrative about expanded speech rights. Beginning in the late 1950s, attorneys such as Charles Rembar mounted victorious challenges in state and federal courts to anti-obscenity statutes prohibiting the expression of everyday intimate human experiences and commonly used words. They rescued from criminalization and banishment a number of now-classic literary texts: Allen Ginsberg's *Howl* (1956, tried in 1957), D. H. Lawrence's *Lady Chatterley's Lover* (1928, tried in 1959), Henry Miller's *Tropic of Cancer* (1934, tried in 1961), John Cleland's *Fanny Hill* (1749, tried in 1966), and William Burroughs's *Naked Lunch* (1959, tried in 1960 and 1966). These cases were bracketed by two landmark Supreme Court decisions, *Roth v. U.S.* (1957) and *Miller v. California* (1973), which established (in *Roth*) and then bulwarked (in *Miller*) the greatly liberalized definition of obscenity that stands today: a work of any kind cannot be judged obscene if, when taken as a whole, it can be shown to have redeeming social value.[3] The road to those expanded rights of free expression was marked throughout the Long Sixties by raids on and prosecutions and convictions of writers, publishers, and performers. U.S. Postal Service authorities seized texts with lines like this one from Ginsberg: "America, go fuck yourself with your atom bomb." Local police targeted stand-up comics who uttered words such as "shit" or "fuck" or "cocksucker," arresting leftist comedian Lenny Bruce at clubs like the Troubadour in Los Angeles (six times in 1963–64) and New York's Cafe Au Go Go, practically hounding the man to death.[4]

Observing these speech restrictions from New York, editor Paul Krassner of the *Realist* (1958–84) and Ed Sanders, editor, printer, and distributor of the irregularly mimeographed underground journal *Fuck You: A Magazine of the Arts* (1962–65, subtitled "Total Assault on the Culture"), both voiced the general sense of outrage at this suppression. They regularly satirized as "Nazis" and "Gestapo" the police and prosecutors whose zeal for restraining speech rights was itself unrestrained, for it included numerous constitutionally forbidden invasions and destructions of writers' and publishers' private property. In January 1966, for example, Sanders became a target when New York police mounted a warrantless raid on his Peace Eye Bookstore, vandalizing the place and arresting him for publishing and holding obscene literature with intent to sell. The offending item: a back issue of *Fuck You* with an enigmatic hieroglyphic or graffiti-like cover sketch depicting a bird with a huge human phallus ejaculating toward a naked, kneeling young man. Sanders won his case at trial. Still, the action forced him into a costly and distracting legal defense that, as prosecutors secondarily intended, broadcast a chillingly repressive message to other underground press editors, like Krassner, whose satires of puritanical government do-gooders remained more circumspect than those of his downtown counterpart, Sanders.[5]

By the late sixties such harassment had become secretly institutionalized in the U.S. federal government. Authorities deliberately employed obscenity and pornography laws as powerful tools for disrupting and suppressing the political and countercultural Left. Covertly, by 1966 the Federal Bureau of Investigation was running what were later named COINTELPRO (Counter-Intelligence Program) operations that strategically targeted leftist underground press editors, arresting them on obscenity charges that—as the release of internal memos later showed—were frankly intended just to shut them down. The record also shows (as many at the time suspected) that beginning with Richard Nixon's presidency in 1969 the FBI, the Central Intelligence Agency, and a specially tasked unit of the U.S. Army coordinated federal efforts to illegally infiltrate, wiretap, disrupt, break and enter, and destroy the activities, press machinery, printed materials, and facilities of underground newspapers, often by using more than two thousand agents to plant evidence, such as obscene material or drugs, so that cooperating local police might justify arrests and seizures, though the political motives were commonly understood.[6] During this "hot" phase of the U.S. culture war the government's "enemies list" included hundreds of leftist newspapers, such as the *East Village*

Other, the *Berkeley Barb*, and the *L.A. Free Press* (or *Freep*), all published using new, easily learned, and relatively inexpensive photo-offset printing techniques. Sanders relied on a still simpler technology, publishing *Fuck You* on a used, hand-cranked Gestetner mimeograph machine. So did his Lower East Side compatriots, Up Against the Wall Motherfuckers, an anarchist collective with an unprintable name ("That which cannot be spoken, cannot be co-opted," they liked to say). From 1966 to 1968 the UAWMF published ten numbers of the hand-stapled journal *Black Mask*.[7] The writer-editor-publishers of these and hundreds of similar papers were amateurs when they commenced the work, and most of them barely covered costs through local sales. Widely circulated titles like the *Barb* and the *Freep* made enough from sales, subscriptions, and advertising to exercise their negative liberty to print what they considered politically significant, and to realize the blessings of positive liberty as well. Their pages included community announcements and news, reviews of cultural productions and events, critical and theoretical essays, investigative articles, national and international news from nontraditional wire services, and strong editorials. Humor was their dominant mode. All understood the use of irony and invective satire in targeting entrenched powers, and liberally sprinkled their pages, covers included, with images defying pornography laws and with the impolite curses, vulgarities, invectives, obscenities, sexually charged metaphors, and street lingo that are age-old rhetorical resources for carnivalesque representation and satirical critique.[8]

Editors' jabs at government's repression of speech could be delightfully, cleverly resourceful. The *Realist* aggravated the establishment's puritanical crackdown on obscenity with a front-cover banner in patriotic red, white, and blue that urged readers to "Fuck Communism." It was available also as a bumper sticker. But would police prosecute, and thus side with Communists? None took the bait. Similarly, the sexually raucous and grotesque language and imagery that underground editors turned against the likes of FBI director J. Edgar Hoover and Presidents Johnson and Nixon, among many others, habitually taunted police to bring obscenity and libel charges. Illustrations on the front pages of underground newspapers depicted Hoover in drag, or a bell-cheeked Nixon with a pendulous phallic nose.[9] In 1968 police arrested and charged with obscenity and criminal libel three University of Hartford students. On the November 13, 1968, cover of the *News-Liberated Press*, an alternative, off-campus paper, cartoonist John Zanzel had depicted the president-elect as the upraised middle finger of a clenched fist, the finger "looking like a penis" as well as like the president, and boldly captioned "Richard M. Nixon." Before the trial, Judge William Ewing dismissed the obscenity charges on grounds the image could be said to have "redeeming social value" as political expression, but he allowed trial on the libel charges. In December 1969 a jury found one of the defendants, twenty-two-year-old editor Jack Hardy, guilty of violating the Connecticut libel statute. Ewing handed down a sentence of ninety days in jail and a stiff fine. The state supreme court later overturned Hardy's conviction on appeal. He remains, however, the only American citizen ever convicted of libeling a president.[10]

As the butts of underground press satires responded using the law's full force, and threats of worse, a certain chill descended. In April 1970, after months of embittered ridicule, criticism, and demonstrations protesting his handling of antiwar resistance at the University of California's most politically active campuses—Berkeley, Santa Barbara, and Los Angeles—an angry Governor Reagan stood against the backdrop of Yosemite National Park and, before the Council of California Growers (large industrial farmers eager to maintain suppression of Cesar Chavez's upstart United Farm Workers union, widely supported by movement activists), coldly threw down a warning to the dissident Left: "If it takes a bloodbath, let's get it over with. No more appeasement." Over the next few months demonstrators protesting the secret, illegal bombing of Cambodia were fatally shot at Santa Barbara, Berkeley, Kent State, and Jackson State universities, and elsewhere. In late 1969 and early 1970, Black Panther Party leader Eldridge Cleaver, having evidently been drawn into a bloody gunfight with police in Oakland, California, fled the United States; Chicago police gunned down Panther leaders Mark Clark and Fred Hampton (killings for which FBI agents were later found criminally complicit); and the overtly violent Weather Underground faction that had spun off from Students for a Democratic Society mounted their "Days of Rage" mayhem in Chicago—and then went underground.[11] The blithe romance of resistance was over.

Countercultural activists occasionally mounted their own secret ops. In 1969 a disenchanted clerk in the California attorney general's office handed the *Los Angeles Free Press* editor confidential documents about University of California campus police break-ins, which listed the names and addresses of eighty state officers engaged in undercover work. Within weeks of publishing these materials *Freep* staff were arrested on felony charges of receiving stolen property; the charges were later dropped because the documents were public property, even if clandestinely taken and shared.[12] In early 1971, unidentified members of the pacifist War Resisters League mounted a daring nighttime raid on FBI offices in Pennsylvania, successfully "liberating" a trove of "political documents." When published in the New York–based underground paper WIN, these memorandums revealed the establishment's siege mentality and disclosed for the first time the extent of highly secret COINTELPRO efforts to disrupt and dismantle the countercultural Left, particularly its presses. Some plots described in the documents turned out to be stranger than fiction, one rivaling even the paranoid fantasies of the great novel Pynchon was then writing. FBI field agents proposed to covertly spray newly printed, baled, and warehoused copies of the *Black Panther Party Paper* with skatole, an organic indole compound naturally available in feces and coal tars. Their idea was that after drying overnight the liquid's powerful fecal odor would make distributing the papers impossible; as an added bonus, it would also symbolically brand such work and its African American authors as *shit*.[13] Other FBI and COINTELPRO operatives tasked with spreading disinformation created and distributed fake underground newspapers whose lame titles—*Armageddon News* or *Longhorn Tales*—and awkwardly written attempts at movement metaphors and street lingo easily tipped savvy readers to the fraud.[14] The core of that federal effort, though, focused on unabashedly repressive tactics. This history was common knowledge on the left and was finally confirmed after the Long Sixties, in documents pried loose by Freedom of Information Act requests, which revealed how agents destroyed newspapers in transit from printers, coerced landlords into raising rents on movement and newspaper offices, and assisted local police in crippling editors with manufactured criminal charges. In 1969–70 the editor of the Miami, Florida, *Daily Planet* was arrested twenty-nine times for selling obscene literature. His costs for bail alone—by arrest twenty-nine, over $90,000, or a half million in 2013 dollars—drove the paper out of business, despite kind fundraising efforts by activist writers like Allen Ginsberg.[15]

Historian John McMillian shows that this covert yet widely acknowledged and systematic federal repression damaged the material resources, morale, and solidarity vital to movement organization and activism. By 1974 more than four-fifths of the over four hundred underground press papers that began flourishing just nine years earlier had vanished.[16] At the same time, overt public repression had equally chilling effects as interest groups and legislatures mounted strong and well-funded threats to new First Amendment freedoms affirmed by federal courts. Throughout the Long Sixties, conservative and religiously affiliated groups like Mothers for Moral America, Citizens for Decent Literature, and the National Organization for Decent Literature kept up the heat on municipal law enforcement to prosecute obscenity cases and lobbied Congress to pass a new court-proof, nationally restrictive anti-obscenity law. They also stoked conservative outrage against the 1970 report of the President's Commission on Obscenity and Pornography.

After two years of considering research and testimonies offered by numerous experts, the commission had found no empirical evidence proving that sexually explicit materials or "foul language" caused deleterious effects to individuals or society. The hearings had also produced another moment paralleling *Gravity's Rainbow* style of chicanery. Thomas King Forcade was the coordinator of the Underground Press Syndicate (a kind of countercultural Associated Press), and he had been closely monitoring government plots to suppress and eliminate underground presses. When granted his request to testify before the commission, Forcade grabbed the opportunity to complain that the commissioners were paying no attention to ways that law enforcement was using obscenity law as a ruse to deny First Amendment press rights. Forcade read from a written statement incisive in its analysis and corrosive in its laugh-out-loud vitriol, as when he accused commissioners of representing the interests of "the Brain Police, Mind Monitors, Thought Thugs," and told them: "you make me puke green monkey shit." In concluding, Forcade reached into a box on the table before him and deftly tossed a cream pie at a commissioner's head.[17] The President's Commission had no interest in counterculture theatrics or Forcade's specific grievances. Nonetheless its report did make quite liberal recommendations. With just three of eighteen bipartisan members dissenting, the commission concluded that minors should be shielded from sexually graphic materials and epithets, but that otherwise Congress should pass legislation repealing *all* federal, state, and municipal obscenity statutes. This would have been a great victory for the interests Forcade represented, but the issue was dead on arrival in Congress. Meanwhile, the report entirely sidestepped charges that secret, "totalitarian" police had conspired to use obscenity and pornography laws in efforts to curb antiwar and antiracist dissent, and thus, as Forcade phrased it, "to stomp out our freedom of the press." Nixon rejected all of the commission's recommendations and denounced the six-to-one majority's "liberalism," vowing his administration would dam up the "flood" of "filthy books and plays" which threatened "the pollution of our culture, the pollution of our civilization, with smut." He might well have done so, had it not been for the ongoing war in Vietnam that he'd promised (while campaigning in 1968) to end, and then (after 1972) the steadily expanding Watergate scandal. A less-distracted and stronger Nixon administration surely would have worked to roll back the new, court-affirmed free-speech rights of 1957–73.[18]

Thomas Forcade's theatrical, pie-throwing rant against congressional and academic "Mind Monitors" and "Thought Thugs" occurred in a much wider political context. Namely, an array of loosely related anarchist collectives, including the San Francisco–based Diggers, the Chicago-based Yippies (of the Youth International Party), and their less remembered cousins from New York's Lower East Side, Up Against the Wall Motherfuckers. The last group took its then unprintable name from a 1967 Amiri Baraka prose poem, or rap, titled "Black People," whose voice urges action among urban brothers surrounded by wonderfully alluring commodities but relegated to abject ghetto poverty: "All the stores will be open if you say the magic words. The magic words are: Up against the wall mother fuckers, this is a stick up!"[19] The name guaranteed they would never be spotlighted, or co-opted, on Walter Cronkite's evening news broadcast. As in the SDS and across the front of loosely affiliated radical Left groups, Digger, UAWMF, and Yippie leaders based their critiques and practices on Norbert Wiener's *The Human Use of Human Beings* (1950), C. Wright Mills's *The Power Elite* (1956), and John Kenneth Galbraith's *The Affluent Society* (1958). The UAWMF manifestos were particularly indebted to Wilhelm Reich's writings in English translation, *The Sexual Revolution* (1936, translated 1945) and *The Mass Psychology of Fascism* (1933, translated 1946). And like other movement theorists, they invoked the writings of Fromm, Brown, and Marcuse, as well as Theodor Adorno and Walter Benjamin, particularly his 1921 essay, "Critique of Violence." They were also following and, if their French was adequate, reading key works of the Situationist International: Raoul Vaneigem's *The Revolution of Everyday Life* (1967), especially its critique of the perverse humiliations in technologized late capitalism of being another person's "thing"; and Guy Debord's widely circulated *Society of the Spectacle* (1967), particularly after its unauthorized 1970 English translation from leftist Detroit publisher Red and Black. Additionally, whenever defining themselves as a political and cultural avant-garde, these groups acknowledged the legacies of dadaist and surrealist aesthetics and their critique of determinist reason, everyday images and commodities, and repressed desire.

The Digger, UAWMF, and Yippie leadership always saw satire and guerrilla theater tactics as means for taking theory into the streets. The Diggers, originally a San Francisco anarchist collective named for the 1649 English revolutionaries who resisted the enclosure and privatization of commons land, drew members from the San Francisco Mime Troupe and, in addition to arranging free food, medicine, and housing, staged theatrical events challenging segregation, lynching, the war in Vietnam, and the draft. They routinely and scathingly satirized Lyndon Johnson and his administration. In contrast, UAWMF activists were more directly confrontational, though less so than the Weather Underground. In October 1967 UAWMF activists broke into the Pentagon building during an occupation of the grounds and suffered brutal beatings at the hands of military police. In January 1968 the UAWMF staged a mock assassination (using a pistol loaded with blanks) of poet Kenneth Koch at a quite apolitical reading—precisely the reason that UAWMF leader Ben Morea decided to put such a fright into Koch and his audience. They demonstrated solidarity with striking New York City sanitation workers, most of them African American, by hurling piles of uncollected, rotting garbage into a Lincoln Center fountain just before elite white Manhattanites arrived in limousines for a grand event. There were also UAWMF filmmakers on hand, cameras rolling, as activists confronted the disgusted men and women in their evening attire, and as squads of baton-swinging city police made arrests.[20]

Yippie satire tended more toward absurdist and surrealist modalities. Months before finding their name at a 1967 New Year's Eve party hosted by *Realist* editor Krassner, future Yippie leaders Abbie Hoffman and Jerry Rubin orchestrated two striking guerrilla theater events. Aided by UAWMF members, they had disrupted the New York Stock Exchange in August 1967 when Hoffman and others tossed fistfuls of money onto the exchange floor, then ridiculed the traders greedily scrambling to gather up the one dollar bills. Two months later they masterminded the mock attempt to "levitate" the Pentagon during the antiwar March on Washington. That day, as military police beat invading UAWMF members for breaching the building, Allen Ginsberg and the masses tried to chant the building skyward, while novelist Norman Mailer made mental notes for *Armies of the Night* (1968), which would novelize the day's skirmishes. In March 1968, the Yippies' antiwar occupation of New York's Grand Central Station ended in a violent clash with city police. And that summer they and others provoked the massive police and National Guard mobilization and violence outside the Democratic National Convention meetings in Chicago, battles punctuated by such satirical media moments as Hoffman and Rubin introducing Yippie presidential candidate "Pigasus the Immortal," a 145-pound hog of whom the campaign literature boasted: "They [the Democrats] nominate a pig and he eats the people. We nominate a president and the people eat him." Other guerrilla theater moments included "news conference" bulletins, one announcing that Yippies planned to lace Chicago's drinking water with LSD, another featuring campaign slogans riffing on what French Situationists produced in the 1968 general strike: "We Demand the Politics of Ecstasy!" and "We Will Fuck on the Beaches!" and "Free Speech Is the Right to Shout THEATER in a Crowded Fire!" In a longer, textual version of the 1968 "Yippie Manifesto," Rubin argued: "Slogans like 'Get Out of Vietnam' are informative, but do not create myths. They don't ask you to *do anything* but carry them." Yippie slogans were instead designed to be performative, to enact inversions of everyday phrases, thus to "make people dream and fantasize" and finally to speak "a magic world which we make real." This is why editor-activist Abe Peck looked back on the Yippies as "flamboyant, but not stupid." Understanding language and media "as a combat zone," they staged situations and deployed subversively ironic words and symbols as means, Peck realized, to create "a united counterculture." When Rubin was subpoenaed to testify before the House Un-American Activities Committee in 1968, he led fellow Yippie witnesses in blowing great chewing-gum bubbles as supporters seated behind them rose to salute congressmen Nazi-style, all of it caught on camera and cycled repeatedly through network news broadcasts, major newspapers and magazines, and underground press tabloids. At their 1969 trial on charges of conspiring to incite a riot during the "Siege of Chicago" in the summer of 1968, Yippie defendants blew kisses to the jury, wore outlandish clothes (one day, judges' robes), and ridiculed Judge Julius Hoffman (no relation to Abbie) as a traitorous Jew and Hitler stooge, his court as "bullshit." They won acquittal on all conspiracy charges but were convicted on some lesser ones, largely reversed on appeal in 1972. Having also paid various fines, many for contempt of court (which none would deny), they were never retried. By then the Yippies were already dispersed, bygones awaiting their chapter in sixties histories.[21]

Skilled as they were at grabbing headlines and getting on television, the Yippies had alienated their more radical, theory-based anarchist counterparts. By mid-1968 the Diggers were chastising Rubin and Hoffman for their merely entertaining and ephemeral theatrics, while demanding that they delink all mentions of Diggers from Yippie attempts to promote "their images as countercultural leaders and spokesmen."[22] The militant Motherfuckers broadcast a more scathing critique. As early as mid-1967, issues of *Black Mask* called on movement activists to set aside "the concept of 'symbolic' protest" as well as the practice of satirical guerrilla theater because those tactics' moral persuasiveness had not generated the broad-based dissident and insurgent movement required to end the Vietnam War and Deep South segregation, much less radically alter U.S. culture and politics. By mid-1968 the UAWMF writings in *Black Mask* and various pamphlets also dismissed the Yippie program as ineffectual "canned pornography" and hypocritical "psychedelic profiteering," and were ridiculing movement elders such as Allen Ginsberg and Norman Mailer as a "new establishment" manifesting "all the mind sapping and anti-revolutionary characteristics of the old" establishment. They further critiqued the Diggers' guerrilla theater efforts and their free institutions (food, housing, medical care, transportation, and so on) as recycled dadaism, on the one hand, and as meekly ineffectual challenges to class and race hierarchies, on the other.[23]

This is the contentious, tumultuous historical context for reading *Gravity's Rainbow*, which Pynchon criticism cursorily acknowledges but otherwise leaves quite unexamined, despite or perhaps because of the subject's breadth and depth, as well as basic difficulties of doing research on the period—that is, until a spate of new memoirs, editions, and histories came into print, and previously rare and ephemeral underground press materials became available in special collections and digital archives. Long Sixties history offers concrete and vitally energizing material enabling literary scholars to rethink the aesthetic practices and political designs of literary satires during the period, Pynchon's great novel centrally among them. For example, the sixties counterculture is obviously crucial to any reckoning of Pynchon's representation of an emergent Counterforce. We think, for example, that even novice readers will recognize in Thomas Forcade's pie throwing and alliterative riffing on brain police, mind monitors, and thought thugs that make him "puke green monkey shit" the kind of seed that grew into the novel's "Krupp Wingding" scene. There, having penetrated the military-industrial complex's innermost sanctum, a private dinner party, Counterforce members just *might*—our narrator remarks—have positioned themselves "to disarm, de-penis, and dis-mantle the Man." Except that he, or rather They, have cannily installed that "branch office in each of our brains" which makes even Counterforce resistance "as schizoid, as double-minded in the massive presence of money, as any." Themselves thus unwittingly de-penised, Roger Mexico and crew commence, at the utterance of a code word ("ketchup"), their requests for non-menu items: *snot soup, pus pudding, menstrual marmalade*, and *vomit vichyssoise*—a long, rollicking Rabelaisian catalog. This leaves the "well-bred gagging" as various international cartel executives and their wives spew rain-bow arcs of "lumpy beige vomit" and, to kazoo accompaniment, our heroes make their escape abetted by black butlers who join the word-play while opening doors for Counterforce anarchists safely to regain the "outside" and freedom.[24] But as the UAWMF and Weather Underground critics were asking: this guerrilla theater accomplishes what, exactly? Or, as agent Hector Zuñiga puts the question to ex-hippie Zoyd Wheeler, in *Vineland*: "ask your-self, OK, 'Who was saved?'"[25] Writing about that novel, critic N. Katherine Hayles has rightly observed Pynchon asking "how profoundly the American revolution of the sixties failed."[26]

We think that the textual evidence put in this wider historical context reveals Pynchon already posing that question in 1973. Initially of course the Counterforce forms for purposes of a search-and-rescue mission into the Zone. Their objective: Tyrone Slothrop, the beleaguered, scuffling ally each of them has in one way or another been complicit in selling out to Them. By the Krupp wingding a few months later, it is no longer clear just what or who is the objective, the liberating desire and/or the salvific mission, of the Counterforce's disruptive guerrilla theater. Certainly they've accomplished nothing more than making Slothrop an underground legend.

We leave that issue for this book's third part, "Freedom." Here we need to recover some core strands of expression and analysis running through the Long Sixties print record, to supplement the issues and problems we have just located in the psychohistorical critiques of Fromm, Marcuse, and Brown. Turning to cultural history, we focus on sixties-era alternative and under-ground writings as efforts in a still wider discursive field, a goodly portion of them comprising the cultural struggle Marcuse rather dismissed in his "Re-pressive Tolerance" essay. While contested from within and without, that field of writings nevertheless wires into Pynchon's narrative discourse and at times lights up in striking ways the particular thematic expressions of domi-nation and of "the chances for freedom" in *Gravity's Rainbow*.

Take Pynchon's numerous and consistently critical references in the novel to "the System," always capitalized to distinguish it from V-2 rocket subas-semblies like the "guidance system," though the narration will often analogize rocket control devices to ideological apparatuses for individual and social control, in Althusser's sense. In *Gravity's Rainbow*, as in sixties counterculture discourse, "the System" is always much more than the military-industrial complex, though that's a core reference. The term also encompasses the legal code and law enforcement, electoral politics and day-to-day governance at all levels (federal to municipal), and a social class hierarchy further overcoded by ethno-racial categories, some of which entail a people's relative rightslessness. Moreover, and centrally, "the System" is a culture conditioned by late modern media and the social management of spectacle. Its aim: to construct the passive citizenry necessary for the commodification and marketing of everything in an affluent West dedicated to "leisure" and "entertainment." That citizenry must be conditioned to accept the deep alienation of work and the repression of desires, conditioned in other words to the forcing of ordinary life into straight and narrow channels of rational and determinist thought, familial and social structures of patriarchy, and strictly regulated desires and fantasies. Interlinking all these aspects, "the System" as a discursive and representational network defines them as "natural" and "just," ultimately as humanity's best bulwarks against the loosing of anarchy, whose end result would be civilization's suicide. Motherfucker Osha Neumann alliteratively summed up the idea: "By 'The System' we meant more than the economic and political institutions by which the rich wage unequal war against the poor, stealing the fruits of their labors, and despoiling the earth in the process. We meant the totality of reality as shaped by, dependent upon, and supportive of those institutions. We meant presidents and penises, the Pentagon and our parents, desires and disaffections, torturers and toothpaste . . . 'The System.' All of it. The whole kit and caboodle."[27] That was the shared sense after 1966, whenever the term appeared in *Ramparts* or *Rat*, in the *Barb* or *Black Mask*. *Gravity's Rainbow* presumes this broad meaning while also stressing the system's linear, deterministic articulation of power: "Taking and not giving back, demanding that 'productivity' and 'earnings' keep on increasing with time, the System removing from the rest of the World these vast quantities of energy to keep its own tiny desperate fraction showing a profit" even while refusing to think of itself as "only buying time."[28]

In formulating analyses of the system, sixties radicals drew much from the texts we have already mentioned and discussed, including Wiener's *Human Use of Human Beings* for its warning about new and more subtle means for repressive social management. These activists developed a critique of systematic power's dependence not just on overt but more invidiously on covert means of conditioning and control—terms often used practically as synonyms. "The Digger Papers" foregrounds questions about "[w]ho's going to control the language . . . the microphone," ultimately one's "phantasies" and thus "one's own mind."[29] In *Black Mask* the Motherfuckers laid out a Reichian analysis of subliminally conditioned submissive mentality, prevalent especially "during periods of social collapse." Understood as requiring Oedi-palized "sexual repression in its formation" during early childhood, this type of regime develops a personality that capitalism markets "by the tens of millions" and catechizes under the everyday domination of "parents, educators, and politicians." The *Black Mask* text concludes with a classic proclamation of negative liberty: "Revolution begins when people take control of their own lives."[30] The primary and urgent task then was to break that mental vise grip, for "the System" seemed hell-bent on its own "death trip" like "a suicidal nation . . . racing to our death in high powered automobiles," argued the Motherfuckers (in a trope the Yippies adopted wholesale). Meanwhile Motherfuckers and Diggers alike foretold how humanity's "giant comedy ends with an explosion" of somebody's errantly launched nuclear missile.[31]

Such pessimism, circa 1967, represented a significant change, or sobering up. Just eighteen months earlier the inaugural issue of *Black Mask* had opened with a Whitmanian chant to the "men at the gates seeking a new world. The machine, the rocket, the conquering of space and time, these are the seeds of a future which, freed from your barbarism, will carry us forward. We are ready. LET THE STRUGGLE BEGIN!" Actually a good deal of that techno-scientific optimism circulated through the late sixties, but chiefly it came from men well ensconced in the system: men like the former Prussian aristocrat, Nazi rocketman, émigré missile builder for the U.S. Army, and Apollo moon program director, Wernher von Braun. His self-aggrandizing and generally panned 1960 bio-pic *I Aim at the Stars* (rather than at, uhmmm, London?, asked reviewers possessing a shred of historical memory) is one likely context when Pynchon's narrator in *Gravity's Rainbow* poses the Manichaean view of "a good Rocket to take us to the Stars, an evil Rocket for the World's suicide, the two perpetually in struggle."[32] Or not so perpetually after all, for we understand Pynchon's storyworld as one dominated by, and captured precariously under, the evil rocket's sign, particularly in the novel's oft-quoted passages on suicide, such as this: "Living inside the System is like riding across the country in a bus driven by a maniac bent on suicide." The driver, wearing "his pressed uniform" and flashing "insane, committed eyes," assigns riders to numbered seats for a trip destined to "end for you all in blood, in shock, without dignity."[33]

Sixties anarchists considered various means for exiting, abandoning, the system. "The Digger Papers" includes a notable unsigned text (the authors renounced ownership of the words, though we know they included Allen Ginsberg, Huey Newton, Lenore Kandel, Gary Snyder, and Norman Mailer) titled "Dialectics of Liberation" (August 1968). This lengthy theoretical and polemical manifesto argues that a countercultural freedom struggle must begin with a deconditioning of the individual psyche. This means breaking down "habit patterns, and our conditioning" to everyday modes of domination, particularly to the "categories" and "hierarchies" governing relations between individuals, within families, and among communal and governmental formations—so much of that order having already been "paid for at an incredible cost in death, slavery, psychoses." Crucial to that deterritorialization of consciousness is the "release of phantasy," a process in which "the private must be made public" so that free thought may begin to recognize, critique, and decommission "the public hallucination—history as it was known." No matter that the expression of individual fantasy life releases extravagantly sexual and violent contents. Such are precisely the signs and symptoms of a patriarchal, Oedipalized social order whose cogs and workings must be known and spoken in order for it to be taken down. In the same spirit, a 1968 Motherfucker manifesto proclaimed: "Until our demands are met, fantasy will be at war with society. Society will attempt the suppression of fantasy, but fantasy will spring up again and again, infecting our youth, waging urban guerilla warfare, sabotaging the smooth functioning of bureaucracies . . . waging pitched battles and winning (its victory is inevitable). We are the vanguard of fantasy. Where we live is liberated territory in which fantasy moves about freely." On the facing page was a photographic image of a threesome engaging in cunnilingus and intercourse, a pie in the face of New York police then working with federal agents to make pornography arrests in order to shut down underground presses.[34]

Looking back on his movement years, former Motherfucker Osha (originally Thomas) Neumann concedes the obvious danger. The son of leftist historian Franz Neumann and, after his father's death, the stepson of Herbert Marcuse (who had resided in the Neumann household throughout Thomas's childhood), he was studying for a doctorate in history at Yale when he left for New York's Lower East Side and the nascent Black Mask–UAWMF anarchist collective. He readily admits that the move was intended to outrage his stepfather's commitment to rational process and analysis by his (Osha's) commitment to a wildly anti-Oedipal politics—that is, one that exaggerates Oedipal fantasy in order to disable it. "The System was our mother and in revolution we fucked her," Neumann writes. Nonetheless he and fellow Black Mask radicals did rationalize their praxis, as Marcuse would want. They argued that igniting revolution in a polity as impassive as that in the United States would require activists to provoke tirelessly "the relation of child to parent." Their aim was to effect a sexual-political repetition compulsion that would drown in fantasy reenactments the system's conditioned reflexes, thus releasing "the genuinely radical and uncompromising elements of their politics."[35] Used as a weapon, then, the movement's guerrilla performances and printed representations of transgressive fantasy were to operate as stimuli—again, as disconnected or scattershot "events"—with the general aim of provoking authoritarian responses. Pornography with a purpose would compel the patriarchal state to act, to arrest desire, thus to demonstrate over and over its own conditioning, its repressive nature, its relative unfreedom, and its hypocrisy. These were traits radical thinkers had already pointed out, yet the hope was that while concentrated in local skirmishes eventually the symbolic and affective power of state repression would ignite general resistance among workers, the poor, and the racially oppressed. That wider insurgency never unfolded. Movement people did open, alter, and raise consciousnesses, yet the behemoth stood rock-solid as ever, as Osha Neumann's stepfather, Marcuse, had predicted. In fact during Nixon's first term the system doubled-down on all major bets: widening the Southeast Asian war (into Cambodia and Laos), doubling budget outlays for the nuclear race and the space race (reoriented to military applications), and suppressing urban racial disorders (and laying policy grounds for a vastly expanded prison system).[36]

Movement radicals were always more realist than fantasist. They observed carefully the cynicism of French workers who at first stood in solidarity with university students during the Paris uprising and general strike of May 1968, and then crassly accepted wage concessions from the de Gaulle government, acquiescing as the president marshaled French military support and returned from a humiliating exile in Germany—of all places for a French leader to find sanctuary. They autopsied the dead-on-arrival attempt at an American version of the general strike, in the streets of Chicago during the August 1968 Democratic National Convention. Yet they had also carried to those frustrations—Paris, Chicago, Nixon—a particular analysis of paranoia that is worth pausing over. An essay in *Black Mask* from the winter of 1968 takes up again the argument that the key to unlocking social and political structures of domination lies in "understanding the role of sexual repression" within the conventional patriarchal family, which is seen as the origin of those structures. Then the writer (probably Neumann) presses further. Remarking that as the work of deconditioning, deterritorializing, and de-Oedipalizing the psyche proceeds—as old hierarchies collapse, categories evaporate, and the laws of domination are revoked—the liberated yet disoriented psyche will initially experience not joy (or *jouissance*) and grace but instead a profound anxiety, a sense of exposure and endangerment, and a fear of persecution for choosing the life of an outsider. Implicitly using Fromm's insights on the terror of real freedom, of existence without submission to authority, and the newly liberated individual's perverse yearnings for a return to order and submission, even in sadomasochistic forms, the *Black Mask* essayist then defines that anxiety of the outsider in terms of paranoia. The "Dialectics of Liberation" piece in "The Digger Papers" made the same case five months later, and both argue that this mode of paranoia is a good thing. Unlike the repressive, covertly fascist, and delusional fantasies of right-wing paranoia that Richard Hofstadter analyzed in his 1965 book, *The Paranoid Style in American Politics*, liberationist paranoia has a kind of term limit. This self-conscious, critical, and thus creative paranoia enables persons and groups to recover "what has been repressed, forgotten, almost lost" under the regime of "patriarchal authoritarian culture." It teaches concrete lessons about the pervasiveness of alienation, fear, and domination in everyday social life, thus coalescing individuals into groups dedicated to "comprehending the profound misery of our lives." Though temporary, a mode of creative paranoia would, in the Diggers' view, unlock progressive change and potentials for a durable counterculture—in new communal spaces for realizing positive liberty. As Pirate Prentice puts the case to Roger Mexico early in part 4 of *Gravity's Rainbow*: "Creative paranoia means developing at least as thorough a We-system as a They-system."[37]

The horrors of failing that kind of liberation, of regressing into delusional and psychotic paranoia, were also readily apparent. Most sixties histories point to the August 1969 Manson family murders of a pregnant Sharon Tate and four others as one object lesson, and the violently dystopian outdoor concert at Altamont, California, four months later as another. Manson's brutal mimickry of the counterculture's project for rethinking the family seemed well capsulized in the bloodlust of his mock children, who rode in from the desert vastness north of Los Angeles wielding guns and knives, one of them telling a victim he was "here to do the devil's business."[38] As for the failed project of deconditioning and deterritorialization in *Gravity's Rainbow*, its closing pages figure that regressive horror in Weissmann/Blicero. He is "the father you will never quite manage to kill" and the reason that the "Oedipal situation in the Zone these days is terrible." The father's mock children perpetuate "the same passivity, the same masochist fantasies" and remain "desperately addicted to the comforts others sell them, however useless, ugly or shallow, willing to have life defined for them by men whose only talent is for death."[39] We think it is important to underscore that phrasing: "the father *you will never* quite manage to kill." Here is an opening into the deep, dark pessimism that haunts *Gravity's Rainbow*. Just pages later, the occupied Zone of 1945 narratively morphs into the freeways and suburbs of Los Angeles in about 1972. Hence the idea apparent to anyone reading the novel, especially when it was first published: the Zone-R-Us.

Increasingly during the period from 1969 to 1972, the project was to get *outside*, in every sense and however dim the prospects. Outside the system, outside the mind-shackling neuroses and psychoses of Oedipal power, beyond the feedback loop of destructive and delusional paranoia, the mechanical, and the urban, and finally beyond the reach of "the Man" and into the natural—simply, "outside." As the anonymous authors of "Dialectics of Liberation" concluded in August 1968, movement people needed to "get in the groove of being way out in the country and walking around with clouds and stars, and talking with trees."[40] And here is another of those wires lighting up Pynchon's text. For *Gravity's Rainbow* is a novel subtly preoccupied with what is materially *counter* to culture: the nature surrounding us all, especially trees. Trees scorched by launches of v-2 rockets, trees perfectly placed to save Tyrone Slothrop, trees dancing in the wind, carved with insignia, decorated for bourgeois holidays, and groves of trees sheltering the Zone's displaced persons: in all, scores and scores of trees (and now that we have the novel in a word-searchable e-text, we can map each one). Trees haunt Slothrop. Puritan ancestors dangling from his family tree felled great stands of Berkshire evergreens "acres at a clip" in order to pulp them, bleach the pulp, and roll it into "toilet paper, banknote stock, newsprint," so that Slothrop sees his life blighted to its roots by the nexus of "shit, money, and the Word." And finding himself in the occupied Zone's great forests, in part 3, he rightly feels "intensely alert" to the trees, recognizes "[t]here's insanity in my family," and "tells them" (the trees, that is) "I'm sorry."[41] The last we see of him in the storyworld, he's out in the German woods. By 1970, a number of movement radicals were also awakening in U.S. woodlands, in a variety of rural communes, some of them entirely off the grid.

The perennial question about the radical Left's dispersal and decline after 1969 is whether that demise constituted a triumph for the society of the spectacle, for the forces of control and domination. That already seemed the case in late 1972 when Pynchon was completing his manuscript. At story's end a version of President Nixon, figured as the jowly, adenoidal Richard M. Zhlubb (shades of Pirate Prentice's giant adenoid!), cruises the L.A. freeways and remarks on stoned hippie "freaks" who are "gibbering . . . swarming in, rolling their eyes . . . playing harmonicas and even *kazoos*." Zhlubb foretells a concentration camp: "There'll be a nice secure home for them all, down in Orange County," then theatrically pauses before delivering the punch line, "Right next to Disneyland."[42] In August 1970 a Yippie faction had occupied Disneyland, establishing a base camp on Tom Sawyer's Island and announcing free Black Panther hot breakfasts at the amusement park's Aunt Jemima Pancake House. More guerrilla theater, symbolic warfare, and grist for the national news mill—for it was still, in every sense, high times.

But there's a still darker historical narrative behind what seems a bit of Pynchon fictional whimsy. Throughout the late sixties and early seventies, unsubstantiated but consistent rumors circulated in the underground presses about government plans to round up and intern movement radicals. It turns out those rumors weren't paranoid fantasy. Even by the early sixties Hoover's FBI had secretly amassed cross-listed information on tens of thousands of American citizens. The "Security Index" of those whom the agency considered a threat to national security during war or other emergency was compiled so that subjects could be "arrested and held indefinitely without judicial warrant." The list included numerous university students and faculty members, including Marcuse and Brown. In the early sixties the FBI also compiled a "Reserve Index," a kind of minor league for subversives. By 1962, reports Seth Rosenfeld, it had nearly eleven thousand names, in two tiers: an A-list of citizens whose "subversive associations and ideology" required them to be rounded up with "Security Index" radicals during an emergency, and a B-list, "considered to be a lesser threat," who would be rounded up after the A-list folks. By the late sixties these lists evidently included some fifty thousand names.[43] In 1975 Americans learned that the rumors, probably spread by dissident army personnel, were true. The Department of Defense had been tasked—after mid-1960s riots erupted in the black ghettoes of Newark, Detroit, and Watts—to develop plans for the roundup and internment of dissident citizens. Code-named "Garden Plot" and finalized in February 1968, this 250-page planning document (fully declassified in 1988) details the process by which two specially designated U.S. Army battalions, nearly five thousand men, would coordinate with state and local police and National Guard units to arrest persons on the FBI lists and intern them at previously designated remote sites, without access to the centuries-old judicial right of habeas corpus. (Disneyland was not among those sites, but Angel Island was the San Francisco area location.) We know as well that Garden Plot went into a partially operational, or "ready," mode several times, particularly during the protests in the spring of 1970 against the extension of the Vietnam War into Cambodia.[44]

That year, monthly sales of the radical Left's most powerful and intellectually compelling journalistic voice, *Ramparts* magazine, rose beyond a whopping third of a million copies. Yet there were signs even in *Ramparts* that movement politics were fragmenting, losing what solidarity they had. As the Selective Service transitioned to a draft lottery in 1970, compulsory military service no longer concerned the one-half of all young men now freed from obligations to serve, and as their concern vanished so did their support for the antiwar movement, particularly with abolition of the draft in 1973. By mid-1972 Richard Nixon had reckoned he would breeze into a second term (and did). *Ramparts* had already passed the *Brennschluss* point of its arc, as V-2 rocketeers would have said, and was commencing its three-year death dive. In fact, in its pages as Pynchon's novel went to press, critics and scholars had already commenced premortem analyses of the Long Sixties legacy. A number of them held that an ineffective counterculture politics—seen as too whimsical and in complicity with repressive tolerance—was responsible for the self-inflicted crash.

For our postmortem we offer one instructive sixties text: the "Youth International Party Manifesto!" in its 1968 posterized version.[45] This widely circulated image, tacked on uncountable walls, measured two by three feet in landscape format: on a black background, a Communist Chinese–type red star was centered, overlaid with a green, seven-leaf marijuana stem, framed on each side and the bottom by white-lettered paragraphs. They open with a proclamation: "WE ARE A PEOPLE. We are a new nation," and the rhetoric sustains that theme of an upstart nation-within-a-nation throughout the manifesto's six hundred words. The writers, evidently Jerry Rubin and Abbie Hoffman, consistently pit "our nation," figured as a cooperative We who "believe in life," against a competitive "Amerika," or They, who constitute "a death machine" dedicated to fascist-style conformity ("We are not good Germans!"), and pitted also against racist and sexist oppression, and against war and "the destruction of the planet." While "They" run a "Pig Empire [that] is ravaging the globe," the new nation promises peace (of course) along with universal health care, access to birth control and abortion, renovated urban housing suitable for communal living, decriminalized and nationally managed free distribution of drugs of all kinds (thus to "stop the flow of bad shit"), and schools liberated from having to teach what "They" deem knowledge. All this was familiar boilerplate in 1968. Some of it still conditions U.S. legislative and political-cultural debates.

Four times, the manifesto rejects state "domination" and "control," figured as patriarchal, whether "They" express it in war, or in the "domination of women by men," or in actions of local "cops and narcs" or federal authorities who "jail us for smoking flowers, induct us, housewife us"—that last, a strikingly gendered and castrating metaphor. To eliminate such dominations the manifesto urges "everyone to control their own life," specifically to "seize control of our minds and our bodies" as a first step toward overthrowing all conditioned, totalitarian practices. Not once, though, does the manifesto mention freedoms, negative or positive. It appears to take for granted that one and all just know what those liberties are, without comment. It does demand "the right of all humans, animals, and plants to play out their natural roles in harmony." Yet that rights claim is so generally biological (but why leave out rocks, whose "mineral consciousness" Pynchon's stoned characters acknowledge) that it offers nothing for communities mired in poverty, for people of color struggling to secure equal rights, for people engaged in labor and freedom struggles (migrant farmworkers, for example), or for women resisting daily subjection to patriarchal authority at work and at home.[46] Like the manifesto as a whole, that formula produced no useful critique of coercions and dominations rooted in Western and U.S. culture and political economy. The same absence surrounds the feel-good ecological gesture about living in "natural harmony." In this light we read the "Youth International Party Manifesto!" as one among many texts and events symptomatic of an apolitical strain in counterculture politics—the butt, even then, of satirical efforts such as Robert Downey Sr.'s film *Putney Swope* (1969) and Little Feat's song "A Apolitical Blues" (1972). The question at hand was whether the "mindless pleasures" and diversions of commodity culture were covertly delinking countercultural practices from the machine, or "Moloch," those practices were supposed to counter. Another question was whether the counterculture had lost in a purple haze the analyses by Fromm, Marcuse, and Brown, whose work had informed movement thought and practice. Capsulized, their analyses sought to reveal the dark side of Cold War American (or, first world) affluence and seeming tolerance as a deeply racist and repressive social order which, top to bottom, needed to secure or else coerce each individual's subservience to a transnational economy of resource extraction, refinement, manufacturing, research and development, and product placement and servicing, particularly in its sales to a ceaselessly hungry buyer: the military-industrial complex, much of it shrouded in secrecy and all of it dissimulated in the society of the spectacle, essential to sustaining the national security state and its "containment culture."[47]

The environmental consequences of that political economy had become central to movement politics by 1970, the year of the first Earth Day gathering, teach-in, and protest. Regarding the wreckage of resource extraction, the pollution of manufacturing, and the specter of nuclear holocaust, New Left thinkers began depicting the system as deadly through and through.[48] The massive February 1969 oil spill off the Santa Barbara coast (just eighty miles north of where Pynchon was then living and writing) provided one among many other object lessons. In June of that year a soup of toxic chemicals and oil drifting down the Cuyahoga River caught fire and spewed deadly fumes across the northern Ohio manufacturing belt, calling attention to the region as one of the nation's most polluted. While the "Yippie Manifesto" writers had fantasized the construction of "transport and communication" networks to bring together "sisters and brothers," other anarchists like the Diggers and UAWMF had been arguing that such networks had to be dismantled entirely in order to nourish freedom, equality, and peace in concert with learning sustainable forms of resource and land usage. By 1969 it seemed clear that this kind of radical change was not going to happen. Stalwarts among the Diggers and UAWMF were making plans to bail out.

By 1969–70 many of them had gone primitive. The UAWMF's Neumann and Morea led the way to remote locations in the Sangre de Cristo Mountains of northern New Mexico, while other Motherfuckers found their way to nascent communes in upstate Vermont. Digger leaders like Peter Coyote made their way to existing northern California communes, most notably Black Bear Ranch in rugged and sparsely populated Siskiyou County, while others established communes in equally isolated places in south-central Oregon and in California's Humboldt County. Pynchon may have had a tie to one of those. Near the end of *Gravity's Rainbow* he includes an untitled song lyric that may express an autobiographical lament: "Sometimes I wanna go back north to Humboldt County / Sometimes I think I'll go back East to see my kin."[49] Morea made the move to New Mexico principally because he was dogged by various legal cases spinning out of his anarchist work. In contrast, Neumann and Coyote recall genuine commitments to projects for realizing new, liberated, pacifist, and sustainable modes of familial and communal affiliation. They believed that the last thing any deconditioned and de-Oedipalized movement anarchist should have desired in 1968–72 was to belong in a *nation*—even in a "new nation" like the "Yippie Manifesto" was advertising. Four decades later a number of the communes they helped to build, Black Bear most notably, are still thriving—along with the anarchist prospect, for some, of leaving the system.

The great and often stunningly corrosive satirical work of Long Sixties print culture also endures. Some of it we know as canonical American literature; the bulk exists as a vast archive of popular writings and ephemera scholars are only now exploring. This body of cultural work helped secure for Americans, and then raucously celebrated, First Amendment rights of free expression the Internet age now takes for granted. These are some particular ways of reckoning the Long Sixties legacy, even as we acknowledge the obvious fissures and failures in movement thought and practice, of which the "Yippie Manifesto" is merely a synecdoche.

CHAPTER 5

The Law and the Liberation of Fantasy

Pynchon wrote *Gravity's Rainbow* during that long culture-war battle over words and deeds, over speech rights in their relation to racial violence at home and war horrors abroad, over late capitalism's ravaging of lands and waters. What scale could possibly balance allegedly obscene epithets and representations against the Martin Luther King murder, the My Lai massacre, the genocidal horrors that Nixon's bombing unleashed in Cambodia? Indeed then the question is not only: "Who was saved?" It must also be: "Who was brought to justice?"—a vital issue in *Gravity's Rainbow* and *Vineland*. Pynchon's writing asks what calculus can reckon the failures of ordinary people such as Franz Pökler and Edward Pointsman really to see their own and others' injustices and to act ethically against them. His work probes the extent to which ideological formations, repressive mass media, and state controls serve to keep individuals and populations ethically dull and impassive. Releasing laughter against those conditions was precisely the object or theme of Thomas Forcade's incantatory curses and pie flinging, and of many sixties street theater events and performative confrontations, pigs and all. Guiding these dissident practices was an age-old wisdom: the satirist's power to unleash laughter rhetorically overmasters the system that would master people. That was the idea of works from Ginsberg's *Howl* through Robert Coover's 1977 novel, *The Public Burning*. Dissident satirists understand why the state deploys libel, obscenity, and sedition laws to silence insurgent movements. Therefore in the sixties they deployed libel, obscenity, and sedition against state dominion.[1]

The specter of systematic mastery over people's minds and mouths swings us back into the Supreme Court's legal reasoning in *Stanley v. Georgia*. Writing the unanimous decision, Thurgood Marshall dismantled the Georgia court's remarkable claim that, just as the state may deploy police powers to "protect the body of a citizen," it also may do so to "protect his mind."[2] Here was the core issue, more so than Robert Stanley's Fourth Amendment protections against an unwarranted police search of his home and seizure of his possessions. Does the Constitution empower authorities to protect people from not just bodily but also mental harms? The Court rejected entirely the analogy supporting that claim. It was repugnant to a first-order human right, namely Stanley's First Amendment right to be free from regulation of the "information and ideas" he might utilize in the privacy of his domicile. In a strong rebuke to Georgia's paternalistic justification, Marshall wrote: "If the First Amendment means anything, it means that a State has no business telling a man, sitting alone in his own house, what books he may read or what films he may watch. Our whole constitutional heritage rebels at the thought of giving government power *to control men's minds.*"[3] In these far-reaching terms the justices affirmed every individual's freedom *as a reader*, in the widest sense. They acknowledged our fundamental freedom from state power in the framing of our own conscience.

In the eighties, biographer Ted Morgan asked William S. Burroughs what Americans had learned from the sixties. The novelist quickly replied: "The lesson . . . was that the paranoids were right." Morgan also reports an eighties conversation in which Rolling Stone Mick Jagger doubted that the sixties counterculture had achieved anything worthwhile, and Burroughs shot back: "Do you realize that thirty years ago . . . a four-letter word could not appear on a printed page? . . . Holy shit, man, what'd you think we've been doing all these years?"[4] Burroughs spoke from the experience of his own fight to publish *Naked Lunch*. The U.S. Postal Service had banned distribution of the 1959 Paris edition (from Maurice Girodias's Olympia Press) on account of its bluntly narrated scenes of homosexuality, pedophilia, and hanging-ejaculation deaths, not to mention its wall-to-wall scatology. In late 1960 Burroughs (and the First Amendment) triumphed in the Chicago courtroom of Julius J. Hoffman, who would be the presiding judge nine years later in the Chicago Seven conspiracy trial. His ruling in favor of Burroughs's speech rights frankly conceded *Naked Lunch*'s "overwhelming galaxy of four-letter Anglo-Saxon words" that were unacceptable in polite discourse yet legal speech in the arts because "the use of shit and fuck violates a cultural and social taboo, to be sure, but not the law." And the law having required him to weigh expert testimony that *Naked Lunch* had some "redeeming social value," he therefore ruled the ban illegal.[5] Conservatives weren't about to give up. The American (Grove Press) edition premiered in 1962, and Los Angeles and Boston sustained municipal bans against its sale until 1966, when a Boston trial finally ended all anti-*Lunch* litigation, an important watershed in literary publishing. Other famously banned books offered nothing like Burroughs's prolonged, graphically violent scenes of sadomasochistic pederasty. By comparison, *Lady Chatterley's Lover* seemed innocently bourgeois. *Naked Lunch* pushed the boundary of obscenity/pornography law deep into wilderness territory.

Consider the context. The *Gravity's Rainbow* that readers know would have posed a difficult, risky decision for publishers if Pynchon had completed his manuscript even seven years earlier than he did. Fifteen years earlier, the

initial release would have happened abroad, perhaps by Olympia (already famous for publishing *Lolita* and other sexually explicit fictions); and then secretly imported copies of *Gravity's Rainbow* would have been tried in U.S.
court as expert witnesses, lawyers, and justices sought to parse the novel's
"redeeming social value." This thought experiment in obscenity law leads to
new and significant literary-historical questions. What scenes and narrative
practices would have brought the heat down on *Gravity's Rainbow*? How
do those passages compare with those of other texts, and would Pynchon's
have been legally defensible in that legal-literary context on the grounds of
his novel's "redeeming social value," namely his intended social and political
themes? Obscenity and pornography trials always foregrounded the very
question—of authorial intent—that formalist New Critics of the fifties and
sixties had taught students to disdain, thus imposing a ban on intentionality
and literature's cultural-social work that leftist students and scholars of the
late sixties and seventies would dismantle, using European structuralist, semiotic, and poststructuralist analyses.

Why had literary fictions become such a mid-twentieth-century legal battle-
ground? Jurisprudential thinking fussed over *content*, over what constituted
obscene or pornographic representation, and then over how to balance regulation against free speech rights. Interrogations of *form*—of discursive and
narrative practices—weren't often hashed out at trial, though from a literary-
historical standpoint form sometimes explained a great deal. In his famous ex-
oneration of Joyce's *Ulysses*, for example, Judge John Woolsey cited the ways
that, as his close reading revealed and "experts" assured him, the novel attempted "to show how the screen of consciousness with its ever-shifting kalei-
doscopic impressions carries, as it were on a plastic palimpsest" not just characters' impressions of external reality but "residua of past impressions . . .
some drawn up by association from the domain of the subconscious" and
some of that content therefore sexual because, well, humans have sexual fantasies.[6] By now, decades of work on narrative art have made it a truism that
the history of the modern novel tracks innovations in techniques for presenting processes of consciousness; also, these innovations have much to do with a
novel's "political unconscious," and thus concern the social work a novel can
be seen to take up.[7] From early on, systematic uses of focalizing characters in
fictions like Austen's *Emma* (1815), Melville's *Benito Cereno* (1855), and Flau-
bert's *Madame Bovary* (1857), through James's development and theorizing
of the "center-of-consciousness" technique in the late nineteenth century and
Joyce's "stream-of-consciousness" narration in the early twentieth, novels increasingly evoked characters' perceiving, thinking, desiring, and fantasizing
mentalities. The novel thus became rather less interested in the social scene
itself than in how the social *is seen*. And with this expanding and interioriz-
ing of the modern novel's scope came a turn into the realities of human inti-

macy, as writers' frankly realized sexual scenes brought more of human experience into fiction, and brought down those infamous bans. Thus decades before counterculture radicals demanded "the private must be made public" in order that "phantasy" might be shared and critiqued, put in the service of resistant and potentially even subversive social and political work, novelists were already doing exactly that—satirical writers in particular. This is the legacy *Gravity's Rainbow* takes up. Indeed, even from a formal standpoint Pynchon's narrative art freely flouts long-standing rules for the writing of focalizing characters, innovations we explore in part three.

As to content, *Gravity's Rainbow* confronted readers (initially, editors) with a gamut of sexualities working within as well as beyond that literary legacy. When censorious officials banned *Ulysses*, one objectionable scene was Leopold Bloom's masturbation in "Nausicaa" (chapter 13). There young Gerty MacDowell leans back on her park bench to watch fireworks overhead, teasing Bloom with her legs open, revealing bare thighs and lacy underthings while Bloom, seated opposite, the fly of his pants open, pumps himself to a climax troped as an arcing "rocket" that "gushed out a stream of rain cold hair threads."[8] In *Gravity's Rainbow* focalization reveals that what arouses Edward Pointsman is not "black lace cami-knickers" or lustful gazing at his secretary, Maudie Chilkes; indeed he well knows "[w]omen avoid him" because "he's creepy" (they're right, as we'll find). Instead Pointsman's erotic trigger is the professional fantasy of arriving in Stockholm to accept his Nobel Prize: pulling up to the Grand Hotel in "the ceremonial limousine," discussing with other admiring scientists the romance in pure research—in stalking dogs and crunching data. He climaxes in a "mad exploding of himself," which is at once his orgasm, his Nobel Prize, and his *"emprise"*—in the sense of control, dominion, and penetration. For the most part Pynchon accomplishes this scene in Joycean style—indirectly, with a metaphorized sexual realism.[9]

In contrast, Pynchon narrates the Roger Mexico–Jessica Swanlake trysts in a more Lawrencian mode, with a direct, middle-class sexual frankness focalized almost entirely through Roger, with his Mellors-like Anglo-Saxonisms (*cock* and *cunt*) that should offend the Connie Chatterley–like Jessica who, by war's end, will return to her boring boyfriend Jeremy. But just not yet, because temporarily Roger and Jessica seem to have detached themselves libidinally from war's dominion.[10] Their affecting scenes recur all through part 1 of the novel, and are stabilized within a conventional narrative realism in concert with their heteronormative sex roles. Perhaps that's the problem. Their passions seem to figure, Roger thinks, potentials for disobedience (they even tryst in an evacuated, forbidden neighborhood) and potentials to get outside the system, to release flows of forbidden desire and so realize themselves as one "long skin interface, flowing sweat, close as muscles and bones can press, hardly a word beyond her name, or his."[11] This is the dream of an all-powerful eroticism fusing the Roger-Jessica dyad into a new monadic being. It's the dream of a paradoxically embodied, romantic idealism with powers capable of launching them on a trajectory beyond what Pynchon names "sterile history" and into "life and joy" in all its "unpredictable" possibilities. Such desires may cast an alluring spell as we move through this eighteen-page episode (number 16), much of it focalized through Roger. What is it, then, that arrests the realization of this dream? Blaming Jessica's bourgeois morality turns out to be too simple. Roger overdubs this romance narrative with his paranoid fantasies that a managerial They have conspired to cast him together with Jessica, beginning with their "cute meet," and that she is likely a player in the controlling plot. If so, the conspiracy is nowhere evident in the two pages focalized through Jessica, which disclose her own analysis of Roger and unmask his romanticism as instead the mentality of an incorrigible "cynic" and "self-centered—boy, really," whose spite for "the System" encloses him (hence, them both) in a solipsistic cave with "only room for Roger, Roger, oh love to the end of breath." This is where Roger's clearly destructive paranoia has led him, and evidently why Jessica will soon leave him for the pipe-smoking, conventional Jeremy, so "familiar, full of trust," however naïve.[12] One of us (Steve) reads the Roger-Jessica story as a critical parable about the romance of the counterculture, while agreeing with the other (Luc) that this historical-political reading may overstrain the story's details.

Next consider the novel's alternative sexualities, including sadomasochism and pedophilia, threaded into *Gravity's Rainbow* by way of two subplots. The first, which we will take up in part two, concerns Franz Pökler's annual quasi-incestuous trysts with pubescent girls resembling his daughter, Ilse, assignations Weissmann arranges in order to realize and control Franz's fantasies and thus discipline the man's engineering work on the V-2. The second subplot involves Slothrop's rough sex with the German film actress Margherita (Greta) Erdmann, followed by his coupling with Greta's pubescent daughter, Bianca. A main motif in the Slothrop-Greta trysting is that it reveals (in contrast to the Roger-Jessica relation) "what happens when paranoid meets paranoid. A crossing of solipsisms." The narration ascribes Greta's sadomasochistic conditioning to her acting in filmed scenes of whipping and sexual domination, scripted for fascist audiences; some of these performances are even taken on the road during the war, played live before troops at rocket sites and even concentration camps—"the barbed wire circuit." They feature Greta bound, whipped, mock raped, all of it hardwiring her desires so that "she couldn't enjoy [sex] any other way."[13] As for Slothrop, what's striking is that while he apparently lacks experience in these practices, he nonetheless slides deftly, knowingly, into the sadist's dominating role, believing "somebody has already *educated him*" to this script, which intersects his paranoid solipsism with Greta's.[14] If so, then They also may have programmed Slothrop's pedophilia, enacted with Greta's daughter, Bianca, aboard the ship *Anubis* in episode 15 of part 3.

The narrative discourse in *Lolita* (rather like that in *Ulysses*) leaves much to a reader's imagination by extensively poeticizing Humbert's couplings with his beloved "Lo." Still, all Nabokov's fanciful literary tropes failed to mollify the novel's early censors and detractors. In contrast there are no kid gloves of metaphor in Pynchon's treatment of Slothrop's rather sadistic pedophilia with Bianca, whom either the narrator, or Slothrop, describes or sees as "11 or 12, dark and lovely." Here the text's language is frank, blunt, and violent. It does represent a Bianca experienced with men, yet she reminds him, "I'm a child." Indeed the text (its perspective being either the narrator's or Slothrop's) repeatedly stresses her small size, her slender girlish limbs and waist, and "her face, round with baby fat." These signs of Bianca's frail and vulnerable childishness, alongside how Slothrop "knows he's vulnerable, *more than he should be*, to pretty little girls," come close to placing a political and ethical frame around depictions of Slothrop's "cruel" ways. He begins by biting her flesh, leaving "red nebulae across her sensitive spaces," as if Bianca's body is contested terrain for him to attack and blast. Then he commences a "very hard" biting of her "pre-subdeb" breasts, and climaxes in a vaginal penetration described, again in the indicative, as "excruciating" to her.[15] Is that the way Slothrop *wants* to see it, just as he desires to see Bianca as "11 or 12"? Readers can have it so, though it will not exonerate Slothrop's character. Indeed much of this scene's frankly described violent pedophilia may be read as unfolding only in Slothrop's imagination; but it is equally possible to read much of it as an omniscient narrator's declaration of fact. Either way—as act or as enacted fantasy—it is still factual in Pynchon's storyworld. In 1973, the text outdid anything then available in the twentieth-century literary canon.

Critics' readings of this scene hesitate over the extent to which its literalism tips into fantasy.[16] The paragraph *after* that "excruciating" copulation certainly does describe Slothrop's post-orgasm fantasy about what's occurred. There the omniscient narrator, focalizing through Slothrop, relates how his conscious being seems to have gone "actually, well, inside his own cock"; and from that vantage he experiences orgasm as a confluence of rocketcraft and imperialism. His penis is a V-2 rocket with its piping and "ducts, his sperm roaring louder and louder, getting ready to erupt, somewhere below his feet," and his penis is a "kingly" and "metropolitan organ" in relation to which the rest of Slothrop's body is "other" and "colonial tissue"—terms most likely inspired by Frantz Fanon's critique of colonial power. So the language itself enables a sharp and even demolishing critique of Slothrop's vulnerability "to pretty little girls," figuring it as (yet another) manifestation of a Western culture given over to forms of patriarchal domination. As for the rest of that scene, we find no persuasive evidence in the narration—in its reported dialogue between Slothrop and Bianca, in the narrator's indicative mood ("He starts taking giant, ass-enthusiast bites"), and in phrases that might or might not indicate focalization ("Such a slender child")—which would authorize readers to unambiguously reject a mimetic reading and conclude that this whole scene of pedophilic fornication unfolds under the sign of fantasy or hallucination. We think that such an interpretive move denies this scene's ethical framing, partly signaled by how Pynchon deploys the semantics of a postcolonial critique that was commonplace in Long Sixties political dialogue. Indeed that language resumes immediately after the brief detour into Slothrop's rocket/penis fantasy. As the narration backs out of the character's consciousness, the narrator describes Slothrop enacting the sovereign's cold "bureaucracy of departure" from the colonized subject, abandoning Bianca—in a profound irony—to the same fascist patriarchy that has hounded *his* entire life. So: has the character understood *anything* from that Norman O. Brown–style polymorphously perverse desublimation of his desires during the *Anubis* orgy, or his tryst with Bianca? Hardly, it seems. For if that event sequence means something, isn't it that desublimation merely enabled his "kingly" dominion over another? This would explain why the narrator judges that Slothrop "is to be counted, after all, among the Zone's lost." A "barren" man, and also a man whose mind and body the sovereign powers have colonized, Slothrop's prospects for liberating, enacting, sharing, and thereby disabling a destructive fantasy, finally to free his own (much less another's) mentality from Their control and into what is presumed to be *natural* and free—well, such prospects seem to approach the zero degree of probability.[17]

In arguing this case, we set our reading athwart those who have interpreted the Slothrop-Bianca scene (and others) as an abyss of ambiguity—and then close down ambiguity by straitjacketing the narrative as fantasy or delusion. Such a reading empties the potentials for judging Slothrop. Further, it vacates judgments by the novel's own characters and narrator(s) and, finally, readers, against the likes of Pointsman, Pökler, or even Blicero, who are figured as equally driven by desires that Western culture and law proscribe as deviant and illicit. This is especially true of Weissmann: the ghastly scenes of his obsessional and sadomasochistic hetero- and homosexual rape-tortures of Katje and Gottfried composing a grotesque mock family (think Charles Manson), which he evidently established as the rocket went operational in September 1944. And most of all General Pudding, whose coprophagia with Katje tops any of the novel's comparable gut-wrenching moments. These scenes, which recur from the middle of part 1 through the novel's last pages, go way beyond Leopold Bloom's fantasia of domination in the "Circe" episode (number 15) of *Ulysses*—where he is willingly slapped around, symbolically mocked, "buttocksmothered," and quite "unmanned" as the Dublin transvestite brothel owner Bella/Bello Cohen sits on his face. In comparison, Blicero's dominations in their content and style approach an extremity or frontier; their nearest landmarks were Burroughs's hanging-ejaculation scenes, themselves warm-up exercises for what Pynchon so graphically depicts.[18]

This returns us to episode 14 in part 1, when Katje, in London, gazes at herself in a mirror and sees only "corruption and ashes," triggering her recall of tortures back in Holland that she reads as a threefold crisscrossing of solipsisms: Gottfried and herself, like Hansel and Gretel, kneeling before Blicero in his "witch paranoia." He wears, incredibly, that "false cunt" made of plastic and studded with "tiny blades" that cut her lips and tongue when she is forced into mock cunnilingus, after which she's compelled to "kiss blood-abstracts" on Gottfried's bare "ungessoed back," an aestheticized abjection that puts the two mock children paradoxically "in play, in slavery"—a stunning contradiction in terms resolvable, it seems, only in the death that Blicero embodies and threatens. The scene's pervasive grammatical mood is imperative. Blicero "commands." Katje and Gottfried "[s]ubmit." They "must" endure restraints and lashings ("the straps and whips leathern") of genitals, backs, buttocks, thighs, hands, and mouths; or "must" perform "metronomic" masturbation, as well as forced oral, anal, and vaginal penetrations, followed by nights "in the cage," like creatures awaiting "the oven"—a doom, Katje realizes even then, assigned only to Gottfried.[19] Redeeming this incredible narration, thematizing it for critical reflection, is its intertextuality: allusions to Germanic folktale, to the deeply romantic and Oedipalized ideology of the *Wandervogel* youth movement that arose in pre-Nazi Germany, and to Rainer Maria Rilke's 1922 book of poems, *Duino Elegies*, which Weissmann has subjected to a relentlessly solipsistic and romanticized reading.[20] These intertexts signal the ways that Weissmann's manias are culturally encoded, and the narration opens the door to historical and ethical critiques of Nazi Germany, in particular, and more generally of fascist ideology and the form of sovereign power it imagines.

So too with the novel's most infamous scene, in episode 4 of part 2: the sadomasochistic coprophagia of old Brigadier General Pudding, which runs *Gravity's Rainbow* beyond any other moment in literary history and into its own heart of darkness. Apparently these pages (more than any others) moved Pulitzer board members to reject their jury's unanimous decision in favor of *Gravity's Rainbow*, and to award no fiction prize for 1974.[21] Reviewers mentioned the scene indirectly; many scholars still shy away. Its elements are these: Katje Borgesius, having previously "learned the proper style" literally at Blicero's feet, now awaits Pudding in the semidarkness of a "cell" deep within the White Visitation; she is elaborately made up, wigged in black, naked "except for a long sable cape and black boots with court heels." She plays Domina Nocturna, a mythic figure out of the Grimm brothers' *Teutonic Mythology*, a night witch who rides above battlefields to gather dead souls, who become her servants for eternity. Pudding is a veteran of the World War I carnage at Passchendaele, where putrefying corpses melded with mud to produce "the sovereign smell" of his first meetings with her, the death-mud now reiterated in her excrements. This night, one in a series of assignations, she stands and he kneels behind, then licks and "bravely clamps his teeth shut" on each "turd" that slides from between Katje's buttocks, chewing each one, his gagging throat spasming so much that the "pain is terrible." She's taken a laxative; the coprophagia continues, with his forced masturbation its epilogue. In leaving, Pudding assures her that the script of utter abjection they've just enacted is far less awful to him than the military bureaucracy, the System. To it and to Pointsman especially, the general's nothing but a funding conduit without which their "whole show"—their experimental conditioning of rats, dogs, and people—"can prang" or crash.[22] They've somehow plumbed the old man's deepest and most horrific fantasies, which are now deployed in scheduled "visitations" to keep the funds flowing—like Katje's excrements. That's the implicit story, another one about the confluence of "shit, money, and the Word," as fascist on this side of the North Sea as anything Weissmann arranged on the other, with Gottfried and Katje in Holland, and all of it part of the same system that uses Slothrop. Months later, Pudding is dead from "a massive *E. coli* infection."[23]

Readers might pose the realist question and ask: how did They fish Brigadier Pudding's awful fantasies from the depths of his mind? We already know. Episode 10 of part 1 narrates one of Slothrop's compulsory sessions where They intravenously inject him with sodium amytal (a truth serum), vanquishing his inhibitions and forcing him to manifest his deepest fantasies: about shit, Boston, anxieties about black-on-white homosexual rape, "Negroes" in general, and the westward course of empire figured as sado-masochistic burlesque. These sessions' ostensible purpose is to work backward from the statistical reckoning of Slothrop's penis as a potentially useful rocket dowser, to the facts of his conditioning as Infant Tyrone in the lab of Laszlo Jamf, thus to understand Slothrop as a mechanism, and then to master and begin utilizing his enigmatic power. How far down that experimental and operational path Pointsman and crew think they were able to get is never clear. By the end of part 3, one of Them, Sir Marcus Scammony, plainly speaks of how They "sent [Slothrop] out" into the Zone to locate and "destroy the blacks," to be a weapon system against Herero rocket troopers wandering through occupied Germany after V-E Day.[24] In sum: up until that moment the entire arc of Slothrop's story, including his mistaken belief (back in Nice) that he was "free," has been under the thumb of elite white men whose scientific and ideological understanding have defined him and his kind as organisms whose conditioning They might utterly control. As such a being, Slothrop's character focalizes a deep anxiety and a consistent rallying cry of Long Sixties history.

Each of the pornographic scenes we have just surveyed turns on a withering satire of control in its psychological, sexual, cultural, social, and ideological aspects. Those scenes may also be read as celebrating speech freedoms newly—yet tentatively—wrested from state control by the era's key court decisions, the last and most thorough of which, *Miller v. California*, would follow four months after *Gravity's Rainbow* arrived at booksellers in February 1973. The novel is political through and through, and never takes its eyes off the machine, Moloch, the System. It may be read as one more dare, one more countercultural liberation of fantasy, thrown against the state's assertion of powers over what people might say and read. But not without a further ironic twist. The novel's narrative practices are living proof that, however reluctantly, the late modern state was easing legal controls over artistic expression. At the same time and not coincidentally, as we often find in Pynchon's storyworld and as Marcuse's theory of repressive tolerance predicted, the system tirelessly devises new and invidious means for conditioning, control, and domination.

TWO

DOMINATION

v-2 rocket engine, including oxygen and alcohol tubing, burner caps, combustion chamber, and frame. La Coupole, Centre d'Histoire et de Mémoire, Pas-de-Calais, France. Photo by Steven Weisenburger, 2009.

For doctors Kevin Spectro and Edward Pointsman it's another of "these habitual evenings" spent chatting over their work in a room "just off the war-neurosis ward" of St. Veronica's Hospital, London. The ward is a "half-open file drawer of pain," each bed a "folder," and the patient between its sheets a document of trauma prone to cry out from the file cabinet. This is Pointsman's view. Spectro, on the other hand, tropes each patient burrowing into bedcovers as a hunted "Fox" seeking shelter in its den. When one cries out, he leaves with a hypodermic syringe to kindly sedate the child's trauma. During a break in their conversation, in a paragraph set within ellipsis points, our omniscient narrator imagines "you" experiencing a v-2 strike: "your sudden paralysis as death comes," the blast first lifting "your" room, then shattering it all around, and "the sight of your blood spurting from the flaccid stub of artery," or alternately "you were pinned and stared at a crumpled cigarette pack for two hours in pain." In what is after all a war novel, this paragraph provides Pynchon's most vividly realized depiction of war's bloody horrors.[1]

Framing that interlude is the men's dialogue, periodically focalized through Pointsman. He confronts Spectro with the need to control "damned Pudding," "the old bastard" and superior officer thwarting their research with his "*plots*" to route funds elsewhere in the bureaucracy. Pointsman speaks especially of Slothrop as their main object of study, and Spectro meekly objects. The plan is to experiment on the man whose uncanny rocket-dowsing penis seems the "perfect mechanism" of "some pathology," which Pointsman is certain their research is destined to decipher. He summarizes relevant Pavlovian theory: how trauma sends victims "transmarginal," a condition that disrupts normative ways of discriminating "pleasure from pain, light from dark, dominance from submission"; and how trauma inverts normally stable opposites and boundaries, plunging the subject into a paranoia where he "would be master, yet now feels himself a slave." The mechanism of this process, exemplified by Slothrop's uncanny reversal and blurring of cause and effect, has become Pointsman's grail. No matter to him what its traumatic etiology may be in Slothrop's case; instead he's awed professionally that while a toddler the American had evidently been "one of Laszlo Jamf's subjects" in conditioned reflex experiments—a likely etiology, as readers will learn.[2] To Pointsman, the American lieutenant's brain simply houses a singular, enigmatic psycho-physical process that seems to reverse cause and effect; once he has experimentally unlocked its mysterious challenge to determinist logic, he will restore the sovereign law of causality, making him a world-renowned behaviorist and winning himself a Nobel Prize. At this juncture, however, Spectro remarks ironically that all Pointsman's kvetching before higher-ups has managed only to "score" from General Pudding's bureaucracy one very large octopus, named Grigori, for experimental use.[3]

This episode, the novel's eighth, also frames a second narrative interlude whose focalization, through Pointsman, reveals the man's pedophilic desires for orphaned, war-traumatized girls. In the hospital ward, Pointsman sees them as "so artlessly erotic" curled between "their virginal sheets," their pain transforming each girl into a "tablet erased" but with "new writing about to begin" as he with a phallic stick of chalk would stand above and inscribe "on them new words" bespeaking his "brown Realpolitik dreams." In the ward these "lusts" are consigned to Pointsman's fantasy. Outside the hospital it appears that he hunts actual girls, or rather "you" do. For the narration has shifted again into second-person address, identifying readers with Pointsman at the same time it implies a schizoid Pointsman addressing himself. Either way, his method is to hunt the war's orphaned, lost, or runaway girls in a London bus station—"You have waited in these places into the early mornings"—where, even though "[y]ou've never quite decided if they can see through to your vacuum," "you" gaze on the way their "knitted stockings droop" and their "little heels kick restless against the canvas bags" beneath the bench, until finally "you" put on the mask of the kindly compassionate helper ("You impress them with your gentleness"; "you are the Traveler's Aid") and target a "soiled sleepy darling beginning to complain." Sometimes "you" succeed: "but only rare nights will even one come in, home to your sprung, spermy bed"—and presumably also to "your" sedatives—where they become "your own fine Foxes."[4] And this night, "you," or rather Pointsman, desires, or demands, "*Damn it*. One, little, *Fox!*"[5]

Foregrounding as it does Pavlovian "ideas of the opposite," this episode counterposes two figures: the "you" who is a v-2 victim, and the "you" who victimizes children. There's also Spectro, who treats pain, who resists the uses of Slothrop as an experimental subject ("I can't"), and who furtively mocks Pointsman with "a Fascist salute." And there's the ethically vacuous Pointsman, who inflicts pain, who certainly will use Slothrop, and whose "brown [shirted?] Realpolitik dreams" stop at no frontier, such as seeking, luring, and raping war's exhausted, lost, and orphaned children. Indeed Pointsman thinks about the girls as war spoils. He seems sure, for example, that the "Fox" he lusts for on this night is "out in the city, a prize of war." One may decode this second-person address in two complementary ways: first, as evidence of Pointsman's double-consciousness, the "you" rhetorically distancing that secret, illegal lust for pedophilic violence from his public, official self; and second, the "you" as an actual other, perhaps the reader, squirming in the chair because of how that rhetoric binds its addressee to the lust and logic of a predatory consciousness.[6]

Perhaps because the narration realizes these extraordinary effects within one of the system's many dull bureaucratic warrens, and during just another of the "habitual evenings" that mid-level co-workers share, a mood of everyday tedium prevails, and episode 8 attracts rather little attention. Yet if only from the standpoint of plot, one must attend to it. The dialogue reveals the extent to which Slothrop's mind has become—or rather, Pointsman has made it—an object of Their interest. This is confirmed almost immediately afterward by how They force on Slothrop a series of exploratory sodium amytal sessions, the mock transcript from one of them providing the text of episode 10. Episode 8 also initiates the subplot involving Katje and the octopus, Grigori, which continues in episode 1 of part 2. It sets up the subplot revealing how these scientists control General Pudding, leading to the elaborate coprophagia scene later in part 2, and ending with the casual aside about his death from an *E. coli* infection three hundred pages after the coprophagia.[7] Spectro's ghostly resistance to Pointsman from the other side, following Spectro's death in a V-2 blast, also follows from this scene.[8] So does Pointsman's role in all of these scripts, revealing him as a kind of plot kingpin even if he's just another vacuously obedient servant of deterministic science, mid-level bureaucracy, fascist domination, and war. Such consequences reach out from these pages like Grigori's tentacles.

Episode 8 is also important for how it names and characterizes the theme of *domination*. It is notable that the condition of *freedom*—the chances for it, what being free means, and how to secure freedom—shows up scores of different times in *Gravity's Rainbow*. With domination, it's quite the opposite. Furniture, people, weather, and buildings will, in a conversational sense, seem to dominate a moment or a space figured in the novel.[9] But forms of the verb "dominate" that signify interpersonal coercion, unequal power relations, and violence occur in the novel only twice, and the first is in episode 8 when Pointsman scientifically (and creepily) discusses "dominance [and] submission." The second occurs seven hundred pages later when Miklos Thanatz defends "S and M" as a resistance to state power.[10] There Thanatz argues that the system "needs our lusts after dominance so that it can co-opt us into its own power game," which has "no joy in it, only power"—a qualification reflecting back on the politics of Pointsman's pedophilic lusts. Indeed we think that once readers have been ghosted into Pointsman's sexually violent consciousness by the text's narrative technique, it should be affectively, dialogically, sociopolitically, and ethically difficult (if not prohibitive) for us to come through any subsequent pedophilic scene—Weissmann and Gottfried, Pökler and "Ilse," Slothrop and Bianca—without pondering our strong, critical reaction against the coercive and traumatizing dominion at stake, summarized in the name of Weissmann's alter ego, Dominus Blicero. After the disclosure of Pointsman's violent lusts it should be well-nigh impossible to read those later scenes as instantiating "mindless pleasures" in any sense that stresses harmless pastiche and playful humor, or a legitimate move in a counterculture or politics of desublimation and resistance. The narrative, leaning as we've shown on a reading of Fromm, and as Spectro's Nazi salute also indicates, repeatedly captions those scenes as fascist.

Pynchon's narration figures the forms of domination throughout the book, even while naming it only twice. The narration both presents and thinks about domination, most obviously in terms of sadomasochism but also quite broadly in terms of repression, mind "control" or behaviorist "conditioning" (a steady and stable nexus of terms), institutional and governmental coercion and force, and corporeal violence and actual killing, which mostly take place offstage—Major Marvy's surgical castration being the memorable exception.[11] Thematically concerned from beginning to end with "ideas of the opposite," this novel focuses on the physical means, figurations, and logics of domination as vital counterparts to its efforts to consider freedom in the age of late capitalism.

Before proceeding, we too should think about domination. After 1945, scholars seeking to understand fascist power and the Holocaust were compelled to study cultural formations. Considering the long run-up to war, scholars asked how the fascist symbolization and representation of supposed racial differences had prepared the ground for catastrophic violence against European Jewry and other ethnic minorities—work that brought us studies like Klaus Theweleit's remarkable analysis of Nazism's affective core, published in English as *Male Fantasies* (1987). The key shift was that postwar intellectuals began to see symbolic and representational practices as themselves instruments of violence. Rethinking violence as more than acts and means for wounding or killing an individual or group, they focused on the ways cultural and sociopolitical institutions that promote and regulate expression—particularly with the spread of modern media—enable and enhance totalitarian controls over persons and groups. Scholars understood, in other words, that violence to persons is the visible, palpable, physically traumatizing aspect of a culture of domination more broadly conceived. Observing how Nazi discourses and institutions constructed and regulated "the Jew" as a degraded identity, an abject form of being, compelled Hannah Arendt, for example, to foreground the political relations of language and action. In *The Origins of Totalitarianism* (1951) and again in *The Human Condition* (1958), she argues that one becomes a political actor "only if he is at the same time the speaker of words," a thesis whose flip-side is that he whose speech is banned from the political stage is effectually dead not just to the polity but "literally dead to the world."[12] Casting a cold eye on fascist cultural practices leading up to the Holocaust, Arendt lays down a stringent norm governing any discourse of and about power. Speech is *justly* human only insofar as one employs it to *persuade*. Speech intended to deceive, coerce, segregate, or eliminate fellow human beings is speech that engages with force, with violence; it is speech whose intent is to dominate, and therefore any society committed to equality, to freedom, and to justice will not tolerate it.[13]

Critics were hard on *The Human Condition* for what many saw as claims argued too abstractly, theorized too metaphysically. In neglecting to demonstrate how domination operates concretely in everyday speech and action, they said, Arendt hadn't effectually drawn the link from action back to speech. Through the 1950s and the early 1960s—until J. L. Austin's *How to Do Things with Words* (1962)—the claim that speech *was* action seemed in itself a disruption of logic, including the logic of scholarly disciplines. But decades of subsequent work drawing from speech act theory, semiotics, and poststructuralist analysis have validated and refined Arendt's fundamental claims for a broad-spectrum analysis of domination. The work of French anthropologist, social theorist, and philosopher Pierre Bourdieu has been especially influential. Extensive fieldwork enabled Bourdieu to describe a "politics of everyday life" in which bloodless and relatively inconspicuous yet powerful modes of control and coercion function relentlessly in culture. His work shows how language is never merely a neutral communications medium but is instead a supple instrument for making and policing distinctions, for muting speech and compelling obedience to power, and for stigmatizing, segregating, dispossessing, and finally banishing or executing individuals and exterminating minorities. Language, he insists, is a powerful means for doing *symbolic* violence. Social and governmental institutions regulate the symbolic order and impose its logic, and thus enact *structural* violence in concert with the symbolic and the visible, one-on-one modes of corporeal, *subjective* violence against persons.

In *Masculine Domination* (1998), the capstone to decades of comparative anthropology and social theorizing, Bourdieu defines symbolic violence as a bag of tricks supposed superiors (particularly those in patriarchal cultures) use to dissimulate the coercions and injustices they ordinarily impose on putative inferiors. In general the trick is to mask how those practices are fundamentally arbitrary, like the relation of the signifier to the signified, or in the sense that one just happened to be born a man rather than a woman. In their particulars, then, the tricks deploy easily recognizable and often vernacular symbolic and representational practices so that the dominated will more easily misrecognize their domination as such, and be more compliant.

Typically this will involve euphemizing the domination according to values and relations defined by trust, loyalty, custom, duty, piety, or just "the nature of things." Or it involves securing consent for what people would otherwise regard as an unjust and violent practice (such as genital mutilation) by appealing to their sense of a divinely ordered world and the proper means to know it—in short, the ontological and epistemological bases of culture. At the very least it is necessary for ordinary persons who regulate and enforce power to believe in the euphemisms and the terms of consensus, even (or especially) when those in subjection refuse to believe. Looking at domination in this way, we can better understand how it coexists with a culture's otherwise liberal ideals and practices; it also "explains how various forms of domination may persist even after their juridical basis has been abolished." This work has folded together analyses of violence and domination, fundamentally reshaping modern work that began with Walter Benjamin's "Critique of Violence" (1921).[14]

Bourdieu's holistic approach is now broadly accepted among anthropologists such as James C. Scott and Nancy Scheper-Hughes, social scientists and historians such as Johann Galtung and Dominick LaCapra, and theorists such as Judith Butler and Slavoj Žižek. How they name the threefold typology of violence and domination varies slightly: symbolic, structural, and subjective in some versions, in others symbolic, objective, and subjective (what Žižek cleverly names S-O-S violence). The three forms of violence/domination are widely seen as differing temporally, in terms of their duration. Subjective violence is more momentous in every sense, often in the sense of being a spectacle (for example, public execution) but also in the sense that its duration is short, its finality often manifested abruptly—as with the assassin's gunshot. Structural or objective violence and domination involves the sustained processes of cultural and social institutions, of governance and statecraft in modernity. And symbolic violence involves cultural practices and institutions spanning long historical ages; it tends therefore to be more durable, deeply entrenched, and embattled. This is why most theorists urge that symbolic modes of domination—such as verbal and visual degradation, psychic wounding, silencing, segregation, and exclusion—must be effectively critiqued. As Žižek puts it in *Violence* (2008), the symbolic register "determines what goes on in social reality." It figures and legitimizes both the objective and the subjective forms domination will take in human experience.[15]

How do these three registers figure in episode 8? The narration presents, as we've seen, imagined scenes of violence wrought by V-2 strikes on London. As for the harm Pointsman will inflict if he manages to "score" one of those "Foxes," that bodily trauma would seem to exist beyond the episode's temporal frame, unsymbolized—except for a stunning phrase which owes its bloody truth to the fact that Pointsman's serial rape of girls has taught him (or "you") to wonder, practically, as "you" gaze upon one of them: "can your lusts fit inside this same white frame"? Otherwise, the modes of objective and symbolic violence relating to Pointsman's mania are visible everywhere. We realize them in his wielding of institutional power (however middling) and especially in the professionalized discourses that dissimulate and shield his objectifications of others, his planned use of psychically scarred human beings like Slothrop, which is okay because, as he puts the case, "It's only one man." We see the signs of symbolic violence throughout the episode, for example when Pointsman tropes the hospital patients as pages in file folders and cabinets, dehumanizing them in the same way as those vulnerable girls he hunts as if they were "Foxes"; or when he sees traumatized girls as blank tablets on which his phallic tool inscribes his power; or when he categorizes Slothrop as pathological, "a perfect mechanism," and of whom he will, just days later, write in his journal: "there can be no doubt that he is, physiologically, historically, a monster. *We must never lose control.*" In moments like this, *Gravity's Rainbow* recognizes the powers of symbolic violence. And of writing as dominating, as when the novel's narrator remarks in the last sentence of part 3 that, in postwar as during the war, "the real and only fucking is done on paper."[16]

CHAPTER 6

Controlling Slothrop

Domination is the default condition in this novel's storyworld, and the clearest illustration of the extent to which They are both willing and technically able to control individual persons is Their use of Slothrop. This operation unfolds in two stages. It has not exactly been planned that way, and it may get a little out of hand. Still, Their control works, and with Slothrop's character Pynchon best narrativizes Marcuse's thoughts on how advanced industrial society degrades individual freedom. Slothrop was first conditioned at age two, a vital clue the reader acquires only gradually. And long before disclosure of that information, the renowned Russian theorist of conditioning, Ivan Pavlov, surfaces. Even as early as the second episode's banana breakfast, the drinking companions slowly start their day searching "cabinets or bookcases for the hair of the dog that not without provocation and much prior conditioning bit them last night."[1] The offhand reference to Pavlov's famous experiments with canines slightly defamiliarizes the fraternal early morning routine. Soon though we've realized the Russian physiologist's high stature among Pynchon's nominees for evil scientist of the century, precisely for the way his work promised ways to better regulate individuals in a well-organized system.

At St. Veronica's Hospital, some of whose staff work on psychological warfare, Ned Pointsman is the resident Pavlovian, indeed a fellow of the Royal College of Surgeons, no small achievement. In episode 7 of part 1 he is out in a rocket-blasted street trying to snare a dog for his own experiments when his foot gets stuck in a toilet bowl. Roger Mexico and Jessica Swanlake lend help but the hilarious hunt ends in failure, a sign to the frustrated Pointsman that he "should be branching out."[2] And he will, using the octopus Grigori and, more important, Slothrop, setting aside Kevin Spectro's strong ethical objections as well as Pointsman's own apparent disregard for the Jamf-Harvard connection in Slothrop's 1920 conditioning.

Eventually we learn that Jamf's conditioning of little Slothrop's penis during experiments on the sexual reflex had become a topic circulating in scientific journals. Indeed the child had become rather a legend, as "Infant Tyrone." For a moment even the narrator seems to share Jamf's scientific pleasure in how experimental stimuli led to a simple, unambiguously measurable response, the child's erections: "But a hardon, that's either there, or it isn't. Binary, elegant."[3] It seems a pure mechanism, off or on, no excluded middle muddying things up and therefore something with which to do real, practical *work*. Eventually Sir Stephen Dodson-Truck tries to help Slothrop recognize these aspects of "the penis he thought was his own" by telling about it in a lyric—"just a big playful boy of a bone,"[4] as the novel's most Pavlovian song (there are several others) puts it. Probably Dodson-Truck is so eager to force this return of the repressed because there's a chance that the same "Mystery Stimulus" Jamf employed to trigger erections links somehow to the v-2.[5] But how would that uncanny process work? The answer: Jamf may have deconditioned the erectile reponse *beyond* the point where Infant Tyrone "showed zero hardons in the presence of stimulus x"; and so having deconditioned the boy too far, taking him "transmarginal," the reversal of cause and effect—hard-on first, then a v-2 strike exactly on that site—just might explain the phenomenon *and* reaffirm causality's sovereign rule over the physical world.[6] Yet Slothrop learns about this first conditioning later than we do, and by then it may not matter that much anyway. In the name of the war effort, Dr. Pointsman has managed the second and more profound programming.

Pointsman seizes on Jamf's assumed deconditioning mistake as a means to gather new information about the rocket: an Allied plan to condition Slothrop for a quest into the Zone, to "expose Slothrop to the German rocket," as Pointsman says, and let his subconscious powers guide him, and Them, to the grail.[7] Having already supposed a connection between Slothrop's sexual-conquest map and Roger Mexico's map of London v-2 strikes, Pointsman's idea, with Dodson-Truck's backing, is to turn Slothrop loose in the occupied Zone, a man thinking he's free, but with his mind crammed with ballistics and aerospace engineering knowledge learned under Katje's care. Thus programmed, his rocket-dowsing power is structured for a quest into the Zone for whatever residues of wisdom, or magic, are there in the v-2's places of origin. This is the novel's most elementary plot structure and what evokes the conventional adventure tale form: an odyssey with helping and hindering characters, plenty of sirens and Circe-like mindless pleasures (even pigs!), some monsters, and a few mock battles. Throughout the novel's part 3, Slothrop will to some extent operate under the control of Pointsman's conditioning and to some extent under the control of quest narrative conventions, both functioning synergistically—but contrary to Slothrop's desires for freedom.

Slothrop's conditioning having been ordered for postwar strategic purposes and under the aegis of science, there's no remorse for how it continues the psychic wounding of Slothrop, which dates back twenty-five years. The process of roping in Slothrop starts comically with Grigori in his glass tank, the octopus's operant conditioning involving repeated exposure to film footage of Katje, as an attractant (octopi having such a keen visual sense), which conditions him to act the part of an attacking sea monster (think: *It Came from Beneath the Sea* [1955], with its H-bomb-mutated octopus grabbing victims from San Francisco beaches), triggering a Slothrop-to-the-rescue reflex and thus a "cute meet" with Katje on the beach outside the casino at Monaco. Indeed on the day They roll out this grand operation, Grigori, Katje, and even Slothrop all react right on cue, our lieutenant battling the creature back into the sea and luring him away with a "found crab." But already quite the paranoiac, Slothrop immediately feels "the conniving around him," thinking: "Oh, that was no 'found' crab, Ace—no random octopus or girl, uh-uh."[8] Nonetheless Pointsman's plotting, realized as if he'd done a turn in some film director's chair, achieves its ends. The ensuing brief but intense affair with Katje at the casino ensures that Slothrop will remain receptive long enough for Them to jam into his mind masses of rocket information useful—though perhaps only bits of it—for his journey into the occupied German Zone.

With this second conditioning now operable, it's no matter that Slothrop's map may have over-exaggerated the number of his "girls." Later, we learn that the investigative work of detectives Speed and Perdoo revealed that some stars may have marked Slothrop's *fantasized* encounters at blast sites.[9] Nor is it a concern that Jamf, according to "world-renowned analyst Mickey Wuxtry-Wuxtry" in another belated disclosure, *may* have been "only a fiction, to help [Slothrop] explain what he felt so terribly, so immediately in his genitals for those rockets each time exploding" around London.[10] *May* have been: because the narrative presentation of this figure, including his name (from the cries of boys hawking newspapers on the streets), can be read as mocking popular media "experts." In any case Pointsman makes a rational application of the two maps, along with existing scientific information on Infant Tyrone, and this effort—despite all the uncertainty—frames Slothrop's actions from the middle of part 1 until he vanishes at the beginning of part 4. Yet even early into that plan-within-the-plan—to condition his paranoid ideations for use in war-torn Europe—it's clear from Slothrop's thoughts while in Monaco that he's partly decoding the daily script, except that he can't quite figure out why Sir Stephen Dodson-Truck would be "consulting a stopwatch and taking notes" as Slothrop becomes sexually aroused looking at graphs of the rocket's "snarled maze of fuel, oxidizer, steam, peroxide and permanganate lines, valves, vents, chambers." He wonders, "what's sexy about that?"[11] In that inquiry Slothrop even gets assists from Dodson-Truck, who in a kind of passive resistance to the system "makes perfectly accessible his disguise, if not his function in the conspiracy." These disclosures soon get him "knocked out" of the project, along with Katje, and panic "the Slothrop group" back in London ("The whole thing's falling apart, Pointsman!").[12] There are hints of sinister forces at work. The last guy to play Sir Stephen's game, Tantivy Mucker-Maffick, seems to have paid for it with his life. Indeed it is interesting that Slothrop "randomly" picks up the news of Tantivy's suspicious death from a *Times* of London column listing "Fallen Officers." In a world where *control* is Their byword, in which "the odds They played here belonged to the past, the past only," and were "never probabilities but frequencies *already observed*," there might be a twinkling of freedom in that moment—in how They cannot control every input of information.[13] Or, They planted that obituary to frighten Slothrop into running, in which case their dominion's working. Either way, the news is just another reminder to Slothrop and the reader looking over his shoulder that this game's played for mortal stakes. Also, that in this game he's never been more than a scuffling knight.

Just what, exactly, "the Slothrop group" expects their subject will locate for them in the Zone is never wholly clear. They do want the mystery plastic, Imipolex G. Understanding the mechanism of Slothrop's enigmatic sexual response to the rocket is another priority, because that gift, skill, curse—whatever it is—might be generally utilized. And They surely also hope to learn something about a certain v-2 Schwarzgerät—a "black-device" or "-tool"—and how it links to black rocket troopers working alongside Nazis. Slothrop only learns about these dark enigmas in the first episode of part 3, after he has "skidded out onto the Zone like a planchette on a Ouija board," a nifty trope for how They see him.[14] There, Geli Tripping tips him to the Schwarzgerät; and the rabidly racist Major Duane Marvy tips him to the Schwarzkommando: "Now we got not just niggers you see but *kraut* niggers. Well, Jesus. V-E Day just about everyplace you found a rocket, you had you a nigger." Nice guy, this Marvy; and insofar as he here indicates a new Slothropian mission in the Zone, he speaks for Them when he voices the terrors, to garden variety white supremacists like him, of blacks with rockets: "You can't trust *them*—With *rockets*? They're a childlike race. Brains are smaller." Slothrop absorbs all of this just after reading corporate documents from a file passed to him back in Zürich, which reveal that his father, Broderick—coded into the files as "B.S." or "Schwarzvater" or "Black-father"—may have sold little Tyrone to Jamf in exchange for the boy's Harvard education.[15]

The "Slothrop group" must have a general sense of their subject's ties to this threatening black web. Putting him through that series of sodium amytal sessions, at least some of which were dedicated "to help[ing] illuminate racial problems in his own country," served those purposes even if it only yielded the surrealistic tale of Slothrop's dive down the Roseland Ballroom toilet after his lost mouth harp and to escape a gang of African American teenagers (including a rag-popping "shoeshine boy" named Malcolm X) he fears are about to gang-rape him.[16] So: there is a nexus evidently linking rocket, Imipolex G, Schwarzgerät, Schwarzvater, Jamf, black Nazi v-2 troopers, and American white supremacist and interracial sexual paranoias. But what does it *mean*? That is, in Pynchon's storyworld is that nexus at all useful? The reader needs a Venn diagram to sort its aspects and graph the links. And finally, it might be only a fantasy, "a conspiracy so immense," as U.S. senator Joseph McCarthy said about China's fall to the Communists, that one *needs* to believe in such a plot in order to hold together the world's inherent disorder. That's how Hofstadter characterized the Puritan legacy of a "paranoid style" in American political culture; and it well defines Slothrop's "operational paranoia" and that of "the Slothrop group," using our hapless hero.[17] This paranoia feeds Their determinist needs for order.

On the flip-side we have the result of Slothrop's second conditioning. It leads him, and readers, into occasional bouts of "anti-paranoia, where nothing is connected to anything" in the world, where causality has vanished, and Slothrop for one feels "vulnerable, uncentered."[18] Disengaging from the ideology of mechanistic rationality that has been activated in him will require a major awakening and change, and in part three, "Freedom," we will consider whether Slothrop actually manages any real exit. Certainly Slothrop's growing awareness of his paranoia does not help. Later in the novel, when actress Margherita Erdmann passes him further information about Their plot against him, while they're aboard the *Anubis*, Slothrop acknowledges that he's captured in that mechanistic paradigm: "Looks like there are sub-Slothrop needs They know about, and he doesn't: this is humiliating on the face of it, but now there's also the even more annoying question, What do I need that badly?"[19] Conscious of his entanglement and how easily he might slothfully set aside real needs and just go along to get along, Slothrop never seems to catch on to what's driving Their uses of him and his own dilemmas: chiefly, his desperate need for simple explanations in terms of cause and effect. In case the reader does not realize how the text puts us in the same predicament, the novel spells it out in a direct address: "You will want cause and effect."[20] One can almost hear the narrator's frustration with and disdain for us determinists out here in the real world, especially when the narrator next says, "All right," and supplies a dose of a supposedly simple, "natural" causality. This comes very late in the novel, after the narration has splintered every which way, so it's as if the text dares us to test our faith in causality against the narrative rubble of those pages, or indeed of the entire text. What good are one's high-cultural training and conventions, one's scientific competence, to rationally explain the information in this novel's pages? Or the information before Slothrop as he rummages through rocket-related and Jamf-related documents?

Happily, many great summaries of *Gravity's Rainbow* attest that readers may largely overcome problems of incoherence and uncertainty.[21] We also don't wish to overstate the degree to which Pynchon deviates from conventional fiction. Unlike Joyce in *Finnegans Wake* and other writers after him, Pynchon rarely devises his own language. Indeed he might be seen to be mocking that tendency in one of the novel's late, fragmentary scenes, when Gerhardt von Göll, stoned on sodium amytal, babbles the phrase "medoschnicka bleelar medoometnozz in bergamot."[22] Ultimately *Gravity's Rainbow* may not quite give average interested readers what they want, but it does not quite decondition them, either. The framework of narrative communication remains in place. The text even nods, warily, to corporatized publishing. Molly Hite has pointed out a remarkable passage in which an authorial voice from outside the narrative frame seems to ask, about our novel, in brackets, "Do you want to put this part in?"[23]

Certainly reader frustration can still run high with *Gravity's Rainbow*. Some would prefer to give up on it, as anyone who's studied the novel with college students will attest. And various critics—beginning with John Gardner in *On Moral Fiction* (1978), through James Wood's chastisements of Pynchon, Don DeLillo, and other "hysterical realists" in *The Broken Estate* (1999)—have filed strong briefs against it, typically for a perceived a- or immorality and/or an alleged infidelity to the realist tradition. We strongly disagree. Along with many others, we find the book's play with realism, its humor, and its morality powerfully engaged with the great tradition and conventionally welcoming enough to attract readers who appreciate a challenge not only to their reading habits but also to the system's logics. Obviously this kind of attraction doesn't warrant a liberated reading experience, even if it moves one to project a highly unconventional poetics or ideology onto the author. Pynchon's difficulty might thus become another example of repressive tolerance, especially when it becomes routinized through academic undertakings that mystify rather than help. There is clearly no need for us to try and look the other way here. Our only point is: Pynchon must have seen this recuperation coming.

James Earl has argued that Pointsman's behaviorism "is only the theoretical and experimental arm of a larger determinism that claims to control all events according to a strict mechanistic causality that denies the existence both of will and chance."[24] In his search for "the true mechanical explanation," the British Pavlovian sees "only chaos in the abandonment of causality," which is what Earl understands as Roger Mexico's goal—a kind of chaos similar to Slothrop's in his moments of anti-paranoia, and to the reader's in moments of incomprehension or downright exasperation.[25] To Earl, then, Pointsman seems a sad and outdated embodiment of a simplistic science. We cannot go that far. Indeed, even as Pynchon's novel satirizes bureaucratic applications of behaviorist science and determinist procedure, what Althusser defines as "apparatuses" for control, it nevertheless depends on realist conventions of plot and characterization; it still represents science and technology as rationally useful enterprises, even if prone to massive abuses; and it declines to throw out the baby with the bathwater. At the novel's end, realism and rationalism remain powerful models and tools, and "Pynchon"—the writer that readers want to imagine—hasn't gone over totally to the Luddites. Thus when Alan Friedman defines three types of science in the novel (Newtonian mechanism, statistical physics, and quantum physics), he never suggests that the first (associated with Pointsman) has been overthrown or that people in Pynchon's storyworld, Slothrop included, no longer deploy science when making decisions about other people.[26] The clockwork model still functions, as do insights into and actions on the basis of chance and uncertainty.

Our experience tells us that this is how the great majority of readers make their way through *Gravity's Rainbow*: reckoning causes, allowing for chance, admitting incompleteness (as the renowned meta-mathematician Kurt Gödel revealed it, and as Pynchon uses it in the song "Sold on Suicide"), while also realizing the ethics at stake in our decisions and factoring in as well the novel's great and disruptive powers of satire.[27] Indeed the Pavlovian's belief in mechanistic rationality and control certainly is not limited to Pointsman or to the Allied forces. It forms an essential part of how They, on either side of the front in World War II, assure Their grip on the individual. This hold is not only necessary for the political status quo, it also enhances profit. Optimally, the subject does not experience this form of domination as coming from without. When Slothrop's paranoia grows during his stay at the casino, the narrator shifts attention to the late Roland Feldspath, a "long-co-opted expert on control systems" and the "spirit" at a séance earlier in the novel. From Feldspath's perspective on the other side, and perhaps in a nod to Fromm's thoughts on the German authoritarian personality, the typical German enthusiasm or "Schwärmerei for Control was used by the folks in power," and They have managed to "put [the control] inside." It's depicted as a momentous turn: "No more need to suffer passively under 'outside forces.'"[28]

The German fondness for control appears in other domains. It comes up when Slothrop may have caught "the German mania for name-giving, dividing the Creation finer and finer, analyzing"; and also in connection with the "Toiletship" *Rücksichtslos* (Ruthless, or Heedless, so also mindless), "a triumph of the German mania for subdividing."[29] Jamf, who first conditioned Slothrop, has a "German-scientist mind"; and as a teacher he has spread the deterministic gospel, for example to former chemistry student Franz Pökler. Franz proudly accepts his wife, Leni's, appellation of him as a "cause-and-effect man," a tribute to the mechanistic rationality and desire for control that Jamf and Pointsman also share.[30] Franz regards his teacher as the latest in a direct line of descent from the originary "hero of chemistry," Justus von Liebig, whose legacy passed to "August Wilhelm von Hofmann, to Herbert Ganister to Laszlo Jamf, a direct chain, cause-and-effect." More important perhaps, Jamf's transnational authority stands like a synecdoche for Their worldwide dominion. German manias for causality and control typify Western authority generally. And those manias are balanced against a method that compensates analysis with amalgamation.

Control requires organization, and "the Slothrop group" is just a branch office (or desk) within the more dominant presence of cartelized economic and political power. Because he worked against the German weakness for organizational subdivision and devised a more unified and efficient, therefore more profitable and *controlled* business environment, the German financier, industrialist, and statesman Walther Rathenau (1867–1922) stands historically in *Gravity's Rainbow* as the founder of "The New Economy," or *Die neue Wirtschaft*, the title of his 1918 book. Known for having coordinated Germany's World War I manufacturers, Rathenau remade the national economy by, as Pynchon's narrator puts it, "cutting across and demolishing the barriers of secrecy and property that separated firm from firm—a corporate Bismarck."[31] If that's the work World War II completed, resulting in the Zone, then Rathenau was modern war's prophet. His innovation was the cartel, "a rational structure in which business would be the true, the rightful authority," closely abetted by science/technology and political regulation. So Jamf's move into organic chemistry, a discipline dedicated to molecular combination and recombination, exemplifies for Pynchon the collusions managed through transnational cartelization.[32] Fully enmeshed in furthering Their methods of control, Jamf eventually receives a medal of honor through IG Farben, one of Nazi Germany's central cartels and in its time one of the ten best-capitalized businesses in the Western world, its reach literally global. An early episode in the novel is preceded by a Jamf quotation out of a (fictional) 1934 advertising brochure from Agfa, the German company (makers of film) that amalgamated in 1925 with IG Farben, whose top managers would be convicted of war crimes after 1945. In the novel, IG Farben has (on the verge of war in 1939) acquired from Jamf the formula for "an aromatic heterocyclic polymer."[33] It's a product exemplifying "[p]lasticity's central canon: that chemists were no longer to be at the mercy of Nature," that they had somehow transcended it.[34] And when we combine this description of Jamf's hubris with the later suggestion that his invention will find use as an insulation device for Gottfried in the 00000 rocket, we think the narration has joined decisively the mastery of "Mister Imipolex" to what Marcuse's work defined as the dominant death drive, or Thanatos.[35] Indeed that conjunction remains tight even as we gather information about how Imipolex, "the material of the future," also serves Eros, for example if (and that's a significant if) it was the mystery stimulus in Slothrop's operant conditioning circa 1920, and it was used again in 1925 when ss men clothed actress Margherita Erdmann in an erotic Imipolex bodysuit, a scene laden with dominance-and-submission overtones.[36] By the novel's end Imipolex seems the cartelized state's main icon. It stands for the system's power to control pleasure and wield pain, and it heightens the symbolic value—and violence—of Gottfried's last ride. We might just be going down with him, corrupted and conditioned as we are by late capitalism.

Working as a technical writer for Boeing in the early sixties, Pynchon became close friends with Fred Gebauer, a mechanical engineer. Fifty years later at a UCLA event, Fred's widow, Phyllis, recalled how "Tom" and Fred clowned around at parties, could not speak of their aerospace work, and called themselves "aero-braceros"—after the migrant Mexican agricultural workers seasonally allowed into the western United States to harvest crops.[37] The average aerospace worker was far better paid, of course, and not nearly as itinerant as his bracero counterpart. Still, within about five years the Gebauers evidently migrated from Seattle, to Houston, and then to Los Angeles. Pynchon ascribed this technocratic nomadism to characters like Pökler and especially Jamf, whose hopscotching around various universities and companies mirrors the growth of transnational research and industrial networks during the early twentieth century. We learn (again looking over Slothrop's shoulder at various documents) that when Jamf invented Imipolex he "was working for a Swiss outfit called Psychochemie AG, originally known as the Grössli Chemical Corporation, a spinoff from Sandoz," and that in "the early '20s, Sandoz, Ciba, and Geigy had got together in a Swiss chemical cartel" (all of this, by the way, deriving from the history of chemical engineering). "Shortly after, Jamf's firm was also absorbed. Apparently, most of Grössli's contracts had been with Sandoz, anyway. As early as 1926 there were oral agreements between the Swiss cartel and IG Farben."[38] As the narrator tells us, this network even breached Switzerland's supposed neutrality, and brought it into the war. And there's more: "Imipolex G shows up on a mysterious 'insulation device' on a rocket being fired with the help of a transmitter on the roof of the headquarters of Dutch Shell, who is co-licensee for marketing the Imipolex," a plastic (but fictional, remember) that Shell got involved with "through an agreement [among the Swiss, the Germans, and] Imperial Chemicals dated 1939."[39] Still more: even Winston Churchill might be implicated through a son-in-law who gathers all the rocket intelligence at Shell Mex House, in London (also historical). And then there's Jamf's (fictional) transatlantic connection. He had wrangled the conditioning of Infant Tyrone (or, "IT," right?) during his post–World War I Boston-area research appointment, evidently after winning a grant ("shoestring funding," but still) from the (actual) National Research Council, "under a continuing NRC program of psychological study which had begun during the [First] World War, when methods were needed for selecting officers and classifying draftees."[40] Still following?

Here's the payoff. When Brigadier Pudding objects that psychological "meddling" with Slothrop would be a "beastly" operation, Pointsman counters by situating his proposal at the end of "a long line of experiment and questioning. Harvard University, the U.S. Army? Hardly shabby institutions."[41] A steady believer in routinized authority as well as the nation-state, Pudding insists on British independence from American methods he regards as corrupt. Pointsman, having evidently wheedled approval from other superiors, wins; British scientists then program an American subject following an American research tradition inherited from the German scientist Jamf, who has Swiss connections, and who seems to have been involved in Slothropiana after 1920. Later, when Verbindungsmann Wimpe tells what he knows about chemistry's secret history to the Russian agent Tchitcherine, Jamf comes up: "[He] was on loan again, this time as a chemist, to the Americans, whose National Research Council had begun a massive program to explore the morphine molecule and its possibilities."[42] This effort was apparently developed together with DuPont, the American polymer company, for the purpose of researching methods of addiction control. That work failed its goal but succeeded in extending still more complexly that transnational academic, business, and industrial web. In its filaments Slothrop seems to have been captured and filed away for decades as the merest of creatures or objects. Then the V-2 links suddenly fascinate Them; in a trice They lock in funding, and manpower, to determine and then to surveil the man's uses. Wimpe's sketch of the transnational web makes clear: American capital and national security interests are keyed into this plot. Hardly surprising, then, that Pynchon starts off the novel with the Wernher von Braun epigraph. The original rocketman's long journey from a privileged Prussian family—his boyhood work with rocket hobbyists, his university degrees, his labor in cartelized rocket development and service as a Nazi V-2 boss and SS officer, his experience as a U.S. prisoner-of-war "advising" American rocket efforts at White Sands, New Mexico, and the Redstone Arsenal in Alabama, and then his becoming a U.S. citizen, writing pieces for *Collier's* magazine, starring in Disney TV programs on space travel, and finally fulfilling a childhood dream by becoming chief NASA engineer in the Apollo moon program—such a life represents just how superficial are nationalities and ideological oppositions when the military-industrial complex and modern media are moving persons around the chessboard.

If Jamf is a German spider working one of the cartel webs, his "pale plastic ubiquity"[43] following Slothrop rather than the other way around, Lyle Bland must be the chemist's American counterpart. Sure enough, the two of them have a central connection. In paperwork relating to German firms, "bootlegged for him back there in Zürich," Slothrop finds "the record of a transaction between Jamf and Mr. Lyle Bland, of Boston, Massachusetts."[44] This is the first time Bland shows up in the novel, but he is no stranger to Slothrop, not least because he "shows up often in the private records Jamf kept of his own business deals."[45] It turns out that Bland was involved in the early twenties with Hugo Stinnes, "the Wunderkind of European finance," who "during the [first] world war worked closely with Walther Rathenau."[46] Bland having let contracts for private currency to the Slothrop Paper Company, the mere sight of his family name in Jamf's records gives Slothrop a fit of nausea, and an erection, "like an instrument installed, wired by *Them* into his body as a colonial outpost in our raw and clamorous world, another office representing Their white Metropolis far away."[47]

It's worth pausing right there. For what does it mean in the storyworld that the character Tyrone Slothrop has just gotten a hard-on from *reading words on a page*: not mid-century, under-the-counter porn fiction words, but boring, fact-laden business records treating contracts, companies, and currencies? Reading the novel under the aegis of mimetic, realist conventions, one concludes that even if the summary of empirical evidence supposedly in those documents weren't enough, the man's nausea and erectile response persuasively indicates that for decades Slothrop has been caught unwittingly in that spider's web of international interests. His responses also indicate that those uses of Slothrop probably did involve some mode of sexual conditioning like the one readers have otherwise learned about. Slothrop's responses may reasonably entitle one to discount other voices in the novel—that of Mickey Wuxtry-Wuxtry, for example—that posit Jamf and the conditioning as "only a fiction."[48] Yet even that option pales beside a further point: Slothrop, reacting as he pores over texts, opens a reading of this narrative text which considers the reading of texts; opens, in other words, a metafictional "scene of reading." What matters here is that Slothrop's somatic reaction to words on pages, even boring business documents, acknowledges reading as an embodied practice, a linking of signification and reaction, words and deeds. This wisdom is available to any *Gravity's Rainbow* reader who feels gut-wrenching revulsion at the plain words relating Brigadier Pudding's coprophagia, who squirms at the surgical details of a castration (even that of war-mongering bigot Major Marvy), or who winces in horror at the words representing Pointsman's wonderment that his "lusts fit inside" the "white frame[s]" of the prepubescent girls he fantasizes about and, according to the details in episode 8 (e.g., bringing them home to his "spermy bed"), sometimes rapes. In episode 9 Jessica intuitively senses that's the man's backstory, which explains why she "shivers" even just thinking of Pointsman. These somatic responses are psychologically and socially determined or, in the novel's word, "programmed," and as such they may commence a process of ethical reading. For a novel seemingly committed to putting causality under erasure, something powerfully significant happens here.

Infant Tyrone seems to have been conditioned through an international cartel that involved his father's business. Confirmation follows almost immediately, at least for Slothrop. On the next page he finds his own initials next to the cryptonym "Schwarzknabe." This "black boy" has been sold by "Schwarzvater" (most probably his father, Broderick) to "Uncle Lyle" in order to finance his Harvard education.[49] Or as Slothrop sees it: "I've been sold to IG Farben like a side of beef."[50] We'll return to Slothrop and blackness. For now let's continue to investigate Bland, who quickly becomes the cartel's archvillain in Slothrop's head. Landing amid a group of Americans and Russians enjoying a beer in the underground tunnels of the Nordhausen V-2 assembly plant, Slothrop thinks that "it's Lyle Bland who has hold of his ankle here."[51] During a short break from being chased by Major Marvy, Slothrop speculates about the major's connections: "Marvy is buddies with GE, that's Morgan money, there's Morgan money in Harvard, and surely an interlock someplace with Lyle Bland."[52] Near the end of part 3, a long section expands on him, including this: "By way of the Bland Institute and the Bland Foundation, the man has had his meathooks well into the American day-to-day since 1919."[53] From a superefficient carburetor to the attention American males devote to their own penis, there's hardly anything Bland has not been involved with. Part of the Business Advisory Council, "whose ideas on matters of 'control' ran close to those of Walther Rathenau," and knee deep in more concrete affiliations with Germany, Bland is so well connected that our narrator, in a moment of typical metafictional irony, muses that if only researchers had the time and resources to trace those connections' full extent, we'd have "a paranoid structure worthy of the name."[54]

It's worth remembering that Pynchon was crafting the character Lyle Bland in a time when a truly legendary, colorful, scheming, and certifiably paranoid military-industrial-complex mogul like Howard Hughes could still intrigue the American popular imagination. As with Hughes, there are untraceable cause-and-effect schemes and plots in *Gravity's Rainbow*, but this hardly prevents the text from offering occasional bites to feed our hunger. An example: Bland has moved one of his German associates, Bert Fibel, to a General Electric plant in the Berkshires so that he may "keep an eye on adolescent Tyrone Slothrop." And even "ten years after the original deal was closed, IG Farben is still finding it easier to subcontract the surveillance of young Tyrone back to Lyle Bland."[55] This comes from an omniscient narrator, apparently guaranteeing verisimilitude at a moment of potential reader duress—our helplessness before all that complexly sequenced detail. So, do we feel easy, comfortable in the strong hands of a controlling narrator? The narrator seems to trump these doubts with a still stronger manifestation of his narrative dominion by referencing a passage more than 125 pages back: "Last we saw of Fibel he was hooking, stretching, and running shock cord for that Horst Achtfaden back in his gliding days."[56] In the grip of authority, are we willing to trust a new bit of information about Slothrop?

In the long section on Lyle Bland, the Freemasons play an important role. Hofstadter's book showed how the Masons throughout the republic's long life have been a staple of many uniquely American conspiracy theories.[57] On an initial reading one might think their usage in *Gravity's Rainbow* stands upon the simple paranoid structure of Them versus the individual. Then we look closer. Initially, the Bland pages play to simple paranoia: "There is a theory going around that the U.S.A. was and still is a gigantic Masonic plot under the ultimate control of the group known as the Illuminati. It is difficult to look for long at the strange single eye crowning the pyramid which is found on every dollar bill and not begin to believe the story, a little."[58] At which point one expects Pynchon's narrator to put on his pop culture mask and exclaim, "Jeepers, Mr. Information!" But the next move upends simple paranoia and any easy equation between Them and the cliché of Masonic dominion. It turns out that Bland was invited to join the Masonic order after solving "the Great Pinball Difficulty," when some machines were misbehaving, deviating from their programming.[59] Already, then, the narration trivializes the Masons and this subplot. In fact the lure of Masonry for Bland involves not his busy role in the worldwide cartel but the order's ancient magic and mythology, as Bland quits "those nefarious tricks of his" in the business world and settles on a sofa for brief, unexpected trial runs at some kind of astral projection that takes him "underneath history." So, at some point (the circumstances and the process are never clear), he vanishes from the living.[60] The perspective in this section is partly Bland's, partly the narrator's, so it is hard to gauge what that independence from gravity means. Bland does disappear from the storyworld, in 1936 according to the narrator, when a commotion erupts among IG Farben management, "all to do with who was likely to take over the Slothrop surveillance."[61] Almost like the Slothrop sightings and mentions in the Zone after his vanishing, Bland also puts in an appearance or two after his enigmatic transcendence, or death. During "The Story of Byron the Bulb" (set in the summer of 1945) none other than Bland is said to have worked out a theory that "consumers need to feel a sense of sin," a conclusion based on how he and his "psychologists had figures, expert testimony and money . . . enough to tip the Discovery of Guilt at the cusp between scientific theory and fact," and thus to put the concept into the businessman's toolkit.[62] There we also learn that Byron labors under the control of the Phoebus cartel, which has made deals with meat and soap manufacturers: "Soap in those days was a booming concern. Among the consumers, the Bland Institute had uncovered deep feelings about shit."[63] Apparently at least the institute operating under his name has survived the vanished Bland. Or is he ghosting this work? It hardly matters. These mentions do the work of humorously tying Byron's story to the rest of the narrative.

CHAPTER 7

War as a Cartel Project

The cartel controlling Slothrop clearly doesn't require Bland; it operates according to its own indomitable requirements. Initially Slothrop learns there were no further business agreements between Germany's IG Farben and Britain's Imperial Chemicals "dated any later than '39," when the nations went to war.[1] But that freeze turns out to have been a ruse, as other documents reveal that certain arrangements continued as ever. Similarly, the morally astute Kevin Spectro would like to think war is not "a laboratory" for experimenting on human subjects, but his own enthusiasm for scientific innovation reveals to him that the war is a massive corporate project bulldozing all manner of human subjects—Slothrop and Pudding, for example—in pursuit of control over processes, products, and markets.[2] By the time he understands how far the corporate octopus can reach, a spectral Spectro must struggle to explain it from the other side. Pynchon carefully distributes throughout the novel this deeper critique of war, often using little more than hints. At the beginning of his personal story, Ensign Morituri avers that "we are conditioned to forget" the days preceding the outbreak of war because of what they reveal: "isn't the hidden machinery easier to see in the days leading up to the event?" he asks. And explains: "There are arrangements, things to be expedited . . . and often the edges are apt to lift, briefly, and we see things we were not meant to."[3] So too when Katje ruminates on her escape from The Hague, and the narrator's overlaid voice summarizes: "Don't forget the real business of the War is buying and selling. . . . The mass nature of wartime death is useful in many ways. It serves as spectacle, as diversion from the real movements of the War."[4] And those movements involve academic disciplines, technological applications, natural resources, product manufacturing, and distribution. When Slothrop enters Zürich, he too gets an inkling of what is really happening: "The War has been reconfiguring time and space into its own image. The track runs in different networks now. What appears to be destruction is really the shaping of railroad spaces to other purposes, intentions he can only, riding through it for the first time, begin to feel the leading edges of."[5] Some characters more deeply embedded in the system can be quite blunt about the war's functions. Wimpe knows exactly how it connects with system-wide repression: "We know how to produce real pain. Wars, obviously . . . machines in the factories, industrial accidents, automobiles built to be unsafe, poisons in food, water, and even air—these are quantities tied directly to the economy. We know them, and we can control them."[6] Citizens are conditioned *not* to see these effects, despite how war ratchets up oppression and violence across the social spectrum.

Postwar needs seem to have pulled back the curtain, made repression visible again for a spell, and defined "peace" as a customary social fantasy screening people from seeing war as the steady-state reality. Watching the police breaking up the black market in a northern German town, Slothrop comprehends just how and why there was so little need for police violence during the conflict: "The War must've been lean times for crowd control, murder and mopery was the best you could do, one suspect at a time."[7] And what about postwar? Enzian considers how his Schwarzkommando had allied during the war with Germans who once sought to exterminate the Hereros in Southwest Africa, and draws a dire conclusion from postwar power shifts: "Perhaps it's theater, but they seem no longer to be Allies . . . though the history they have invented for themselves conditions us to expect 'postwar rivalries,' when in fact it may all be a giant cartel including winners and losers both, in an amiable agreement to share what is there to be shared." He reflects on how Germans, even the scavenging poor, will betray his Hereros, without a thought, to the Russians or the Americans under Major Marvy, himself allied "with General Electric."[8] Later, Enzian gazes at a Hamburg refining plant and understands why even the bombed ruins reveal Their modern view in action: "It means this War was never political at all . . . secretly, it was being dictated by the needs of technology . . . by a conspiracy between human beings and techniques" to raze old factories and make room for the new.[9] Pointsman's aide, Dr. Rózsavölgyi, indulges in a utopian vision of postwar predicated on faith in technocracy. During the strife, he recalls, thinkers believed "that behind the War—all the death, savagery, and destruction—lay the Führer-principle. But if personalities could be replaced by abstractions of power, if techniques developed by the corporations could be brought to bear, might not nations live rationally?"[10] In the twentieth century's first half, many agreed with Max Weber that a rationalization of charisma would prevent charismatic dictators and mass violence. By 1945 that hope lay in ruins, while it became clearer that rationalization would also only tighten the system's grip on individuals by incorporating them into bureaucratic and managerial structures where their regulation and domination might proceed by subtle coercion rather than overt violence, by enlisting people in the mindless pleasures of consumption rather than in military regiments which limit their abilities *to buy*. Not to mention the disciplining authority legitimized through a permanent state of emergency—the Cold War that Enzian already glimpses on the Zone's horizon. Just prior to "The Story of Byron the Bulb," our narrator takes on the guise of Mr. Information speaking to Skippy, a naïve, gee-whiz modern teenager he first mocks ("Skippy you little fool") and then cynically reeducates: "Skippy, the truth is that the War is keeping things alive. *Things*. The Ford is only one of them. The Germans-and-Japs story was only one, rather surrealistic version of the real War. The real War is always there. The dying tapers off now and then, but the War is still killing lots and lots of people. Only right now it is killing them in more subtle ways. . . . These are the ones the War cannot use, and so they die."[11]

Cartelized war, hot or cold, affects everything and everyone in *Gravity's Rainbow*. In "its glutton, ever-nibbling intake," it literally incorporates the entirety of human experience; its inexorable logic of conditioning dominates all classes and kinds of people in the storyworld.[12] Indeed, if one wanted an exemplary fictional treatment of the extent and means of structural or objective violence in modernity, it would be hard to do better than *Gravity's Rainbow*. And the wall-to-wall proliferation of structural domination in the narrative highlights even more sharply the near absence in it of conventional, subjective wartime violence. Pynchon's focus is fundamentally, and politically, different.

What happens to the symbolic, in war's totalizing regime? At the V-2 battery operating in The Hague, Katje, Gottfried, and even Blicero feel helpless: "the War" with its "absolute rule of chance" forces them to recognize "their own pitiable contingency here, in its midst."[13] Gottfried thus tries to shift the symbolic register, to imagine a replacement narrative for the Hansel and Gretel game Blicero forces him to play; but he gets no further than "the War itself as tyrant king."[14] A sillier example: in London, Mrs. Quoad makes Slothrop go through a disgusting candy drill, telling him to "show a little backbone" and swallow another of her gut bombs; he holds out until Darlene, his girlfriend of the moment (therefore, doomed), gives her assent: "Yes," she tells him, "don't you know there's a war on? Here now love, open your mouth."[15] The point being, while there might be an important example in the novel of a temporary reprieve from all these subtle dominations large and small, in the end it never amounts to anything substantial. So while Jessica and Roger represent love—*the* iconic and idealizing sixties condition—nonetheless their occasional "Fuck the war" attitude cannot overcome their dependence on the conflict.[16] They wouldn't be together without the war, for one thing. More important, Roger's "mother is the war"; and rather like Ezra Pound's post–World War I vision of "civilization" as an "old bitch gone in the teeth," this one too has "leached at all the soft, the vulnerable inclusions of hope and praise scattered" formerly in Roger's being.[17] As his mother, "the War must disapprove of [Jessica's] beauty, her cheeky indifference to death-institutions he'd not so long ago believed in."[18] Later, Roger will come to see the life his "Jess" inspires him to imagine as mere illusion. And Jessica will also drop *her* romantic illusions about Roger. He thinks her being infected by the war explains her desire, after V-E Day, for a return to the simpleminded complacency of her fiancé, Jeremy, aka "Beaver." Roger may like to believe that Jeremy epitomizes "every assertion the fucking War has ever made—that we are meant for work and government, for austerity: and these shall take priority over love, dreams, the spirit, the senses and the other second-class trivia that are found among the idle and mindless hours of the day."[19] Yet is Roger greatly different? He isn't, though he does voice a criticism of his rival seemingly cribbed from Marcuse's analysis of the deeply repressed one-dimensional man, mindlessly deferring recognition of his own domination. Yet what resistance, mindful or mindless, is possible against the system, against war as a wholly repressive regime? *It* need not fret over disturbances in the standardized flows of things, including people like Roger. So when Jessica is detaching from his affections, Roger faces a grim future: "There's something still on, don't call it a 'war' if it makes you nervous, maybe the death rate's gone down a point or two . . . but Their enterprise goes on." He knows that with war's continuance comes the same old repressive tolerance.[20] From there, Roger's anger will veer into an activism against Them that is still hobbled by an outdated notion of "war" as clear-cut conflict, as subjective violence and domination rather than this ceaseless version of war, the looming Cold War, and its insidious objective and symbolic control over everyday life. So he futilely sings a sixties-style chant: "But we're bringin' down Their system, / And it isn't a resistance, it's a war."[21] Roger cannot conceive of power and subversion working in any other mode.

The novel's narrator thinks Roger should know better, and a scene in part 1 explains why. It takes place just a few days before Christmas 1944, somewhere near the coast in Kent, southeast of London and right across the English Channel from Dunkirk and Calais. Roger has evidently picked up Jessica at the coastal anti-aircraft battery where she serves, and, driving north, they stop at an Anglican church where servicemen are filing in for evensong. Jessica, feeling a weight of "nostalgia" for prior Advents, wishes to "be home"; Roger, normally a "snide" unbeliever, wants to go in "[t]o hear the music." Inside they sit amid deep tradition: sixteenth- and seventeenth-century caroling in English, Latin, and even a German macaronic. But they are also (though neither is said to realize it) awash in "imperial outcomes," figured not only by the multilingual texture of the service but by the presence of a black Jamaican conscript, his baritone "riding above the others . . . out of the honest breast." Jessica is struck by how Roger is quite absorbed in the singing and so evidently restored, even his pink skin, to a flush of childlike delight. Just there, the narrator executes a lengthy backward pan: above the soggy, farting congregants, out of the church, over the Kentish coast, the wide-angle focus taking in women and men, pipefitters and shipbuilders, hull plates swinging overhead, to warehouses of metal toothpaste tubes ready for recycling and a return not to commodity flows but "to the War," a great "continuity" of materials—metal, paper—flowing into, well, "paper routines."[22] If Thomas Pynchon were Walt Whitman, whose spirit rises above busy Manhattan in "Song of Myself," the narration would here commence a paean to the people, to democracy, to progress. It won't, for reasons those "imperial outcomes" have already suggested.

This church scene may *seem* to demonstrate *Gemeinschaft*, the traditional, horizontal community that binds individuals together in equality, in shared belief, custom, morality, and myth. But Pynchon's panning out and especially the narrative voiceover stress how those congregants—all of them military people—are instead enmeshed in a larger *Gesellschaft*, a vertical society of rationalized, monetized, and corporatized interests that supersede and subordinate the individual, who chiefly matters as a unit of labor.[23] In that sense Roger and Jessica truly do attend "the War's evensong, the War's canonical hour." This night's worship is only ostensibly for the mythic advent of a savior; more properly, it is for the war. The war has come inside this chapel that had seemed to rise organically out of the English soil as if it were "a hummock in the dark upland"; the war machine is sovereign in the church pews just as it is sovereign in Kent, and globally, in December 1944. There is no place of sanctuary. And this is why "the night is real" among these worshipers, with a Lord of the Night present in their midst. The plain fact is: "The War does not appear to want a folk-consciousness, not even of the sort the Germans have engineered, ein Volk ein Führer—it wants a machine of many separate parts, not oneness, but a complexity"—the cartel.[24] War alone and not the Christ child in his manger is the "true king." And what this sovereign demands from "the serai" following the star of wonder this Advent season are "gifts of tungsten, cordite, high-octane" fuels. The war machine "needs coal" and it "needs electricity," power in its latent and manifest forms, power whose essential importance, again, supersedes individual persons.[25]

That claim about power rather than "oneness" marks a good point for a return to Slothrop's sodium amytal session, sixty pages before this church service. Toward the end of his session Slothrop's fantasia veers into the American Southwest and introduces "Crutchfield the westwardman," a figure who's always rather baffled old Pynchon hands, particularly the singularity defining his world. For he is *the* "westwardman": "Not 'archetypal' westwardman, but the *only*." In the westward world there is "only one Indian who ever fought him," and just "one fight, one victory, one loss"; and in his desert domain there exists precisely "[o]ne of each of everything," which our narrator concedes is "not so bad. Half an Ark's better than none."[26] There's something more to Crutchfield than whacky surrealistic fantasy, however, and it relies again on Calvinism, Weber, and modern concepts of the individual. By

1940 it was more or less a given—from the work of Ferdinand Tönnies, Max Weber, and French anthropologist Marcel Mauss—that the West had derived from Protestantism a new idea of the person, as radically individualist and self-reflexive. For the first time the person had an all-important inner life that he or she was supposed to attend to, think about, and always control. Indeed that new subjectivity was structured, its uniqueness set forward as a *story* that manifests selfhood temporally as the progressive, inexorable line of unique events whose telos optimally is one's realization of grace with the one true God. For Weber especially, Calvinism's crucial move was to dismiss priests and sacraments as intercessors with the divinity, because believers had unmediated access to the divinity through the Holy Spirit all around them.

Yet that crucial move had additionally required Calvinist theology to reconceptualize the Trinity, which, since the Councils of Nicea (325 CE) and Constantinople (360 CE), had been figured as an equilateral triangle, a threefold godhead in which the being of Christ and the being of the Holy Spirit (understood as Christ's earthly sojourn and teachings promulgated in the Gospels and by true believers) were conceptually equal with God's being, or creation. Calvinism's radical revision was to rethink the Holy Spirit as, in Weber's words, "a consciousness of divine grace," a feeling within the individual that gave the believer direct access to the godhead. Thus Calvinism rationalized, disenchanted Christian practices, and deconstructed the Trinity into a vertical line. A core precept, expressed in the Westminster Confession (1647), was that God exercises "his Sovereign Power over his creatures,"[27] and that man, as the topmost creature, has "sovereign power" over his inner life and faith. Believers answer directly to God, using Christ's earthly sojourn, as narrated in Scripture, as their model. Thus radical Calvinists conserved the hierarchical concepts of sovereignty all around them in Western monarchies. Having shattered the trinitarian triangle, Protestantism rearranged things hierarchally, in descending order: God, then Christ the God-man, then the Holy Spirit surrounding the true believers, or elect, with the preterite occupying the bottom. On this hierarchical great chain, Weber argues, Calvinism also created something else new in the world: alienation, or "a feeling of unprecedented inner loneliness of the single individual." Damned or saved, "he was forced to follow his path alone to meet a destiny which had been decreed for him from eternity. No one could help him." This is the new individual's storyline, in Bunyan's *Pilgrim's Progress* and all those personal narratives from the pens of New England Puritans, narratives that Pynchon's story of William Slothrop satirizes. Compounding that profound worldly alienation, Calvinist Protestantism also radically redefined the concept of brotherly love. Since no amount of aid will benefit brothers-in-the-flesh, their fate being sealed, the individual's only answer is in work, selfless impersonal work, the only means by which the elect, "God's invisible church," might know themselves as such.[28]

Calvinism's gospel was that, in Pynchon's phrasing again, "we are meant for work and government, and austerity."

To Weber, industrial capitalism derived its essential ideas about individuals and work from Calvinist theology. Yet as Calvinism migrated from Geneva to London to Boston, it also brought along a core contradiction. For even as Puritanism stressed sovereign individualism, one's lonely decision-making powers on the pilgrimage to grace, it also devised a profoundly illiberal and in Weber's view a downright "despotic" political order. It *seemed* to empower the individual even as it more thoroughly dominated him. So while political historian Quentin Skinner argues strongly for Calvinism as a model for the development of popular sovereignty as a cornerstone idea in revolutionary America, he also stresses the ways that it brought along deeply illiberal assumptions about "the people" as inherently depraved, in need of strong rule and social controls. And without venturing as much into American Puritanism, Edmund S. Morgan's *Inventing the People* argues the same point: that "popular sovereignty" was by and large a means for the early republic's elite few to speak upliftingly of "the people" in the abstract, while subtly dominating the "actual people" they conceived as cantankerously, bumptiously difficult, if not ungovernable.[29] We suspect this problem is what swung Pynchon into eighteenth-century America, in *Mason & Dixon*. Here the problem swings us back to Crutchfield, whose "westwardman" label invokes Bishop George Berkeley's famous poem of 1752, "Verses on the Prospect of Planting Arts and Learning in America," with its oft-quoted last lines: "Westward the Course of Empire takes its Way; / The first four Acts already past, / A Fifth shall close the Drama with the Day. / Time's noblest Offspring is the Last."[30] Bringing along the Calvinist seed from continental Europe to England to America, the "westwardman" stands for a doctrine of personhood according to which, just as there is one God, beneath whom are one Christ and one Holy Spirit, each human being is a singular, sovereign individual, a monad on his quest to decipher his grace, or doom, all by his lonesome. Here as throughout the novel, Pynchon mocks a theological politics, or political theology, that conceives the divinity, spirit, man, and all worldly things as a one-off deal. A world of no returns, ever. A world governed, in other words, by death. That logic explains why, earlier in the Advent episode, Roger considers the prospect of Jessica dying in the rocket blitz and romanticizes his life afterward, thinking how she'd always be to him "the *only one* who ever mattered."[31] Elsewhere the novel consistently reckons the Western logic of identity as inherently fascist, as when Pointsman justifies experimenting on Slothrop by saying, "It's only one man"—as in the German motto *Ein Volk, ein Führer*. In the Kent church that evening in late December 1944, Roger, Jessica, and the congregants bear witness to the westward world: its one nativity, its one crucifixion. What they cannot quite bear to witness, though Pynchon's narrator does, is the starkly real *Gesellschaft* of that world, its symbolic and institutional presence in their lives as a logic and practice of sovereignty and domination, and the endless war which They regulate. And that is what the novel's narrator would have Roger know.

In *Gravity's Rainbow* the integrative Western business cartel, melded with Protestantism's alienated and monadistic individual, and armed with an ideology of technical rationality sufficiently commonsensical to keep people marching to its beat, is the perfect instrument for a permanent state of emergency, the Cold War our narrator absurdly hymns: "Whin this war is over, / How happy Ah will be, / Gearin' up fer thim Rooskies / And Go-round number three."[32] Especially since go-round number two taught Them how to divert attention away from the strife, the business of the business cartels will still be war. Pointsman, Jamf, and Bland—and Blicero, too, if indeed he emigrates to the United States—have shown the transnational potentials for sustaining things. Of that crew, Pointsman is the loser, perhaps because he has no ethical understanding to balance the stark economic dimension of his seemingly objective science. When the war is almost over, he thinks of it as "this State he'd come to feel himself a citizen of," realizing only belatedly that, "professionally speaking, he'd hardly got a thing out of it."[33] Recall the "pointsman" in the Skippy passage, just before Byron the Bulb's story, his face always shadowed as Lord of the Night, controlling happiness and pain. Yet despite all that power he is a nice man, seemingly, as he throws the lever, "making big things happen all over the world," like wars, assassinations, romances. Think of him as a Walther Rathenau or a Lyle Bland, or think of him as an omniscient narrator, or even the reclusive Mr. Pynchon: "he knows just where the points and the lever are."[34] A "pointsman's" always in command, directing this world, or the storyworld, and rarely if ever showing his face—just the way They do.

CHAPTER 8

Working for the Nazis

Once conditioned at the Casino Hermann Goering, Slothrop seems so well synced to the rocket that They can set him quasi-free in the Zone to see what he turns up, his colonized mind posing little threat to the system. His case represents the extent to which domination in *Gravity's Rainbow* depends on institutions that condition subjects' behaviors in ways simulating self-control and masking the *Manchurian Candidate*–style mind control that it actually entails. Slothrop embodies the workings of such powers on the Allied side. Others, on the Axis side, make equally compelling cases. For example, the engineer Franz Pökler, a garden variety Nazi, realizes only belatedly how he willingly gave himself over to domination. Long before that, Pynchon has provided us with a telling character sketch so that we might follow the process, although he reveals none of the behaviorist conditioning that was applied to Slothrop. With Pökler, what does the job is a much more ordinary, cultural, and smartly managed ideological manipulation and coercion.

We first meet Pökler through his wife, Leni, a taking-it-to-the-streets Communist Party activist. In this flashback to the Weimar Republic (1919–1933), with Nazism ascendant, she decides to leave her dreary "Piscean husband, swimming his seas of fantasy, death-wish, rocket-mysticism—Franz is just the type they want. They know how to use *that*."[1] Knowing all "about the German male at puberty," Leni understands his love for her as little more than a romantic desire to be released from a typical German future determined by a middle-class family ideology—*Bürgerlichkeit*—destined to destroy all his youthful ideals: "Franz loved her neurotically, masochistically, he belonged to her and believed she would carry him on her back, away to a place where Destiny couldn't reach."[2] Leni refuses to play that role, which is both physical and virtual, knowing Franz will better satisfy that kind of hyper-romantic desire in the *Technik* of rocketry, increasingly a German army item of interest: "Let him look for flight out at the Raketenflugplatz, where he goes to be used by the military and the cartels." Thanatz captures the same sense when, in a dialogue with Slothrop, he sexualizes the rocket's ascent: "cruel, hard, thrusting into the virgin-blue robes of the sky, my friend. Oh, so phallic."[3] If Pökler embodies the German male's wish to rise in that metamorphosed sexual sense above the boring role set for him by society, then rocket technology functions as his release from a critical, uncooperative wife and, more generally, serves as a virile symbol of Nazism's transcendent promise. As a "steel erection," the v-2 appeals to young men who wish to compensate for their impotence with dreams of technological power, unaware of the violence inherent to the project.[4]

As a Piscean, mutable creature, Pökler's soul stirs when he witnesses a static rocket test in a Berlin suburb. Afterward, an encounter with an old college classmate, Kurt Mondaugen, stirs his enthusiasm still more, though what's striking is how the real attraction is quite impersonal, involving "not persons but forms of energy, abstractions." In Pökler's sublime experience of it, the small silver rocket bolted to its test stand "didn't sound ominous to Franz in his wonder," even when it blows apart in "a terrific blast."[5] Not the rocket's thingness but its aura of power—its power in motion—moves him. Later, in part 3 of the novel, in a long episode devoted to work on the v-2, Pynchon focalizes through Franz to resume that flashback on the Weimar years. In this memory, leftist Leni tries to instruct Franz in the cartel structure enmeshing his work; and he, aggravated that she will not submit to him, resists taking her criticisms seriously and then flips the dominant-submissive script, by accepting a submissive relation with Major Weissmann, the new kind of military man, "part salesman, part scientist," and the epitome of the mutable or octopus-like cartel structure.[6] Franz comes to know Weissmann first at the amateur rocket field, later during the design and testing phases of the v-2 project. Thus readers witness Weissmann's tightening grip on Pökler, though the engineer hardly acknowledges it, even early on when Leni is still around to needle him. Affecting to struggle with "the burden of his poor Berlin self," he still relinquishes himself to the v-2's aura, well knowing that a weaponized rocket might fulfill Nazi desires for political dominion, for *Lebensraum*, for revenge against the humiliations of 1918 and any nation that would dare counterattack. He senses in a significantly ambiguous way that the rocket is out to *get him*, to make him its own or (virtually the same thing) to kill him: "The fear of extinction named Pökler knew it was the Rocket beckoning him in. If he also knew that in something like this extinction he could be free of his loneliness and his failure, still he wasn't quite convinced." Such misgivings turn out to be quite superficial. They are not moral concerns because he's utterly shallow, which is to say, rocket-centered. In fact Pökler only *imagines* for a number of years that he is dithering between two equally interesting possibilities: on the one hand, "personal identity," which might mean resisting the rocket's lure and securing himself a measure of positive freedom in Fromm's sense, and on the other, "impersonal salvation," which would mean entirely surrendering to Nazi dominion in the person of Major Weissmann.[7]

An alternate way of putting it is that "personal identity" means being *one* with the rocket, in the monadistic, Calvinist/capitalist, "westwardman" sense, which the narrative already has tied to Nazi culture. In that instance, submitting to the rocket and to Weissmann are one and the same. How *Gravity's Rainbow* resolves that identity issue becomes clearer when we witness Pökler's readiness to accept the stipulated identity of the girls Weissmann sends him—each of seven summers, beginning in August 1938—to keep his libido disciplined. The characters never speak that motive, however, for Pökler and Weissmann agree to relabel each girl's visit as a "furlough" from the stresses of working at the Peenemünde rocket facility. The first two girls in the series call themselves Ilse; they speak and act as if they were his daughter; yet Pökler's doubt prevails, as does our own, for how could a man not know his own daughter from a stranger? That question only leads to the next. Pökler learns from the first Ilse, perhaps the real one, that she has been sent down from a place "surrounded by barbed wire and bright hooded lights that burn all night long," so why does the man stop short of questioning, much less doing something, about his daughter's (or any girl's) internment with her mother in a concentration camp?[8] What kind of regime does that? Mondaugen easily thwarts Pökler's anger and intuitive resolve to do something: the camps do not matter, he advises Pökler, for there is nothing "sinister" about them.[9] Sure there isn't. So, choosing silence and reinforcing the "past neutralities" of his colonized mind, Pökler's initially righteous anger cools to a "vexed engineer-elitism" he thereafter sustains in his exchanges with Mondaugen and Weissmann.[10]

Pökler's tense sessions with Weissmann in the winter and spring after "Ilse" number one's visit validate Mondaugen's insight that "Pökler needed to be at someone's command"; also, that he's cultivating his status as a victimized underling.[11] Perhaps that explains Weissmann's choice for "Ilse" number two, who arrives just before Germany invades Poland, on the morning of September 1, 1939—the outbreak of war. In the first place she's an impossibly taller girl, Franz thinks, and her darker hair color, the "set" of her eyes, and her darker complexion—a "dark, long-legged, Southern creature"—seem to clearly define her not just as a different girl but as an epitome of the erotic southerner sent for his diversion.[12] Assured, now, that it's all Weissmann's plotting, for five more Augusts (1940–1944), Pökler and each new (or the same?) "Ilse" furlough at Zwölfkinder, a kind of Aryan Disneyland that the narrator describes as an official site for the Nazi state to cultivate its citizens' racist ideology as well as a belief in their innocence for the nation's genocidal crimes. In August 1943 Pökler is there on furlough when a British bombing raid kills hundreds of workers, an attack well documented in Pynchon's historical sources. In 1944, Pökler and "Ilse" journey separately to Zwölfkinder from the Nordhausen area, and there she tells Franz of witnessing increasing horrors (such as hangings) in the Dora camp, most of this also deriving from Pynchon's historical sources. These revelations force the man at last to confront "the inconveniences of caring"—even if it's "a bit too late for it."[13]

Indeed it may be "too late" for Franz to atone not just for his sins of omission but also for his sins of commission. For what, after all, do we know of the man's relations with those serial Ilses punctuating each year? When Ilse Two arrives at Peenemünde, she kisses him; he thinks about her tall, dark, erotic southern difference; and that night before bed she will "come into his arms and kiss him again," sparking fresh ruminations about Weissmann's apparent Ilse plot. Franz wonders if, as the girls "grew more nubile," would he "fall in love" with one? Indeed he wonders if doubts about an Ilse's identity finally would trump "any fears about real incest," releasing him into a lawless zone where they "could make up new rules." The next day Franz and Ilse Two journey to Zwölfkinder, described as an inverted world with the children on top, running everything from the mayor's office on down. There, visiting children literally command their parents and their enjoyment of the park's pleasures, marking it as a space ideally suited to Franz's passivity, controllability, and guiltlessness. That night at Zwölfkinder, Pynchon's narration veers into a vividly realized scene of incest/pedophilia, its technique profoundly complicating our reading of it.

The scene unfolds in simple indicative sentences. In their hotel room Franz unlaces his shoes, Ilse's hand comes "lightly to rest" on his bare leg, and their eyes meet. Pökler thinks once again of Their plot to use him, whereupon he apparently "hit[s] her upside the head with his open hand," and father and supposed daughter begin pulling at each other's clothing, she declaring "*how I've wanted you*" as they commence "hours of amazing incest." Any reader will be sucked into viewing the scene in the terms of mimetic realism. Except that it appears to veer off into a fantasy—of escape from Germany to a "free" and welcoming Denmark—but that scene trails off in ellipsis dots, and the next paragraph negates the fantasy. "No," says the narrator, then assures us that Franz only held in his arms an "Ilse" who "wanted comfort that night." Finally acceding to the terms of Weissmann's game, Pökler thinks that "while he played, this would have to be Ilse"; and on those terms he realizes a "real moment of conception, in which, years too late, he became her father." Yet that "conception" seems no more "real" than Franz's fantasy, entered by way of a realist narrative discourse, may be interpreted as "unreal." Indeed, since the sentences never signpost a detour into fantasy, the presentation of events here is as ambiguous as any comparable moment in the novel. In Zwölfkinder's space of inversion, the textual hinge (or pointsman) swinging us from real to unreal, from guilt to innocence, and from adult to child has become nearly indecipherable. We may only say with certainty that Pökler entertains vividly realized fantasies of pedophilia and incest, for which readers may justly hold him to account. How he lives with or lives out those fantasies during his later furloughs with Ilses Three through Seven is non-narrated stuff, vaporous matters that an ethical reading must reckon by dim if not dead lights.[14]

We can also say with certainty that Pökler, having settled into that annually recurrent, incest-accented mock parentage, crosses the threshold into full obedience to a fascist and patriarchal authority. He sustains a hunch that "somewhere in the State's oversize paper brain a specific perversity had been [wrongly] assigned" to him. Still, giving his mind over to violent incest commits him to the role the authorities have programmed.[15] As we already indicated in our pages on Fromm, Their script lets Pökler compensate his masochism with a sadism singularly his own, whether or not the system, or Weissmann, erroneously understood his desires. His continuing tensions with Weissmann further reinforce the tacit agreement, and Pökler nurtures his fear of the man to the point that, as before with the rocket, his submission to Weissmann realizes his own self-identity: "Weissmann was the sadist, he [was working] toward a maximum cruelty in which Pökler would be unlaid to nerves vessels and tendons . . . nowhere to shelter, entirely his master's possession."[16] With Weissmann as his master, his dominus or lord, Pökler and the rocket complete a perverse trinity (sadistic father, tormented son, holy ghost) that satirically realizes Pynchon's critique of capitalism. For Pökler, though, the paranoia attendant on this kind of radical deterritorialization becomes almost unbearable, and the narrator is keen to point out that while Franz rather clearly recognizes what's controlling him, he never quite understands how being in that particular relation to Weissmann coincides precisely with his need to self-sacrifice for the program. The engineer's domination is complete; he's the perfect fascist subject, Fromm's ideal Nazi. Pökler will always function as planned because the lever Weissmann has installed in his psyche enables the major, like the pointsman, always to exploit it, particularly because its masochistic function depends on the absence of free will.

Slowly but surely feelings of guilt do undermine what can only be described as Pökler's perverse sense of comfort in Weissmann's hands. After his transfer in late 1943 from Peenemünde on Germany's north coast to the underground v-2 production site near Nordhausen in the nation's heartland, Pökler concludes at the next summer's Zwölfkinder reunion (in 1944) that this year's "Ilse" must have come from the nearby Dora forced-labor camp: "For months, while her father across the wire or walls did his dutiful hackwork, she had been prisoner only a few meters away from him."[17] There is no overwhelming evidence for this, however. First, "Ilse confirmed—or was told to answer—that it was Dora," and later she simply says that Zwölfkinder is her alternative to "the camp," but as a true paranoiac Pökler quickly connects the dots once he is no longer completely blind to the truths of Nazi terror.[18] Sad and disgusted, he breaks down and seems prepared to quit the game. But in an amazing development that proves his great weakness in the face of power, Pökler easily assents to another Weissmann work order. Returned from his v-2 battery in The Hague and now fully enacting his role as Dominus Blicero, Weissmann is in central Germany during the late winter or early spring of 1945 to prepare the 00000, the special rocket redesigned to launch a human payload, Gottfried. Pökler becomes his insulation engineer, responsible for developing "a plastic fairing," presumably of Jamf's Imipolex G, though he seems unaware of its intended use as a shroud for the boy about to ride in what is both a vehicle and the coffin of "God's Peace."[19]

It, or rather the boy inside the Imipolex, seems to have been code-named "Schwarzgerät." This information, scattered mostly through dialogues midway into the novel and confirmed only in the final pages, continually supplements Slothrop's idea of the "Black Device."[20] And it enables at last a reading of these details under the aegis of realist fiction. The "Black Device" need not be a figment of Schwarzknabe's (Slothrop's) imagination. It isn't a figment for Pökler, who, good Calvinist and Nazi that he is, considers his role on the 00000 team as his "special destiny." That phrase not only connects with his early, Berlin-era understanding of "Destiny" as the force that kills youthful ideals, but it also links with Weissmann's own sense in The Hague that "his Destiny is the Oven."[21] Weissmann and Pökler will each in his own way, master or slave, consider himself a "Wandervogel in the mountains of Pain," think of himself as the mortally destined soul of tragic romance, longing for destiny/death as a reading of Rilke's *Duino Elegies* would teach them to do. Ironically, though, the novel's storyline denies Pökler the deviant pleasure of seeing that *Wandervogel* fantasy through to its violent, sacrificial conclusion.[22] For Franz, work on the special rocket fulfills his German adolescent dreams—and the boyhood space flight fantasies of the historical von Braun who haunts these pages. Weissmann's reward to Pökler is a permit for a reunion, "after hostilities end," with a girl who "has been released."[23] The arrogant leniency of this favor pushes Pökler to a final insight into his commanding officer's control: "How long had Weissmann been keeping him deliberately on ice, all so he'd have a plastics man he could depend on, when the time came?"[24] Something seems to have snapped in Pökler, but we cannot be sure. Pynchon finishes the episode on a small but grotesque hint of goodness lurking beneath the character's impotence. Leaving the underground works at Nordhausen and crossing into the Dora concentration camp just before Allied troops liberate the internees, Pökler must at last confront the stark realities of the violence in which he's been implicated: "the odors . . . the naked corpses being carried out . . . and the living, stacked ten to a straw mattress, the weakly crying, coughing, losers."[25] In a foul, dark corner, he sits briefly with a woman barely breathing, "holding her bone hand," and gives her his wedding ring to pay for whatever she might need.[26] Compared to the enormity of the German violence inflicted in the camps, this gesture obviously amounts to little, and its importance in Pökler's development is difficult to gauge at this moment in the text. Whether mechanical sympathy or a genuine act of compassion, his futile gift might be the vehicle of just another illusion—that it's not too late, and he can buy off his guilt.

We encounter Pökler again much later at, of all places, Zwölfkinder, where he has moved into the basement of the resort's faux town hall. Does he return there to regress into blameless childhood? Perhaps to recoup his Ilse, or one of the "Ilses"? Or even to reenact the pedophilia/incest script? Pökler's dialogue with Slothrop in that later scene offers nary a clue. The setting and his characterization both imply that he's clinging to a Nazi-style organization of society and innocence. In a plot development worthy of their joint paranoia, a pig named Frieda brings Slothrop, in his Plechazunga pig suit, into Zwölfkinder where Franz, initially suspecting the American of pig thievery, whips "out a Luger as big as a house." Tyrone, thinking the German suspects him of bestiality with Frieda the pig, wonders "if there is about to be a shotgun, or Luger, wedding here—in fact the phrase *unto thee I pledge my trough* has just arrived in his brain," when the danger wanes, as readers ponder the implication that Franz, given that shotgun-wedding trope, has at Zwölfkinder lapsed still further into his illusion and made Frieda into a surrogate daughter. That we never know, because Pökler, though evasive about the Schwarzgerät and talkative enough about Imipolex to confirm its existence, instead wants to talk about German movies. He launches into capsule summaries of Fritz Lang's *Metropolis* (1927) and *Der müde Tod* (1921), so that things get interesting on the topic of domination, even if off the topic of Slothrop's quest for the Schwarzgerät and Imipolex G. Pökler's film critique of *Metropolis* rather closely rehearses Fromm's argument about the German disposition toward authority, evokes Rathenau's idealized cartel structure, and confirms Siegfried Kracauer's thesis in *From Caligari to Hitler* (1947): that German film during the Weimar Republic reflects a mentality awaiting the seed of Nazism to be planted in it.[27] We learn that *Metropolis* presents "a Corporate City-state where technology was the source of power, the engineer worked closely with the administrator, the masses labored unseen far underground, and ultimate power lay with a single leader at the top, fatherly and benevolent and just."[28] The narration here is about to segue into tales about Laszlo Jamf, then Lyle Bland, but first the narrator links Pökler with "ritual submissions to the Master," the embrace of "power not for its social uses but for . . . chances of surrender . . . to the Void, to delicious and screaming collapse," a longing for death that is described on the following page as holding "joy and defiance, nothing of . . . bourgeois death."[29] This states exactly what Pökler always avoided by giving himself to romanticized dreams of rocketry, and just what his wife, Leni, the materialist and revolutionary, also had detected and detested in Franz. And that's the last we know of Pökler, who has been judged rather clearly as a man loyally submissive to the dominations of a violent patriarchy.

In Pökler we have a man trained by his authoritarian Nazi culture, German cinema for example, to desire submission. In film actress Margherita (Greta) Erdmann we witness that conditioning from the standpoint of one put before the camera, as was Katje for the behavioral training of the octopus Grigori. In comparison to Pökler's story, Erdmann's goes to further extremes and has elements of pathos. She's introduced as the lover Slothrop will spurn, an aging and somewhat decrepit movie actress with a terrible desire for men to chastise her flesh. They meet at a dilapidated studio in Neubabelsberg (literally, New Babel Mountain), where she has detoured nostalgically from a search for her lost daughter, Bianca. The opposite of man-eaters such as Marlene Dietrich, Greta has played the "doll—languid, exhausted," in a prewar series of "vaguely pornographic horror movies" from the studio of fictional director Gerhardt von Göll.[30] Erdmann was "his creature," always chased and tortured, even whipped to death in one of her roles. In a gender twist on the Pökler script of a young German male longing for that special destiny, the actress has submitted to von Göll just as the engineer continues to genuflect before Weissmann. Indeed the two compliant characters are linked: when Pökler and Leni make love on the night they may have conceived Ilse, Franz is spurred on by a fantasy of ravishing Erdmann, the "delicious victim bound on her dungeon rack" in the movie he has just seen, *Alpdrücken* (Nightmare).[31]

Here is a cross-character suggestion that under the Nazi regime in *Gravity's Rainbow*, as Fromm suggested about the historical period, sadism and masochism easily combine, with Pökler and Erdmann a particularly helpless pair in relation to power. Cause and effect in Erdmann's career are difficult to determine. Maybe her own wish for a special destiny, as a movie actress, has brought her to accept all those passive roles, leaving her with a constant masochistic desire for pain. Or perhaps her masochism has been there all along, and the movies merely gave her work—during the Weimar-era depression—that paid well for enacting long-held paraphilias. Either way, she exists beyond repair. After the surrender, in the Berlin episode with Slothrop, she has come down with a tremor and requires her daily dose of brutality. Slothrop "has to draw blood before she cleans up the fish" that she has thrown against the wall to provoke him into sadistic violence against her.[32] Then, aboard the *Anubis*, where Erdmann reunites with Bianca (perhaps conceived during the violent orgy scene that drove Pökler wild), it is Erdmann's time to turn the tables and punish: "It's as if Greta is now releasing all the pain she's stored up over the past weeks onto her child's naked bottom."[33] As Pökler's case has shown, sadism and masochism combined in the same person compellingly illustrates the psychosis in Nazism's generalized state of repression. In the postwar Zone's state of abandonment, Erdmann has nowhere to go, no evident means to survive, leaving violent domination her only chance—as subject or object.

Also onboard the good ship *Anubis* is Slothrop, to whom the Japanese ensign Morituri provides part of Greta's backstory. After her return from a failed prewar attempt to make it in Hollywood, rumors that she is part Jewish brought on a paranoid fear of Gestapo violence, thus the onset of painful "symptoms" seemingly impossible to cure.[34] At Bad Karma, the fictional spa whose name riffs on a common sixties phrase meaning bad fortune, or more colloquially, bad shit, Erdmann obsessively takes part in a murderous ritual as the Shekhinah from Kabbalah, not in the positive role as the earthly presence of Yahweh but in the negative role of a demon gripped by dark forces.[35] Her victims are Jewish children, and the forces in question are not hard to figure out. As the next flashback section also reveals, Erdmann's malleability has clearly carried over from her movie parts into roles for the SS, with none other than Weissmann apparently in charge, just as with Pökler. "It was always easy for men to come and tell her who to be," she thinks. In one of her final roles before the surrender, she is brought to a petrochemical plant and dressed in an Imipolex bodysuit rather like Gottfried would have worn on his death trip, and around the same time.[36] The experience erases her sense of self, of identity. Erdmann thinks: "Blicero had brought [her] across a frontier. Had injected [her] at last into his native space without a tremor of pain. [She] was free." Simultaneously the torture has evacuated all her thoughts and memories, reducing Greta to a familiar attitude, taking her "transmarginal" (in behaviorist lingo) and erasing her sense of opposites so that, seeming to start over from zero, she asks just what the system wants her to ask: "Was this 'submission,' then—letting all these go?"[37] It surely is.

From here on, the narration ambiguously reckons the value of Erdmann's attitude in the presence of Weissmann and the V-2. Slothrop understands Thanatz's repeated whipping of his wife, Greta, as a way for her to reach the rocket test stand, the novel's "holy center." To Thanatz himself, she has glimpsed a map of the "kingdom" in Weissmann/Blicero's eyes. Yet when she receives a final mention, the narrator associates her identity with "dames whose job it is always to cringe from the Terror" (like Fay Wray in *King Kong*) and then only dream, in the comfort of their beds, of "plots against good and decent men."[38] In this final reckoning, Greta's lack of any actual freedom signals things to come: her rapid decay, miserable addiction to the whip, and fear of revenge. Thus if Pökler exemplifies the habitual escape from *Bürgerlichkeit* into a masochistic steady-state accented with romantic idealism, we might say Greta takes the same trip but that her steady-state masochism is accented with pathetic decadence.

Then there's the escapism of Pökler's rocket-team colleagues Mondaugen and Fahringer. They represent even more strongly the illusions of German technicians under Nazism, not least because they seem capable of reconciling a non-Western striving for mindless serenity as they both advance the war effort. As college students Mondaugen and Pökler "lived in the same drafty mansarde" near the Technische Hochschule in Munich.[39] An engineering student, Mondaugen "[o]n graduating [has] gone off to South-West Africa, on some kind of radio research project."[40] Pynchon readers will remember Mondaugen from V., where he's chapter 9's central character. Integrating a version of that chapter with the rest of the novel at the end of his composition process, Pynchon achieves a balance between historical accuracy and creative fictionalization that turns Mondaugen's story, as retold by Stencil, V.'s main character, into a disconcertingly bleak and compelling narrative about colonial dehumanization, genocide, and the origin of the German *Konzentrationslager*.[41] *Gravity's Rainbow* picks up many of those threads, as if it were partly spun off from the first novel. In V., the electrical engineer has come to Southwest Africa in 1922 on a research project to study "atmospheric radio disturbances: sferics"; and after seeking refuge from a local rebellion in the fortified villa of a landowner named Foppl, he eventually deciphers a code in recorded electromagnetic signals.[42] The debauchery at Foppl's centers around efforts to restage the great Herero uprising of 1904–7, when Germans carrying out an "extermination order," or *Vernichtungsbefehl*, nearly brought the Herero people to extinction. Near the chapter's end, Pynchon offers Mondaugen's dreams of white violence as an intersubjective experience that yields insights into a reality more profound than those available in conventional realism. His use of the dream rivals similar achievements in the work of Joseph Conrad, Thomas Mann, and Hermann Hesse, among others, and climaxes in a mode of antirealism that offers a narrative means to probe for truths otherwise hidden by requirements for chronology and conventions of verisimilitude. In *Gravity's Rainbow*, Pynchon returns to that ambitious representational method to unfold the self-delusion crucial to Mondaugen's character. We learn that in early stages of his amateur rocket work at the suburban field in Berlin, he "could come up with solutions to cooling problems." Yet what really distinguishes Mondaugen to Pökler is his capacity for "Demian-metaphysics" as a way "to accept Hitler."[43] In Hermann Hesse's novel *Demian* (1919, but obligatory sixties reading), the existence of mutually opposing forces provides the conceptual framework for a story in which the protagonist, Emil Sinclair, finds himself with the help of a spiritual leader, Demian, by learning to accept a dualist ideology pitting war as a logical, necessary corollary to peace. This view sets Mondaugen at ease with Nazism and the impending catastrophe of World War II. His antirealist way of seeing the world blocks the moral questions that Pökler's witnessing of the horrors at the Dora camp may have—indeed should have—raised. Instead Mondaugen impassively accepts the necessity of it all.

In *V.*, some of the white characters at Foppl's, including a young Weissmann, seem to anticipate *Gravity's Rainbow* and play the Demian role to Mondaugen, a relatively innocent and likable character rather like Sinclair in the Hesse novel. In *V.*, however, Weissmann's grip on Mondaugen is nothing like his dominating hold on Pökler in *Gravity's Rainbow*. The Mondaugen of *V.* can, for instance, apparently dream nostalgically for the good old days of German general von Trotha and not be irredeemably corrupted. The narrator suggests that "[p]ossibly Mondaugen alone among them was escaping" Foppl's rigidly imposed "common dream" of reenacting 1904–7, because Mondaugen employs "his peculiar habits of observation," surely referring to both his voyeurism and the detachment of his scientific objectivity.[44] By *Gravity's Rainbow*, Mondaugen's engineering work on the v-2 project under Weissmann's heavy-handed supervision may make us wonder whether he escaped anything, and particularly a blind allegiance to the bloody horrors of colonial domination, when he left Foppl's. *V.* sends Mondaugen off with a hopeful pat on the shoulder: "Whatever it arose from . . . he was starting to feel those first tentative glandular pressures that one day develop into moral outrage."[45] By *Gravity's Rainbow*, the v-2 program and Nazism's ascendancy have ended his sense of morality and justice, which was only subconsciously "glandular" and "tentative" anyway.

In *Gravity's Rainbow* Mondaugen's backstory continues where *V.* leaves off. As Pökler hears it from his friend, "Weissmann was one of the people who had driven Mondaugen, finally, away to live in the bush" while in Southwest Africa, and there he "ended up living with the Ovatjimba . . . the poorest of the Hereros."[46] Paradoxically this contact with colonized others leads to the "electro-mysticism" that will make it possible for Mondaugen to relativize Hitler later on: "Think of the ego, the self that suffers a personal history bound to time, as the grid. The deeper and true Self is the flow between cathode and plate."[47] The goal is "signal zero," the state of purity which one just might achieve by disregarding the ego's constant demands, thus also the superego's moral demands.[48] Clearly, electro-mysticism and Demian metaphysics are both means to look the other way. When Pökler is trying to decide between the seeming opposites of personal identity and impersonal salvation, Mondaugen "had no free advice for his friend. Pökler would have to find his own way to his zero signal, his true course," which seems improper for a man billing himself as a "bodhisattva" or enlightened mentor.[49] Pökler's a practical man who does things by steps, and this may be why Mondaugen's mysticism fails his friend but attaches him to Weissmann: "they had found a rapprochement here, among the rockets, either for sunblasted holyman reasons it was not for Pökler to understand or because of some deeper connection which had always been there."[50] Still, they are an odd pair, Weissmann the sadistic authoritarian and Mondaugen the transcendentalist soaring above categories like master and victim, but nevertheless linked. Is it that both have to reconcile with the terror and violence their rocket will inflict? Mondaugen comments quasi-mystically that identity or "personal density . . . is directly proportional to temporal bandwidth." This means, as we understand the phrase, that as available frequencies, or "bandwidth," narrows so does the "density" or compressed heaviness of selfhood increase. This is a way of saying, then, that the individual secures a denser, stronger identity by narrowing his bandwidth frequencies, dialing back the signal of selfhood, the "width of your present, your now," until frequencies having to do with "the past" and "the future" no longer get through and there's just one frequency, such as a here-and-now mania for rocketry. Narrowing "temporal bandwidth" according to Mondaugen's law therefore also means eliminating frequencies that involve (for example) love, community, ethics, morality, or war crimes guilt. All of that noise, gone! On this reading, Mondaugen's enigmatic phrase is just another way of troping the Calvinist/fascist political theology of the one, and the romance of identity as Weissmann's favorite poet, Rilke, spells it out. This is what working for Nazis means, in Pynchon's evocation of the deal. Whether or how Mondaugen's law relates to the narrator's remark about Tyrone Slothrop, who already in part 3 of the novel "has begun to thin, to scatter," is a question we leave for part three, "Freedom."[51]

Fahringer the aerodynamics specialist is still more eccentric in comparison to other engineers working on the v-2 at Peenemünde. At least that's how Franz Pökler remembers him. When colleagues working on guidance obsess over "getting the Rocket's long axis to follow the tangent, at all points, to its trajectory," Fahringer goes into the woods to practice with his "Zen bow and roll of pressed straw"—his way of meditating on the technical problem of the *Folgsamkeitfaktor*.[52] The adjective *folgsam* means "obedient" and that is just how They want the rocket to behave, while Fahringer may not seem *folgsam* with his unorthodox, Zen Buddhist approach to the problem. Actually, though, he is. Pynchon's idea behind the character derives from the German philosopher Eugen Herrigel, who tried in the 1930s to combine Japanese Zen teachings with National Socialist ideology.[53] The war got in his way, but in 1948 Herrigel published his short treatise, *Zen in the Art of Archery*, which brought Zen practices to Europe and, with the 1953 English translation, eventually to American readers, including Pynchon.[54] So in the novel Fahringer approaches the guidance problem by comparing the v-2 to a "fat Japanese arrow," mystifying Franz Pökler, who summarizes for us: "It was

necessary in some way to become one with Rocket, trajectory and target—
'not to *will* it, but to surrender, to step out of the role of firer. The act is un-
divided. You are both aggressor and victim, rocket and parabolic path.'"[55]
This may be an apt summary of Herrigel, but one cannot help noting how
it also replicates the erasure of opposites that characterizes the "transmarginal" phase, after trauma, in Pointsman's discussions of Pavlovian behaviorism with Kevin Spectro. In any case, the utility of this view seems clear. As
D. T. Suzuki summed it up for a 1971 paperback reissue of Herrigel's book:
"The archer ceases to be conscious of himself as the one who is engaged in
hitting the bull's-eye which confronts him. This unconscious state is realized only when, completely empty and rid of the self, he becomes one with
the perfecting of his technical skill."[56] What Fahringer gets out of Zen archery is yet another rationale, along with Mondaugen's law, for utter oneness
with the object of one's technological expertise, a narrow and mindless ("unconscious") devotion to things—arrow and target, rocket and London—that
just naturally translates into perfect obedience before the master, whether
Weissmann or Hitler. Pynchon's narration has been working the changes on
his motif of the one, and Fahringer characterizes yet another change of key,
another way of working for the Nazis, guilt-free.

Another of the engineers, aerodynamics specialist Horst Achtfaden, remembers "mad Fahringer" as a unique member of the Peenemünde team
"because he couldn't bring himself to kill," and thus didn't sport "the ex-
clusive pheasant-feather badge in his hatband."[57] So it's no surprise but also
a dark irony that Fahringer, whose Zen practice synced beautifully with his
Nazism, is the "first at Peenemünde to fall to the ss." Before they seize him,
Fahringer seems finally to have confronted his guilt for working on a weapon
for mass death; but by then it is too late. Achtfaden is another good Nazi
worker, but is at least capable of seeing beyond pheasants to the mass killing
that their rocket engineering is about to visit on people in London and Antwerp. He sees Zen practices as the way Fahringer initially had "found his way
free of guilt, fashionable guilt"—to us, a fair judgment. Postwar, guilt is back
in circulation and "becoming quite a commodity in the Zone," as Achtfaden
puts it. Yet he too manifests that canny, obedient-to-authority means of laying aside guilt, arguing to himself that his specific task at Peenemünde never
involved the rocket's reentry, much less finding and hitting targets. Achtfaden
recalls Fahringer's opinion on the subject: "You are either alone absolutely,
alone with your own death, or you take part in the larger enterprise, and you
share in the deaths of others. Are we not all one?" Still, is not being "all one"
in death really just being too late, *for all*? But not for Fahringer, who stops
short of such a question because he has found his way free of guilt about
death while still holding in his mind the death that he, as a cog in the system,
is involved in. Another contradiction transcended: and this is how Zen self-

lessness synced with National Socialism, even if thick-headed ss men didn't get that *this*, and not disobedience, explains why "mad Fahringer" went out to the woods with his bow and arrows. As Fahringer puts it to Achtfaden, explaining the central physical activity in meditation: "*Atmen* [to breathe] is a genuinely Aryan verb." In his Zen practice, Fahringer was *breathing* Aryan/Nazi idealism and ideology. Achtfaden just can't figure out if the man was talking "gibberish" or giving him "a *koan* [or enigmatic saying] that Achtfaden isn't equipped to master, a transcendent puzzle that could lead him to some moment of light." Unlike Pökler, Mondaugen, and Achtfaden, who are burdened with doubts, Fahringer entertains none at all. His obedience most nearly perfected, his oneness with *Technik* and his fellow technicians more fully realized in him than in any other character that *Gravity's Rainbow* sets before us, except perhaps Weissmann, "mad Fahringer" best represents fascism's ideal mode of domination. Its grand project is to devise means for asserting cultural and social control over masses of individuals. Optimally this means governing those masses by installing the control *within* each citizen-subject, who also thinks of her- or himself as being fully invested with freedom. On those terms, Fahringer is this novel's ideal Nazi.

CHAPTER 9

The Logic of the Camp

To think about Nazism and the representation of the masses in *Gravity's Rainbow* requires swapping in a wide-angle lens. Novels are the great art form of the modern individual, and especially of an individual character's mentality in relation to others'. And our analysis to this point has focused on the particular thoughts and tropes defining the mentalities of the dominators and the dominated during fascism's peak years in Pynchon's fictionalized presentation of history. Yet this novel does not forget the greater view, the masses of people World War II touched: the tens of millions killed, the civilian populations uprooted and compelled to live in stateless and rightsless conditions, the millions consigned before and during the war to slave labor or the ovens in the ss network of *Konzentrationslager*.

On its very first page *Gravity's Rainbow* figures the plight of displaced, orphaned, traumatized souls en masse, the "second sheep" fleeing the rocket blitz raining death down upon London: "drunks, old veterans still in shock from ordnance 20 years obsolete, hustlers in city clothes, derelicts, exhausted women with more children than it seems could belong to anyone, stacked about amongst the rest of the things to be carried out."[1] That phrase referring to children "stacked about" with other "things" haunts the text. Instantly it recalls a shared history constituted by a multitude of news stories, photos, and film footage of emaciated prisoners stacked in liberated concentration camps like Buchenwald and Auschwitz—and Dora, the camp in central Germany where tens of thousands of slave laborers helped build Germany's v-2 weapons. Pökler, when he wanders through Dora in the spring of 1945, sees the living-dead slave laborers "stacked ten to a straw mattress."[2] In this way and many others, *Gravity's Rainbow* evokes Holocaust history. As the narration represents persons and masses, the work in rocket development facilities and that done by camp laborers threatened with extermination, how does this novel reckon such horrors and the West's accommodation to them?

Take Wernher von Braun, his voice being the first in *Gravity's Rainbow*. In 1960 the former German rocketeer was fifteen years down the road from his surrender to the U.S. Army and the head of aerospace operations at the army's Redstone Arsenal (since June 1961, part of the Marshall Space Flight

Center) in Huntsville, Alabama. There in 1960 he oversaw the work of just under four thousand employees. What little spare time he had, von Braun was using to collaborate on the script for *I Aim at the Stars* (1960), a Columbia Pictures film about his adventuresome life. It was supposed to be a blockbuster, capitalizing on von Braun's rising fame and a keen nationwide interest in "the space race." Biographer Michael J. Neufeld remarks that by the late fifties von Braun was "never more famous." The protagonist of numerous journalistic stories about rockets, he wrote popular articles on space exploration for *Collier's* and starred in Disney TV programs—a photogenic, dashing, aristocratic genius. To tell this life on the big screen, Columbia Pictures opened its wallet wide, for a collaborative effort with a German production company directed by Friedrich Mainz and for extensive shooting at locations in Berlin, rural western Germany, Austria, and the American Southwest. Scenes in a mock-up of Peenemünde (the actual site being in Soviet hands) featured one of the last operational V-2 rockets then known to exist in Germany. Then there was the star-studded cast with Gia Scala, Herbert Lom, and Victoria Shaw as von Braun's wife, Maria. For the Wernher role, director J. Lee Thompson (*Cape Fear* and *The Guns of Navarone*) cast the handsome, six-foot-four German-born star Curt Jurgens, known for his parts as a Nazi U-boat captain and a German army general, and the envy of middle-aged men everywhere for his part as Brigitte Bardot's older lover in Roger Vadim's *And God Created Woman* (1956). In the run-up to the von Braun film's release, magazines and newspapers touted the story and Dell publishers released a comic book version capsulizing the script for American adolescents. Alas, *I Aim at the Stars* was a dud. Reviewers found the story simplistic and melodramatic, pitting von Braun—as the heroic genius of space flight—against evil ss generals wanting only to put English citizens into early graves. *Time* thought it offered empty platitudes about "the moral dereliction of the scientific community—personified by von Braun." About the title, comedian Mort Sahl famously quipped that it needed a subtitle: "But Sometimes I Hit London." At every major premiere, in Munich in late August, in Washington, D.C., in late September (at which von Braun escorted First Lady Mamie Eisenhower), and in New York City in early October, ban-the-bomb protesters thronged the streets, some with signs condemning von Braun as a Nazi war criminal. Critics in London barely contained their outrage; the city of Antwerp, the target of even more V-weapons than London, simply banned the film. Wernher Magnus Maximilian, Freiherr von Braun had found once again that he could run but he could not hide from his reputation as a Nazi rocketman.[3]

Neufeld rightly judges the film "an act of hubris." In startling ways, the script set aside the question of von Braun's involvement in war crimes in order to burnish his star as *the* transnational wunderkind of rocketry. Just how the film does that work, and how it bears on Pynchon's novel, and matters of war guilt, are questions worth considering. For example, there's the way the von Braun character refers to fellow scientists—in Berlin, in Peenemünde, and in White Sands, New Mexico (where they were taken beginning in October 1945)—as "family." This follows an opening scene, before the credits roll, that depicts a boyish von Braun launching an errant little rocket that destroys a neighbor's greenhouse, and Papa von Braun covers the financial cost of Wernher's damages with only a warning that from now on, "if a von Braun shoots off a rocket, it should go where it's supposed to go." This basic trinity—father, funding, and success—governs everything that follows. Whether working with *Verein für Raumschiffahrt* amateurs, managing his project crew at Peenemünde, or managing them again at White Sands or the Redstone Arsenal, the film-Wernher's constant needs are on-target test flights, funding to make those flights happen, and being in the good graces of paternalistic leaders in German or American military bureaucracies who deliver those funds. This creates two basic tensions in the film. First it pits the *Gemeinschaft* of idealistic rocket experts bonded together in an idealistic quest for "space flight," against the cynical *Gesellschaft* of the army officers wanting rockets as weapons of terror and able to provide what's needed to make a missile "go where it's supposed to go." Second, it erases any political or ethical distinction between the kindly *Vater*, or the Pernicious Pop of Nazism, or of America, behind Wernher's rocket science. And this erasure ruins one of the film's key claims on us: that democratic America is different, for it provides a culturally and politically free climate for capital *S* Science to succeed at rocket mastery and space flight, whereas, in contrast, the dominations and terrors of German fascism had *failed*, launching only the bad rocket, which is just how Soviet Communism would fail in its turn.[4]

While von Braun is working at Peenemünde, the Nazi ss is depicted as constantly threatening his intellectual and physical freedom to do rocket research and development *his* way or, after a series of failed launches, to do it all. With the failures, ss men arrest him on a treason charge and promise immediate execution—a short version of what actually transpired. He's saved by a fatherly General Dornberger, who also promises better funding. His mother having earlier confronted him about bargaining with evil, Wernher understands from this point on that he's struck a Faustian pact with the devil, especially as a fictional ss general named Kulp assures Wernher that with an operable v-2 Germany can "level any major city on earth" and then dominate the world. Kulp and others constantly lean on him to attach his space flight dreams to their dominion, to join "our little circle"; but stalwart Wernher resists. Indeed the script frequently insists on his steady course. "I haven't changed," he tells his future wife, Maria, who frets about him making the Faustian pact. To Dornberger he insists: "Look, I'm a scientist. I couldn't care less about party stuff. Hitler, or the man in the moon, it's all the same to me. Come to think of it I prefer the man in the moon." Aiming at the moon and stars is, he admits to Maria, his "addiction," a telos for scientific achievement that, he constantly assures people, will never take his own trajectory off course. In fact even his wardrobe never changes: not once does the film's Wernher appear in a military uniform, instead always wearing a business suit, or a sport coat and shirt (perhaps a fashionable turtleneck), or at his most leisurely a cardigan sweater, a wardrobe befitting a man not just from the German nobility (though a *Freiherr* is merely a baron) but a man representing the emergent technocratic and meritocratic elite, whose constant admirers—German and American—all say (in Dornberger's words) that "von Braun's brain power puts him in another class." Even the film's sets remain weirdly static. Though punctuated with a few exterior panoramic shots that repeatedly gaze skyward beyond an upraised, steaming, phallic rocket on its launch pad, the camera in *I Aim at the Stars* spends the bulk of its time indoors. In the forested Peenemünde compound buildings, or in the U.S. facilities set in the vast New Mexico desert, we see repeatedly different but the same interiors: the launching blockhouses with banks of electronic equipment and viewing scopes, the offices and design rooms with the same desks and drafting tables, the same machine shops and fabrication facilities with their gantries and busy welders. Perhaps this is the film's main triumph: representing techno-scientific modernity as a mobile, transnational venture while also contrasting the utterly mundane and tedious reality of scientific work against the singularly romantic and idealistic frisson of rockets erect on their launch pads, then roaring aloft.

Yet none of this fabulation disguises the film's obvious historical lies, beginning with a seemingly small one: in *I Aim at the Stars*, Dornberger and von Braun order workers to abandon Peenemünde after an early spring 1945 Allied bombing raid devastates the facility and leaves seven hundred dead, as Soviet guns pound a front line some miles off to the east. In fact that move commenced with an August 18, 1943, Allied bombing and it stretched through January 1945. This change cannot only have to do with the temporal compression and leapfrogging required of a one-hour-and-fifty-minute film. Instead, the film's hasty escape to Austria and the rocketeers' surrender to the U.S. Army's Forty-Fourth Infantry Division in early May 1945 enables von Braun to entirely efface the facts of his lengthy involvement with what many thought, and still think, were war crimes. This aspect of von Braun's life was widely circulated for decades after 1945, but Neufeld's archival work nails down a damning case. Its prelude was that von Braun had joined the ss in 1940.[5] Then in 1943, after he had a run-in with ss officers that nearly got him executed for treason, Hitler gave in to Albert Speer's pleading and restored von Braun to power, made him an ss *Sturmbannführer*, and personally awarded him the Reich's highest honor, the Knight's Cross. After that scare von Braun was often seen in his ss jackboots, black uniform, and armband.[6] This is precisely how a Columbia Pictures promotional photo presents him, flanked by two other actors in full ss regalia (see our book's cover photo), an image that had to have been made while the second unit was filming on location in Germany. That wardrobe never found its way into the finished cut, however, which literally clothes von Braun in the lie that he was merely a business-suited civilian scientist unshy about speaking his antipathy to Nazism and Hitler. The historical von Braun, records reveal, wore his ss uniform on at least seven official visits to Nordhausen and the Mittelbau-Dora manufactory/concentration camp, beginning in late August 1943 and ending in January 1945. During those site visits he consulted on the construction and installation of v-2 manufacturing equipment in the underground tunnel network, and on the uses and management of the concentration camp's slave laborers. Their numbers ratcheted up tenfold from August to October 1943, by which time there were four thousand people living in wretched conditions, and then rose approximately six times more in the following months. Neufeld has shown also that von Braun knew very well that the camp internees were being overworked and undernourished, and some were tortured or executed for underperforming. He probably ordered or at least assented to the brutal corporal punishment of one laborer for poor performance. The archive also shows that he did visit the nearby Buchenwald camp to consult on the selection of prisoners, many of them French, for forced labor at Dora. He also had to have known from his last visit in January 1945 that, as the Reich collapsed around them, the ss at Dora continued to carry out hangings and firing squads, culminating in the grisly stacks of bodies that U.S. troops discovered when they liberated the camp that spring.[7] Neufeld's moral and legal reckoning from these facts is cold, clear, and just: there was more than ample evidence for von Braun to have been indicted for war crimes under the Nuremberg protocols.

Scriptwriters working up von Braun's draft certainly must have foreseen the public relations nightmares, and so went beyond merely putting Curt Jurgens's ss uniform back in the wardrobe locker. They also revised an early script to include two other fictional characters. The first is Elizabeth, a German-born secret agent working as von Braun's secretary at Peenemünde, but passing rocket information to the Allies because the ss killed her husband. The second is Taggart, a fictionalized American information officer who, having lost his wife and daughter in the London v-2 blitz, insists that the captured Peenemünde rocketeers, von Braun most of all, must be tried for war crimes. Together they voice the film's strongest case against von Braun but also, especially in Elizabeth's words, against the evil marriage of science to war. She tells one of von Braun's top assistants: "You are so blind to the misery you've caused" and charges further, "You're just like a slave to Wernher, as if he was God. You'll do anything he wants you to do, anything, anything! Scientist, without thinking," she sneers, "scientist!" Such charges continue till the film's end, when Wernher matches the Soviets' Sputnik I victory by successfully putting an American spacecraft into earth orbit, lifting the old clouds of suspicion gathered over his record. In real life the film only darkened the clouds, as protesters outside the theaters showed. The worst of it was some film dialogue charging von Braun with enslaving a fellow German technocrat, a trope deflecting attention away from the actual slave labor at Dora. In so many ways the film's representational strategies, dialogue, politics, and ethics were like an inchoate miasma, indicating—we think—the obfuscation, denial, double-think, repression, and sublimation complicating this chapter of recent history, as the sixties began. The only justice Neufeld finds in all this: von Braun's share of the box office income from *I Aim at the Stars* was zero.[8]

We have no way of knowing, but do like to think that Pynchon saw *I Aim at the Stars* in the autumn of 1960, perhaps at Seattle's Varsity Theater, several blocks north of his apartment in the University District, or at the Neptune, a short bus ride south. After living in Greenwich Village in the second half of 1959, he'd moved to Seattle in February for work as a technical writer at Boeing, in the company's BOMARC guided missile division. And why wouldn't he want to see the film? He was working in rocketry, and the film treated the most famous rocketman of all. Assuming he bought a ticket, Pynchon surely would have been taken by some of the characters' critical remarks about science and their cynicism about war: an American officer's complaint that "it always takes a war to make people see how useful scientists are"; or von Braun's observation that if he were prosecuted for war crimes then "everyone who worked in a munitions factory" should be in the dock with him; or Maria von Braun earnestly advising that conscience is something a free person "can't leave to others." Such condemnations should have pricked Pynchon's conscience. Perhaps he also held onto the film's subplot involving Elizabeth, the secret agent planted among German rocketmen, eventually morphing her into the figure of Katje.

If Pynchon saw *I Aim at the Stars* in late 1960, it would have been just weeks later that he took in the implications of outgoing President Eisenhower's January 17, 1961, "Farewell Address." The last of Eisenhower's occasional talks, this speech sharply criticized the powers of the very type of company, and political economy, in which the aspiring novelist was then enmeshed. Eisenhower described it as an "immense military establishment and a large arms industry," which annually spent "on military security more than the net income of all United States Corporations," words Ike double-underlined in his reading script. He further warned that this "military-industrial complex" already posed "grave implications" for "the very structure" of American society because it wielded inordinate and dangerous power over all facets of national life. His concerns also extended to American universities and to scientific progress generally. Observing that research and development had become so "formalized, complex and costly," and that national priorities had become so focused on Soviet nuclear threats, Eisenhower regretted that the competition for funds nationwide had prioritized research with military applications over any others. The lucrative and prestigious potentials for weapons-oriented research were irrevocably altering "the free university" in America and also interlocking it with the new and vast technocracy, thereby raising "the prospect of domination of the nation's scholars by Federal employment, project allocations, and the power of money." The ultimate danger, in the president's view, was that this new, national security state would make government "the captive of a scientific-technological elite." Asked afterward who he had in mind in the role of captors, Eisenhower immediately answered: the father of nuclear weapons and the father of rocketry, "[Edward] Teller and [Wernher] von Braun."[9]

Some details about Pynchon's Seattle years have surfaced: Phyllis Gebauer's recollections of her husband's friendship with Pynchon, formed at Boeing; archived interviews with other co-workers at the Boeing plant; and a substantial portion of Pynchon's published technical writings for Boeing.[10] From this emerging archive we get images of a long-haired and mustachioed Pynchon remembered for meticulous and tireless research, who wrote with more stylistic flair than anyone else in his department and sprinkled through these dry pieces his folksy anecdotes and humorous asides. During this time, he also made his first in-print mention of the V-2 missile, in a September 1962 article titled "Hydrazine Tank Cartridge Replacement." Pynchon wrote most extensively on the BOMARC winged, surface-to-air missile, quite similar to the A-9 that von Braun's team had been designing at Peenemünde for targeting New York City. He also wrote on the Minuteman intercontinental ballistic missile, or ICBM, a solid-fuel multistage rocket built by former Peenemündans to fling a payload six thousand miles and strike within a one-mile diameter target area (von Braun's film-father would have been proud). Tipped with a nuclear warhead, it was touted as the "ultimate weapon" in 1961. It also raised the ante against Soviet competitors, eliminated the (mythical) U.S. "missile gap," and touched off the series of events leading to the Cuban missile crisis of 1962. Writing about the BOMARC and the Minuteman, Pynchon addressed his prose to mechanics, technicians, and missile-transport specialists whose jobs were quite similar to those that German V-2 troopers performed during World War II, men who got their instructions and advice from the A-4 *Fibel*, a manual for operating the Aggregat-4, or V-2.[11]

What then were the ethical and political implications of Pynchon's daily work, in relation to these greater concerns about science, militarism, and missiles popularly expressed in a film like *I Aim at the Stars* and officially voiced in Eisenhower's "Farewell"? Fears of a nuclear holocaust peaked during the years he worked in Boeing missile support. Throughout the fall 1960 campaign, presidential candidate John F. Kennedy harped on claims that Republican leadership under Eisenhower had allowed the United States to lag behind the Soviets in the number and power of ICBMs. Told shortly after taking office in early 1961 that the so-called missile gap was "a fiction," Kennedy nevertheless ordered increases in missile production and research, and built new launching sites nearer than ever to Soviet soil. When Soviet leaders countered with launch sites in Fidel Castro's Cuba, Kennedy's duel with Nikita Khrushchev brought the world's peoples nearer than ever to the brink of nuclear annihilation.[12] At that moment Pynchon had just left off writing for Boeing to finish his first novel, his thirty-one months as a cog in the U.S. war machine over. He had, as they say, "interfaced" with technicians, engineers, managers; knew the warrens of beaverboarded work spaces; and had grown accustomed to synthesizing and translating for ordinary usage the system's top-secret "work product" for field applications. He had produced those writings at *the* historical moment when any kind of labor on behalf of nuclear armaments was the subject of public scrutiny, when peace activists and protesters worldwide were making clear that workers in that system were cogs turning the wheels toward an unspeakable violence. Like any drone producing and servicing the "pilotless aircraft" for either side, Pynchon's work—his gift for writing—had made him inescapably complicit in a technocratic political economy specializing in mass destruction and terror. The questions circulating widely in early sixties America were the same questions Pynchon, and his co-workers and friends, had every reason to share. Were they "slaves" to a military-industrial regime, as the character Elizabeth puts it to von Braun in the film? Was their work implicated in a wider "domination," as Eisenhower darkly warned? What was the logic of that system, then seen as barreling toward annihilation? Writing *V.*, Pynchon was thinking historically and fictionally through these issues, beginning a narrative discourse he would carry into *Gravity's Rainbow*.

Pynchon's first novel invokes the 1922 Bondelswarts rebellion in Southwest Africa to look back upon the 1904–7 extermination campaign against the Hereros and to look forward to the Holocaust. He carefully grounds discrete details of that chapter in historical sources, while also staying mindful of those events' wider implications. In a January 1969 letter to an inquiring Thomas F. Hirsch, then a graduate student writing his thesis, Pynchon indicates that he saw the Herero genocide as "a sort of dress rehearsal for what later happened to the Jews in the '30's and '40's." That violence was preceded by the extermination of American Indians and was succeeded by "what is now being done . . . in Vietnam," the result, Pynchon states, of "a culture

valuing analysis and differentiation."[13] This is the view that found its way into
V. and brought queries from Hirsch, perhaps because of how Pynchon's narrator comparatively tallies the Jewish lives lost in the Holocaust: "Allowing
for natural causes during those unnatural years [1904–7], von Trotha, who
stayed for only one of them, is reckoned to have done away with about 60,000
people. This is only 1 per cent of six million, but still pretty good."[14] Some of
that violence occurred in the field, some in special encampments: "The barren islets off Lüderitzbucht were natural *concentration camps.*"[15] Actually
there was nothing new in that name, which was routinely applied to internments of Native Americans in the late nineteenth century and again during
South Africa's Second War of Independence (1899–1902), fought over the
Transvaal region's mineral riches. During the strife, the British moved Boer
women and children into "refugee camps" and black Africans into desolate
tented sites, "concentration camps," and then sat passively by as many died
of disease and starvation. The novelties in von Trotha's campaign were an
expressed military policy and a systematic campaign of active violence, murder on a mass scale.[16] The facility at Shark Island, a small peninsula close to
the coastal town of Lüderitz, now a holiday resort for Namibian and foreign
tourists, was arguably the world's first "concentration camp," in the sense
widely shared after 1945.

Genocide as a rationally planned government policy is the most radical
form of human domination: subjective violence against entire ethno-racially
defined populations. Pynchon's approach is to tackle the matter sideways.
In *Gravity's Rainbow*, the Mittelbau-Dora camp has to stand as a synecdoche for the entire Nazi camp system. And while it was networked to other
internment facilities, indeed originally constructed as a Buchenwald satel-
lite camp, Dora was Pynchon's focus because of its role in producing V-2
rockets.[17] The histories he consulted detail how rocket technology and industrial cartels converged at Dora, in stark, ironic contrast to the transcendent
urges of German romantic ideology. Not that Pynchon disregards the Nazi
genocide of European Jewry. Dora had some of that, though so many others
also were held in slave labor and murdered there: French, Dutch, and Belgian
workers, along with Eastern Europeans and for that matter anyone trained in
tasks like precision lathing and welding. We've noted that *Gravity's Rainbow*
scarcely figures the one-on-one subjective violence of war. And in its treatment of Dora we do not find any directly figured torture or execution scenes,
though Pynchon would have known about such war crimes from his reading. The closest the novel comes to such moments is the narrator's recognition that workers turning the lathes in a Nordhausen manufacturing tunnel
had their "knuckles . . . bloodied against grinding wheels, pores, creases and
quicks [of fingers] stabbed by the fine splinters of steel."[18] That's an exqui-
site feat of imaginative detailing, but merely hints at the horrific violence in

Dora's last days. In this connection, too, remember the seventeenth-century dodo extermination episode on Mauritius, in the flashback to Katje's ancestor Frans van der Groov. That scene displaces human genocide onto birds, a move readers may rightly find trivializing or insensitive, given the enormity of the Holocaust evidence. Yet Pynchon's language leans, somewhat, toward that greater world historical sense: "Frans could not know that except for a few others on the island of Reunion, these were the only dodoes in the Creation, and that he was helping *exterminate a race.*"[19] All of this is further presented in context with colonial conquest ("the purest form of European adventuring"), which also brought the (fictional) Schwarzkommando to the German metropole from their periphery in Southwest Africa. As the narrator puts it: "Colonies are the outhouses of the European soul, where a fellow can let his pants down and relax, enjoy the smell of his own shit."[20] In the white supremacist worldview Pynchon ascribes to such a "fellow," the colonialist then brings that "shit" back to the metropole in the form of African menial labor.

The tendency in these moments is to avoid realism in favor of parody and black humor, as in Vonnegut's *Slaughterhouse-Five*. Uses of the word "holocaust" in *Gravity's Rainbow* offer no help, and tend to run in a black humor mode rather like Vonnegut's. The world war's actual Holocaust remains dormant, even repressed, at most a kind of latency in the novel's verbal and moral texture. Whether applied to a sunset panorama over London, a garishly illuminated Monaco casino, or an image of St. Veronica's Hospital consumed by fire, a range of small *h* "holocaust" images hang over the non-German landscape of this storyworld. In those moments the capital *H* "Holocaust" comes barely to the surface, perhaps giving the word a subtle foreshadowing power, evoking with minimal historical weight what might be learned about the camps, or perhaps what is already widely recognizable: images of crematoriums and stacked bodies. But that might be pushing the textual traces in a way that over-ascribes intentions to Pynchon. Maybe these uses of "holocaust" are merely symptomatic of avoidance, a subtle concession that he's not up to "Holocaust" realism, unwilling to try the detailed descriptive version of camp experiences, or to try a Brechtian strategy of defamiliarizing the topic so that readers see beyond the genocidal violence. What that "beyond" might be is unclear—though the novel's last page implies it is world-ending nuclear holocaust.

What little *Gravity's Rainbow* does with the dehumanizing violence of concentration camps is worth a closer look. Earlier in this part on domination, we considered Pökler's tour through Dora on the eve of its liberation, noting that his small altruistic gesture of giving away his wedding ring may come off as incongruous and futile, considering the scope of the murder there. How does this scene compare to the way Pynchon evokes Dora? When first mentioned, as Slothrop arrives in Nordhausen, Dora is identified with "slave laborers," and soon after, as Private "Micro" Graham tour-guides Slothrop around, with "the prison camp next to the Mittelwerke," the v-2 production plant with its "secret doors."[21] In these pages the living internees are faceless, nationless, their ethno-racial identities unmentioned. Graham warns Slothrop and other visitors they may see ghosts of dead prisoners, then the tour quickly veers into the Mittelwerke tunnel system, its architecture and machinery. In cross-tunnel 41, Slothrop finds "a crowd of Americans and Russians gathered around a huge oak beer barrel"; there follows some quaffing, raunchy rocket limericks, and an appearance of Major Marvy and his "mothers" that sends Slothrop running, whence the episode breaks into another of the novel's humorous chase scenes—guns blazing, great leaps—that riff on film conventions (think: James Bond). Humor and over-the-top action thus leave behind us the prospect of dead bodies and emaciated internees. As in the dodo yarn, we find a calculated exaggeration: the same defamiliarizing technique but laying before us a far more obvious ethical problem. Readers cajoled into thinking, dark humorously, about the relation of Nazi ideology to the Holocaust are quite different from readers addressed using a realism that would take them inside the horror and help to develop compassion for the victims. Finally it's a matter of how we feel *addressed*, how we construct the writing, and whether we want to be the person we believe the text is addressing.

Pynchon goes even further in two subsequent scenes, using the same technique. The first unfolds when former Peenemünde engineer Horst Achtfaden focalizes our view of the "Toiletship" *Rücksichtslos*. He thinks that, postwar, guilt will become a Zone commodity, and sarcastically suggests: "Extermination camps will be turned into tourist attractions, foreigners with cameras will come piling through in droves, tickled and shivering with guilt."[22] Pökler was moving toward a sense of guilt only at the end of his stint in the Mittelwerke, and Fahringer realized guilt when it was too late, but when Achtfaden phrases Holocaust guilt as a pop cultural "attraction" he undermines even that microgram of Pökler's or Fahringer's ethical growth. Much as we might agree with Achtfaden's sarcastic assertion that late capitalism will commodify anything and everything under the sun, the rhetoric nonetheless has the same distancing effect, and one might feel the same ethical wince.

The second scene unfolds when Miklos Thanatz steps ashore from a rowboat that's saved him just in time from drowning, and finds his way blocked by "175s—homosexual prison-camp inmates" from Dora, who have come north and "set up an all-male community."[23] Surprisingly, "none of the men can bear to be out of Dora" for it had become their home; and in a perverse nostalgia, these masochists now feel their "liberation" as banishment. Moreover, in this makeshift concentration camp they've even made up their own version of the "ss chain of command."[24] Once more avoiding specific mention of Jewish and other ethnic prisoners put into forced labor at Mittelbau-Dora, Pynchon again stretches our credulity to a snapping point. Of course we *get* it: these guys represent the Nazified, colonized mind taken to a limit of possibility, finding comfort, even pleasure, in their fascist domination and taking Fromm's *Escape from Freedom* argument to an overdetermined absurdity. The description of their "phantom ss command" culminates in two paragraphs about Blicero's supremacy, his name having ghosted its way into their hierarchy as an eminent title for the commanding "officer" among the 175s, evidently mirroring Weissmann/Blicero's reputation among Dora guards during the war. Notably also, this passage mentions two infamous concentration camps, but only in order to point beyond them: "[The guards'] fear kept echoing: fear not of Weissmann personally, but of the time itself . . . a time which was granting him a power different from that of Auschwitz or Buchenwald, a power they couldn't have borne themselves."[25] The mention of those two iconic names is as close as *Gravity's Rainbow* comes to identifying, much less representing, the Holocaust as systemic catastrophe. And how is "power different" at Dora, compared to Buchenwald? One difference is that the rocket rationalized power and domination at Dora. It brought cartelized capitalism and a German version of the military-industrial complex into Mittelbau-Dora in ways similar to but different from other camps. It operated as a forced-labor plant for the manufacture of v-2 rockets; Auschwitz and Buchenwald were manufactories for exterminating European Jews. Krupp and Siemens manufactured the steel and components for the v-2; the Bayer AG plant produced the Zyklon B used to gas victims at Auschwitz and Buchenwald, which were end points of a telos begun decades earlier, in Southwest Africa for example. In contrast the operations at Peenemünde and Mittelbau-Dora were the inception points of the rocket and the rocket age, whose terminus is the Orpheus Theater at the novel's end. Extermination is the logic driving both historical processes. The rocket is the novel's master trope for this moment, when the West can be seen to have pivoted from a mode of ethno-racial extermination, soon to be named genocide, into a process for incinerating the globe. The rocket *is* destiny.

The dodo extermination flashback comes near the end of the episode about Blicero's sadomasochistic domination of Katje and Gottfried in The Hague. Evidently Weissmann/Blicero has been invoking the Hansel and Gretel tale to narrativize his sadism. Following the brothers Grimm plot, he's the evil witch threatening the boy-girl pair with the "oven." This analogy might once more threaten to trivialize the Holocaust, if it weren't for how the analogy cannily implies that generations of children raised on the Germanic folktale were subconsciously acculturated to what German men did in the death camps. But then in another strong moment of defamiliarization, the narration frustrates any simple equation. Weissmann revises the plot's iconic moment, which ironically, justly, ends with Gretel tricking the cannibalistic witch into a position where she can kick *her* into the oven. Weissmann/Blicero, in contrast, *desires* the oven precisely because he understands it as *his* "Destiny," the telos of his plot and his (perverse) ticket to immortal recognition. Yet things don't turn out that way either. The narration erroneously suggests that the "children," Gottfried and Katje, "will survive and prosper long beyond his gases and cinders, his chimney departure."[26] Instead the novel figures Gottfried's end in Rocket 00000, while also reckoning Katje as a survivor destined in a practical sense for freedom from Weissmann's witchcraft. But is she *free*, really, from this past, which They have built around her?

This raises larger questions. Who or what defines the political subject, as *Gravity's Rainbow* represents it? Is there any mode of subjectivity that does not entail subjection? Given how the novel represents persons in their relations with power, in late capitalist nation-states, the answers to those questions look grim. Liberal political and jurisprudential thinking has always framed the relations of persons and powers according to whether subjects are represented as having certain rights, privileges, and immunities, the blessings of negative liberty with which individuals may form just communal relations and realize the greater blessings of positive liberty. Yet even some of those elementary, negative liberty blessings will depend crucially on whether one is a citizen or a noncitizen. And in a modernity defined by world wars, by displacements of whole populations, the kinds of belonging and the rights secured for citizens shrink and increasingly become matters of great historical contingency. The making and breaking of nation-states and their borders has been incredibly fluid, as Europe's constantly morphing map demonstrates, since the age of revolutions. Throughout those centuries, citizenship has been further complicated by shifting identifications of race or ethnicity as decision points for sovereign powers to confer citizenship on some, while assigning others to inferior grades, perhaps consigning them to outright subjection and rightslessness as slaves. This is one of Pynchon's great subjects even from his earliest work, particularly when it involves how persons are transformed into things.

Consider a passage in *Gravity's Rainbow* that one might read quickly, without much mindfulness, as just another of Pynchon's laundry lists. The scene unfolds shortly after the opening of episode 25 of part 3, "In the Zone." Slothrop's just awakened in a village locksmith's somewhere near Rostock and, walking out the door dressed in Tchitcherine's Red Army uniform, he gazes over a landscape seemingly reverted to Viking times, a Europe with "no clear boundaries." He enters that vastness, which our narrator then describes in its human terms, with this long catalog:

The Nationalities are on the move. It is a great frontierless streaming out here. Volksdeutsch from across the Oder, moved out by the Poles and headed for the camp at Rostock, Poles fleeing the Lublin regime, others going back home, the eyes of both parties, when they do meet, hooded behind cheekbones, eyes much older than what's forced them into moving, Estonians, Letts, Lithuanians trekking north again, all their wintry wool in dark bundles, shoes in tatters, songs too hard to sing, talk pointless, Sudetens and East Prussians shuttling between Berlin and the DP camps in Mecklenburg, Czechs and Slovaks, Croats and Serbs, Tosks and Ghegs, Macedonians, Magyars, Vlachs, Circassians, Spaniols, Bulgars stirred and streaming over the surface of the Imperial cauldron, colliding, shearing alongside for miles, sliding away, numb, indifferent to all momenta but the deepest, the instability too far below their itchy feet to give a shape to, white wrists and ankles incredibly wasted poking from their striped prison-camp pajamas, footsteps light as waterfowl's in this inland dust, caravans of Gypsies, axles or linchpins failing, horses dying, families leaving their vehicles beside the roads for others to come live in a night, a day, over the white hot Autobahns, trains full of their own hanging off the cars that lumber overhead, squeezing aside for army convoys when they come through, White Russians sour with pain on the way west, Kazakh ex-P/Ws marching east, Wehrmacht veterans from other parts of old Germany, foreigners to Prussia as any Gypsies, carrying their old packs, wrapped in the army blankets they kept, pale green farmworker triangles sewn chest-high on each blouse bobbing, drifting, at a certain hour of the dusk, like candleflames in religious procession—supposed to be heading today for Hannover, supposed to pick potatoes along the way, they've been chasing these nonexistent potato fields now for a month—"Plundered," a one-time bugler limps along with a long splinter of railroad tie for a cane, his instrument, implausibly undented and shiny, swinging from one shoulder, "stripped by the ss, Bruder, ja, every fucking potato field, and what for? Alcohol. Not to drink, no, alcohol for the rockets. Potatoes we could have been eating, alcohol we could have been drinking. It's unbelievable." "What, the rockets?" "No! The ss, picking potatoes!" looking around for his laugh.[27]

Reading those lines invokes a common aesthetic experience in *Gravity's Rainbow*. So often the narration gives one the feeling of being buried under a rubble of words naming things, concepts, techniques, and peoples; words with no clear reason for being tumbled together and that challenge us therefore to seek meaningful order and readerly control. That task is all the more challenging, alluring, as Pynchon's verbal embrace draws in so many nouns from technical jargons, historically specific slangs, and foreign languages. Once upon a time, reading the lengthy catalogs in Walt Whitman's "Song of Myself" was supposed to invoke visions of the new, variegated, or "melting pot" democratic body politic the poem celebrates. But what shall we make of Pynchon's passage? It begins with the expelled ethnic Germans, or "Volksdeutsch," trekking westward out of liberated Poland, imagined as an "Imperial cauldron." It ends with a Wehrmacht soldier telling the bitter irony of his fellow refugees' collective starvation, then waiting in vain for them to reward his black humor with a "laugh." It is framed on one end by émigré Germans, on the other by German citizen-soldiers. Thus framed—cataloged in

a 370-word sentence grammatically and thematically realizing their jurisprudential in-betweenness or rightslessness—the Reich's randomly arrayed former enemy aliens trek across our field of vision.

With their deep-set eyes and emaciated "white wrists and ankles," and in
their "numb" and silent "drifting" on waves of "momenta" generated from
somewhere deeper than any potential or actual "nationalities" indexed in this
catalog, Pynchon's refugees, denationalized families, former concentration
camp inmates, and prisoners of war collectively represent the multitude of
stateless persons streaming over occupied Europe in the months following
V-E Day. The passage focalizes through their collective consciousness. But
what is their relation to those "Imperial" powers on whose cauldron surface they drift? Put differently, what form of body politic might one's reading
bring forth from this passage? The figures set before us are "white," a sign
that skin color alone cannot account for the ethno-racial marking of bodies
that modern state powers have demonized, interned, murdered. So in this sentence their ethnic identities pile up like blasted bricks: Tosks, Ghegs, Vlachs.
English-speakers might read such tongue-stopping monosyllabic proper nouns
as exemplary "material typonyms," what Alec McHoul and David Wills define
as post-rhetorical, semiotic prostheses for that which is absent but could (or
should) fill the spaces between Western culture's overdetermined binaries:
white and black, law and anarchy, and—especially in this passage—sovereign power and its subjects.[28]

But there is a hitch in that approach. McHoul and Wills regard Pynchon's
practice as bringing forth the *positive* potentiality of critique to cleanse what
Pynchon elsewhere (in *The Crying of Lot 49*) terms the "bad shit" of binary
rhetorics by opening speech to formerly excluded middles—such as those
refugees. Yet the passage above implies that a sovereign authority has reckoned these persons through the lens of an ethnic type of humankind, and deployed the name for their kind within a mode of statecraft dedicated to their
abjection, to the "bad shit" of their dehumanization. Thus they represent
an excluded middle well along the way to becoming a midden, mere human
trash. In fact the grammatical subjects of this compound, complex sentence
are represented as no longer standing in a relation of citizen-subjects to *any*
sovereign power. The imperium has abandoned them to what the text depicts
as long and "deep" wave forms practically beyond reckoning, and according
to whose inertias they are "supposed" to do this or that mindless labor. For
sovereign authority still needs them after all, needs especially their reduction
to menial, emaciated, naked being, and needs them not only as slave labor
but just thus, as an index of its total power. Historically grounded figures,
still human but nonsubjects vis-à-vis the state, these refugees represent a paradoxically included-excluded middle. Politically, they embody the staggering
consequences of a modern dominion hell-bent on producing ever more of

them. Alienated from homelands, banned from membership in any citizenry, denied the protective tent of any nation-state, and therefore beyond the protection of constitutions and of authorities warranting their claim on basic negative liberties, such persons figure a humanity apparently outside of the political yet posing a core political problematic of modernity.[29]

This was a central thesis of Arendt's *Origins of Totalitarianism*, whose chapters on statelessness most likely suggested some of those ethnic names to Pynchon.[30] And suggested, as well, the historical thesis that European colonialist outposts like German Southwest Africa were seedbeds for the concentration camps, spaces for the manufacture and control of death-in-life. Always lacking character names in *Gravity's Rainbow* and appearing most frequently in parts 3 and 4, but imaged with striking power in those refugees in the novel's opening pages, or in the orphaned "Foxes" Pointsman hunts in a London bus station, these figures of bare life have walk-on roles throughout Pynchon's novel. Yet even some of its major characters become stateless and rightless in the same sense, though under the more expansive circumstances of the camp and the Zone. Take Leni and Ilse Pökler, for example, or Miklos Thanatz and the Schwarzkommando. Still more: what is Slothrop's progress? Or the reader's? The text opens in mid-December 1944 with "fantasist surrogate" Pirate Prentice dreaming he is seated in the "velveteen darkness" of a railway car, surrounded by other London evacuees such as "derelicts," "drunks," "old veterans," and "exhausted women with more children than it seems could belong to anyone." Where is this train taking these passengers, and why, as they "pass under archways," is their destination figured as "a judgment from which there is no appeal"? Indeed a judgment of dereliction seems to rest upon them all, Pointsman included. In the post-Holocaust decade of this novel's writing, these figures seeming to have been "stacked" in the railcars implies a deeply ominous answer to our questions.[31] The camp thus shadows the novel from its beginning. And then at the last, as our reading approaches its terminus, in the "Orpheus Puts Down Harp" section of the final episode, our narrator represents just outside the windows of the "black Managerial Volkswagen" carrying Pynchon's thinly disguised Richard M. Nixon a host of countercultural "freaks . . . swarming in . . . in full disrespect for the Prohibitions," and showing most of all their disrespect for the sovereign Nixon. But "Relax," the manager advises: "There'll be a nice secure *home* for them all, down in Orange County. Right next to Disneyland." So the *Konzentrationslager* stalks sixties America too.[32]

We understand "the Zone" as a chronotope of statelessness and bare life that poses the novel's theme of domination in its most general form, encompassing concentration camps as well as the wider condition of stateless, rightless human existence that so concerned Arendt. In a rare moment when criticism has verged on treating such matters, Stefan Mattessich in his 2002 study remarks that the Dora concentration camp "would seem to be a radical limit to Pynchon's strategies, the arrest or suspension of the joke." He further argues that "the holocaust is never submitted to its parodic mutations of form" and even remains an "exteriority or muted presence in the background" of *Gravity's Rainbow*.[33] We disagree, arguing above that the novel's uses of parody and black humor are notably problematic in its treatment of camp realities, however brief in (but not exterior to) the novel. Our sense instead is that the Zone generalizes camp space and camp dominion. The Zone is that space where sovereign power operates with a certain invisibility (named They) that is normal to it. The Zone also defines that space— camp or wide-open frontier—where sovereignty performs its greatest magic, lawfully declaring the absence of law, declaring forfeit all guarantees of individual rights, for *some* people. It's the space in which power enforces a state of exception, normally invoked only during war, and over which law declares a profound anomie, a lack of law whose instrumental purpose is to enable the production of human beings stripped down to bare biological life, mere creaturehood or objecthood. This is the condition Giorgio Agamben defines as that of the *homo sacer*: the form of human life included *in* the juridical order only by his codification as one excluded *from* that order's privileges and immunities. *Homo sacer* defines that human being who can be killed with impunity, and defines all who are entitled to visit punitive violence on him as sovereigns, not as kings per se but as individuals with a pro rata share of that elemental dominion.[34] Without that share as a minimal entry requirement, forget about joining Them (though consider being a useful tool, and cultivate what They call "prospects"). In *Gravity's Rainbow*, "the Zone" is any space that manifests that logic of power, which is ordinarily hidden and latent. Zone spaces proliferate throughout the narrative—in Pointsman's lab, in St. Veronica's Hospital where Slothrop's very dreams are invaded for purposes of control—and we find Pynchon generally mindful about just where, and why, the Zone's frightful realities should suspend the wise-guy joking. At the end of that 370-word sentence, for example, the starving DP's don't give even a nervous laugh at the Wehrmacht soldier's black humor.

We should also be clear about what these zones are *not*. The irrepressibly nostalgic Tyrone Slothrop, for example, considers the Zone a space where "maybe for a little while, all the fences are down, one road as good as another, the whole space of the Zone cleared, depolarized, and somewhere inside the waste of it a single set of coordinates from which to proceed, without elect, without preterite, without even nationality to fuck it up."[35] To him as to many others the Zone symbolizes the *seeming* suspension of bad rhetorical binaries and the promise of a return to primal homelands where some originary historical and cultural singularity might point a way out of current political dilemmas. In sum, this passage (like many others in the novel) de-

scribes what we might name the Romantic Zone: a cleared ground bloom-
ing with chthonic potential, an atavistic yet opportunistic wilderness space
where the individual subject and individualism itself seem sovereign.[36] "It's
so *unorganized* out here," Geli Tripping tells Slothrop soon after he's entered
the occupied Zone of Europe. But the novel clearly represents that as a delusional view, as if persons like Geli were all watching the same movie, groov-
ing to some intersubjective fantasia. Slothrop, chief among them, might be
"as properly constituted a state as any other in the Zone these days," a fantasy of the sovereign, a shell of that self-reliant soul figured repeatedly in the
novel's pop cultural riffs, figured, as one song lyric puts it, as a westwarding
hero "Zoomin' through the Zone, where the wild dogs roam." In *Gravity's
Rainbow*, other instances of the Romantic Zone are the American Southwest
of fiction and film, the nineteenth-century Argentine Pampas of the *Mar-
tín Fierro* epic (specifically, during the time of Fierro's first avatar, *before* he
sells out to General Roca's Indian hunters), the desert wastes of Südwest Af-
rika (where von Trotha's troopers hunted the Hereros as if they were game
animals), and the high deserts backgrounding Tchitcherine's sojourn in the
"wild East" steppes of Kirghizstan, where related atrocities occurred.[37]

So that we might be undeluded, *Gravity's Rainbow* typically inscribes
signs of domination and extermination either within or immediately adja-
cent to scenes of the Romantic Zone. Just before Geli Tripping's remarks
about the Zone's "unorganized" and supposedly liberating spatiality, for
example, Slothrop notices emaciated old refugees, along with former Dora
camp "slave laborers" and homosexual inmates still wearing "175 badges" on
the chests of their camp pajamas. With such instances of total dominion thus
stalking the edges of perception, the incisive question is: How are the dominated subjects of the total state encouraged by such romantic fantasies? Late
in part 4, Gottfried "believes he exists *for Blicero* . . . [and] that in the new
kingdom they pass through now, he [Gottfried] is the only other living in-
habitant."[38] This passage illustrates precisely what Arendt in *Origins of Totalitarianism* and then Agamben, fifty years later in *Remnants of Auschwitz*,
define as the slave or camp inmate's apotheosis: a mentality inculcated with
and disciplined to the perverse belief that submissive abjection constitutes
his proper and just condition, and ultimately that his transformation into
what Arendt names "inanimate man" and Agamben the *homo sacer* will enable deserving persons, the elect, to achieve and sustain a singular and transcendent being.[39] In Gottfried's case, the narrative represents this belief as
growing from Blicero's schooling the boy in late romantic *Jugendstil* fantasies of the solitary *Wandervogel* alone in his mountain wilderness, precisely
the anti-industrial ideology encoded by Rilke's lyrics yet made to serve the
project of this boy's total "immachination." In a telling observation, Agamben warns that the spaces sovereignty carves out during colonialist adventur-

ing and during emergencies and wars must never be mistaken (nostalgically romanticized) as some originary, pleromatic state in which a fullness of executive power seemingly anterior to law enacts all by itself the functions normally reserved to other governmental branches. He shows that all such spaces are always already coded into law under the aegis of emergency powers, the "state of exception." Hence any belief that they are just returning power to its full and originary juridical condition amounts to nothing other than "a legal mythologeme analogous to the idea of a state of nature." As a particular chronotope of state power, the Romantic Zone constitutes the sort of myth that will, we are told in one of Pynchon's moments of second-person address, make "you lindy-hop into the pit by millions, as many millions as necessary."[40]

Pynchon shares with Arendt and Walter Benjamin a critical (but, in his case, also satirical) rejection of the romantic chronotope. The Zone is for Pynchon, as for Arendt, always historically contingent; it is represented in part 3 as a space to contain and regulate the flows and labors of stateless persons. And the Zone appears more generally in the novel as any topology—at home, at work, out in the world—within which totalitarian power has demolished individuality, replaced it with the delusion of a monadistic and seemingly sovereign self, and realized its deepest desires for control and dominion. It is the space wherein sovereignty denationalizes and denaturalizes the subject, then achieves its abject devolition, transforming the human into a laboring machine until, its productivity exhausted, comes the time for its extermination. The novel also represents the global extension of such spaces. St. Veronica's Hospital or the White Visitation thus constitute kinder, gentler versions of the Zone, tasked to develop psy-war options and develop ways to better behaviorally test and condition subjects, as we've seen. The Kamikaze training facility in wartime Japan may be read as an Asian cultural variant on the same structure.[41] And this list could go on: the Mittelbau-Dora KZ lager, Zwölfkinder as a mirror image of Dora (call it a ZK lager), and all of the novel's colonial territories in the Americas and Africa and Central Asia—where Europeans hunt dodoes and men, "Sarts, Kazakhs, Dungens," for example, "like wild game. Daily scores were kept . . . [while] Their names, even their numbers, were lost forever."[42] These sites function as seedbeds for reproducing the exterminationist logic that Europe reimported from its colonies, as Arendt argues. Back home, such spaces spawn a myriad of avatars: even, for example, Gerhardt von Göll's movie sets and film work for the popular screen, promulgating sadomasochism, thus serving the total state, as Fromm described. Finally this mode of fascist sovereignty, this topology of dominion, must be inscribed on bodies and programmed in mentalities. Slothrop, remarks Sir Marcus Scammony at the close of part 3, was first sent out in the Zone "to destroy the blacks"; as a kind of terminator robot he was, says

Marcus, "a good try at a moderate solution" to the Herero problem. Slothrop having failed at solving it, Sir Marcus warns: "We've got the Army, when the time is right."[43] As an instrument of state power, Slothrop's colonized mind-body reproduces imperialism's geography. In language much like Fanon's, his cock works "like an instrument installed, wired by them into his body as a colonial outpost" answering to the imperial "Metropolis." Programmed to signify in the "kingly voice of the [A-4 rocket] itself," it should have taken the Allied powers straight to the 00000 rocket and the Hereros who wish to emulate it. By the end of part 3, however, Slothrop's constant sidetrackings have demonstrated that, in the words of Sir Marcus, "it's obvious . . . he won't do the job." We leave the issue of his fate after that to our discussion of freedom.[44]

Aside from these functions of domination and exterminationist violence, Pynchon is also quite specific about the form of politics emerging from the Zone. In a telling remark near the end of part 3, the Zone's "skeleton-functional" refugees contrast with well-fed Soviet and American rocket and Herero hunters, like fat Major Marvy. Those Allied soldiers are wrapped in the protective mantle of sovereign nations, while the DPs are stateless, therefore rightsless too. Tchitcherine, who seems to think about multiethnic DPs as stray mongrel dogs, thinks (shades of Sir Marcus Scammony) it may be necessary "to send in combat troops" as a last-ditch means for saving their "garrison state."[45] Thus even beyond "the awful interface of V-E Day, on into the bright new Postwar," war as sovereignty's ultimate state of exception, with its racist and colonialist logic and its fascist culture, will continue the work of subjection in new guises, continue especially as a series of police actions (Korea, the Bay of Pigs, Vietnam, and so on)—each revealing war-ending treaties and "peace" as dissimulating public rituals.[46] This realization—or rather, prediction—of the total state's perpetuation of "emergency" powers was a principal thesis of the sociologist Harold Lasswell's influential 1941 essay, whose title first introduced to political theory the concept of the "garrison state." Lasswell realized even before the United States had joined the conflict that world powers had entered an age of permanent strife, in which militarized modern states, including Western democracies, would radically revise and extrapolate the monarchical/imperial form of sovereignty. Looking to the garrisoned territories of colonial empires, Lasswell foretold a new "national security state" whose driving needs are a ceaseless defensive posture combined with aggressive expansion. This new polity would combine the industrial state, operating on the basis of contract, with the military state, which operates according to coercion. It would centralize government bureaucracies, create a universally regulated, military-driven economy, and establish state monopolization over all means of coercion, including police power and "compulsory labor camps," an effort requiring especially the expertise of elite industrial managers capable of fully rationalizing production and effectively deploying materials and forces.[47] Wimpe realizes the essence of Lasswell's argument when he looks out over the Zone with Tchitcherine and remarks to his Communist counterpart that "our little chemical cartel is the model for the very structure of nations" emerging from war's cauldron.[48]

This emergent corporatized power has little to do with traditional, nationalized forms of sovereignty and explains why the figures of Churchill, Truman, and Stalin appear in *Gravity's Rainbow* only as simulacra: as enormous chromolithographs decorating Berlin's Potsdamer Platz or—still more satirically—as figures on "square after square" of toilet paper onboard the *Rücksichtslos*, each decorated "with caricatures of Churchill, Eisenhower, Roosevelt."[49] Pynchon's text thus understands all too well the ways that heads of state in late capitalism merely encapsulate, and dissimulate, the real workings of sovereignty in this corporatized and governmentalized form. Indeed we think this is just where Arendt's study offers so much when put alongside Pynchon's novel. Her principal goal in 1951 was to rebut claims that, after all, concentration camps were superfluous, because unnecessary, strategic facets of Nazi totalitarianism. Then, examining how the major continental powers all moved to denationalize their own minority populations in the twenties and thirties, Arendt narrates how the reimportation, especially from Africa, of colonialist white supremacy served the project not only of legitimizing the newly imposed statelessness of Jews, Slavs, and Gypsies, but of deploying "race" as the core issue of post–Great War power struggles. As a prophetic early example, Arendt points to the 1922 decision by French authorities to garrison the occupied Rhine River zone with twenty thousand black troops imported from Africa, forces intended to humiliate German racial sensibilities as well as to remind them of their lost colonies in the Südwest. More important, the power to denationalize whole populations implied a state structure which, Arendt argues, even if it were not yet a fully totalitarian garrison state, had already constituted itself around the essential operating principle of such a polity. Denationalization and forced emigration demonstrated that not only in times of war but even during supposed peacetime the rights of legalized citizens could be zeroed-out. The camps, Arendt argues, were thus not only spaces for quarantining newly rootless former citizens but also for making the state of exception permanent and for realizing the principle that stateless persons "belong to the human race in much the same way as animals belong to humans"—"living corpses" or "inanimate [men]."[50]

Arendt analyzes how this form of the total state requires a vast bureaucratization of power and a new managerial class. She understands the work of that technocratic and managerial elite as analogous to that of the camp's head officer, or *Sturmbannführer*, whose objective is to conduct daily a "ghastly experiment of eliminating, under scientifically controlled conditions spontaneity itself as an expression of human behavior and transforming the human personality into a mere thing, into something even animals are not; for Pavlov's dog, as we know, was trained to eat not when it was hungry but when a bell rang." There, and in the last chapters of *Origins*, Arendt returns repeatedly to the trope of Pavlov's dog as an exemplary case of the total state's desire, as she puts it, to mobilize on behalf of the military-industrial complex great masses of men constituted as "bundles of reactions that behave in exactly the same way."[51] So we find in Arendt's *Origins of Totalitarianism* a critique of modern powers and dominations seminally important to understanding the political subjects of Pynchon's novel. Her book yielded a host of minor as well as certain major figurations for Pynchon's great story, including its lists of stateless refugees in the occupied Zone of 1945, the 1922 *Schwarze Besatzung am Rhein* reference in Pynchon's novel, the all-important trope of Pavlovian-style pseudo-sciences of control, and the idea of colonialist domination reimported to Europe.[52] Finally we see Pynchon's novel standing with Arendt's book in another critical respect. She concludes her study with a warning that statelessness, the space of the camp or the Zone, and extermination are all realizations of this new mode of total sovereignty, what Eisenhower would soon name the "military-industrial complex," a form of power that seemed likely, in her concluding phrase, "to stay with us from now on."[53] *Gravity's Rainbow* shares this dark, post-romantic pessimism, despite or even because of the humorous movie theater hand-holding and blithe yet mechanically orchestrated chorus of its closing page. The deathly domination is total, apparently final, already beyond a point of no return. "It is too late," as the novel's third sentence laments, phrasing that recurs nearly thirty more times by novel's end. And is there no hope, then, for justice?

One recurring allusion in Pynchon's work is to a paragraph from an 1878 Ralph Waldo Emerson essay, "The Sovereignty of Ethics." At a key moment, *Vineland* quotes the passage at length, a replay of the words after a more veiled usage in *Gravity's Rainbow*. There, it introduces a "balancing" act of justice that might be visited on Lyle Bland for having called upon "machineries committed to injustice as an enterprise," particularly in the plot to sell Infant Tyrone into the bondage of his operant conditioning, a process that may look harmless (after all, the toddler's only being aroused) but that Slothrop recalls in the terms of terror and trauma—a psychic wound.[54] The Emerson essay recycles familiar themes from American romanticism, positing in the place of divine justice a wellspring of balancing forces in nature, imagined as the source of a "latent omniscience not only in every man but in every particle." This worldly, organic omniscience invests all natural beings with sovereign powers to rectify evil. For Emerson, indeed, nature's beneficent sovereignty was ultimately attested in the history of warfare, from "Savage war" that gives way to strife predicated on "limitations and a code," thus to yield in a utopian twentieth century "the finer quarrel of property, where the victory is wealth and the defeat of poverty."[55] We argue that *Gravity's Rainbow* militates against that progressive and romantic dream. Its counterpart, which Emerson surely never saw coming down the road, is the military-industrial state, figured in Pynchon's novel as the ghastly sovereignty of Dominus Blicero. No more can "nature" save, much less give justice to, those rightsless people streaming across Pynchon's post-Romantic Zone. The Zone defines the entirety of the storyworld; its topology figures that steady-state of emergency in the coming Cold War. What Walter Benjamin wrote in mid-1940 shortly before his own death defines that new reality: "The tradition of the oppressed teaches us that the 'state of exception' in which we live is the rule."[56]

Death rules.

THREE

FREEDOM

The Hanged Man in "reversed" position. Illustration by Pamela Colman Smith, from A. E. Waite, *The Pictorial Key to the Tarot* (1910).

In the first place, note how he's liberated from gravity. The Hanged Man drawn from the tarot deck in "reversed" position paradoxically floats. His foot impossibly supported by the rope binding him to the tau cross, he stands tiptoe on thin air, and even his hair defies gravity. Flip the page to restore gravity and see him in his proper, upside-down position. Then the Hanged Man will symbolize human potentials for acceptance, for inner harmony in relation to the divine, perhaps for the martyr's contemplative nonresistance and patience, aspects T. S. Eliot's *The Waste Land* (1922) references ironically.[1] For Slothrop, though, the card came out reversed and when this happens (for any card) during a tarot reading, it does not signify simple negation or contradiction. Instead it invites the client to meditate on his inability to realize the potentials, the perspective and wisdom that the card symbolizes. Reversal indicates that those boons will remain latent, repressed or thwarted, because something nags from below or behind, in the unconscious or the past, something he might work on after his reading. When the Hanged Man is reversed, it indicates blocked access to the martyr's contemplative acceptance of violence, his gravitas or wisdom enabling sympathetic communion with others. Reversed, the card signifies selfishness, alienation in the crowd and, according to A. E. Waite, in "the body politic."[2]

In the second place, it's clear that anything we might say about Slothrop's cards as "a reading" of his character or fortunes within or beyond the story-world would be based on incomplete information.[3] Unlike the full detailing of Weissmann's tarot eight pages later, we aren't told the "significator" that the diviner deliberately selected from the unshuffled deck to symbolize the client's query (also unknown) for Slothrop. Worse, we are told only two of the nine other cards the diviner selected from the newly shuffled deck and sequentially laid down, to form a cross of six, then beside it a vertical line of four, the cross providing symbolic recognitions of the client's current conditions, and the vertical line, his future hopes. From these the diviner would state potential meanings of the cards and their arrangement so that the client, or "querant," may decide on a pathway ahead. In Slothrop's case we are told only that the first card "covering his significator," limiting or conditioning the unknown query itself, was the 3 of Pentacles reversed, even after a "second try" (surely a bit of cheating). That reversed 3 of Pentacles would attach Slothrop's question to his "mediocrity in work" as well as to his "puerility, pettiness, and weakness"—traits that jibe with the Tyrone Slothrop we've come to know. We're told that each of his four "hopeful cards" also come from the deck "reversed," particularly the Hanged Man for his ninth and penultimate card, revealing his desires and fears. The reversals indicate that Slothrop's road promises a great deal of blockage and repression, consequences (it might seem) of Infant Tyrone's traumatic conditioning. Especially with the Hanged Man reversed, Slothrop's tarot reading casts one's "hopes and fears" for his story to climax in redemptive martyrdom as quite unlikely, particularly because the novel has abundantly presented a Slothrop deeply blocked, alone, and captive to his past. His "are the cards," our narrator says, "of a tanker and a feeb" with a "long and scuffling future" in "mediocrity" ahead of him. His story will end neither in comic "happiness" nor in the tragic irony of "redeeming cataclysm." Apparently Slothrop's post-romantic, foolish, and satirical end was already assured, despite what would have come up if the countdown of his tarot cards had reached the tenth and most powerfully predictive card.

Yet what, in the third place, ought readers *do* with such a presentation of divinatory practice? Elsewhere *Gravity's Rainbow* has shown or mentioned related practices, such as astrology, séances, Ouija, I Ching, automatic writing, trance speaking, Kabbalistic divination, and spirit possession. Characters take very seriously and even study scientifically the processes and results of these divinatory occasions, observing sessions and analyzing transcripts for telling patterns and data. Not that readers should be so serious in their turn. Still it can be useful to consider divination as a discursive practice, but one that defies—in relying on chance—modes of meaning making taken for granted in ordinary discourse and in the storytelling art. We are not so interested in speculating on what divination may reveal about characters and events in the storyworld, but we *are* interested in how divinatory discourse backlights narrative practices. Our interest is less in content than on formal matters and what they indicate about "chances for freedom."

Historical fiction and divination each speak about a world that does not exist but that stands in a near space-time relation to one's familiar world. One reckons with what occurred in the past, the other with what to do in the future. Each presents statements about otherness or alterity. Indeed, some forms of divination and any modern historical novel worth its price will specialize in providing access to others, to the mentalities of the dead. Each does this in order that clients or readers may know differently and, optimally, may realize better the conditions of their being in *this* world. Stated in terms of linguists' speech-act theory, fiction and divination both deal in performative, or illocutionary, statements. Simply by being said, their sentences index a change of state; they enable speakers and auditors to posit or project a world, one they might inhabit. What sets historical fiction and divination decisively apart, however, is that divinatory speech acts create meaning without intention. This is because they lack a personal origin, a responsible speaker accountable for the efficacy, much less the veracity, of each divinatory statement. In tarot the cards speak, in Ouija the planchette, in a séance it's the dead voicing through a medium. Practitioners of tarot, I Ching, and Ouija use aleatory methods to produce speech acts pertaining to an alterity—the future. Doing so by way of randomness and chance further underlines the apersonality and absence of intentionality of divinatory discourses used as means to meditate on rather than to predict the future. Moreover, that lack of intentionality takes us into a vexed and contested corner of twentieth-century thinking about language and art. For even as early as 1921 the linguist Edward Sapir insists that inarticulate vocalizations, such as a grunt from exertion or a scream in pain—when a "screaming comes across the sky"—are involuntary acts, thereby excluded (he argues) from the category of language and consigned to that of noise.[4] In *Speech Acts* (1969), John Searle similarly claims that any disembodied, decontextualized mark or sound must be excluded from the category of speech because there is no *communication* process involving an addresser and addressee sharing a code and context, and therefore no *intention* either.[5] Intention also had dogged literary analysis after W. K. Wimsatt and Monroe Beardsley argued in 1946 that critics were committing an elemental fallacy when they attributed authorial intention to literary works, which instead had to be treated as apersonal and autonomous meaning makers.[6] For a time the rule of "intentional fallacy" commanded critics to make sense of literary texts as if they were the supposedly autonomous art objects of high modernist practice and theory, while it also propped up disciplinary purists' desired barriers against psychoanalytical and sociopolitical interpretive work on literature. All of that was passé by the early eighties, for example when Walter Benn Michaels and Steven Knapp invoked Searle while arguing, in "Against Theory" (1982), that literary meaning requires one to posit a speaking subject and hence an intention, and that even if—following Roland Barthes and Michel Foucault—criticism should conceive of an "author-function," it would still have to regard *un sujet de l'énonciation* with its own operative intentions.[7] Thus for nearly a century, excepting the decades when Wimsatt-Beardsley apersonalist true believers held sway, ascribing intention to discursive practices has been a mainstay of literary-critical theory and practice.[8]

Lately however, claims for meaning in apersonalist, non-intentional meaning making are back, and the scholars giving it fresh attention are anthropologists. Studying second and third world peoples who employ divination in everyday life, not as a way to "see the future" but to make decisions taking them into their future, social anthropologists trained in linguistics have looked to the ways that speech act theory's foundational, universalized claims for the intentionality of enunciating subjects do not always hold up, particularly among non-Western peoples. Studying divinatory practices such as Afro-Cuban uses of Santeria or the practices of the Yoruba in West Africa, scholars have shown the ways divinatory discourses constitute an important method for people to produce meanings about the future, but do it outside the discursive forms common to the totalitarian and late capitalist dominions that otherwise determine their daily lives.[9] Typically their uses of aleatory methods in soothsaying diminish or displace control or authority for meanings: in the Yoruba ceremony Ifa, sixteen cowrie shells are tossed and shaken in a basket, then the diviner recites lengthy memorized verses determined by how the shells come to rest (with the open side up, or down), some verses running over a hundred lines and relating canonical tales and sayings of emissary deities (the Orishas) from whose mythic doings and traditional wisdom the attentive client alone must derive meaning and direction for her or his life. Field studies worldwide find that people turn to divination especially in times of critical decisions, traumas, and significant changes or catastrophes sweeping through households, communities, and nations. This work also finds that divination is a mode of non-authoritative decision making in such times, and that it benefits social cohesion because it depersonalizes responsibility for decisions, thus disabling processes of blame and retribution that would otherwise alienate people from one another and further disrupt and erode social solidarity just when it is most needed. In divination, moreover, propositions for action into the future are entertained and appreciated (or not) in the subjunctive rather than asserted in the indicative. In this regard researchers also find that divination is deeply pragmatic. Its uses and truth value rest wholly on how divination brings one up to and through a life change—to marry, move, take a job, select a cure for a disease—decisions whose efficacy can be tested and validated only in an immediate time frame, a time of now-and-next-week instead of in the frame of some distant and abstract telos or ideal.

A key aspect of divination's practical efficacy is that clients must judge its utility through a recursive process.[10] Indeed, as early as 1961 the anthropologist Victor Turner realized the importance of recursion when he described "the 'cybernetic' function of divination."[11] After a divination and a subsequent action, clients must look back, evaluate a prophecy's utility—gauge how efficaciously it enabled them to confront change—then adjust their prospects by scheduling another reading with the diviner. It's a business model with built-in sustainability! It also reminds us of a song early in part 3 of *Gravity's Rainbow*, "Sold on Suicide," about which the narrator remarks that because the singer may have omitted some reason or another for ending one's life, the prospective suicide must recursively "go back over the whole thing, meantime correcting mistakes and inevitable repetitions, and putting in new items that will surely have occurred to one, and—well, it's easy to see that the 'suicide' of the title might have to be postponed indefinitely!"[12] In many ways that's the kindly and generative, even if temporary, work that divinatory practices carry forward, recursively.

A previously overlooked motif that runs from early to final episodes of *Gravity's Rainbow*, divination represents ways of knowing that are radically different from modern science and stand outside a Western epistemology which organizes meaning, deciding, acting, progress, fortune, and history according to deeply entrenched individualistic, deterministic, and teleological frames. This epistemology is embedded in the West's long theological history and its chief idea of sovereign power in nation-states, what German National Socialist thinker Carl Schmitt named in the title of his 1922 study, *Political Theology*.[13] Crucially unlike Western religions in general, divinatory practices—the Yoruba uses of Ifa, for example—are not based in eschatology, in an ideal or myth of "last things" that imperatively orients one to ordinary things in the here and now.[14] In divinatory practices, it's never too late—to change course, or oneself. This is a view of divination Pynchon might have picked up from Victor Turner's work. In any case, in the way it is threaded all along this novel's arc, divinatory discourse does suggest radical alternatives to the system and its dominant cultural ideology and political theology, which imagines each individual as invested with sovereign, free, and seemingly plenary decision-making powers gathering him into the great project: the westward course of empire whose ending is the day of revelation and judgment. Pynchon's novel describes the price of accepting that social contract, of accepting a veil of invisibility and unspeakability drawn over the realities of "free" persons existing in manifestly unfree circumstances. Divination has long provided limited alternatives to modernity's unfree freedoms.

Judging from Pynchon's consistent scenes of divination in *Gravity's Rainbow*, we suppose he recognized in tarot, séance, trance speaking, and other divinatory methods an alternate approach to historical fiction, a potential to innovate on and perhaps subvert the form's determinist and teleological underpinnings. We aren't saying *Gravity's Rainbow* is an antirealist novel. Only that Pynchon's writing sought means to push back on the Western novel's commitment to determinist logics, on particular rules for presenting minds, and on ways of working out a story-within-a-story and of disorienting a story in relation to its ending. We think such narrative practices may be read as his effort to stay on the grid of historical fiction while also doing a bit of rewiring. His riffs on the form may be understood as vital aspects of his novel's place in the literary canon. Other Long Sixties fiction writers were realizing rather more extensively the attractions of nondeterministic composing practices: see William Burroughs's cut-up process that Julio Cortázar adopted for *Hopscotch* (1963), Robert Coover's hilariously recursive method in "The Babysitter" (1969), and Walter Abish's mechanical abecedarian process in *Alphabetical Africa* (1974). By such lights, we turn to some ways that *Gravity's Rainbow* humbly, and strikingly, committed storytelling to—

CHAPTER 10

Liberating Narration

The novel's first séance scene unfolds, in episode 5, at a many-roomed Victorian-style London building named Snoxall's. Roger and Jessica attend: she to sight-see the oddly assorted bunch of spiritualists, scientists, and military men; Roger to pick up microfilm of Slothrop's map and to get a firsthand aspect on work he's done for Milton Gloaming—statistical analyses of word-occurrence ratios and patterns in transcripts of paranormal events. Attendees at the séance this mid-December night include Gloaming; Selena Feldspath, there to contact the spirit of her deceased husband, Roland (his death a mystery); and Carroll Eventyr, the spirit medium seated opposite Selena. From the other side, in death's kingdom, Roland speaks through "the Control," a German named Peter Sachsa, killed by the blow of a police truncheon during a 1930 Berlin street demonstration. Roland's message, of no discernible solace to the grieving widow on this side of death's great wall, concerns *control*: how regulatory apparatuses were "put inside," supposedly giving systems such as apparently free financial markets their "own logic, momentum, style," and thus giving financial managers an insider's "illusion of control." Later, in conversation with Jessica, Gloaming characterizes Roland's message as that of "a classical paranoiac," and the narrator describes Roland, Eventyr, and séances as aspects of a wider wartime pathology "useful" for "the Firm to study."[1] Readers, however, will take from this scene the generalized problem of internal control mechanisms and processes: operant conditioning, or "guidance" mechanisms in the broadest sense, including their inescapable vulnerability to noise, chance, and accident. The episode also introduces the technology and protocols of divination, especially how the recent dead speak through an experienced spirit (Sachsa as "the Control"), then through a living "medium" (Eventyr), to the client (Selena).

The second séance comes in episode 19, a flashback to Berlin circa 1929–30, where Leni Pökler has just left her husband, Franz, and taken their infant daughter, Ilse, to the home of her lover, Peter Sachsa. There she finds a séance in progress: Sachsa (still among the living) is the medium and the client is an IG Farben managing director named Smaragd, eager for contact with the spirit of industrialist Walther Rathenau, the minister of reconstruction after World War I and the foreign minister when two proto-Nazis assassinated him on a Berlin street in 1922.[2] While Smaragd and colleagues "from the corporate Nazi crowd" seated around the séance table are obviously there for financial tips from the "prophet and architect of the cartelized state," the messages that Sachsa mouths for Rathenau are dissatisfying economically and politically to Smaragd and his Nazi friends. Rathenau's spirit tells them that their ideal of a natural, organic, cartelized marketplace is illusory, the actual market being little more than a "very clever robot" whose internal control mechanism is hardwired for death: "Death converted into more death." He understands that logic in reference to organic chemistry research efforts and manufacturing processes dedicated to "the impersonation of life," especially in polymerization, which produced all manner of new plastics during the twenties and thirties. To Rathenau this impersonation defines "the real nature," the logic and telos, "of control." The session ends with one of the Nazi attendees dismissing Rathenau with an anti-Semitic joke.

The novel supplements these episodes with an array of other information about divinatory processes, scattered through the text. Just before the narration flashes back to 1930 and the Sachsa séance, we are given background on Carroll Eventyr. We're told how he "feels a victim of his freak talent," which descended upon him years earlier when "all at once someone was speaking through Eventyr," some unknown "soul that took and used him."[3] This casts his trance speaking or spirit possession in the same mold as Pirate Prentice's freakish fantasist-surrogate abilities, figured in the novel's opening pages as a matter of his being used, as though he were merely Their tool. Episode 5 of part 2 further develops this view, as Slothrop, still awash in v-2 paperwork some three months after They sent him to Monaco, experiences a "reverie" of spirit occupation—by none other than Roland Feldspath. Slothrop's been deep in rocket guidance formulas, and it turns out Feldspath had worked as an aeronautical engineer "on control systems, guidance equations, feedback situations," and now from a position hovering five miles above the earth, his spirit has been awaiting contact with the living, though "not necessarily for the aimless entrances of boobs like Slothrop." ("Is *this* the one?," Roland asks. "Oh, dear. God have mercy.") He makes the best of it, explaining to Slothrop how "folks in power" have developed a kind of fanaticism (Schwärmerei) about control and "the deep conservatism of feedback," all in a quest for war mastery. When this visitation ends, Slothrop lacks any sense of a "clear symbol or scheme" to what he's heard, feeling only an "alkaline aftertaste" and a hardening of his alienation and psychological armor, a "self-sufficiency" that will soon carry him out of Monaco on a quest/journey he wishes to think is free, even after Feldspath's warning.[4]

Episodes in part 3 add to this emerging picture. At Peenemünde sometime in the early 1940s, for example, Franz Pökler recalls the séances Leni had attended and feels they offered a useful opportunity for IG Farben and Nazi leaders to bureaucratize "the other side." And Greta Erdmann recalls another Smaragd-sponsored séance, this one apparently at an IG Farben boardroom during the war's latter days, when she got a first glimpse of Imipolex G on a table around which attendees sat, "waiting for Blicero." This is a striking bit of information for any reader trying to detect lines of influence and power. It ties Weissmann/Blicero to military-industrial interests evidently conspiring toward such a moment for decades. It also ties in global interests, apparent from Rathenau's caution at the 1929–30 Berlin séance that beyond the German industries "[t]here is a link to the United States" as well as a "link to Russia," ties he thinks only Wimpe the Verbindungsmann understands.[5] And the information loops us back to that initial séance in episode 5, where Dominus Blicero, Lord Death, first appeared—in Peter Sachsa's enunciation of Feldspath's thoughts, spoken by spirit-captured Eventyr at Snoxall's. Having "been brought up a Christian, a Western European, believing in the primacy of the 'conscious' self and its memories," Eventyr finds the séance "abnormal" and deeply troubling.[6]

These supernatural byways and signposts are helpful in any reader's detective quest through the *Gravity's Rainbow* storyworld. Equally important is the divinatory process for acquiring that information. The modes of spirit possession and trance speaking gathered in the séance take a particular discursive form: multiple intermediaries each "speak" at a further, or deeper, remove. The client seeking access to the spirit of a deceased person engages a medium who, from this side, accesses on the other side a capable spirit, the control, who translates and transmits the deceased's message back up the line, through the entranced medium, to the client. Séance discourse has to cross or translate an ontological boundary that divides living persons from spirits of the dead, and even in the world of the living and the world of the dead the discourse must be transmitted expertly, by "sensitives"—the "medium" on this side, the "control" on the other. The dead spirit's discourse is mediated by, sequenced in, this recursive structure. This is how *Gravity's Rainbow* represents it, while also marking for us a certain tradition or *genealogical* consistency: Peter Sachsa, who was a medium on this side, became a control on the other. But whether the speaker is a control or a medium, the process involves knowledge of or access to another's mind. That's a supernatural power that novelistic discourse traditionally accomplishes using techniques of first-person narration or third-person with internal focalization. At the same time realist conventions limit the practice: characters (even narrators, if participants in the storyworld) aren't allowed to access other characters' thoughts, memories, or fantasies. *Gravity's Rainbow* chucks that convention in its opening pages, with the introduction of fantasist-surrogate Pirate Prentice. And, once liberated from that conventional restraint, the narration gives us, with an entirely straight face, séances, sodium amytal sessions accessing Slothrop's fantasies, spirit possession, and more.

Consider a moment near the end of episode 14. Frans van der Groov stands before an assembly of dodo birds on the island of Mauritius.[7] The surviving remnant of a once-great population presently subjected to random slaughter by Dutch colonialists, these flightless birds, so easily hunted, are rapidly approaching the zero point of extermination. Now having "waddled in awkward pilgrimage," they stand before Frans, he thinks, dreaming of baby Jesus. So, is he "witnessing a miracle: a Gift of Speech . . . a Conversion of the Dodoes" to Christianity, thus to the logic of messianic sacrifice? Or is the moment his projective fantasy? Either way, their "Conversion" happens on several levels: from mere creatures to beings with "souls," thus from narrated *objects* of van der Groov's story to "dreaming" or narrating *subjects* whose religious conversion he (thinks he) is accessing; this leads to their final conversion into dead beings, but now at least with savable souls. Yet in this scene Frans himself is already the object of Katje's genealogical recollections, even while, throughout episode 14, Katje herself is being filmed by a "secret cameraman" (under the authority of Osbie Feel), who is making a brief clip to be used in a further act of conversion or control, namely the operant conditioning of Grigori. The octopus's motor reflexes will then behave themselves on the beach at Monaco, where Slothrop is supposed to think he saves Katje from an octopus attack, which we realize loops back thematically to those dodoes, whose "conversion" in the presence of a baby Jesus will not, alas, save them from extinction.[8] All of this comes under the authority of an omniscient narrator's voice—itself, as throughout much of *Gravity's Rainbow*, problematic, as we'll see.

This example of deeply and recursively sequenced narrative moments is complicated yet by no means the hardest one to follow in a novel rather full of similar instances. Take episode 9, just after the Pointsman-Spectro episode revealing Pointsman's pedophilic fantasies and bus-station girl hunting. Episode 8 ends with him at St. Veronica's Hospital uttering, sotto voce, desires not for "an octopus" but a little girl—"*Damn it*. One, little, *Fox!*" Then in a neat and telling segue, episode 9 opens with Jessica's partially wakeful thoughts while lying in bed, realizing that "Something's stalking through the city" and it is "gathering up slender girls, fair and smooth as dolls, by the handful," a subconscious recognition registering our worst apprehensions about the pedophilic Pointsman.[9] Then, jolted from her bed by the distant blast of a v-2, Jessica wanders to a window as Roger sleeps. She lights a cigarette, thinks of rockets, the war, and Roger's statistical work, and recalls talking with him about that work. At that point the narration passes into Roger's consciousness and his memories of applying Poisson's equation to the dispersal of v-2 strikes on London, of a conversation he had with Pointsman, of another with the Reverend Paul de la Nuit (who discusses randomization in Roman methods of divination), of still another with Prentice, and another with Jessica, who seemed to "know so exactly what Roger meant to say." On that (vaguely paranormal) cue, we revert back to Jessica at the window as she lights another cigarette, and tellingly "shivers" at the mere thought of Pointsman, a man—she thinks—who "could as well torture people as dogs and never feel their pain."[10] Indeed. The episode ends with her at the window, Roger still sleeping. But it has done a remarkable thing: Jessica's past-tense thoughts about Roger have enabled that pass into sleeping Roger's mind, his conversion from a flat, grammatical object of Jessica's thought into a mentally deep, thinking subject—yet without any formal signposting in the text. It just happens.

Classical narrative theory is grounded in a distinction between who speaks and who perceives. This difference leads to a rule formulated by Susan Lanser: A can tell what B saw and felt, but in the moment of seeing and feeling B cannot know that A is (or will be) relating it or for that matter how efficaciously, truly, A does so.[11] *Gravity's Rainbow* cuts itself loose from these rules for narration's foundational, or "natural," practice of integrating focalizations, particularly as Pynchon's writing recursively relates the focalizations, one into another into another. Take the entirety of episode 14, rather than just the isolated moment of the dodoes' "conversion." Like others we might take up, this episode interlinks multiple focalizations. It begins with a sentence from the omniscient narrator, to which the last words of the episode will loop back—a technique employed also in episodes 5, 9, and 10 in part 1. But the narration in episode 14 quickly leaves behind the omniscient view for that of Osbie Feel's man filming Katje Borgesius on that December day. From the cameraman's focalization—literally, through the camera's viewfinder—we are delivered into Katje's consciousness, focalizing through her as she moves about and remembers episodes of sadomasochistic sexual domination at Captain Blicero's rocket battery in Holland during the autumn. Her focalized recollections initiate still another pass, into Blicero's mentality as he reckons with v-2 rocketry in the context of memories of his service in German Southwest Africa, putting down the 1922 Herero uprising. His focalized memories barely invoke the figure of the Herero boy Enzian, also subjected to the man's sadomasochistic games, which then enables a further pass into the consciousness of young Gottfried, the latest "boy." This invokes Gottfried's mock sister, Katje, to whom we briefly return before the narration makes a further pass backward in time and into the consciousness of Dutch colonizer Frans van der Groov and then, as we've observed, into dodo bird consciousness (which is both an epistemological and ontological breach), before the episode in effect crashes these nested-box focalizations and returns us to what initially seems to be the cameraman's view. Except that it is no longer *his*, because by then the episode has (without saying so) moved forward in storytime, and someone is screening the film for Grigori in his glass fishtank.

Following those complex transitions—and episode 14 is still more complicated than the above summary—requires a reader with either a great deal of patience and skill, or a certain intuitive willingness to roll with the text's free transitions, or some mode of stoned consciousness—or perhaps all three playing in combo. As Samuli Hägg wisely puts it, these "mind-to-mind" moments, which seem illicit, beg for a reader actually "to play the text to comprehend it, even in the most basic sense of figuring out the relationships" between the text's sequenced or nested-box views.[12] By our count there are six major recursively related passes in this episode, though at times the text will loop us back to a prior one, for instance from Holland back to Katje's mind in London, before leaping back to the island of Mauritius in the seventeenth century and Frans's view. At different moments in the episode, however, we find ourselves out there in the wild blue, four or five minds away from the omniscient narrator's position we started from, and just as we get used to it the narrative will loop us back. There is little symmetry, much less any spatiotemporal stability, to these recursive changes, which leave one wondering, Where and when am I?, and Who am I seeing and thinking with? One reason for that confusion is that the narration neglects any of the conventional signpostings, the phrases that attribute thinking or seeing, as in "she recalled" or "he sees," "it occurred to her" or "this reminded him of"—phrases that normally mark ontological or epistemological passages in narrative time-space. Often *Gravity's Rainbow* will signal the jump-cut with the merest sensory trace affecting a character, as when we are told that Frans's gun, his *haakbus*, was warm from killing birds so that he feels "its heat on his cheek"—a phrase that immediately begins our focalization through Frans's consciousness. Or the subtle signal will be merely a repeated word or phrase. Nothing in Pynchon's writing gives novice readers more fits than these liberties he takes with long-standing narrative conventions.

Add to that the ways that these shifts of focus in *Gravity's Rainbow* refuse conventional sense making in still another way. From the moment we jump from the view of that "secret cameraman" into Katje's consciousness, then into Blicero's, and Gottfried's, and back for a moment to Katje's before leaping into Frans's consciousness, then into the dodo's, and back out—we are making moves and transitions previously prohibited, that is, unless the fiction has constructed a storyworld whose people have evolved quite novel mental capacities or developed fantastic scientific devices. Luc and Steve cannot know, nor can the characters know, other minds, especially those of the dead. Nonetheless, with Katje Borgesius we access the memories of her ancestor Frans van der Groov, deceased two centuries earlier. Sci-fi and paranormal stories accomplish such leaps by imagining them in terms of some newly devised or alternately evolved capacity, understood as the realism of the future or of some alternative world. Pynchon's historical novel makes no such future fiction or fantasy fiction claim, yet it does take—somewhat seriously, or just usefully—the discursive practices of the séance as one model for the mental calisthenics required of ordinary readers. Pirate Prentice's fantasist surrogacy is another model, as are trance speaking and tarot. And the ways that *Gravity's Rainbow* anchors narration so thoroughly in historical realities, even in the deepest realistic minutiae of ordinary life such as popular programs on 1940s London radio or the taste of a Thayer's slippery elm throat lozenge, only increase the bright light that realism turns upon the paranormal, or irreal, effects the narration also achieves.

Pynchon's focalizer-to-focalizer (or mind-to-mind) shifts do violate both narrative convention and common sense. Yet other than a few pecksniffian guards in the house of realist fiction, we know of no one who really minds the liberties *Gravity's Rainbow* takes. Years of bringing this novel before nonprofessionalized (student) readers have taught us that the dizzying transitions and irrational jump-cuts do require some attentiveness and getting used to but soon seem "natural" and even rather exhilarating. Soon enough, the question turns to what the techniques themselves are doing or revealing. The easy yet unsatisfying answer to that question would be to nod our assent with the character Edwin Treacle, who considers Their keen interest in séances and other divinatory and paranormal events and then advises a cynical Roger Mexico: "There are peoples—these Hereros for example—who carry on business every day with their ancestors. The dead are as real as the living. How can you understand them without treating both sides of the wall of death with the same scientific approach?"[13] Two things trouble that rhetorical question. The first is that Treacle (as his name suggests) begins by merely offering the kind of hyper-sweet nostalgia that moderns feel for so-called primitive consciousness. The second is how that nostalgia leans right into, in fact that kind of sugary discourse always seems to buttress, the "scientific" justification—for pushing knowledge past frontiers, conquering them all, space for example and even the frontier of other minds, and finally death. "Jeepers, Mr. Information!," we should all exclaim. But we don't. For if the novel's description of the séances means anything alongside Prentice's utility as a fantasist surrogate or the uses of Slothrop's sodium amytal–induced dreams, it is that They are engaged in scientific projects to instrumentalize paranormal practices, even to *weaponize* them. Slothrop, for example: when Sir Marcus Scammony wipes our scuffling hero from his conscience in an offhand reminder to Clive Mossmoon, we learn that after Slothrop's conditioning at St. Veronica's in London and in the Monaco hotel rooms, he was "sent out [into the Zone] to destroy the blacks, and it's obvious he won't do the job."[14] So if incorporating divination, trance speaking, and spirit possession into the military-industrial regime weren't the objective, then those military-industrial types—ss men like Blicero, Nazi industrialists, English officers in parade dress, IG Farben and PISCES men—would not be gathered so eagerly around séance tables in London and Berlin. The issue is domination. As They see it, the divinatory process and discourse seems to access a frontier, a "Free Zone" with the fences down or yet to be built, and They mean to colonize it. Death rules, as we've argued, and on the other side is a charisma They mean to routinize.

This way of reading divination alongside the mind-to-mind jump-cuts in *Gravity's Rainbow* ascribes a *potentially* liberating power to both kinds of discourse. We need to be cautious, though, and not only about the lure of nostalgia and charisma. For the wider problem is whether these somewhat liberated narrative techniques connect to a politics, a practice, capable of addressing the alienated individualism, the thwarted prospects of nurturing and community, and the deathward trajectory of all the plots *Gravity's Rainbow* otherwise represents. The novel's dark ending gives no hope for such a politics; it gives only song. Still, Pynchon does free his book from some prohibitions, especially in its deployments—for a narrative and ideological critique—of what had only recently been judged legally punishable obscene and pornographic representations, and in its irrepressible dark humor, right down to songs like "Red River Valley" (sing along now: "Down this toilet they say you are flushin'— / Won'tchew light up and set fer a spell?").[15] By those lyrical lights, who among us would give in to final despair and the deadly sin of acedia? The sociopolitical ideas implicit in this novel's references to and scenes of tarot readings, astrological divination, fantasist surrogacy, trance speaking, spirit possession, and out-of-body journeys (by Lyle Bland), no matter how whacky all of them may seem or be, include at least the following three. First, the persistent suggestion that models for intersubjective communication and solidarity may exist outside routinized channels. Second, that the very apersonality and non-intentionality of the divinatory processes of non-Western societies might have something to teach first world people. And third, that people might also learn from those practices' acausal, nondeterminist, and recursive ways of knowing what it is right and just to do. (Here, sing choruses of the never-ending "Sold on Suicide.")

Before turning from these supernatural means, we should also reconsider Walther Rathenau's remarks at the Berlin séance. He enjoins the skeptics: "ask two questions: First, what is the real nature of synthesis? And then: what is the real nature of control?"[16] Pynchon's innovative practices of focalizing not only set a rhythm of unconventional and dizzying transitions that challenge and surprise even experienced readers. They may also, despite Their colonizing efforts, suggest needs and even potentials for counterdiscourses against synthesis and control. In *The Final Frontier*, a remarkable interdisciplinary study of aerospace industrialism in relation to *Gravity's Rainbow*, Dale Carter shows that even while the "Rocket State" synthesized production by integrating horizontally, extending its octopus-like reach into far-flung international markets, nonetheless its fundamental mode of organizing control over production was hierarchical integration. The ideal "organization man" of this regime, as Pynchon well knew from his stint with Boeing, was the worker who knew his place and role in a sub-sub-unit. Real power ascended vertically. Researching the American aerospace industry circa 1958–1963, Carter found that Project Mercury "provided work for 12 prime contractors, 75 first order subcontractors, over 1,500 second tier, and around 7,200 third tier suppliers." And he found that "between 1961 and 1973 the Apollo program drew on the resources of at least 20,000 and possibly as many as 80,000 firms at all levels."[17] These figures only describe the space program, its data publicly available because NASA's nonmilitary budgeting and resourcing was open. The military aerospace budgets, especially for highly secretive weaponry like the BOMARC and Minuteman missile programs once employing Pynchon, were far greater and the programs much more extensively and recursively networked. Huge corporate entities like Boeing, Lockheed, Teledyne, General Electric, and Northrop interfaced closely with the military, and the resulting corporate hierarchy was much more finely reticulated, which explains why the Raketenstadt, or Rocket City, in *Gravity's Rainbow* needs a fantastically extended elevator to whisk employees up and down to its uncountable levels, and why the equally fantastical "Toiletship" includes bulkhead after bulkhead laterally dividing its interior space into smaller and smaller worker cubicles troped (hilariously, especially for anyone who's done such labor) as toilet stalls. This then is the nature of synthesis and control. And it's why Pynchon's trippy uses of recursion and mind-to-mind shifts are more than playful postmodernist breaches of old storytelling conventions. At once they mimic and disrupt narrative authority, disrupt both "nature" and "the real" of late capitalism by confounding them with the irreal and the supernatural.

The rocket's parabolic flight path, arcing from the first to the last page, tropes the arc of *Gravity's Rainbow*: with a beginning or launch, the middle or *Brennschluss* of Slothrop's and the Counterforce's feeble lurches at freedom, and an end one instant before the impact on the Orpheus Theater. That arc is also the text's principal sign of Dominus Blicero. And about him or it, our narrator advises: "nothing can really stop the Abreaction of the Lord of the Night unless the Blitz stops, rockets dismantle, the entire film runs backward: faired skin back to sheet steel back to pigs to white incandescence to ore, to Earth. But the reality is not reversible. Each firebloom, followed by a blast then by sound of arrival, is a mockery (how can it not be deliberate?) of the reversible process: with each one the Lord further legitimizes his State."[18]

Gravity's Rainbow enacts a mockery of that "mockery." And it pays heed to that passage's main trope: the hysteron proteron, or reversing figure. This figure plays a familiar event sequence *backward*, invoking the law of cause and effect by turning it around. It's a rare trope, one to which Richard Lanham's classic *Handlist of Rhetorical Terms* (2nd ed., 1991) rather gives the boot, naming it one of the literary "vices," thus following the lead of Renaissance scholar George Puttenham, who thought it was a deformity and classed it with figures of the "preposterous," the "absurd," and the "intolerable." Pynchon does tolerably well with it, though. In the text, hysteron proteron figures crop up fifty-nine times—unless we've missed a few. And there's far more at stake than when Kurt Vonnegut makes absurdist or black humorist uses of reversing figures in *Slaughterhouse-Five*, as when Billy Pilgrim comes "unstuck in time" and watches guns or "tubes" that "suck" bullets back out of dead men's bodies, which return to life.[19] In the passage quoted above Pynchon's narrator frames the backward-running process—faired metal back to pig iron back to earth—as proof of a causal worldview, reactionary desires, and totalitarian politics whose ne plus ultra is a fantasy of world dominion. For ordinary people, its cruel slap-in-the-face recognition is that weird hysteron proteron, that scream of an arriving supersonic missile preposterously and intolerably *trailing* the blast. What freedom is there under that arcing sign of the rocket, and that terminus, witnessed as the very reification of terror?

What *Gravity's Rainbow* does, then, is to deploy the reversing figure against Western ways of knowing and of storytelling that depend on causality and reversal. The novel's satirical energies target the narratives of reversal troped in the core knowledges of modern science and philosophy, Laplacean physics and Cartesian metaphysics. Both are understood in the novel as leaning on the same reductive plot: positing an atomized or monadic physical state or biological self, then reasoning knowledge and civilization progressively, causally, from that origin and figuring deterministic human rationality as that creation's crown, in dominion over what the novel's narrator names "lovable but scatterbrained Mother Nature."[20] The role of hysteron proteron in that dominion is equally clear. Reversibility and repetition are fundamental ways of verifying an empirical equation or scientific process, of revealing proof, and mastery; therefore each proof upholds the monolith of Western knowledge, itself a kind of reversible macro-narrative. The novel's principal characterization of that verification process is the rocket. But also and more problematically, Slothrop: an atomized man, a lost nomadic monad as the novel concludes, but maybe (we'll see) no longer a rocketman.

The reading of stories depends on a cognate process. While the order of events in a story proceeds in a one-two or proteron-hysteron order, interpretation typically works backward from effects to causes in order to realize the hysteron proteron logic that is plot. So foundational and conventional is this retrospectivity of reading practice that, as Hayden White puts it (para-phrasing Benedetto Croce), "Where there is no narrative" to instantiate cau-sality in that way, "there is no history."[21] Initially this is as much Slothrop's job as it is the reader's; and for so many other important characters—Points-man chief among them—this is the only proper detective work during the novel's first half. The question for the second half of *Gravity's Rainbow* is whether narration, itself so committed to teleology, can find a means to ar-rest—before it is too late—the deadly telos of Western history and especially its traditions of knowing time by working backward from time's eschato-logical denouement, or untying the judgment which paradoxically ties up all loose threads. In a work that both presents and theorizes a politics of bond-age and discipline, the issue is whether narration can free itself, find some kind of errant and truly novel potential outside the tradition of Laplacean physics and Cartesian metaphysics leagued in a chilling Axis pact with forms of Pavlovian, behaviorist, and cybernetic sciences in a seemingly unstoppable regime of "control."

But how can a writer mount an effective, liberating resistance to that domi-nant way of knowing, especially in a novel, an aesthetic form (like narrative film) deeply committed to seriality and determinist plotting? Any wholesale disruption of form would hazard the novel's intelligibility for the sake of its historico-political critique, or "theme." What we find instead is that our text builds momentum for its case in scores of moments. As, for example, when Jessica recalls first having sex with Roger and how "she came twice before cock was officially put inside cunt, and this is important to both of them though neither has figured out why, exactly."[22] Readers do, because of course that reversal of cause and effect, of intercourse and orgasm or stimulus and response, replicates what's going on with the rocket, in Pointsman's labs, and in a traumatized Europe that has gone "transmarginal" under the sign of war. The ways that Roger and Jessica's story is given to us—in some of the most conventional, continuous, realistic portions of narration in the novel—sucks readers into the vortex of romance conventions and may indicate not only why the subplot dooms Roger and Jessica's relationship but also why early critics were attracted, nostalgically, to their story.

One alternative would be to read their story as symptomatic evidence of their desires to be overmastered by texts, by plots, beginning with their Hollywood-style "cute meet." Not the least of these plot figures is the inani-mate "text" named the "v-2." This may be why many of the really madcap fantasies in *Gravity's Rainbow* unfold under the sign of hysteron proteron. Rollo Groast, for example, desires to recognize his own central nervous sys-tem in "some surviving cell-memory" of the primitive, "retro-colonial" cen-tral nervous system.[23] Or: In the German actor Rudolf Klein-Rogge's star-ring role in Fritz Lang's film *Doktor Mabuse, der Spieler* (1922), Franz Pökler thinks he witnesses onscreen "the savage throwback, the charismatic flash" whirling him back "toward myth" as a way of understanding his own sadomasochistic drives—a moment that clearly parodies modernist writers' trust in what T. S. Eliot named "the mythic method." Similarly, at the Dutch rocket battery, Katje, Gottfried, and Weissmann grotesquely enact a "formal, rationalized version" of the Grimm brothers' fairytale, which itself derives from older versions of the Hansel and Gretel story.[24] As for Weissmann's progress into the Blicero identity, validating his increasingly atavistic realizations of sadistic domination, the narrator will name his plot also as a reversion "to some ancestral version of himself . . . back into the pre-Christian earth we fled across." Note also the subtle work of that "we," inter-implicating the book's audience in the very atavism driving Blicero's plot.[25]

So dizzying and challenging are the novel's mind-to-mind shifts, linked as they are to chronological jump-cuts, that finally our narrator relents and accedes to readerly desire: "You will want cause and effect. All right." And since the proteron-hysteron ordering is what "you" think is needed to master the text, causality is what "you" get. But—in the form of a convoluted account summarizing how Miklos Thanatz is saved from drowning after he slips overboard into a storm-tossed Baltic Sea from which he's rescued just in time by a Polish undertaker. This tale then launches a digression on Ben Franklin, lightning, and what surviving lightning-struck persons know about rates of change and reversal, a "discontinuity in the curve of life" so total that it seems the apotheosis of hysteron proteron: "do you know what the rate of change *is* at a cusp? *Infinity*, that's what! A-and right across that point, it's *minus* infinity! How's that for sudden change, eh? Infinite miles per hour changing at the same speed *in reverse*. . . . That's getting hit by lightning."[26] If readers are thinking about the obsessional qualities of moments like this one, which so digresses from the details of how Thanatz was saved, they are on to something. That Polish undertaker out in his boat in an electrical storm surely parodies the well-known moment in *Moby-Dick* when the obsessional Ahab seizes the *Pequod*'s twin lightning rods in his hands to tempt fate, which leaves him "branded," like a whip scar or a "birthmark on him from crown to sole."[27] Obsession is thus character trait, theme, and narrative practice, as *Gravity's Rainbow* imagines a world whose science and instrumental fantasies have enshrined absolutely the "preposterous" and "intolerable" logic of hysteron proteron, of a perverse determinism seen as plotting humankind's final reckoning.

As the novel spins toward its ending, characters fantasize the potential for *return*. Slothrop thinks wistfully about "a way to get back," return "home" to an America that betrayed him decades ago. Among the Hereros, a group that calls itself the Erdschweinhöhle fantasizes a (suicidal) return to their earthly mother. And child murderer Margherita Erdmann, whose name encodes the regressive Germanic fantasy of earthiness, the Nazis' ideal of *Blut und Boden* (blood and soil) defining a mythical Aryan identity, mythifies her murders by casting herself as the Kabbalistic Shekhinah in the tenth and last of the Sephiroth, or levels of being, figured as a messianic bride who gathers in all the shattered pieces of being in an eschatological climax or cosmic hysteron proteron, while along the way making mere robotic shells, Qlippoth, of her devotees.[28] Her subplot incisively figures imperial colonization as a reverse flow, or expropriation, even of those core mythic materials sacred to the collective mentality of those the Reich seeks to exterminate. Reversal also marks what it means to integrate with the rocket, whose countdown toward launch—as Fritz Lang devised it for his 1929 film, *Die Frau im Mond*—assumes the same mock mystical fantasia.[29] So while *Gravity's Rainbow* cannot live and prosper as a novel without linear plot lines and causality, it insists at the same time that earthly survival demands the disruption and abnegation of the determinist logics bringing humanity, represented in those Orpheus Theater film fans, to the brink of catastrophe.

The changes *Gravity's Rainbow* works on conventional third-person narration are also consistent with that politics. Even some early reviews and scholarly articles remarked without going into much detail how this book's narration seems to modulate, helter-skelter, into a great range of voices that destabilize, even if they do not upend, conventional third-person authority. Here also there's a kind of shattering and scattering. Whether objective or personalized, omniscient or limited, the uniquely individuated and masterly third-person narrators from Austen to James to Faulkner established and sustained a *coherence*, a set of individuated semantic, stylistic, and sociolinguistic features both pliable and always identifiable, because vital to ongoing recognition and success in the literary marketplace. Pynchon's short stories and two novels leading up to *Gravity's Rainbow*, all of them in the third person (to date, he hasn't written a first-person fiction), follow the trajectory of the gifted young novelist developing that coherence, or voice. Then the third novel disrupted that trajectory and the long history of his medium. This is why scholars eager to define postmodern narrative practices or to develop poststructuralist theories of narrative often turn to moments in Pynchon's novel as demonstrations. In terms of third-person narrative authority, his book seems to have tossed a bomb into the House of Fiction, for it has a voice—perhaps schizoid—inhabited, defined, by a multitude. By now it's a critical commonplace that *Gravity's Rainbow* levels narrative omniscience and its presumptive hierarchy by giving readers a narrator riffing on, modulating among, ventriloquizing within, an extraordinary range of voices: the mathematician, aeronautics expert, and engineer—about whose fields (as we now know) Pynchon had written copy for Boeing's in-house publications; the behavioral and the neo-Freudian psychologists his studying had taught him to "do," along with the linguist and cryptographer and lexicographer (with mini-dissertations on "ass backwards" and "shit 'n' shinola"); then, persistently throughout the text, the historian, whether the sober, frank spokesman for plain fact as in TV documentaries like *Victory at Sea*, or the optimistic, folksy old-timer of countless Western fictions and films, or even the professional film historian (thanks in part to Siegfried Kracauer's work); and many more, a great miscellany, including the musicologist and lyricist, the tarot reader and paranormal aficionado, the European tour guide (thanks to the Baedeker books), the action-hero comic book narrator, and the street-savvy guy who offers hustler lingo, doper jargon, and sixties underground newspaper–style obscene and pornographic humor. And don't forget Mr. Information, whose brief visitations mock the entire assembly cataloged above. The shifts in this extraordinary pastiche of voices occur horizontally across the entire fabric of Pynchon's text, within episodes, at times on the same page, or even in the same paragraph.

Equally powerful changes occur vertically. Conventional third-person realist fictions structure authority top-down. Typically, the omniscient narrator who speaks from without and focalizes through characters has more force and truth value than the characters themselves. And as we've said, in conventional third-person mode, these figures—narrators and characters, and one or some of their minds—occupy different orders of being or ontological frames that shall not overlap. Pynchon repeatedly bends and breaches the frames, which is why narrative theorists reach into Pynchon's novel for examples. What has most interested them are the ways Pynchon's narration seems to put third-person narrative authority under attack (if not deconstructionist "erasure"). Critics have noted how the narrator (narrators?) will make and then debunk a claim, leaving unresolved "whether it is the narrator or its audience that is being fooled" or otherwise manipulated.[30] Equally disruptive to narrative authority are the ways that the narrator(s) will trot out pseudo-experts—figures such as film specialist Mitchell Prettyplace, Mickey Wuxtry-Wuxtry, an unnamed "spokesman for the Counterforce," and Steve Edelman—who speak from within the storyworld yet also from positions equal (or superior?) to that of our (no longer?) omniscient narrator. Readers have also remarked on Pirate Prentice's peculiar powers of fantasist surrogacy as an instance of a character manifesting and so perhaps metafictionally commenting on what omniscient narrators do when they focalize.[31] They've also noted the ways that the narrator's speech seems so infected by other characters' jargon and colloquialisms as to trouble deeply, if not to erase entirely, the putatively airtight ontological boundary separating them.[32] We do find that infectiousness, but see it as subtle, not world shaking.

Having a word-searchable text, since 2012, enables us to study more closely what the narration actually achieves at the level of semantics. Take, for example, one of the earliest appearing and most sustained verbal tics: that little stutter in the conjunction "A-and," typically used at the beginning of a sentence or clause. A computer-assisted census reveals what readers probably suspect, namely that this is one of Slothrop's characteristic speech tics in his dialogues with others and in his inner speech. In part 1, it is ascribed almost entirely to him, the only exception being Roger Mexico, who uses it in moments of inner speech.[33] Excepting Roger, the text ascribes "A-and" only to Americans: Major Marvy, Clayton Chiclitz, Alfonso Tracy, Seaman Bodine, Albert Krypton, and Skippy. By the middle of the novel "A-and" has found its way into songs like "Sold on Suicide," "Victim in a Vacuum," and "Bright Days." Then, in the last hundred or so pages, it has migrated into the narrator's discourse, as in "do you know what the rate of change *is* at a cusp? *Infinity*, that's what! A-and right across the point, it's *minus* infinity!"; or again in "A-and wait'll those *kazoos* come on!"[34] We've found the same tendency for other exclamations, interjections, and colloquialisms like "sez," "jeepers," "Ace" (as a mode of American English slang address to another), and "hmm"—all slang and vernacular that have installed themselves in the narrator's speech by part 4. These verbal symptoms loosely manifest the shift from conditions of paranoia in the novel's first half to accelerating conditions of anti-paranoia in the second. Put differently, at first the authority, control, and connectedness of seemingly everything gathers securely around the omniscient narrator's position, voiced in moments of colloquial humor but generally in standard, university-educated English. But then that voice gives way to a flattening and decoupling of meaning making, signaled by how certain semantic features have infectiously migrated from characters' inner speech and dialogue into the narrator's discourse, which is not discredited so much as it is democratized. Indeed it may be one of the novel's darkest ironies that this democratization occurs at the same time Pynchon's storyworld screams toward total demolition—commencing with passages like our narrator's relation of Alfonso Tracy demonstrating to Lyle Bland the quirky malfunctioning of a batch of pinball machines he's just bought, particularly the "Folies-Bergères" model. Play begins with a "*Chunng*, boing there goes the ball just missing a high-scoring hole, hmm looks like a permanent warp there ahnnnggghk knocks a flasher worth 1000 but only 50 lights up on the board— 'You *see*?' Tracy screams as the ball heads like a rock for the bottom, outside chance get it with a flipper *zong* flipper flips the other fucking *way*, and the board lights up TILT."[35] It's a stunningly vernacular moment from the days of pinball, now gone.

With this novel's proliferating obscenities and profanities there's something just a bit different going on. Take George Carlin's seven infamous "filthy words" (fuck, shit, piss, tits, cunt, cocksucker, and motherfucker), supplemented by Lenny Bruce's additional two (ass and balls). It will surprise no

Gravity's Rainbow reader that, excepting the words "cocksucker" and "moth-erfucker," which are absent, Carlin's "filthy words" are scattered (with others like asshole and cock) liberally through the book. What's notable is that from the first to last pages these words show up in characters' inner speech and voiced dialogue, as well as in the narrator's discourse. And there's the hitch. That ubiquity through all levels of the narrative discourse breaches a long-standing convention. For even as the twentieth-century novel began opening narrative art to forbidden words, it did so by maintaining a membrane of pro-priety around the narrator's discourse. In the *Lady Chatterley's Lover* trial, for example, defense counsel pointed out that the obscene words cropped up in the characters' dialogues, Mellors to Constance Chatterley for example, while in a kind of gentlemen's agreement with bourgeois readers the narrator (and therefore "Lawrence") had responsibly wrapped itself in a kind of pro-phylaxis against all such verbal filth. *Gravity's Rainbow* doesn't just pierce, it destroys that membrane against vulgarity and obscenity; it *profanes* the omniscient narrator's imperial position. There's nothing quite like it in Long Sixties American fiction outside of Burroughs's novels. Even Mailer, in *Why Are We in Vietnam?* (1967), finesses this prohibition by having his narrator—the expletive-inclined Texas good ol' boy named DJ—speak of himself in the third person, Henry Adams–style. *Gravity's Rainbow* simply refuses the con-ventional novel's grant of prestige and power to the omniscient narrator's dis-cursive position in the text, and most particularly it declines the narrator's authority to reinstantiate propriety, to enact a regulatory control or dominion over speech. Perhaps Pynchon's refusal to play by that rule factored into the Pulitzer board members' 1974 decision to reject the fiction jury's unanimous recommendation of *Gravity's Rainbow* for the prize. By any view of it, here was a novel that liberally used vulgar, "filthy" language, and that was bad enough. Yet throughout the novel, we witness an omniscient narrator whose discourse the profane world has entirely, even proudly, infected. For evidence of that seeming transgression, one needn't have read more than fifty or a hun-dred pages into this book.

That "Pynchon" foresaw the likelihood of such summary judgments is clear from the striking metafictional moment near the novel's ending, brack-eted in the middle of a paragraph in which the seemingly authorial voice of a Counterforce "Spokesman" admits to a *Wall Street Journal* reporter that he is "a traitor." What follows is his confession to acts of subversive and vio-lent resistance in a revolutionary cell, the speaker's "initiation" to it occurring in urban subway "tunnels," with a chase and capture of multiple "enemies," when, he says, "I tasted my first blood" and commenced the "years of grease and passage, 1966 and 1971." Most striking about this moment, beyond how it names the years when Pynchon was writing the novel, is that this poten-tially authorial, metafictional voice—a unique instance in the novel—identifies the revolutionaries' own bloodthirstiness with a Christian tradition of gnosticism, grail questing, and eucharistic blood drinking entirely shared by that "you" to whom the passage addresses these words. This is why the first-person "I" traitorously admits to carrying the same "virus" as the imperial "you." And the only difference between the first- and second-person positions in these sentences is that the revolutionary cell is defined by "friends" that are "cherished," in other words by an organic community, or *Gemeinschaft*, that pitches itself against the mechanistic officialdom, "penal code," and domin-ion of a corporate *Gesellschaft* to which "editors" are also connected.[36] We read this passage as a diagnosis of what ails the fictional Counterforce, and by close analogy the sixties radical Left, both represented as afflicted with the same (mindless?) attachment to counterrevolutionary needs partly expressed in bloody violence. Therefore, striking as we find this moment, when a seem-ing authorial voice breaches the narration's uppermost boundary layer, where the conduit for us between storyworld and historical world is the image of the writer, we nevertheless think it would be foolish to take too seriously the passage's revolutionary hyperventilating and obviously overcoded romantic melodrama. We do in any case read it as a backhanded slap at sixties revo-lutionary fantasies, and as one way to diagnose their failure. Also, as a chal-lenge thrown down to the editorial bureaucracies that Pynchon might have had good reasons to believe, around 1971–73, were liable either to mute his freewheeling novel or decline to publish it, as written, in the United States.

CHAPTER 11

Narrating Liberation

As we hope these pages make clear, Pynchon's song lyrics for *Gravity's Rainbow* bring onstage some of its most freewheeling, entertaining, and satirically effective moments. As much as possible one ought to stop, recognize the known or likely melody, and *sing the text*, feel its powers as a performance in a mock musical. Pynchon's ear is attuned to modern rock 'n' roll, country, folk, jazz, and blues, as well as to classical music and opera. In 1959 he applied to the Ford Foundation for a grant to work on a libretto, an application the foundation declined, whereupon he found employment at Boeing and began writing about rockets—an ethically troubling business that the novel might be read as redressing.[1]

His novel about V-2 rockets explores the freedom in music. While in Berlin, Slothrop witnesses the composer Gustav Schlabone and his friend Emil "Säure" Bummer ("Acid Bummer"—right, sixties hands?) debating who is better, Rossini or Beethoven—an argument that initially seems a doper's divertimento or mindless pleasure, but certainly is up to something. As David Cowart suggests in a seminal contribution on music in *Gravity's Rainbow*, "the common denominator of the political and geometrical metaphors with which Gustav talks about music is freedom: freedom from tonality, freedom from gravity, freedom from oppression."[2] The debate does hold up Beethoven as a champion of musical freedom, but Rossini too, though without Beethoven's seriousness and with a sense of freedom as a much more fleeting quality. The Italian composer already appears a few times before the Berlin debate, suggesting Pynchon's preference for him. The prior mentions also give an advance perspective on the Berlin discussion, and connect Rossini to Slothrop, who senses freedom on the Rue Rossini. At the casino in Monte Carlo, even before fleeing for Nice, Slothrop, while hunting for three young French girls, finds himself in a theater where, later that night, the performers "will play an abbreviated version of *L'Inutil Precauzione* [The Vain Precaution] (that imaginary opera with which Rosina seeks to delude her guardian in *The Barber of Seville*)," and moments later he hears the casino orchestra rehearsing "a lively Rossini tarantella."[3] Already the novel takes a certain improvisational liberty with Rossini's *Barber* (1816), in which Rosina only refers to *L'Inutil Precauzione* to account for an amorous note she's dropped indiscreetly from her balcony, and then sings only one aria from it. There exists, in other words, no full opera score to abbreviate, though the tarantella Slothrop hears might be Rossini's trademark *La Danza* (1835), a stand-alone piece with which the casino orchestra might seek to fill the gaps. In any case, either the musicians or Pynchon have taken significant liberties in putting this imaginary "opera" on the program.

Months later, when Slothrop escapes from the casino, he takes a room "on Rue Rossini," an actual street (in fact 44 Rue Rossini is the Beethoven Building. But, then, so what?); his stay there will be quite short. Slothrop has "no time even to get to know" the street, but it does give him "the best feeling dusk in a foreign city can bring . . . some promise of events without cause, surprises, a direction at right angles to every direction his life has been able to find up till now." On the Côte d'Azur he feels freedom in the air, and there Slothrop will rightly ask himself: "Free? What's free?"[4] Rossini's musical liberties accord with Slothrop's political liberties, it seems; or at least they index his (temporary) sense of happiness at the prospect of self-liberation. Even our narrator signals allegiance to the Italian composer. In episode 8 at the close of part 2, set on the English seaside near the end of May 1945, an organ grinder at the pebbled beach "plays Rossini's overture to *La Gazza Ladra* [The Thieving Magpie, 1817]," and in an uncommonly strong display of omniscience the narrator gives advance notice of the novel's upcoming music debate, and doesn't hesitate to take sides. The overture, "as we shall see later, in Berlin, marks a high point in music which everybody ignored, preferring Beethoven, who never got further than statements of intention." In contrast, Rossini, even played on a barrel organ at the English seashore, "is mellow, full of hope, promising lavender twilights, stainless steel pavilions and everyone elevated at last to aristocracy, and love without payment of any kind." In Nice, Rossini had referenced the random delights of freedom. Now at what is most likely Brighton Beach, on Pentecost Sunday, the thieving magpie ironically brings down to attentive disciples a secular musical message about a possible future, a utopia of natural, cultural, and amorous delights that foretell potentials, at least, for realizing the political romance of democratized, anti-capitalist, and anti-elitist pleasures. And even if that reading overdetermines the presence of the political in the liturgical symbolism of Pentecost, still we are free to do with the music what we will—take in the mere fun of it, or perhaps find release from the worries of the day.[5]

Thus even before the debate begins, readers know the narrator's favorite, and Säure's too. In conversation with Slothrop, Säure refers to "the Sublime Rossini" and never swerves from that position while arguing the case with his "doping partner," Gustav. Säure finds Rossini realizing "more of the Sublime in the snare-drum part to *La Gazza Ladra* than in the whole Ninth Symphony." He resolutely clings to his unsophisticated understanding of Romanticism's strong conception of the sublime, merely seeing it as the experience of feeling good and thus, to him, self-evidently an aesthetic and moral good. That experience results mostly from Rossini's music but is amplified by his lyrics, with their sense of humor and especially, for Säure, their emphasis on love: "lovers always get together . . . *love occurs.*" This is the same (small *r*) romantic Rossini that our narrator praised on the English seaside, and now Säure explains the composer's importance: "isolation is overcome, and like it or not that is the one great centripetal movement of the World": "The world is rushing together." For Säure, the Italian composes in music and words the prospect of a world that brings atomized individuals into community, even in a time and place—mere weeks after the war's end, in a Berlin reduced to rubble—whose divisiveness and centrifugal, scattering forces would seem to blight any prospects for unity. Now *there's* a relevant composer! Or perhaps just another good Nazi, like Margherita Erdmann, murdering Jewish children as if she were the Shekhinah gathering shattered bits of the profane world. In any event, Beethoven, Säure wants to think, does exactly the opposite of Rossini: "All you feel like listening to Beethoven is going out and invading Poland. Ode to Joy indeed," for that historical reference—to September 1, 1939—promises only the restart of war's horrors. So we have Säure's Beethoven, virtually a Nazi world destroyer, and his Rossini, by implication in this black-and-white dialectic a world restorer, a guarantor of freedom. When the narrator ends the Berlin debate by confirming Säure's outcry to Gustav that a tarantella from the opera *Tancredi* (1813) is a wonderful tune, one's clear understanding is that Säure, the narrator, and probably also Pynchon share the contagious, passionate optimism of Rossini's music.[6]

Most of Säure's arguments are cribbed from Stendhal's 1824 biography of Rossini, and Pynchon may have wanted readers to know this.[7] For example, when he lets Gustav attack Säure by calling him old-fashioned, an "antique," and when he claims young people no longer go to concerts because the halls are full of "snow-topped old rascals" who provide the music with a "background murmur of wheezing, belching, intestinal gurgles, scratching, sucking, croaking," and all they listen to is Rossini, "drooling away to some medley of predictable little tunes," he's colloquially summarizing Stendhal. To Gustav also, Rossini is an irrelevant entertainer for the elderly whereas Beethoven endures primarily because of his role in the forward march of music history. As a composer of contemporary classical music, and a German arguing his case in 1945, Gustav is attracted unsurprisingly to high modernist Viennese composer Arnold Schönberg and his pupil Alban Berg, whose modern, twelve-tone technique gave the world a "democracy" (he says) in which "all notes get an equal hearing," a "freedom" that Beethoven foreshadowed, having learned composition from Bach, the forefather of "an expansion of music's polymorphous perversity till all notes were truly equal at last" in modernist works. We find Gustav's way of collapsing "equality" and "freedom" problematic, an issue we'll soon take up. Pynchon likely derived Gustav's argument for Beethoven's historical significance from the Robert Schauffler hagiography, *Beethoven: The Man Who Freed Music* (1933), whose argument is no less reductive than Säure's for Rossini. And the (anachronistic) use of the Freudian "polymorphous perversity" concept, popularized by Brown, further burnishes Beethoven's genius, ascribing to it a sixties neo-Freudian aura. It suggests again the realization that this music has evolved toward a practice liberated from tonality. However, dodecaphonic music's last genius has been snuffed; its moment of maximum freedom murdered, Gustav laments, when an American soldier shot the atonal composer Anton Webern. (And here is another anachronism, for Webern died on September 15, 1945, at least six or seven weeks *after* this debate.) Gustav rejects Säure's consoling remarks and a little later "raves" to an Allied forces officer that he and his American countrymen cannot resist "the simple-minded German symphonic arc, tonic to dominant, back again to tonic. Grandeur! Gesellschaft!"—again, a rationalized economy typified, one supposes, by popular German (note the pun: "to tonic"/Teutonic) symphonic composers such as Haydn, Brahms, Bruckner, or of course Beethoven. These historical errors and manipulations of terms show that Pynchon's narration stacks the deck against Gustav's argument, and if one had the feeling that Säure and his beloved Rossini had come out on top, then these details may close the issue. If not, consider how Gustav's symphonic arc recalls the rocket's parabolic flight path, a figure and a serial technology that the German space program geniuses von Braun and Dornberger have translated to America. The "pleasures" of Rossini are of another kind.[8]

Much later in the novel, perhaps still in Berlin or somewhere else in the Zone (the place is indistinct), Gustav and Säure briefly resume debating. Gustav reproaches his friend for being "caught in tonality," for being incapable of understanding the importance of the dodecaphonic "Row," which he names "enlightenment." Säure retorts that the row, like conventional tonality, is just another game; indeed, "*Sound* is a game" and that's why he listens to "Spohr, Rossini, Spontini," musical gamers "full of light and kindness," and why he finds Gustav's "enlightenment" an idealistic-sounding word to mask the "dullness" of serial music. Gustav will have none of it, deriding his opponent's "light and kindness" as "the jigging of the doomed," the "mortality in every one of those bouncy little tunes." Of course, for Säure, bouncy is good, just as it's a good thing for those Orpheus theatergoers at the novel's end, and for readers too, as all "follow the bouncing ball" marking the words of the old William Slothrop "hymn" that They had consigned to the dustbin. As for Gustav, in his last appearance the man has joined a string ensemble "suicidally depressing everybody inside 100 meters' radius." Still, it seems, the once-raving atonal composer is beginning to come around. Instead of the violin he's playing the kazoo in the slow movement of a "suppressed quartet" by Haydn, enjoying mindless pleasures à la Rossini, it seems. At the Krupp wingding, Gustav even jumps into the Counterforce's game of insolent and awful alliterations batted around the elitists' dinner table—putting down the kazoo for a moment and "screaming" out "Wart waffles!" It seems that even though Gustav confessed to having been "a Storm Trooper" with the Nazis, Counterforce members have welcomed him into the fold.[9]

Slothrop's main instrument is not the kazoo but the equally unassuming and vernacular harmonica, which he accidentally drops out of his shirt pocket down a Roseland Ballroom toilet, then recovers it (after giving up on bagpipes) from a stream somewhere in the Zone, about seven years and six hundred pages later. As if it were the Rossini-Beethoven debate's final word, or coda, this recovery seamlessly warps into a consideration of Slothrop and his "harp," as early American bluesmen popularly named it. "Just suckin'" on it, playing a simple blues, Slothrop is said to approach the state of a "spiritual medium," which is just how the Counterforce will soon understand him. From the earliest days of *Gravity's Rainbow* criticism, Slothrop's bluesharp playing has been taken as signifying that he is a latter-day Orpheus, doomed to fragmentation and "scattering"—the repressive fate of polymorphously perverse souls. "An instinctual musician" is how Cowart defines him; and there he is after recovering the harp, shed of civilization's order and decency—he prefers "to spend whole days naked, ants crawling up his legs" and "just feeling natural"—as he begins to vanish from the plot. And while it might be nice to think of Slothrop as inspiring the "irresponsible use of the harmonica" that brings to "a state of near anarchy" the filmgoers queued up outside the Orpheus Theater, a disruption that enrages the manager, still if we look close it's only a very minor disorder. Not long afterward, the descending ICBM will still freeze-frame over their heads. Perhaps we're too cynical, but music may also only be what was once called a "lifestyle marker" for those who were mildly derided as "nonconformists" as the sixties began, and disdained as "filthy hippies" as the decade ended. Or maybe we should be less cynical. Gustav, having learned from ex-Peenemünde engineers that the kazoo has the "perfect shape" for smoking dope, reveals to Säure that a controlling financial interest behind the kazoo-hashpipe connection is the Phoebus light-bulb cartel, and—lo and behold—one may screw into its threaded bowl a *light bulb!* He demonstrates with none other than Byron, who wishes he could tell them this revelatory tale isn't about the romance, or the schadenfreude, of installing vast and conspiratorial powers and dominions over ordinary humanity. Instead, it's simply about solidarity, even between kazoos and bulbs, and however fleeting.[10]

In pitting the serial composing style or ideology of the (dead-end) Bach-to-Beethoven-to-Schönberg-to-Webern tradition against that of the populist pleasures and compassion of "Spohr, Rossini, Spontini," the Gustav-Säure debate plays out this novel's core dichotomies: the rational and the instinctual, the mechanical and the organic, *Gesellschaft* and *Gemeinschaft*, rocket and blues harp, tragedy and comedy, war and peace, They and We, domination and freedom. Looks simple, and pat; but as Pynchon's narration plays them out, such themes are never clear-cut. Bearing in mind this attention to the midfield, to the space between one and zero, the zone of probabilities and affinities, we move the analysis of "chances for freedom" from the close focus on musical technique to the novel's wide-angle representation of technology.

The rocket, a supersonic missile achieved by laboratory breakthroughs, mechanical problem solving, manufacturing, and field operations, gives technology a certain primacy. Without it, there'd be no story. In *Gravity's Rainbow* the rocket, the Raketenstadt (Rocket City), its economy and sociocultural order, trope the great historical turn from classical industrial capitalism to the late capitalist and neoliberal formation that prevailed in the Cold War decades. The critical importance of this theme was apparent in the earliest reviews and essays. Joseph Slade cautioned against a reductive treatment of its importance in *Gravity's Rainbow* when he wrote that it is "difficult to overstate the ambivalence of technology as Pynchon assesses it in [the book]: it represents the worst and the best in man, his limitations and his potential for perfection, entropy and entelechy."[11] Two relatively simple elements—one applying to the novel as a whole, the other specifically relating to its technological themes—bring about this uncertainty. First, Pynchon regularly endows his narrator (and sometimes his characters) with an ethical consciousness. The narrator's statements may be inconsistent and multivocal at times, but do generally relate a stable and sustained belief in individual responsibility over and against the system's dominion. Second, characters express variably cautious and incautious opinions on technology, and these come to us in both dialogue and interior monologue, sometimes seeming to influence the narrator's view. These instabilities in narrative technique generate the "ambivalence" Slade and everyone after him has duly noted. How then may we summarize or generalize the novel's take on technology's—which is to say, the rocket's—seeming determinations of human desires and liberties?

One useful place to open that inquiry is episode 21 of part 3, set in the German city of Hamburg. Members of the Schwarzkommando are looking for salvageable parts to build Rocket 00001, which ought to give them a new lease on the transcendence they feel has been lost during their diaspora. Riding his motorcycle through the city's ruins, Enzian realizes that World War II's violence determined only the surface of what, within people and culture, is far more devastated. With that recognition he goes further:

It means this War was never political at all, the politics was all theatre, all just to keep the people distracted . . . secretly, it was being dictated instead by the needs of technology . . . by a conspiracy between human beings and techniques, by something that needed the energy burst of war, crying, "Money be damned, the very life of (insert name of Nation) is at stake," but meaning, most likely, *dawn is nearly here, I need my night's blood, my funding, funding, ahh more, more . . .* The real crises were crises of allocation and priority, not among firms—it was only staged to look that way—but among the different Technologies, Plastics, Electronics, Aircraft, and their needs which are understood by the ruling elite.[12]

Enzian's rather studied use of the word "technique" suggests the influence, here, of French philosopher Jacques Ellul, whose book *The Technological Society* (1954, English translation 1964) treats the threat to human freedom in what the French text named *technique*: "the totality of methods, rationally arrived at and having absolute efficiency (for a given stage of development) in every field of human activity." Technology is only a byproduct of this totality. In the Pynchon passage, technology both resembles and does not resemble Ellul's "technique." It has become an autonomous entity, but for the gratification of its needs it conspires with Them. For all the angst this passage displays, we shouldn't forget that the thought of technology as an autonomous and conspiring entity is Enzian's vocalized paranoia, expressing his need to get a grip on the obvious chaos around him. In the rest of the Hamburg passage, however, the narrator and Enzian develop a dynamic consciousness that, certainly at first, appears much more agile in its moves toward an ethical position on technology.[13]

The very next paragraph, which begins "Yes but Technology only responds," sets out the doubled or dynamic consciousness that interests us. In whose voice is that assent, the "Yes"? Is it Enzian's, whose interior monologue then continues through the paragraph and into the next, which begins "We have to look for power sources here"? Or is this the narrator's voice, which might be seen as taking up (or over) the argument and even monopolizing it? There are few semantic or grammatical cues enabling us to answer. In these paragraphs we find a degree of formality, hence distancing, conventionally associated with a third-person narratorial voice—in particular, the phrase "among the younger Schwarzkommando," which we wouldn't expect one of them, even their leader, to use. This also holds, but to a lesser extent, for the paragraph's comment that the argument over technology has been reiterated humorously "as a Gaussian reduction," an allusion to advanced mathematics typical of our narrator(s) but never of Enzian. Other uncertainties crop up. Shall we read the uses of the second-person "you" in these paragraphs as moments when Enzian addresses himself, or the narrator addresses Enzian, or addresses the readerly audience? And what does one do with the comment "Well, this is stimulant talk here, yes Enzian's been stuffing down Nazi surplus Pervitins"—which makes it *seem* clear that our narrator has let Enzian ramble on until, having exhausted his own argument in manically drugged chatter, it's time for the voice of authority to step back in? One could try to stabilize the reading of this page by deciding this is an imaginary dialogue in which the narrator stages a response to "Technology," giving the floor to Enzian in the we-paragraph, then challenging his speech with the next paragraph's critique. Finally, the text offers no decisive cues for how to read "YAAAGGGGHHHHH!"—which someone screams at the end of this confusion. Or does that yell express *our* response?

What is the confusion's effect? We might construe it as an old-fashioned case of form working in unison with content. Thus the ambiguity of voice could be read as mimicking the paragraphs' ambivalence concerning autonomous technology, its different aspects ("Plastics, Electronics, Aircraft") functioning like gigantic robots (shades of Fritz Lang's 1927 movie, *Metropolis*). But does that really do justice to the text? Here's what's crucial about how "Technology . . . responds," in Enzian's insights: "Go ahead, capitalize the T in technology, deify it if it'll make you feel less responsible—but it puts you in with the neutered, brother, in with the eunuchs keeping the harem of our stolen Earth for the numb and joyless hardons of human sultans, human elite with no right at all to be where they are." This passage unmasks Enzian's revelation of "Technology" as an autonomous entity, or being, revealing it instead as a projection, perhaps a genuine (that is, paralyzing) paranoia. Notably, too, this unmasking occurs in a paragraph opening on "Technology" with a capital *T*, so that the writing ironically takes on itself. Of course this self-referential paradox cannot brush aside the ambivalence of this entire page on technology; nevertheless it may constitute the grounds for developing an ideological position. Indeed, in that capital *T* Technology paragraph the speaker appears outside the conspiracy posited in the prior paragraph, a conspiracy whose existence the writing confirms. The resulting dichotomous structure (in which the neutered are opposed to the elite) leads to the use of a cohesive "we" for what seem to be the neutered—a "we" that at least includes Enzian and the voice(s) of the paragraph starting with "Yes," and may also include the readers who buy into the dichotomy as a result of earlier episodes in *Gravity's Rainbow*. This "we" gives itself a community-structuring task largely based on the projection of yet another duality, which takes up the metaphor of the theater ("the politics was all theatre") from the already quoted revelation: "Up here, on the surface, coaltars, hydrogenation, synthesis were always phony, dummy functions to hide the real, *the planetary mission* yes perhaps centuries in the unrolling." Theater versus reality, surface versus a presumably "deeper" reality: these oppositions both imply a level of truth upon which (for example) the status of technology might be settled once and for all. However, and here the ideological position in sight already starts to undo itself, these oppositions rest squarely on the deification this page also calls into question. They result from the paranoia that capitalizes the *T* of technology. Take this paranoid projection out and the entire argumentative construction, ending perhaps in a mode of anti-paranoia in which nothing is connected to anything, reduces itself to rubble. This is what the rocket is designed to do—and perhaps what Tyrone Slothrop is designed to do, if we understand him as destined, or rather programmed, to scatter.

We put this closely argued pressure on one page out of 760 to remind ourselves how this novel's narrative technique may trouble readers doing their detective work and coming to rash conclusions about ethical values and moral truths. The page just before it produces a related instance, this one involving references to Kabbalistic mysticism as a source of metaphors for reckoning possibilities for spiritual truth in relation to the truth of technology in Pynchon's Zone. Kabbalah comes in, or rather it *"breaks,* as that light you're afraid will break some night," as an "extraordinary understanding" to Enzian. This occurs in two paragraphs of the character's inner speech as he looks at the ruins of a Jamf oil-processing plant, rubble which is just awaiting "the right connections to be set up" for operations to resume. As throughout this episode, it is difficult in these paragraphs to establish what speech may be ascribed to the narrator, what to Enzian. It's not exactly an imaginary dialogue, something that does occur later in the episode. Instead it's more like this narrator speaks from inside Enzian's mind in order to walk the character through an explication, about explication: "yes and now what if we—all right, say we *are* supposed to be the Kabbalists out here, say that's our real Destiny, to be the scholar-magicians of the Zone, with somewhere in it a Text, to be picked to pieces, annotated, explicated, and masturbated till it's all squeezed limp of its last drop . . . well we assumed—natürlich!—that this holy Text had to be the rocket." Indeed this voice regards the rocket as "our Torah."[14]

Kabbalah claims secret knowledge of the unwritten Torah (the divine revelation) that God communicated to Adam and to Moses. They and their heirs were given means for approaching, for hearing God directly (also a cornerstone of Puritan theology), not through rational exegesis but through mystical knowledge (for example, about the numerical values of Hebrew letters and words) that was passed on, through adepts who tease meaning from closely interpreted sacred texts. The quote about Kabbalah provides two more instances of dichotomous structure. First of all, the real text "persists" in darkness. The possibility of a true, magical approach to divinity has remained hidden so far, just as the Hereros were misled by their own assumptions about the rocket. Furthermore, even when the holy text is found it will require adepts to decipher the meaning. So it will have "to be picked to pieces," as if shattered Kabbalistically, in order to reveal, and be regathered around, its transcendent truth. Interpretation is of course the key commitment here.

This should be a chastening thought, especially when we consider the capitalized *T* on "Text" and the projection it seems to imply when read along with the paragraph about the deification of "Technology." If "Technology" and "Text" are similar, if they are only synecdoches for a greater, unified, and divine revelation, the disclosure of entelechy or final cause, then the hermeneutic endeavor may fail or suffer permanent delay because of the ways interpretation is so recursive, without end (which as we've said, seems a good thing).

The Kabbalah passage does not explicitly link text and technology, however. The narrator's masturbation metaphor surely confounds the issue because of how it pulls spiritual questing down into the nitty-gritty of profane and autoreferential desire. On the one hand, it signifies exhaustion ("squeezed limp"); on the other, it may promise hermeneutic satisfaction, though lonely and momentary. If text equals penis, that interpretation must bring a climax—that is to say, transcendent truth—but the achieved end hardly puts a period or eschatological end to things. Since desire is recursive, the text/penis (or rocket) will rise again for satisfaction/interpretation, which is just what Enzian realizes. Indeed, later in his interior monologue the text turns out to be a much more unstable, fluid concept than technology, witnessed under the sign of war: "the bombing was the exact industrial process of conversion, each release of energy placed exactly in space and time, each shock wave plotted in advance to bring *precisely tonight's wreck* into being thus decoding the Text, thus coding, recoding, redecoding the holy Text." The code alters, because context changes historically, yet the text's meaning (its entelechy) remains essentially the same because war has become a constant, as the novel repeatedly advises. What the narration seems to be pressing toward in these two densely inscribed pages is a perfectly regulated communications system. In it, They conspire with an ever-evolving technology ("auto, bomb, gun, v-1, now v-2") that alters both context and code while the text messaged to recipients (to us) remains identical: war. War has morphed into its own autoreferential system. This is consistent with Enzian's circular logic for understanding technology. As an autonomous entity, technology is determined by a conception of the text, which turns out to be a product of technology seen as an autonomous entity.[15]

This chicken-or-egg conundrum suggests why Enzian cannot get outside his way of understanding technology in terms of dichotomies: neutered versus elite, theater versus reality, surface versus depth, the really real text (of the conspiracy) versus the imaginary real text (of the rocket). And we take this limit on Enzian's understanding as the reason that an analysis of "ambivalence" cannot unfold the problem of technology and freedom as *Gravity's Rainbow* evokes it. If the individual submits his or her freedom to technology's ever-increasing demands, and if the individual simply sees no way out from under that domination because the problems of textual under-standing and technological problem solving are captured in the same auto-referential and recursive cycling around the same old stable dichotomies, then our chances for freedom reduce to nil. Unless there's a different way to con-sider the text-technique interaction.

One of the novel's best meditations on this problem unfolds in episode 24 of part 3, when Father Rapier propounds an alternate approach. Rapier is one of several memorable Jesuit fathers in Pynchon's work, including Father Fairing in *V.*, who leaves the island of Malta for New York and a mission cat-echizing sewer rats, and the lapsed Jesuit priests in *Mason & Dixon*—Father Zarpazo, the "Wolf of Jesus" and "Lord of the Zero"; and Captain Zhang, the freelance feng shui master who contributes to important conversations about lines, borders, and emergent nation-states. *Gravity's Rainbow*'s Father Rapier seems stuck in a very unsightly place. His office "is a little corrugated shack, stovepipe coming out the top, rusted automobile parts lying around the yard, piles of wood under rain-colored and failing canvas, a house trailer with its tires and one wheel tilted forlorn in the spanging of the cold rain at its weathered outsides." Rapier's nameplate reads "DEVIL'S ADVOCATE," which accords him a certain official stature in the rather mundane and enjoy-able hell that is this episode's scene.[16]

Given this mock supernatural setting it's hardly surprising that the episode also lacks temporal coordinates, other than that Pirate Prentice is ambling through on "tour," implying that this linear episode is his own fantasy and "Nobody else's," for a change. The episode follows number 23, which is set back in England and which takes a break from Slothrop's tribulations in "the Zone" of occupied Germany in the summer of 1945. Indeed the sequencing here is notable. As episode 23 begins Katje Borgesius is still stationed at the "White Visitation," the seaside headquarters where a variety of (mainly Brit-ish) psychologists have been developing bizarrely original contributions to the war effort. There Katje watches—or she is made to watch—a film that incites her to leave the White Visitation and join Pirate Prentice and a nascent Coun-terforce in London. It turns out Prentice is "out scouting up some transporta-tion" for a sojourn into the Zone. As the episode ends Osbie Feel—the man They had assigned to help with that film used to condition octopus Grigori—reveals the beginnings of a Counterforce to Katje and mentions an important "division" between kinds of people, rather like that dividing elect from pret-erite in Calvinist theology. Episode 24 then commences with an epigraph at-tributed to the Gospel of Thomas (Pynchon?): "Dear Mom, I put a couple of people in Hell today." What follows is a topology that could be right out of Eliot's *The Waste Land*: "Who would have thought so many would be here?" Or it's out of Milton, or better still Dante's *Inferno*: "It seems to be some very extensive museum, a place of many levels, and new wings that generate like living tissue." When Prentice "looks up through all the faintly super-imposed levels above," he and/or the narrator recognize these levels as "the milieu of every sort of criminal soul." Then his "tour" brings us to Father Rapier's decrepit shack, which seems to cross some saint's hovel in a Hieronymus Bosch painting with a coal-miner's cabin in Appalachia.[17]

So this is not hell as we know it from Dante, Milton, or Eliot. When newly arrived, Prentice finally "understands where he is" and realizes he'd best "stay down among the Preterite," who will not be among the saved on Judgment Day. All along, *Gravity's Rainbow* has given these second sheep a sympathetic treatment, and even here in hell conditions are far from hellish. Indeed it seems more like a consolation prize, with its "cafés to sit in and watch the sunset," fantastic "pastry carts" pushed by vendors, and chefs "with ice-cream scoops at the ready." Katje will also come touring through, but before that happens Prentice passes down a "Beaverboard Row," remarking on the neatly bureaucratized "offices of all the Committees, with the name of each stenciled above the doorway—A-4 . . . IG . . . OIL FIRMS . . . LOBOTOMY. . . SELF-DEFENSE . . . HERESY." Walking through this corporatized hell, Prentice eventually arrives at Rapier's little stand-alone shack. Actually there's no need to get the preaching straight from Father Rapier because residents and evidently even hell's tourists can "tune in from anywhere" thanks to a radio network. The narrator kindly summarizes and quotes from Rapier's message, especially his thoughts on freedom. Rapier, it turns out, is "here to preach, like his colleague Teilhard de Chardin, against return. Here to say that critical mass cannot be ignored." In *The Phenomenon of Man* (1955, English translation 1959), Pierre Teilhard de Chardin describes humans as the "omega-point" of an irreversible evolution. A paleontologist and geologist in addition to being a priest, Teilhard sought to meld evolutionary theory and Christian theology, arguing that humanity will achieve on earth no return to the primitivity, naïveté, and supposed innocence of some prior Edenic condition. Hegelian in his logic of unstoppable linear evolution, Pynchon's fictionalized Teilhard de Chardin ranks with other characters in *Gravity's Rainbow* who believe in forces working against entropy, though they lack Rapier/Teilhard's philosophical and theological Christianity. Love in Teilhardian theology is a cosmic energy, and under divine guidance it will ensure humanity's continuing potential for transcendence.[18]

In a reversal typical of this novel's satirical practice, we are getting this sermonette from a Jesuit working for the devil, thus getting a certain unmasking of Christianity—as in Feuerbach and Marx—as an intrinsically evil ethos, one of whose main functions is to check individual freedom by keeping the masses opiated. In fact for Rapier too the loss of freedom in the Christian era is a first-order problem. He argues: "Once the technical means of control have reached a certain size, a certain degree of *being connected* to one another, the chances of freedom are over for good. The word has ceased to have meaning." This dark warning recalls earlier ones, such as the comical lyric "The Penis He Thought Was His Own" and the novel's recurring and grisly scenes of extermination (the dodoes on Mauritius, the Hereros of Southwest Africa, the dead at Dora). Yet those moments are relatively straightforward ethically, compared to Rapier's more complicated pronouncement on freedom. After all, his job description can be read in at least two ways. Since Rapier resides in hell, he works for the devil, particularly in attending to certain satanic legal projects. But as a devil's advocate, in the term's common sense, he is one who attacks a point or cause in order to strengthen it, all along agreeing with the point. This may explain why Rapier at first sight seems to deliver a message about freedom that contradicts that of "his colleague" Teilhard.[19]

Teilhard in a postscript to *The Phenomenon of Man* specifically considers the question of freedom: "what place remains for freedom (and hence for the possibility of [its] setback in the world)?" He is quick to mention that "*the final success* of hominization" (that is, the evolution and eventual domination of key human traits) is by no means "necessary, inevitable and, certain." And he argues that the driving forces of cosmogenic development, "compression, organization and interiorisation," "do not at any moment relax their pressure on the stuff of mankind." However, the "very nature" of this entire developmental process, natural and human, which Teilhard describes as "the arrangement of great complexes," is such that it involves "two uncertainties": there is "chance at the bottom," he claims, "and freedom at the top."[20] Having Teilhard's words in front of us here seems crucial, not least because Rapier's phrase "chances for freedom" doesn't just collapse the two concepts at either end of Teilhard's hierarchy; it assigns to aleatory forces the primary importance that Teilhard ascribes to "freedom." So it seems that Rapier *is* at loggerheads with Teilhard. It turns out, however, that Teilhard is the devil's advocate—for he brings up freedom only to retract it—and Rapier even borrows from him the idea of critical mass. Teilhard's first retraction of the possibility of freedom posits that when the human population reaches a certain mass, "the process tends to 'unfallibilise' itself." In other words, as uncertainties decrease and the process approaches zero potential for fallibility, "the likelihood of success grows on the lower side [chance] while that of rejection and error diminishes" the possibilities of freedom on the other side. Teilhard then hides his second retraction in a footnote to the first retraction: "For a Christian believer it is interesting to note that the final success of hominization . . . is positively guaranteed by the 'redeeming virtue' of the God incarnate in his creation. But this takes us beyond the plan of phenomenology."[21] While Teilhard likely put in that footnote to trump church criticism or censorship of his writings, this second retraction nonetheless reveals his difficulty in trying to meld his Catholicism with his evolutionary science. His unwavering sense is that the successes of evolution doom human freedom. With no exceptions—not even for Americans who love to tell exceptionalist stories about their great, industrialized, progressive, westwarding national project.

Father Rapier borrows only from Teilhard's science, and for good reason. How could he litigate for the devil if he rejected freedom with reference to God's "redeeming virtue"? In any case, Teilhard's secular argument against the prospects for freedom is the only one that made it into the pages of *Gravity's Rainbow*. The formulation "critical mass," instead of Teilhard's "very large numbers" of people on earth, refers to "the smallest amount of fissionable material necessary to sustain a nuclear chain reaction." Thus Father Rapier is actually, and rather uncannily, referencing the atomic bomb, as becomes clear in the narrator's reference to the "Cosmic Bomb" just a few lines later, though its worldwide debut at Hiroshima (August 6, 1945) is still weeks in the future as this scene unfolds.[22] In that historical context the narrator's term, "Cosmic Bomb," nicely evokes Teilhard's cosmogony. Yet the ghastly difference in this new outcome of techno-scientific advances, especially in the military-industrial complex, is that it inaugurates man's power to terminate earthly life. And *that* is the new "exceptionalist" story.

In the crucial "chances for freedom" passage, Rapier associates the definitive loss of freedom with total control through technological progress. Although, as we have seen, the various points about technology in *Gravity's Rainbow* cannot simply be compressed into a stable, unambiguous ideology, Rapier here clearly generalizes the principle of molecular connection—which operates on various levels in the novel, from banana breakfast to chemical polymerization in plastics, and which may not be all that different from Teilhard's process of "organization"—and thus includes "the technical means of control." As a creative achievement, then, atomic weapons clearly illustrate technology's progress in the same light that a few players in *Gravity's Rainbow* also shine upon it. Various "technical means" or innovations (such as elaborate lenses) had to be developed and combined in order to produce controlled fission in a deliverable bomb. As bearer of this news, Father Rapier is one of the novel's few hyphens connecting v-2 missiles screaming into *Gravity's Rainbow* on its first page, with the image of a nuclear-tipped ICBM forever dangling like the tarot deck's Hanged Man over Los Angeles on its last page.

Those who have the bomb control the world. Rapier enters into a disquisition about Them and Their power, using the same pronominal designations for the world's invisible rulers that have been circulating in *Gravity's Rainbow* since its opening episodes. Rapier submits that now They may have achieved such powers that They may no longer die, for perhaps "it is now within the state of Their art to go on forever—though we, of course, will keep dying as we always have." But not stopping at the distinction between Them and us, Rapier goes two steps further. First he plays devil's advocate and calls for a new faith resting on the belief in Their mortality. Then he offers an alternative to act upon: "But rather than make that leap of faith, perhaps we will choose instead to turn, to fight." It's the novel's first call for active resistance and is not lost on Pirate Prentice, whose descent into central Germany will be motivated by the project of growing a Counterforce against Them. As such Rapier's sermon assumes the status of a briefing from hell. Yet the Counterforce's failure to take root and grow a resistance movement remains a crucial fact about Pynchon's storyworld. At their best, the Counterforce's pursuits never go beyond mildly subversive performances (such as their Yippie-style pranksterism at a formal dinner), silly skirmishes They effortlessly brush aside or tacitly moot through repressive tolerance, one of modern liberalism's subtler methods. Therefore Rapier's proposed new faith may be the more important of his two solutions for the coming Cold War world's endless state of emergency. In what looks like one more reversal, Rapier ends up preaching *for* instead of (as the narrator first indicated) *against* return: "'To believe that each of Them *will* personally die is also to believe that Their system will die—that some chance of renewal, some dialectic, is still operating in History. To affirm Their mortality is to affirm Return. I have been pointing out certain obstacles in the way of affirming Return. . . .' It sounds like a disclaimer, and the priest sounds afraid."[23]

Rapier here perhaps tries to out-Hegel Teilhard. Yet his formulation—"some chance of renewal, some dialectic . . . in History"—seems marred by his insistence on renewal's subversive aspect, which, as Teilhard knew only too well, would disappear into the synthesis. More important, Rapier emphasizes that any chances of affirming return (implying residual freedoms) would confront "certain obstacles." What the narrator hears as a "disclaimer" may imply that, just like Teilhard in his postscript, Rapier also retracts the suggestion of individual freedom his Christian faith seeks to mute—in collusion with Them, as Marx said. The Jesuit also "sounds afraid" to the narrator because Rapier realizes he has gone a little too far on behalf of that resistant ideology he's trying to underwrite. So, maybe Rapier is here to preach against return after all, because They might come and get him! Yet Rapier's subversive inspiration hasn't been lost on Pirate Prentice, who takes it into Germany as a kind of mantra to motivate the Counterforce—whose actions amount to little, and their conviction perhaps all that counts, on the They-system/we-system scoreboard. The resisting consciousness may be all that remains of freedom as *Gravity's Rainbow* jump-cuts to the Orpheus Theater. Yet even that consciousness looks false, because so evidently indebted to Their power structure and logic, especially its dichotomized practices. Indeed, the discourse on technology and freedom occurs in a fictional world that, in the Hamburg episode, exposes as aporetic the dichotomies shaping Rapier's thought. No wonder the Counterforce does not get very far: it plots with Their logic, within parameters They control. Failing to reckon the "chances for freedom," the Counterforce acts on cue.

"Suicide is a freedom even the lowest enjoy," claims Josef Ombindi to Enzian, near the novel's close. The time is mid-September 1945, and references put them in northern Germany near the Elbe River and Cuxhaven, where Allied forces have been gathering captured v-2 missiles for testing and shipment to America. The Schwarzkommando have come there via Nordhausen and the Mittelwerke and before that Peenemünde—all along seeking rocket parts and subassemblies. Evidently in Cuxhaven the Schwarzkommando have gathered liberated components for this 00001 rocket, soon to be assembled, "painted black," and—and what? It's unclear just *what* Enzian plans to do with this rocket, and probably that's the point. There are in any case other positive indicators. Katje Borgesius is with them, and so is the orphaned German kid, Ludwig, from way back in episode 25 of part 3. Seventeen episodes ago Slothrop had ended a "Partial List of Wishes on Evening Stars" by wishing for the boy to recover his pet lemming, Ursula, lost in the Zone. And here they are, reunited, trekking alongside the Schwarzkommando. We know the Hereros are going to the Lüneberg heath, where Blicero had launched Rocket 00000. And now we learn Enzian has "objectives" in mind. Ten objectives to be exact, each introduced with an infinitive construction: "To make the run over tracks," "To have to stay out in the rains of early Virgo," "To brew tea," and (the ninth) "To keep faith that it is not trek this time, nor struggle, but truly Destiny" moving this v-2 along, and then (tenth) "To take this most immachinate of techniques, the Rocket—the Rocket, this most terribly potential of bombardments." The paragraph, or rather the countdown, ends (rather like the novel) in uncertainty, incompletion, and (here) ellipsis, its destiny unstated, though Enzian does seem to have the heath "firing site" in mind even if he does not have in mind (and this seems vaguely significant and symptomatic) a target. A moment later a young Schwarzkommando named Christian interrupts Enzian's thoughts, arguing that although a natural "society," or *Gemeinschaft*, is "created among men" in order to "protect you each from violence, to give shelter in time of disaster," even then—says he, pointing at the rocket—"what protection *is* there? what can protect us from *that*?" Enzian agrees: "Nowhere is safe." Yet he also argues that the fact of this danger, and particularly the sheer randomness of it penetrating from the sky "at any given point," constitutes an existential threat that finally has severed the diasporic Hereros from Them, from the colonial masters who brought them north some two-thirds of the way around the globe to this cold and rainy heath: "We can't believe Them any more. Not if we are still sane, and love truth."[24]

Ombindi's claim, that even the "lowest" soul still has the liberty to deny a master bodily ownership of her- or himself by means of suicide, is always the last-ditch claim freedom makes against total domination. Available equally to slaves and to concentration camp inmates, it is negative liberty's lowest common denominator, next to its absolute zero or null point. Christian's rhetorical argument is that the human condition at this nearly null point erases any potential for communal solidarity, for it casts each survivor as an alienated, solitary monad. Against that view, how shall we gauge Enzian's project as he exits the novel? First consider the history behind it. We recall that Enzian "had been walking only for a few months" when his mother took him, in late 1904, on Herero leader Samuel Maharero's "great trek across the Kalahari" desert—fleeing German general von Trotha and a genocidal campaign that would take the lives of at least sixty-five thousand Hereros.[25] Maharero's remnant of one thousand souls made it to British protectorate lands in what is now Botswana. This makes Enzian about forty-two years old in 1945, and makes Weissmann's sexual and quasi-legal enslavement of him— back in Southwest Africa in 1922, when he was nineteen or twenty—part of a greater (but when Pynchon was writing, still a largely untold) history of extermination, enslavement, and diaspora. Now, there are significant problems with this chronology, which conflicts with information the omniscient narrator provides just thirty pages later. Most likely it's an authorial error, like that involving Bianca Erdmann's age.[26]

Here, we see Pynchon picking up historical material he had developed in V., using what was then a limited archive of primary source materials and a few secondary scholarly works to reference a history, now known in much finer detail, about the Herero genocide and the early twentieth-century African diaspora in Europe. West African young men were brought to France, Congolese to Belgium, South Africans to Holland, and Southwest Africans from the colony in what is now Namibia to the German metropole. These Afro-Europeans were a constant thorn in the side of the German Weimar Republic, especially when the French garrisoned Senegalese troops in occupied Rhineland, leading to a vast outcry in 1922 against what British journalist E. D. Morel infamously named the "horror on the Rhine," foreshadowing Nazi atrocities in the early years of World War II: massacres of African soldiers fighting with the Allies, and concentration camp internments of many noncombatant blacks.[27] Afro-German rocket troops constitute a fantastical rewriting of this historical record, which nevertheless indicates that a tiny remnant of Hereros did work in Germany during the war as servants and laborers. The point though is not historical verification or even contextualization of narrative detail but Enzian's idea of "the trek." He understands the Schwarzkommando journey as reiterating Samuel Maharero's rescue of his people from total elimination—from the fate, say, of the dodo bird—

by leading them into exile, though just where Enzian would take them, in Europe or beyond, is untold.

We understand that to be Enzian's implicit "objective." Explicitly "the trek" stands as a testament against Ombindi's argument for suicide. Indeed Enzian's mock countdown of the trek's ten objectives only underscores that point, not with argument per se but by way of a technique or praxis whose infinitive verbs ("To avoid," "To sleep," "To hide," "To disperse," "To keep faith") must be seen as mediating and middling actions in a sequence without end—other than in ellipsis dots irrupting (perhaps infinitely) between the one and the zero, between "a good Rocket to take us to the stars, [and] an evil Rocket for the World's suicide." The narration thus enacts a set of mundane deferrals focused in the moment but also in a larger pragmatic and communal resistance to "this most immachinate of techniques"—a phrasing that surely applies the word "technique" in Ellul's sense. Thus in a suspensive but perhaps hopeful irony, Enzian's ten-item list of objectives counters the "good" as well as the "evil" rocket, both its transcendent "destiny" and its worldly "suicide." His list logically and ethically disrupts, answers that dichotomy (or rather excuse) with which Wernher von Braun tried (especially in *I Aim at the Stars*) to rehabilitate his reputation amid persistent war crimes accusations. Enzian's countdown might also be read as commencing the same recursive logic as "Sold on Suicide," a song lyric bookended by the episode's narrative summary of the Herero factions gathered around Ombindi on the one hand, Enzian on the other, and laying out a minimal Herero history readers will need, here at the novel's close, as they work through this fictional yet historical people's gnarled actions and motives, in what is after all a desperate diaspora. Enzian's practice also bears the marks of a divinatory method. The narrator represents him as literally *finding* the refugees' way across the Zone by mystically reading various signs he recognizes, strung haphazardly along the way, at times seeing with "X-ray vision."[28]

And there's more. The following episode, number 11 out of 12 in part 4, narrates the accidental meeting (on a bridge over a stream) of Enzian and his sworn enemy Tchitcherine, who has obsessionally pledged to hunt Enzian down and kill the man who is both his racial other and his biological half brother. That plot fails, or rather evaporates. And the reason may have to do with the magic spells that Tchitcherine's devoted witchy-woman lover, Geli Tripping, has cast over her man from a distance, using every device and invoking every spirit being she knows. Especially, she uses a fragment (the crotch) of her underwear to cast a spell over Tchitcherine's eyes, so that he will not recognize Enzian. As things happen we cannot tell if it's Geli's witchcraft or mere happenstance that structures the half brothers' meeting and lack of recognition. They exchange greetings in "broken German"; then Tchitcherine requests and Enzian offers him "half a pack of American cigarettes and three raw potatoes." Whereupon Enzian tools off on his motorcycle, while Tchitcherine lights a cigarette and returns to "his young girl beside the stream." Their failed recognition may seem magical "but [is] not necessarily fantasy," the narrator remarks, reminding us that it may be read as an accidental passing-by in dim light, "at the edge of evening," and as such a moment of secular grace. Rushing streams have tended to be signs of such moments, even if associated with Rilke's problematic romanticism; and certainly that rushing stream in episode 1 of part 4 seemed to bode well for Slothrop, since in it he finds his long-lost blues harp. The point being: while Teilhard and Rapier may win the argument about no chances for freedom, in the meantime people's best remnant of liberty may be found in the accidental, in chances realized in the moment, and at the transient, micro-level of social organization. In episodes 10 and 11, one kid with a lemming, or two people together, or even the remnant of Herero exiles sustains a desire for freedom. The singular refugee, the couple, at most some minimalist form of familial or communal existence may still have access to the accidents, the moments, beyond Their control. This would explain why Ludwig sheers off from the trekking Schwarzkommando with his Ursula, why Geli alone and then together with the alienated and immachinated Tchitcherine just might have decent chances, and so might Enzian's sizable crew. As for Slothrop, we'll see.

Among the novel's array of ethno-racial figures, one of the most curious is the character Gavin Trefoil (a teenager like Gottfried), an epitome of the Teutonic type, with his "pale freckled redhead's complexion." But that's in his "rest state." When he's active, and feels like it, Trefoil can willfully modulate his complexion through a spectrum of colors from "most ghastly albino" through magenta to a "very deep, purplish black." The narrator even offers a quasi-scientific explanation: this boy can freely will his body to metabolize the amino acid tyrosine, thus to "produce melanin, which is the brown-black pigment responsible for human skin color." This singular talent, which physicians (in the novel) name "autochromatism," has earned Gavin a residency at the White Visitation, where he's an object of study among "the freaks" collected there, and a helpful one after all.[29]

The supreme commander of the Allied Expeditionary Force, General Eisenhower, calls for a propaganda campaign using a "strategy of truth" to turn Nazism's distortions and lies back against German society. One plan is to agitate German racial fantasies and fears using resources of the London-based Psychological Warfare Department. All of this is more or less historically based. But then Pynchon spins his own yarn. Within the PWD, a special group named Operation Black Wing has hatched a scheme to spread stories of black rocket troops in the war zone, armed, potentially on the loose, and posing a mortal threat to Aryans, especially women. The PWD-OBW's idea is to turn against Nazi society the same kind of anxiety that erupted in 1922 over the (actual) garrisoning of Afro-European peacekeeping troops in the Rhine Valley—the "Schwarze Besatzung am Rhein!" crisis fomented by German media. Now, in 1944–45, the specter of actual black troopers loose in the (story's) war zone with phallic v-2 missiles certainly will stoke the racist fears of ordinary Nazis—or so the (fictional) thinking goes.[30] The propaganda vehicle OBW decides on is a film, to be shot in England and scripted to represent the black rocket troops who, according to hearsay testimony Pirate Prentice's spycraft has turned up, are in the field, quite unbeknown to ordinary Germans, who will be properly shocked and worried if the film works its magic. The problem is that OBW lacks black actors. So, calling on the one "magic negro" they have available, a Zouave from the North Africa campaign, while also drafting the autochromatic Trefoil into service from the White Visitation, and using white actors in blackface, they set émigré German film director Gerhardt von Göll scripting and directing the short film he will later consider his "greatest work." Along the way They also draft Slothrop into service, setting up a sodium amytal session (in episode 10 of part 1) specifically so that he might "help illuminate racial problems in his own country," where fears of black-beast rapists are staple figures in American racial mythology. (And thus readers learn one reason that Slothrop was put under narcosis.) It's hard to tell how They would derive anything useful from that session, which features Slothrop's fantasies of interracial homosexual rape (at the hands of Malcolm X), a deeply unconscious cathexis of blackness and shit ("Some of it too must be Negro shit, but that all looks alike"), and a brief fantasy involving an Afro-Scandinavian kid named Whappo, whose buttocks "combine the callipygian rondure observed among races of the Dark Continent with the taut and noble musculature of Olaf, our blond Northern cousin."[31] What *we* learn can be quickly summarized. One is that Slothrop's unconscious horror at interracial homosexual rape has its counterpart in his interracial homosexual delight in the "callipygian rondure" of Whappo's buttocks. And that language, incidentally, indicates that in reading up on race Pynchon has come across the history of the "Hottentot Venus," a Khoikhoi woman, Saartjie Baartman, who was brought in 1810 from Cape Town to Europe, then exhibited to paying spectators wishing to gape at her famously large callipygian buttocks, a spectacle accompanied by supposedly eminent anatomists who would expatiate on her features and the supposed degradation of her racial type, as she stood and turned about for the customers. Another thing this material teaches is that American racial fantasies, and British too for that matter, are close cousins of those of good Aryan Germans. Certainly the narrator's discourse—about "races of the Dark Continent" and "our blond Northern cousin"—mimics satirically the turns of phrase common in countless nineteenth-century classics of racial pseudo-science.[32] Finally, these scenes suggest there is no "free" human potential, no matter how freakish, that They will not seek to control and exploit. How Trefoil responds to Their uses of him is untold; he remains a cipher with a quaint name and a bizarre talent but no degree of represented mentality.

That Pynchon does relatively little with racial domination and liberation in *Gravity's Rainbow* is itself notable. The civil rights movement is one of three major narrative threads running through Long Sixties history, its stage of passive resistance running up until the 1968 assassination of Martin Luther King Jr., and followed by more confrontational, militant liberation struggles—black, Chicano, Native American. The other two major threads involve fifties and early sixties opposition to nuclear weapons and the increasingly resistant anti–Vietnam War movement, sometimes gathered under a big tent as the peace movement. Pynchon first developed his fictional critique of Herero history in *V.*; and that novel was also revised before publication to accentuate racial identities as sociocultural constructs, particularly in the fictional depiction of African American jazz and of saxophone player McClintic Sphere. Yet even those revisions hardly pushed the representation of race beyond "beat-inspired clichés, garden variety liberal sentiment, and limited personal experience."[33] Pynchon's 1964 short story, "The Secret Integration," also treats race as a sociocultural construct though again it hardly gets beyond rather stock characterizations and conventional liberal sentiments for change. A 1966 essay on the Watts riots for the *New York Times Magazine* indicates a slight alteration in Pynchon's outlook, particularly in his laconic yet more deeply witnessed insight that black anger and impatience at a deeply rooted "white version of what a Negro was supposed to be" (as he phrased it) seemed to foretell long years, or decades, of struggle for justice and equality. Finally, a key scene set in San Francisco in *The Crying of Lot 49* (1966) engages a subtle satire on the idea that a white liberal (such as Oedipa Maas, or for that matter the Pynchon of "A Journey into the Mind of Watts") will find the holy grail of racial understanding and peace by visiting a ghetto flophouse and feeling the pain of its denizens, before returning home to the 'burbs. This is a scanty yet self-aware record. Pynchon's extension of his Herero fabulations in *Gravity's Rainbow*, the representation of Slothrop's racialized fantasy life, and the brief Trefoil subtext are consistent with the practice of his prior fictions. Still, the absence—really—of meaningful fictional engagement with race and, more particularly in the case of *Gravity's Rainbow*, with the Holocaust and anti-Semitism makes us wary of those who want to make a strong case for a committed antiracist and in general a more politically active Pynchon. Evidence in the writings up to and including the 1973 novel, the slim pickings available in the extremely sparse biographical record, and the materials now available in special collections libraries do not advance such a view. If it even matters in the first place.

The novel Pynchon published in February 1973 is fundamentally concerned with the dominion of globally corporatized techno-scientific powers, for which nations still were effective constructs, but whose ICBMs and threats of nuclear annihilation better manifested their new global domain. The rocket not only defies national borders and oceans, it knows neither race, gender, nor class (excepting perhaps special dispensations for Them). "It's eminently fair," says Roger Mexico to Jessica Swanlake early in the novel. "Everyone's equal. Same chances of getting hit. Equal in the eyes of the rocket." Roger is riffing on the phrase "equal in the eyes of the law," signifying on how the rocket has *become* the law, sovereign unto itself. As Enzian's fellow trooper Christian insists nearly seven hundred pages later about life under the rocket: "what protection *is* there? what can protect us from *that?*" And just before Christian poses those questions, our narrator has insisted that "heretics" refusing this new rocket state sovereignty "will *all* be sought out. Each will have his personal rocket," programmed with his or her vital signs so that "each Rocket will know its intended and hunt him." Just so. In September 2011, a CIA-controlled drone aircraft launched a Hellfire missile that obliterated a car racing across the desert of Yemen and carrying a U.S. citizen named Anwar al-Awlaki in addition to several top Al Qaeda militants. The killing sparked a heated debate over what the *New York Times* story framed as "the legality—and morality—of putting an American citizen on a list of top militants marked for death."[34] The state's killing of a citizen without due legal process puts before one a problem for U.S. and international law. The *idea* of this, as Pynchon well understood in 1973, involves other magnitudes of inquiry. The questions at stake are not only legal and moral but ontological, involving an order of quasi-beings, or programmable (even, decision-making) robots, to do Their killing. Thus also at stake are matters of political theology, entailing what if anything a sovereign power may *not* do, a question of just whom executive authority may count as having reached a degree-zero of humanity, a rightless condition warranting enslavement or killing. The matters at stake are also theological, as new practices of utterly inescapable and seemingly random "death from above" tend to signify. The Calvinist Jonathan Edwards, who famously sermonized on "Sinners in the Hands of an Angry God" (1741), understood quite well the holy terror of such a death.

These thoughts return us to Roger's trope "equal in the eyes of the rocket," which he utters in a novel that wisely delinks the problems of equality and freedom, perennially muddled together in the history of Western democracies, particularly during the Long Sixties in the United States. The principle of equality under the law pertains to individual citizens of particular nations, and has involved matters such as guarantees of access to the ballot box and to nonsegregated public facilities, means of travel, and housing. It involves equal access, in other words, to constitutional rights such as the Fourteenth Amendment right of due process, formerly extended even to an allegedly traitorous citizen such as Anwar al-Awlaki. This is the history of *equality* in Anglo American jurisprudence that Roger's comment invokes. Yet the philosophical ideal of *freedom*—freedom of conscience, work, movement, and becoming—pertains to *all* human beings in its aspects of negative and positive liberty. Not legal equality but existential freedom is what's ultimately at stake in *Gravity's Rainbow*, as the dialogues involving Roger Mexico or Enzian or Father Rapier remind us. The difference is crucial. On this view, at the moment when a Hellfire missile obliterated him and his equal rights to due process before U.S. law, Anwar al-Awlaki might nevertheless, and despite the extent to which he may have understood himself as enacting Allah's divine edict, rightly have regarded himself as a perfectly free man. Free in accordance with his understanding of human existence. And so might Enzian, or Slothrop.

CHAPTER 12

Tyrone Slothrop's "Fuck You!"

And so we finally take up Tyrone Slothrop and the question of freedom. Among the strangest plot moves in the annals of literary fiction, our scuffling hero exits from *Gravity's Rainbow* when one-fifth of it still lies ahead. His disappearance leaves unresolved the specific enigma of his childhood traumas that might, or might not, unravel Slothrop's relation to the V-2 rocket. Yet that issue—the erection question—is overshadowed by others. Slothrop and the rocket are the focuses of an ellipse within which circulate world historical themes of patriarchal power, bureaucratized domination, and sovereign violence, forces the narration represents as trending deterministically toward a moment of annihilation. That moment haunts *Gravity's Rainbow* from its opening dream sequence to the closing figure of a nuclear-tipped ICBM descending at "nearly a mile per second" yet captured imaginatively, cinematically, in its last instant above the theater roof. In the hands of a more conventional fiction writer, Slothrop's rocket link would open a way for readers to reckon that historical arc, to complete their detective work in reading and deciphering the novel's clues. Instead, standing somewhere in northern Germany, Slothrop witnesses "a stout rainbow cock driven down out of pubic clouds into Earth," the contrary of that descending ICBM. He witnesses this vision without "a thing in his head, just feeling natural"; and four ellipsis dots then signal, it seems, his vanishing. Afterward his name resurfaces in the expressed desires of Counterforce characters, such as Katje Borgesius and Pig Bodine, who would find and help him, and in the desires of others, such as Tchitcherine and Enzian, who would only use him. Otherwise he exists in the subjunctive mood: Slothrop *may* have bumped into Tchitcherine's young driver, Džabajev, in a German village, and he *might* have played harmonica and kazoo for a sixties English rock band named the Fool. He seems to have become a byword and legend—a mock heroic, postmodern Orpheus—scattered, if only through other characters' memories and motives. To some of them Slothrop no longer "matters." In a focalized passage Tchitcherine considers that Allied bureaucracies have, by midsummer, lost interest in Slothrop because "he has still not recorded, tagged, discovered, or liberated a single scrap of A-4 hardware of intelligence" and reports "to no known Allied office" any longer.[1] He's of no *use* to anyone, yet still a danger because of what he knows. This is why we're shown in the novel's final episode that should Slothrop attempt a return to his Massachusetts home he'd be "interdicted" by occupying forces deployed there to seize him.[2] Slothrop also seems either deliberately or willy-nilly to have become, in every sense, a free radical, a missing-in-action soldier, a stateless person.

Critics read Slothrop's scattering or disappearance in various ways. One tendency is to interpret it as a consequence of Slothrop's moment of "visionary transcendence," seen as cosmically synthesizing "the subject-object duality." Another is to read it in the terms of techno-scientific metaphors, thus to define a Slothrop who may be pulled by gravitational forces into a "singularity" or black hole, or pulled by the gravitational collapse of his own psyche into a vanishing point on the "temporal bandwidth" defining stable human selfhood. In either case, this view reads him as effectively dying. Further possibilities include reading his disappearance as the ironic end of either a failed quest or a frustrated night journey, or as an evocation of Pynchon's own flight from public life, a variant of which is Harold Bloom's idea that Slothrop's vanishing realizes an "anarchic visionary ideal that animates much of Pynchon's fictions." All such interpretive strategies address the striking liberties Pynchon takes with narrative conventions by invoking—but in the novel's fourth part denying—the schematizing force of particular spiritual, philosophical, cosmological, cultural, or sociopolitical idealisms, each with its own intellectual and affective allure, and each typically pitched in the terms of romance narrative.[3]

We choose to stay with the narrative's messy and material stuff and the historical contexts of state power and domination, of texts and expressive freedom, of struggle and means of resistance. To begin with, consider Slothrop's disappearance in its twofold aspect. First, there's the "Fuck You!" he utters, or flings (four times), against the agents of a globalized military-industrial regime bent on using him as its instrument, and how this figures his fugitive relation to the last fifth of the novel. Second, consider how these narrative representations take on a concrete and vivid existence if read in context with one of the persistent questions of political life during the years Pynchon was writing *Gravity's Rainbow*: namely whether, and how, nonviolent (but still active) resistance should answer imperialist forms of domination and violence. This resistance crucially involves the free speech rights we surveyed in part one, as writers and publishers in the fifties and sixties confronted a legal regime that criminalized startling, strong words and representations targeting state-sponsored repression and violence. Bringing those cultural, political, and legal struggles back into view enables us to read *Gravity's Rainbow* as one obvious beneficiary of that struggle's eventual successes in the Long Sixties. Pynchon's stunningly explicit figurations of pedophilia, coprophagia, sadomasochism, and homosexual and heterosexual rape are all vital to his critique of fascist domination and simply would not, as we've shown, have found a U.S. publisher without the success of that free speech movement. Applying the lessons of that history to the disappearing-Slothrop problem also enables us to read his "Fuck You!" and his fugitive status in the terms of a compelling philosophical dialogue on nonviolent resistance to imperial aggression. A persistent topic of intellectual and political struggle during the 1966–71 years, this debate over forms of resistance reemerged during the second Iraq war, when thought again had to reckon with new/old political realities posed by the radically enhanced surveillance techniques and methods of control available to late capitalist sovereignties. At times that critique turned to literature, most notably to the minimalist idea of resistance posed in Herman Melville's "Bartleby, the Scrivener," a story Pynchon has also noted. So we are interested in the textual facts and the enduring politics of Slothrop's psychological and political dilemma, and how that approach opens critical understandings of his fugitive status in the novel's dark ending.

Slothrop's disappearing act commences in Monte Carlo. Initially a virtual or attitudinal shift, it depends on his recognitions, in a casino gaming hall where everything ought to depend on chance, that instead "everything in this room is being used"; that there are "two orders of being" and he's glimpsing the second and newly revealed one; and that this plot that They have scripted in order to make him instrumentally useful involves "the Forbidden itself"— the erection question, especially what is alleged to have been done to him in Jamf's lab. In the text there's a paragraph break, then this: "'Fuck you,' whispers Slothrop. It's the only spell he knows, and a pretty good all-purpose one at that." With that utterance Slothrop exits the casino, runs through a hard rain that's begun to fall, and recognizes his action as "flight. It is flight" (he repeats to assure himself). Two further recognitions accent this moment. The first is that Slothrop takes encouragement from the remembrance of Teddy Bloat's recent promise to assist: "if you need help, well, I'll help you." The second, a moral and spiritual imperative, is that this revelation requires him to meet the future with a "kind of grace."[4] Eight pages on, as Slothrop finds himself back in the company of Katje Borgesius and Stephen Dodson-Truck, but now having to act from the basis of his new double-consciousness, Slothrop recalls that injunction: "Grace, he warns himself, grace." Before he disappears Slothrop will twice more remind himself to act with the "Grace he always imagined himself short on," because if he can maintain even a "state of minimum grace" then, he thinks, "this network of all plots may yet carry him to freedom." That last reminder, incidentally, occurs just before he becomes "a crossroad" and disappears.[5]

Back to Monte Carlo for a moment. Rejoining Katje after his "flight" through the rain, Slothrop follows up on his recognitions. Now seeing himself as "a victim" who has been "conned" into Their plot, he also understands Katje, Bloat, and others as persons equally coerced into Their confidence game. Thus he recognizes himself as, potentially, one among others in a makeshift network. Moreover, in realizing that the great military-industrial powers have linked him and his cohort bodily and mentally to the war machine—"their iron-clad engine" of death—Slothrop understands that his newly realized double-consciousness has installed within his psyche "a clutch he can disengage." Yet he also understands that declutching from the war might only liberate him into "his inertia of motion, his real helplessness." The point is that Slothrop does not yet know enough about that con game, or his options within it that might reveal a way out of it. This unknowing defines his inertial helplessness. The narration from early in part 2 thus represents Slothrop recognizing that "all in his life of what looked free or random" turns out "to've been under some Control." The text metaphorizes that domination in the form of an arc running backward to a room "where something was done to him" as a child, and forward into his present, uncanny link to v-2 rockets.[6] As for the affective signs of this new double-consciousness, they involve his "scared-elated" anxieties, confronting both imminent danger and possible liberation.

Staying in Monaco, playing along in order to better calibrate the scope and powers of what controls and threatens him, Slothrop commences the rocket technology crash course They have designed especially for him. During that stretch he gets confirmations of the big plot, for example as They remove Bloat, Dodson-Truck, even Katje. He learns "to hear quote-marks in the speech of others," finds documentary clues about people and institutions apparently related to his operant conditioning as Infant Tyrone, and learns so much about the rocket that, by the time he flees Monaco for Nice, then Zürich, and into the Zone, Allied intelligence, "naturally, is frantic about Slothrop's disappearance. Here's a man running loose who knows everything possible to know—not only about the A-4, but about what *Great Britain* knows about the A-4."[7] That passage precisely identifies the ways that Slothrop and the sovereign powers controlling him are reciprocally dangerous to each other. Indeed, any reading of *Gravity's Rainbow* attending to the text's command of realist conventions, often so stunningly accomplished, should see in that reciprocal threat a key dynamic driving this novel's plot. No matter how surrealistic the narration in some episodes, or satirically disruptive in others, Slothrop's imminent endangerment naturalizes a good deal of one's reading experience as this storyworld takes shape. Throughout part 3 of the novel, U.S. Army major Duane Marvy is hunting Slothrop, blazing away at him with two .45 automatic pistols, for example in the chase scene through the tunnels at Nordhausen, a parody of the Hollywood big-budget thriller. And it's only because of Slothrop's purely accidental or improvisatory costume switch (at the end of part 3) that English operatives mistakenly castrate Marvy, in Slothrop's stead. Even after Slothrop's final disappearing act in part 4, readers are given several intimations, recollections delinked from any identifiable chronology, that somewhere in a "Transvestites' Toilet" our antihero wonders if those sent to kill him will "come in person" or if his father might "send a hit man" to beat them to it. Eight pages later our narrator remarks: "Eventually Jack [Kennedy] and Malcolm [X] both got murdered. Slothrop's fate is not so clear. It may be that They have something different in mind for Slothrop."[8] The threat from above is certainly clear.

Slothrop's dilemma seems sharply defined as part 3 ends. On the one side we have Slothrop with his knowledge of, and his evident psychosexual enmeshment with, the rocket. On the other stand the sovereign powers—Britain, the United States, and the Soviet Union—with their broadly and deeply capitalized, bureaucratized, and militarized potentials for surveillance, domination, and violence. Slothrop and the several state powers may be reciprocally dangerous to each other, yet their abilities to inflict violence are totally asymmetrical. As the doctors Muffage and Spontoon's castration of Major Marvy at the end of part 3 suggests, Their powers to find Slothrop and inflict trauma might make the earlier Marvy chase scene read more like that "disgusting English Candy Drill" back at Mrs. Quoad's London flat—just another exercise in black humor. For the more likely scenario, see another of the part 4 moments decoupled from any identifiable chronology: when Pig Bodine tells Slothrop how FBI agents gunned down the outlaw John Dillinger on a sidewalk outside Chicago's Biograph Theater in 1934.[9] So the dilemma Pynchon's plot sets up is that Slothrop might well sustain his old, pre-rocket life by repressing his new knowledge and performing flawlessly his familiarly hedonistic, apolitical self. Yet all of the novel's uses of modern psychology— behavioral (Pavlov), psychoanalytical (Freud or Jung), neo-Freudian (Fromm, Marcuse, Brown), or even pharmacological (injecting a truth serum, for example, as narrated in part 1)—would argue that some uncontrollable abreaction, some return of the repressed, or some recursive divination would sooner or later disclose Slothrop's dangerous mind. Seen as a literary character inscribed largely according to realist conventions, and defined by his particular traits and peculiar dilemma, Tyrone Slothrop's best (or only) choice is to resist Their plot—which is also to say, the novel's deathward trajectory— by giving Them, or it, the finger and fleeing the ellipse in which he has been Their captive subject.

When Slothrop utters his first "Fuck You"—whispering it, in fear They might be listening—he's shown thinking of it as an all-purpose "spell," while also considering how he might sneak back into the gaming room named for ss head Heinrich Himmler and "paint FUCK YOU" in a dialogue balloon rising from "the mouth of one of those little pink shepherdesses" depicted on the casino walls. After that moment, the "Fuck You" epithet appears five more times in *Gravity's Rainbow*. Two of those instances are merely vulgar come-backs in response to a humorous situation: Slothrop to Der Springer, after the man farts in his face, and to Eddie Pensiero, in reply to an ethnic joke. These ways of brushing off someone, of obscenely expressing disregard or dismissal, do not interest us here. As the *Oxford English Dictionary* etymologist Jesse Sheidlower reminds us, they operate as crass retorts to ironic situations, often among friends. That usage lacks the contemptuous and more overt and uncanny hostility of the kind of "Fuck You" we are considering.[10]

That species of "Fuck You" entails real aggressive potentiality. It is commonly classed and legally recognized in U.S. jurisprudence as "fighting words"—speech understood as liable to provoke violence and therefore legally proscribed and punishable. Indeed this kind of speech may, depending upon context, perform a legally actionable incitement to violence, whether one-on-one or one-to-many. In a well-known 1971 case, *Cohen v. California*, the U.S. Supreme Court ruled that nineteen-year-old Paul Cohen did *not* speak "fighting words" when he appeared in a public space—a Los Angeles courthouse, where he was about to be conscripted into the army—wearing a jacket blazoned with the words "Fuck the Draft." Notably, the justices ruled that unlike epithets such as "Fuck You," which *are* addressed to someone and which municipal and state courts had previously found, depending on the situation and verbal context, to be illegal "fighting words," Cohen's phrasing neither explicitly nor implicitly incited action against a specific person or persons. The justices ruled that Cohen was instead "informing the public of the depth of his feelings against the Vietnam War and the draft"; also, that this context defined Cohen's use of an obscenity as a constitutionally protected free speech right. On those grounds the Court overturned the man's 1968 conviction for—and here's a neat irony—"disturbing the peace." Pynchon captures the crucial difference in Cohen's case when *Gravity's Rainbow* represents the resisting residents of Kirghizstan using a new, Soviet-imposed writing—the New Turkic alphabet—against Soviet apparatchiks: "On sidewalks and walls the very first printed slogans start to show up, the first Central Asian fuck you signs, the first kill-the-police-commissioner signs (and somebody does! this alphabet is really something!)." Such instances in fiction as in real life require one to analyze the context of illocutionary utterances, in which the word is reckoned as effectually linked to the deed. This understanding is exactly what made the f-word subversive and legally hazardous speech during the Long Sixties.[11]

Another Slothrop "Fuck You" occurs in part 3. Slothrop's aloft in a hot-air balloon piloted by a German named Schnorp when Marvy attacks in a reconnaissance plane. Slothrop shouts the epithet at Marvy, then flings custard pies, one nailing the major in the face and another hitting the plane's engine, forcing him down and saving our scuffling hero from certain death. The scene unfolds as pure slapstick. More seriously, Slothrop in another moment is shown to understand that some things evidently were done to and with his body and mind when he was a child. The terms involved a contract worth five thousand dollars and the boy's guarantee of a Harvard education, a complicated and pathetically monetized life history that raises fears he cannot keep "down with a simple Fuck You." It's as if They have put him and kept him under "a spell."[12] What then might Slothrop effectively say and do by way of a counterspell against such powers, thus to claim some measure of freedom? We understand this as, arguably, *the* key problem in *Gravity's Rainbow*. And in the approach we are sketching here, the Supreme Court's jurisprudence in *Cohen v. California* points up the need for one to tease the politics out of scenes in *Gravity's Rainbow* that may wrongly seem, forty years after their writing, to be merely farcical. To Justice John Harlan, who wrote the Supreme Court's majority opinion in this case, Paul Cohen's wearing of that infamous "Fuck the Draft" jacket had interjected both humor and righteous anger on the day when, as federal law required, he dutifully reported to his local draft board. That offensive jacket was Cohen's own "spell" against state power—and by the way, it worked. His protracted legal journey enabled Cohen to avoid the draft and likely army service in Vietnam.[13]

Here then is a vigorous and compelling historical backdrop of social, political, and legal struggle—of resistances to and evasions of a massive and invasive sovereign power—against which we must read Slothrop's "Fuck You" and his disappearance. It is a history, in brief, according to which we would find in *Gravity's Rainbow* a principled disturbance of the peace, wonderfully clad in its jacket of fictional art. Consider the discursive repressions and countercultural resistances in play during the late fifties and sixties, when first as a Cornell University student Thomas Pynchon started writing literary fiction and when using the f-word was prohibited in American print culture. Norman Mailer's characters' prolific usage of the f-word had been infamously revised out of his 1948 war novel, *The Naked and the Dead*, as his editors at Rinehart substituted the words "fug," "fugger," and "fugging." Three years later J. D. Salinger's *The Catcher in the Rye* barely made it into print without his Little, Brown editors having to revise a scene set at Holden Caulfield's school, where a student had "written 'Fuck You' on the wall." And these were texts the reviewers treated as major fictions by up-and-coming writers. As we argued in part one of this book, the smaller underground presses pushed much more vigorously against that prohibitive regime, and wound up in court. The 1957 San Francisco municipal court obscenity trial of Lawrence Ferlinghetti and Shig Murao for publishing and disseminating Allen Ginsberg's 1956 chapbook, *Howl and Other Poems*, surely is the most widely recollected instance, not just because literary luminaries testified for the defendants, who won their case when Judge Clayton Horn decided that "Howl" had "redeeming social value," but because it commenced a nationwide movement for writers' free speech rights to so-called obscene and subversive utterances, like Ginsberg's curse on the American war machine: "Go fuck yourself with your atom bomb. / I don't feel good don't bother me."[14]

By mid-1965, when Pynchon returned to the United States, eventually residing in California, the Berkeley free speech movement had transformed significantly. The key seems to have been the arrival on the University of California campus of John J. Thompson from New York's Lower East Side, where he'd been interacting with Ed Sanders (of *Fuck You* magazine fame), William Burroughs, and the *Realist*'s editor, Paul Krassner, among others. One day while watching the free speech movement scene in the Berkeley campus's Sather Gate area, Thompson took out a felt-tip pen and made a makeshift sign that the campus newspaper, the *Daily Californian*, described as "a four-letter word for sexual intercourse." When a conservative UC Berkeley student attacked Thompson and tore up his sign, Thompson made another, at which point police moved in and arrested him on an obscenity charge. Next day, supporters set up a table with two large signs: "FUCK DEFENSE FUND" and "SUPPORT THE FUCK CAUSE." They were soon arrested, along with an English major reciting pages from *Lady Chatterley's Lover*. Mass rallies followed, at one of which someone led protesters in a cheer—"Gimme an F, gimme a U . . ."—spelling out the offensive word and originating, as legend tells it, the "Fuck Chant" with which rock band Country Joe and the Fish would introduce performances of their anti–Vietnam War song "Feel Like I'm Fixin' to Die Rag," notable also here for its famous kazoo accompaniment. There was a clear politics at work in such moments, involving perfectly ordinary sexual acts, commonly used obscenities, speech rights, and then antiwar activism. So the free speech movement had spun off a more confrontational, raucous, and humorous brother—the "filthy speech movement."

As that movement went national, and especially as it merged with civil rights and anti–Vietnam War movements, the liberty of speakers, writers, and artists to utter obscenities in the public sphere, particularly in opposing state-sanctioned violence that movement activists depicted as far more obscene than usage of the sexually charged f-word, became a key rhetorical, cultural, political, and legal aspect of sixties activism. These resistances typically took on a sharp and subversively satirical edge—as antiwar rallies featured poetry (Ginsberg reciting "America" or "Howl"), fiction writers (Mailer essaying the situation with obscenity-laced analyses), and music by the Fugs or Country Joe. During these events police invoked local or state obscenity statutes to arrest numerous dissidents, most of whose cases were either dismissed or thrown out on appeal. By late 1968, when three student editors of the University of Hartford campus newspaper were charged with obscenity and libel for depicting Richard Nixon as an upraised "fuck finger" (see part one of this book), these law enforcement tactics had become a police standard—promoted, as Seth Rosenfeld has shown, by Ronald Reagan (then the California governor), FBI chief J. Edgar Hoover, and numerous U.S. senators and congressmen. By 1971–72, according to one legal historian, the U.S. Supreme Court had a backlog of more than sixty appeals of obscenity convictions, half of which involved political speech rights.[15]

A long tradition dating to early sixties obscenity arrests of leftist standup comics like Mort Sahl and Lenny Bruce persistently regards the uses of "crude" or "vulgar" language as unnecessary and in any case degrading to the "high ideals" of equality, justice, and peace for which movement radicals were advocating. So Reagan said over and over, during his 1966 run for governor. He was typical, and the claim still has some traction. Even McMillian's superb history of Long Sixties underground presses finds Ed Sanders's *Fuck You* to be "a crude journal." It was, and proudly so. And what the literary historian can teach the cultural and political historian is that all of these practices, those of Sahl and Bruce, Ginsberg and Mailer, Sanders and young John Thompson, grew out of a much deeper literary-cultural tradition of carnivalesque and satirical work. Also, that the flowering of this cultural moment may be seen in *Gravity's Rainbow* and in Robert Coover's comparably transgressive novel *The Public Burning*. Sanders's irregularly mimeographed magazine was just much more in your face with its rejections, as when it periodically featured Lower East Side anarchist Norman Barr's column, titled "Bouquet of Fuck Yous," maledictions that he launched against the likes of neo-Nazi white supremacist George Lincoln Rockwell, the FBI and CIA, and the far-right Republican wing called Young Americans for Freedom. Police and FBI agents regularly harassed Barr, as they did Sanders, who finally shut down the magazine because the people distributing it in shops and newsstands were also being threatened with obscenity charges. Eight years later, when *Gravity's Rainbow* appeared, that kind of police pressure had mostly ended. In June 1973, four months after Pynchon's novel was published, the U.S. Supreme Court handed down the long-awaited, landmark ruling in *Miller v. California*, allowing any work that "taken as a whole" can be found to offer "serious literary, artistic, political, or scientific value."[16]

In 1993 Thomas Pynchon broke his customary public silence with a humorous essay for a *New York Times* series on the seven deadly sins. His assignment: the fourth sin, sloth. Pynchon addresses his topic by way of the Latin term Thomas Aquinas used, *acedia*, which names the inability to commit oneself to action in the world, thus a somatic condition of sloth but, more important, a lack of moral and spiritual will. Walter Benjamin, we should add, analyzed the tragic condition as an "indolence of the heart"; thus, more than transient apathy, acedia is for Benjamin an abdication of sovereign selfhood on a path to suicide—turning on whether "to be or not to be." In the "Sloth" essay Pynchon has in mind much the same thing, drawing one of his prime examples from Herman Melville's "Bartleby, the Scrivener." He reads the story's title character as redefining acedia for a secular mid-nineteenth-century America, seen also as an offense against the reigning capitalist economy. In repeatedly addressing his boss's demand that he do his assigned office work—the tedious copying of legal papers—Bartleby's "I would prefer not to" signifies a lack of desire, expressed as a negated existential preference, *not to* meet the demand and the prospect of his continuing to sell his middle-class soul for what Pynchon typifies as "a paycheck and a hassle-free life." This means, though Pynchon doesn't explicitly say so, that he reads Bartleby as expressing disobedience, however passive, in response to another's willful demand, although the character's passive resistance required a bare minimum of free will. This is crucial, because Pynchon next sees twentieth-century sloth becoming the norm of modern political culture. For him, modern acedia demonstrates a lack even of a minimal disobedience. Pynchon claims this has led to a general "failure of public will [in] allowing . . . the rise of evil regimes," especially "the worldwide fascist ascendancy" of the 1920s–'30s and, "not far behind" in governmental evilness, "the Vietnam era and the Reagan-Bush years"—the Cold War, in other words. One clear context for understanding Pynchon's critique is, again, Marcuse's idea of repressive tolerance—the concept that state powers will tolerate a certain degree of dissident, culturally resistant behavior in exchange for the sustained repression of people and populations, which repressed subjects impose *on themselves*. The true acedia Pynchon defines entails the absence even of Bartleby's bare-bones mode, so meek and ineffectual that the story's narrator, the Wall Street lawyer, grossly misreads it, though he does *feel* a resistance.[17]

Pynchon's way of using Bartleby to historicize sloth in relation to a cultural and political critique and resistance, however minimal, returns us to Tyrone Slothrop's "Fuck You." How does it relate to his disappearance and its politics? Indeed, how does the phrase parse the chances for freedom figured in *Gravity's Rainbow*? First consider the ways Bartleby's sentence "I would prefer not to" differs from Slothrop's reiterated "Fuck You." Grammatically, Bartleby's syntax is a maddening mix of the subjunctive (would) with the negative (not) in relation to a verb expressing weak desire (prefer). Gilles Deleuze is one of many who read Bartleby's sentence as cannily disconnecting words from deeds, language from reference, for it is a sentence without an object: prefer not to do—uhm, what? As such, it erases the boss's demand that Bartleby *copy*. Deleuze thus finds in the sentence's elemental indifference to that labor an expression of the speaker's subtle rebellion, which is enabling passively a process by which the boss will introject Bartleby's own madness (caused by that labor of being a human copy machine). Giorgio Agamben, in an essay that partly responds to Deleuze (and to another essay by Jacques Rancière), argues that Bartleby expresses not indifference but a condition of suspension. Specifically, his sentence would suspend in pure potentiality the law itself, would suspend law's power to do (what it alone defines as) justice. To Agamben the sentence expresses neither civil disobedience nor quiet rebellion. Rather, it instantiates the messianic moment absolutely outside human law. This is why constituted authority legally *sentences* he whose sentences seek to deny sovereign power, as Bartleby's death in prison indicates.[18]

Slothrop's tarot with its reversed Hanged Man contradicts his potential for a messianic moment. Yet if that divinatory reading has any efficacy, then why would state power need to martyr a fellow defined by his "mediocrity" and his future as "a tanker and a feeb"? One reason is that Slothrop's "Fuck You" must be understood as a quite different mode of utterance than Bartleby's. For one thing, it is not even a sentence. We owe this recognition to a brilliantly funny 1971 essay published in what has been called "the most unusual Festschrift in the history of academic publishing." In it the eminent University of Chicago linguist James D. McCawley, writing under a pseudonym as Vietnamese linguist Quang Phuc Dong, puts "Fuck You" under the analytical microscope of transformational grammar. (He was one of Noam Chomsky's early and best students.) We have no idea whether Thomas Pynchon knew of this well-circulated piece, though we'd like to believe so. McCawley finds that "Fuck you!" does *not* fall into the category of subjectless sentences (like "Damn Lyndon Johnson"), nor can it be transformatively embedded in a sentence (though of course it can be quoted in a punctuated sentence, as we do here). Indeed this locution resists analysis using the tools of transformational grammar because it is *not* a sentence. Rather it is a species of pure epithet expressing hostility, rejection, dismissal, resistance, abjection. This is why it operates as such an all-purpose spell or malediction. There is negation and indeed abnegation but nothing subjunctive or impassive much less messianic about it. If the epithet really were magical, then it would (in the illocutionary sense) express the addressee becoming gone, different, or dead. It is perhaps the purest of vulgar, secular curses. Speech act theory understands a proper "Fuck You" as a performative: an illocutionary expression that does what it says—it *fucks* (in all possible vernacular meanings) the second-person addressee.[19] That is its power.

This returns us to Slothrop's scattering or disappearance, which by contrast, says something in what he *does*. To be concise, Slothrop first chooses to go AWOL (absent without leave) from his post in Monaco in order to chase down clues about the erection question, then finalizes his desertion at the beginning of part 4. If captured, like some twenty thousand World War II deserters, he would face prosecution and potentially execution, according to the Uniform Code of Military Justice (to which Pynchon would have been introduced after enlisting in the navy). Actually, though, in this matter the relevant context for *Gravity's Rainbow* is not World War II but the Vietnam War, from which some fifty thousand draft resisters and AWOL soldiers found sanctuary abroad, mostly in Canada.[20] As antislavery activists in the antebellum United States commonly said about fugitive slaves running to Canada, such persons were "voting with their feet." And that history and rhetoric was exactly what sixties antiwar activists such as Carl Oglesby and Daniel Berrigan drew upon, when they publicly urged resisting U.S. military personnel or potential draftees to speak the truth of their conscience by becoming fugitives—their numbers nearly equal to the number of war dead whose names are on the Vietnam Veterans Memorial in the nation's capital.

While Slothrop is a fugitive but still on the narrative's radar screen in parts 2 and 3, he's assisted by fellow AWOL soldier Blodgett Waxwing and by "semi-AWOL" sailor Pig Bodine, among others. While offscreen in part 4, he supposedly encounters—is said to have encountered—the equally AWOL Soviet soldier Džabajev in the village of Niederschaumdorf.[21] The problem, however, is that once Slothrop slips out of the novel's mimetic frame, readers get nothing further in the way of direct discourse telling his whereabouts, actions, thoughts, and reasons. Our detective work is further frustrated by the ways that our third-person narrator(s), as we've noted, will make contradictory statements about Slothrop, and complicate things further by bringing in characters' hearsay remarks and those so-called experts, like Steve Edelman, who either repeat or contradict earlier information. The narration thus providing no evidence with which to naturalize, much less stabilize, claims about Slothrop's disappearance, how can we reckon with that strangest of all plot moves?

One way to infer its meaning is to analogize Slothrop's predicament to the novel's narrative practices. *Gravity's Rainbow* relies on omniscient narration to penetrate the consciousnesses of characters, to evoke their perceptions, idle thoughts, reasonings, fantasies, and obsessional desires as well as the deepest recesses of their traumatized and self-abjected, subconscious minds. In other words, this novel's uses of narrative "authority" operate at a level of supreme and total power or dominion. Seemingly nothing escapes the narration's penetrating eye and rationality, not even the consciousness of a dodo bird. The novel's narrative practices mimic the surveillance apparatuses in the cartelized, global state that Pynchon represents as emerging after 1945. This novel may have been titled "Mindless Pleasures" when he submitted the typescript, but its métier is nothing less than the total *mindful rationalization* of characters, events, and actions. One trenchant, self-reflexive view of these practices, which occurs relatively early, in episode 10 of part 1, is Slothrop's sodium amytal session, which They schedule in order to pierce his deepest anxieties about shit, race, blackness, and sexual domination—indeed, domination in general. All such practices, executed in the name of "the war effort," of "saving lives," as They would say, nonetheless instrumentalize Slothrop in ways that reiterate his earliest trauma (real or imagined), ways further reiterated in later episodes. So whether we think of Slothrop as a natural man or as a textual construct, still the only way "he" may avoid that iterative violence is by exiting the novel's frame—achieving a fugitive self, going underground, scattering the remnant items and memories of his existence in the storyworld. However we choose to think of it, this seems to be all we know, and all we need to know. Slothrop's disappearance is his own version of Ginsberg's "Go fuck yourself with your atom bomb / I don't feel good don't bother me" malediction to "America."

Tyrone Slothrop certainly is represented as a scuffler and an idler and to some extent as a (Harvard-graduated!) "feeb," an apolitical late twenties guy with an all-American lineage. He's a man who for much of the time we know him mainly lives up to the deadly sin indicated in his patronymic. One might even make the case that he, duly prepared by enterprising Pop, Broderick, and Mom, the aptly named Nalline, exemplifies the acedia-defined, soulless modern who impassively watched the "worldwide fascist ascendancy."[22] But early in part 2 and throughout part 3, Slothrop has been leaving the sin and the name behind. Out in the Zone, he's attentive to the workings of "grace" and at times thinks it has operated in his life; surely it blesses him at Putzi's, near Cuxhaven, when by accident he escapes castration and leaves behind the last of his multiple alternate identities, from Ian Scuffling through Plecha-zunga. His vanishing in part 4 puts a period to those metamorphoses, a kind of stability, and grace, after all.

Let us also be frank about the strict limits on this kind of freedom. As with Vietnam-era war deserters, Slothrop's freedom entails the conditions of a perpetual banishment and excludes any right of free return to his home and community, his habitus, forswearing practically all that human beings iden-tify with "the good." We might well read that self-banishment as a gauge of his frustration and his precarious life, perhaps symbolized partly by his drawing the Hanged Man reversed. We should also read Slothrop's disap-pearing act in context with our last glimpse of Enzian, discussed above. The recognition that Christian and Enzian share in late 1945, the Cold War ef-fectually born but still lacking its name, is that no place and no one can pro-tect against the rocket, against modern state power. It can penetrate and find one "at any given point." From that realization Enzian has put his remnant of a people on course for a long trek into uncertain exile—himself included, unless he's going up in Rocket 00001, as Gottfried did in the 00000. Mean-while their condition is utterly precarious; enemies—especially the Soviets—are hunting them down and picking them off one by one. They are homeless and without rights, all questions of "equality" before the law simply inap-plicable to their condition. As such they are shown as persons and as a com-munity existing on the threshold just above that condition of total dominion that might make suicide their last "free" option after all. But Enzian commits himself to resisting that null point. His Herero survivors have a minimal social organization, and possess a spiritualized, haunting object for which They will hazard anything. Whatever Enzian may do with it, the 00001 is the Herero war survivors' totem, its number—one—signifying its entelechy and perhaps also their identity as its death-driven counterpart. Or perhaps not. We might read it as the Hereros' "Fuck You!" thrown in Their face. In these ways they are the same as but, with their minimal community, just a little better off than, say, Geli and Tchitcherine, Ludwig and his lemming, and Slothrop alone with his blues harp and *his* "Fuck You!"

More than a freedom to "prefer not to," as in Bartleby's case, Slothrop's favorite malediction is conditioned by an actual, not a potential, negation. There is nothing idealistic, much less transcendent, in such a self-alienating decision. It is selfish by definition, hence elementally political for it rejects domination and claims the right only to abide by one's own lights, to sustain the integrity of and sovereignty over one's own body and mind. Again, it enunciates a minimalist claim of negative freedom, deeply alienated and individuated. It may sign the achievement of a psychological identity, but only in resistance to or flight from or scattering before an otherwise crushing power. Thus it signs a wholly dangerous resistance, which the subject who yells the obscene malediction more or less accepts, along with the proviso that this single-minded resistance likely accomplishes nothing of political or historical importance. *Gravity's Rainbow* presents the facts of that ineffectuality and futility in the missile descending on the Orpheus Theater, some twenty-seven years after Slothrop's vanishing act. It's an utterly dark ending, uplifted only momentarily by song.

Seen against the backdrop of U.S. history, Slothrop's disappearance does make sense. Sustaining one's non-narratability can be seen as a primary condition of one's survival. By 1972, as we've shown, Hoover's FBI had compiled its "index" of "subversives," with Pynchon and others in his circle included on it, and the Defense Department's Garden Plot document had marshaled resources and readied troops for rounding up the "indexed" people, down to the selection of detention sites. So the project of staying off Their radars in a late capitalist world of mechanized informatics and surveillance did stand on a plain logic and a basic rationale by 1973. We cannot know what the character Tyrone Slothrop thinks about these matters in his fictional 1945 because after a point relatively early in part 4, the narration no longer reveals his thoughts. Still, readers have been given copious evidence that he resents being grievously violated in childhood and unforgivably manipulated during the nine months of the novel's main chronology. Slothrop therefore may be understood as one brought to the threshold of freedom's minimalist position, short of killing himself. More than that dark and empty prospect, human beings should at least possess the negative liberty not to be implicated in evil, by whatever lights they reckon evil. Also, human beings may at least realize their negative liberty by articulating their "Nay." Like Bartleby, or any of us, Slothrop is shown to realize that possibility of resistance, even if he declines to express it in league with any wider collective of fellow freethinkers. Any human being in his situation always has access to the "carefully crafted *Fuck You!*"[23]

v-2 damage to Van Straelenstraat, Antwerp, February 9, 1945. Photo by Frans Claes. Courtesy of the Claes Estate.

"Too Late" (A Conclusion)

Pynchon's 1990 novel, *Vineland*, ended a seventeen-year stretch of near silence after *Gravity's Rainbow*. He sets the novel in Ronald Reagan's United
States in 1984 and flashes back to sixties radicals in Berkeley "going around
in battle fatigues with their hair in matching oversize Jewish Afros, spray-
painting SMASH THE STATE on public walls and keeping plastic explosives in
Tupperware containers"; "[p]retending to be film editors but . . . really anarchist bombers."[1] In some ways these characters reprise the Argentinean anarchists of the 1973 novel, who fancy themselves using insurgent art to bomb
"down your fences and your labyrinth walls," thus to lead people "back to
the Garden [they] hardly remember." Like its sixties American counterpart,
the 1945 anarchist revolution in the Zone never materializes. Instead, some
of the Argentineans imagine a cinema that captures on film a "mineral consciousness" which reckons temporality from the fanciful standpoint of sentient stones, witnessing time in "frames per century" or even "per millen-
nium." Others follow the lead of Beláustegui, whose yearning for mindless
pleasures takes him on a quest for an equally stoned "moment-to-moment"
consciousness. Alone among this crew is Graciela Portales, worrying about
the coming repression and asking herself: "what will the military government
think of a community like this in the middle of their garrison state?"[2] Notably, she also feels deep dependencies that reveal her *desire* for just such a
repressive state. More or less the same dynamic defines the regressive turn
of *Vineland*'s anarchists: stoners and pretenders and cop-outs who actually
want the coordinated police and military repression that inevitably comes
down, as Erich Fromm warned in 1941.

Gravity's Rainbow and *Vineland* present characters romancing the idea
of revolution but failing to carry it through, failing to realize even their own
radical desires for a "natural" and "free" individual existence, much less one
in community with others. In both novels the realities of insurgency over-
whelm the romance. Both texts partly assign this failure to the persistent
grip of primitivistic and Edenic fantasies, shown as reactions against increasingly pervasive and technologically sophisticated modes of control and violence, which are often depicted as frankly patriarchal. So the wannabe rebels
tie themselves up in Oedipal knots. Yet both novels also assign failure to the

ways in which, as Fromm and Marcuse argue, prospects for real freedom send people scurrying either backward into age-old forms of domination and violence or forward into ever-morphing modes of repressive tolerance. In either case, failure validates the authority of an existing dominion and reproduces the inferiority or preterite condition that capitalist and state powers have ascribed to the insurgents.

The final irony in *Gravity's Rainbow* is that for *all* the characters, it is simply too late. The narrator repeatedly says this about many of the novel's main preterite figures. Enzian is shown thinking to himself that for him and his exiled, trekking Hereros it is "too late, miles and changes too late"; and later we learn it's also "too late" for his half brother, Tchitcherine—a good thing for Enzian, at least. Roger laments the irony in how the war's end means it is "too late" for his romance with Jessica.[3] Frans van der Groov, after months of wantonly shooting the dodoes in company with fellow Dutch colonialists, momentarily thinks of putting a stop to the extermination but decides the effort is so far along it is just "too late" for the remnant of dodoes standing before him. So he blasts away. Gottfried, snugged into Rocket 00000 before launch, thinks of something he wanted to say to Weissmann, but now "it's too late." And about Slothrop's persistent nostalgia for Massachusetts, the narrator says it is "too late to get home." This belatedness afflicts all the novel's characters, including Them. In part 1, Ned Pointsman thinks of abandoning his already passé Pavlovian research "before it's too late," and by the novel's end he realizes the doors to scientific renown and especially his shot at a Nobel Prize are "closing behind him forever," leaving the man "only with Cause and Effect, and the rest of his sterile armamentarium," while "Mossmoon and the others" smirk behind his back. Then there's the adenoidal Nixon figure, "Richard M. Zhlubb, night manager of the Orpheus Theater on Melrose" Avenue, who is shown rolling down the L.A. freeways in his "black managerial Volkswagen" while wrestling with a prophetic dream about smothering in a plastic bag, a sign to him that it's "too late."[4] It surely is, and too late as well for all of humanity under the sign of that descending, nuclear-tipped ICBM poised over the Orpheus Theater on the novel's last page.

This situation might invoke apocalypse, but it ought not. The specific contexts for each claim in *Gravity's Rainbow* that it is "too late"—and there are many more than the examples we've listed—lead us to an alternate reading. The Judeo-Christian idea of apocalyptic end times, or eschatology, pivots on the ultimacy of divine judgment, on a final separation of the saved from the damned, whose evil deeds bring down divine wrath. Pynchon does riff (humorously) on this traditional idea, particularly when his writing lays out the Puritan division of elect from preterite. This seems to align *Gravity's Rainbow* with the Western scriptural tradition of apocalyptic interpretation, or hermeneutics, and some early critics ran with the idea.[5] Thus they tended to read the characters' fantasies and actions as displaying various libidinally degenerate, morally atavistic behaviors typical of the end times—more "mindless pleasures," in other words.[6] Pynchon's humorous riffing on apocalyptic thought should have raised a caution flag, though the real hitch is in that concept of God's wrath answering men's evil agency, and perhaps their acedia. Imminent apocalypse ill defines this end-times belatedness in *Gravity's Rainbow*, and not just because many characters do not do, or serve, evil. The novel presents most of its humanity as existing in the grip of massive military-industrial power, relegating any resistance to experiences of helplessness, futility, and death. Those terms don't jibe with the tradition of apocalypse. Indeed *Gravity's Rainbow* ascribes the helplessness and futility of its preterite folks entirely to the rule of vastly greater and manifestly evil powers and dominions, to the elect, thus satirically inverting the standard New Testament plot of apocalypse. This too may seem a seductive reading, because the inversion appears to stabilize the novel's complex ethical cruxes.

Yet a troubling fact is that *Gravity's Rainbow* thoroughly democratizes the pending doom. Indeed an intriguing consequence of working with the "too late" trope is that it erases the elect-preterite model set up in the book's beginning and sustained nearly to its end. By then, it's too late for everybody, from Pynchon's Nixon caricature right on down to the novel's lowliest souls—such as the random woman at the Dora camp to whom Pökler gives his wedding ring. Elsewhere, we read helplessness in the rocket-traumatized St. Veronica's Hospital children burrowing into their bedcovers like frightened "Foxes," and in old Pudding's tired submission to the coprophagic mania that will finally kill him. And we read the futility in, for example, the Counterforce's efforts to disrupt the Krupp dinner party, in Enzian's attempt to save the remnant of his people by committing them to scavenging the parts for and then firing Rocket 00001, in Tchitcherine's mission to find and kill Enzian, in Katje's and Roger's desires to find Slothrop and save him, in Zhlubb/Nixon's inability to interpret the portent of his dream, and finally in Slothrop, whose acedia sets the futility gold standard. All these characters keep doing what they do, futility and helplessness having become a minimal form of passive resistance that scarcely fazes the system. Indeed it's as if the system has gone on autopilot, its Clive Mossmoons and von Brauns and Zhlubb/Nixons all soullessly going about their work, the system meantime throwing everyone, right down to the last Bartleby, into the Tombs. There is no judgment, much less redemption for some, hence no apocalypse. All are equally doomed and damned. It's game over. It's been "too late" for a long time.

After the "screaming comes across the sky" in the novel's nineteen-word opening paragraph, the second one begins: "It is too late. The evacuation still proceeds, but it is all theatre." Yet is not "evacuation" also futile, even absurd, when a V-2 rocket may seem to find one anywhere? Or when nuclear war will crisp all of Mother Earth? The first V-2 missiles fired against Antwerp struck in early October 1944, as German forces sought to thwart Allied uses of the Scheldt River port to resupply troops. Like Londoners, some Antwerp residents evacuated to the countryside or to Brussels; but most stayed and worked their jobs, and learned to live with the rocket, which blasted their lives daily, utterly without warning. Just at the noon hour of November 27, for example, at the large and busy Teniers Square next to the city's central train station, a V-2 exploded just above the ground—it probably struck overhead power or tram lines, which touched off the nose cone's ton of amatol explosive—unleashing a lateral blast that left an incredible debris field of scorched and smoking automobile parts, luggage, paving stones, and human limbs and torsos, killing 126 and wounding twice that many. One victim's body was later found atop an undestroyed nearby multistory building, where the blast had flung it. The city imposed restrictions, for example against large gatherings of people; yet such efforts really were "all theatre," dramatizations of rule and bureaucratic order against indiscriminate annihilations. For the missiles simply rained randomly from the sky, obliterating a cemetery or a span of row houses on this or that city street, like Van Straelenstraat, captured days later in a Frans Claes photograph. Each blast sent up a mushroom cloud of debris—grit that used to be brick, along with tiny bits of metal, wood, and fabric that once made people's homes, all mixed with organic matter from vaporized residents—that would sprinkle down in a kind of mist for minutes afterward. At 3:30 on the afternoon of Saturday, December 16, a V-2 made a direct hit on the roof of the Rex Cinema, on one of the city's major avenues, De Keyserlei, as an audience of about eleven hundred watched Cecil B. DeMille's *The Plainsman* (1936), with Gary Cooper as Wild Bill Hickock trying to stop a bloody war with Cheyennes who've traded with greedy white gunrunners for the latest in repeating rifles. Assisted by Calamity Jane and Buffalo Bill, Wild Bill succeeds, and in the nick of time, of course! For the majority of that day's filmgoers, though, it was too late for that triumphal ending. The Ciné Rex death toll was 296 soldiers and 271 civilians, who were pulled and dug from rubble up to fifteen feet deep.

Whether it was the lure of mindless pleasures that took patrons to the Rex on that day, or a matter of playing the odds even if death is the croupier, or just the intrepidity and audacity of those who would tell Hitler, and death, "Fuck You!," this is some of what it meant to be human, in late 1944 and early 1945, under the reign of such incredible new weaponry. Pynchon's novel evokes this new world, which is not brave but exists under a new, dark cloud of not-knowing. This new dispensation, or "Rocket state-cosmology," is laying down fresh rules.[7] It has already quite displaced former ways of knowing morally a world governed by an eschatological concept of time, a concept necessary for judging that one is too late, an irredeemable sinner. After all, in traditional eschatology one can only be too late *for* something, namely too late cleaning up your life before the hellfire-and-brimstone consequences of Judgment Day. Now, however, the hellfire and brimstone is of another sort, not divinely intentional but humanly launched and robotically controlled, yet still at the mercy of chance. Moreover, even if the supersonic missile were far enough above the roof to allow a split second for you to think of your belatedness, you still couldn't do so because supersonic missiles disable the operation required for the phrase "too late" to have meaning. In the rocket's world, people simply lack legible or audible advance warning signs pointing to the consequences of a causal process they might avert, or escape from, or meet with repentant hearts. Therefore you can no longer sigh and say, "Too late!" Not that it matters existentially, because you will be vaporized before you can know enough to think it.

Throughout its pages *Gravity's Rainbow* evokes this new way of not-knowing, or at least mis-knowing, the manmade world. Think of it as an epistemology of ignorance. Figured initially in the paradox of supersonic speed, as the novel proceeds it is generalized to a postwar mindset that generally mis-knows things, events, and people because it lacks ways of understanding a world in which randomness trumps causality, in which Aristotelian concepts of character and plot long essential to theatricality are bankrupted. In that radically blasted sense, even saying "it's all theatre" on the first page of *Gravity's Rainbow*, as on the last, is too late. In between the first and last pages the narrative frees us, however ignorantly, to reinterpret or deconstruct or recuperate theatricality or dramatization. With time (for singing and other forms of recursive practice) we begin to recognize in theatricality itself a self-conscious nostalgia for the old world before Wernher von Braun's team took the V-2 to war; we realize characters' yearnings for their former home, the old familiar moral law or economy in a scriptable, predictable, determinist world. This is why a self-conscious mode of dramatization inflects and shapes so many of the novel's moments and scenes: the fantasies Pirate takes on as surrogate, Slothrop and Katje's "cute meet" which recalls Roger and Jessica's, the many chase scenes, the moment when Franz Pökler thinks he and Leni conceived Ilse, nearly all the scenes of paraphilia, the various guises Slothrop takes on and so easily performs—this list could go on at some length. This is how the rocket creates a subject that may think it is someone, a free agent enacting a script where he or she still has some kind of chance, and is still on her or his way to something, perhaps something big, like building an intercontinental missile or winning a Nobel Prize. But that's all a delusion, isn't it? As fantasy, it is thoroughly complicit with Their needs and aims. Or, more accurately, it serves technology's needs and aims, against which all people are just "too late." For the problem was never simply, or only, the rocket. The general problem throughout *Gravity's Rainbow* is the reign of technology, of techno-scientific knowledge and its methods of control over people, thus a thoroughgoing dominion serving the belligerent requirements of nations, which themselves serve a cartelized capitalism—the System—seen as endlessly hungry for natural resources and development and powers in an ever-expanding military-industrial complex. Individuals, populations, nations, and cartels *all* serve techno-scientific militarism. Once that historical process has reached critical mass, it is too late. No hods-full of cocaine with which to zap *this* giant adenoid!

In *Gravity's Rainbow*, Pynchon begins working that motif in the earliest pages, keeps it running throughout the novel's episodes, then brings it to a brilliant fulfillment at the end. In the ironically titled "Chase Music" interlude, the narrator imagines Sir Denis Nayland Smith of Sax Rohmer's Fu Manchu novels arriving, "my God, too late" to thwart a looming world crisis. Similarly, "Superman will swoop boots-first into a deserted clearing" where v-2 rockets were launched—but too late. Same for novelist Raymond Chandler's detective hero, Philip Marlowe, who, realizing his belatedness, will reach "by reflex for the pint of rye in his suit pocket, and feel homesick for the lace-work balconies of the Bradbury Building" where he rented an office. Comic book hero Sub-Mariner will have "battery trouble" and arrive too late; so will Plastic Man, and ABC Radio's Lone Ranger, whose belated arrival finds "his young friend, innocent Dan, swinging from a tree limb by a broken neck." For all of them, the narrator concludes, "'Too late' was never in their programming." But now, in the new age of rocket cosmology, as Superman explains it to young newshound Jimmy, heroes like himself "will go on, kicked upstairs to oversee the development of bright new middle-line personnel, and they will watch their system falling apart." They will "call it cancer," he tells Jimmy, and people "won't know what things are coming to, or what's the meaning of it all."[8] These are not the end times. They are middle times, for "middle-line personnel" like us. They are times, then, of unknowing or institutionalized ignorance to which the old words, old plots, don't apply. It is too late for adventure tales, detective stories, westerns, action hero and superhero yarns, romantic comedies, romances of nation building and science, and perhaps for storytelling in general. *Gravity's Rainbow* will not supply a name for this condition; Pynchon's readers would soon enough draft his novel into the service of postmodernism. In any case the condition's governing spirits would seem to be Dominus Blicero and Domina Nocturna.

We take that dark view of technology and capital and war as the deeply cynical recognition that germinated *Gravity's Rainbow*. The novel imagines no way out from under the dominion of that trinity—what Ginsberg, in "Howl," gathered around the name Moloch. And it presents that dark cul-de-sac by innovating on the conventions of realist fiction for which Pynchon, in that June 1963 letter to Kirk and Faith Sale, considered himself rather inadequately equipped. In the manuscript that became *Gravity's Rainbow* he surely did not write the "traditional realist kind" of novel, but his capacities as a "surrealist, pornographer, word engineer," *and* historical thinker give this novel a certain "can't-put-it-downness," however dark and cynical.

Finally, if one wants a name or definition or at least a demonstration of this new world and its ignorant ways of knowing, think of it as a condition comparable to "riding across the country in a bus driven by a maniac bent on suicide." As in that hypothetical vignette, so in the novel you *may* be free to smile at the driver's lame jokes, hum along to his familiar, corny songs, even amuse yourself at rest stops with other passengers "throwing down the swords and cups and trumps" of somebody's "oily and worn" tarot deck, because the driver—who could just as well be our narrator on this novelistic bus ride—has got you covered; he'll make sure you get back aboard after the card games.[9] There, check, is your name on the passenger manifest! For this is a one-way ride and you're on it to the bitter end. You still cannot wholly answer the question Slothrop posed on the Rue Rossini in Nice: "What's free?" But it's become clearer how and why your "chances for freedom" were never really chances. That too was a useful fantasy.

Notes

"What's Free?" (An Introduction)

1. *Gravity's Rainbow* (New York: Viking, 1973), 256. A word, also, on why we use endnotes rather than parenthetical page citations in this book. The first edition of *Gravity's Rainbow*, issued in hardcover and paperback (New York: Viking, 1973, 760 pp.), is the one scholars, including us, cite. Yet the Viking edition is rarely the one used by contemporary readers, who will need a bit of patience, perhaps an arithmetic scheme, to coordinate Viking page numbers with the different lengths of their editions: the Bantam paperback (1974, 887 pp.); Penguin Great Books of the Twentieth Century paperback (1987, 776 pp.); Penguin paperback (1995, 760 pp., and the only one paginated like the first edition); Penguin Classics paperback (2006, 784 pp.); and Penguin e-text (2012, 768 pp.). In these circumstances we decided on endnotes and less cluttered, more readable pages.

2. *Gravity's Rainbow*, 38.

3. Tony Tanner, *Thomas Pynchon* (London: Methuen, 1982), 75.

4. For the best poststructuralist study of Pynchon, see Hanjo Berressem, *Pynchon's Poetics: Interfacing Theory and Text* (Urbana: University of Illinois Press, 1993).

5. See David Chalmers, *And the Crooked Places Made Straight: The Struggle for Social Change in the 1960s* (Baltimore, Md.: Johns Hopkins University Press, 1991); Terry H. Anderson, *The Movement and the Sixties: Protest in America from Greensboro to Wounded Knee* (New York: Oxford University Press, 1995); Ian Lekus, "The Long Sixties," OAH *Magazine of History* 20.2 (2006): 32–38; and "Time Is an Ocean," the introductory statement of editors Michael Foley, John McMillian, and Jeremy Varon in their scholarly journal, *The Sixties: A Journal of History, Politics and Culture* 1.1 (2008): 1–7; they date the Long Sixties from 1954 to 1975.

6. In *Pynchon and the Political* (New York: Routledge, 2007), Samuel Thomas provides detailed readings of Pynchon's novels in context with the work of Frankfurt School theorists, including Marcuse and Arendt.

7. By "social death," sociologist Zygmunt Bauman means the ascription of non- or subhuman characteristics to groups as a means of discursively, legally, and governmentally dividing them from the social body, denying their rights and humanity—slavery and genocide being the main examples. See Bauman's *Modernity and the Holocaust* (Cambridge: Polity/Blackwell, 1990), and Orlando Patterson, *Slavery and Social Death: A Comparative Study* (Cambridge, Mass.: Harvard University Press, 1985).

8. George Levine and David Leverenz, "Introduction," in their *Mindful Pleasures: Essays on Thomas Pynchon* (Boston: Little, Brown, 1976), 3.

9. *Gravity's Rainbow*, 6–7, 10.

10. Ibid., 12.

11. Ibid., 14–16.

12. Ibid., 12.

13. Ibid., 71.

14. Ibid., 647–55.

15. Steven Weisenburger, *A Gravity's Rainbow Companion*, 2nd ed. (Athens: University of Georgia Press, 2006), 337.

16. *Gravity's Rainbow*, 640–47. The program ran each Saturday on most NBC affiliate TV stations. Pynchon riffs on the program's children, exclaiming, "W-well gee" (644) and "Jeepers" (645), common moments on each show, dedicated as they were to increasing American children's enthusiasm for science studies. See Joel Sternberg, "Watch Mr. Wizard," in *Encyclopedia of Television*, 2nd ed., ed. Horace Newcomb (New York: Museum of Broadcast Communications/Routledge, 2004), 5:2487–88.

17. *Gravity's Rainbow*, 655.

18. Ibid., 760, 64–65, 652.

19. Ibid., 590. Alan Wilde, *Horizons of Assent: Modernism, Postmodernism, and the Ironic Imagination* (Baltimore, Md.: Johns Hopkins University Press, 1981), 127–31.

20. *Gravity's Rainbow*, 355–56 (our ellipsis); Weisenburger, *Companion*, 10–11.

21. Khachig Tölölyan, "War as Background in *Gravity's Rainbow*," in *Approaches to Gravity's Rainbow*, ed. Charles Clerc (Columbus: Ohio State University Press, 1983), 31–67.

22. On such comparisons, see, for example, Peter L. Cooper, *Signs and Symptoms: Thomas Pynchon and the Contemporary World* (Berkeley: University of California Press, 1983), 40–41; Bill McCarron, "*Catch-22, Gravity's Rainbow*, and Lawlessness," *Oklahoma City University Law Review* 24 (1999): 665–80; and David Cowart, *Thomas Pynchon & the Dark Passages of History* (Athens: University of Georgia Press, 2011), 84, 200.

23. See Richard Poirier, "Rocket Power," *Saturday Review of the Arts*, March 1, 1973, 59–64, reprinted in *Pynchon: A Collection of Critical Essays*, ed. Edward Mendelson (Englewood Cliffs, N.J.: Prentice Hall, 1978), 167–78; Michael Wood, "Rocketing to the Apocalypse," *New York Review of Books*, March 22, 1973, 22–23; and *Gravity's Rainbow*, 616, 521.

24. Stefan Mattessich, *Lines of Flight: Discursive Time and Countercultural Desire in the Work of Thomas Pynchon* (Durham, N.C.: Duke University Press, 2002), 1–5.

25. See Molly Hite, "'Fun Actually Was Becoming Quite Subversive': Herbert Marcuse, the Yippies, and the Value System of *Gravity's Rainbow*," *Contemporary Literature* 51.4 (2010): 677–702; Hite, "Reading the Value System of *Gravity's Rainbow* with Marcuse, Freud, and the Yippies," in *Approaches to Teaching Pynchon's The Crying of Lot 49 and Other Works*, ed. Thomas H. Schaub (New York: Modern Language Association of America, 2008), 39–45; and Lawrence Wolfley, "Repression's Rainbow: The Presence of Norman O. Brown in Pynchon's Big Novel," PMLA 92.5 (1977): 873–89.

26. A word on our studied use of the word "bullshit" here and in what follows: we mean it in the sense set forward in the philosopher Harry Frankfurt's *On Bullshit* (Princeton, N.J.: Princeton University Press, 2005), a revision of his classic 1986 essay

in *Raritan*. Regarding "bullshit" as false claims advanced on behalf of selfish ends and typically using the persuasive forces of affect—e.g., nostalgia, sentimentalism, romanticism—Frankfurt argues that bullshit is pervasive in modern, media-driven societies. It is in fact "a greater enemy of the truth than lies are" (61). Satirizing modern bullshit is a key aspect of Pynchon's anti-romantic criticism in *Gravity's Rainbow*.

27. *Gravity's Rainbow*, 539.

28. For its thorough analyses of negative and positive liberty and the long history of liberal theory on the subject, we are indebted here and throughout to Cyrus R. K. Patell, *Negative Liberties: Morrison, Pynchon, and the Problem of Liberal Ideology* (Durham, N.C.: Duke University Press, 2001).

29. Pierre Bourdieu, *Masculine Domination*, trans. Richard Nice (1998; rpt., Stanford, Calif.: Stanford University Press, 2001); Giorgio Agamben, *Homo Sacer: Sovereign Power and Bare Life*, trans. Daniel Heller-Roazen (1995; rpt., Stanford, Calif.: Stanford University Press, 1998).

30. Orlando Patterson, *Freedom*, vol. 1: *Freedom in the Making of Western Culture* (New York: Basic, 1992), 10–12; Charles Mills, *The Racial Contract* (Ithaca, N.Y.: Cornell University Press, 1997), 16–17, 31–32.

31. See two essays by James Farr, "'So Vile and Miserable an Estate': The Problem of Slavery in Locke's Political Thought," *Political Theory* 14.2 (1986): 263–89, and "Locke, Natural Law, and New World Slavery," *Political Theory* 36.4 (2008): 495–522. Also helpful: Martin Cohen, "John Locke Invents the Slave Trade," in his *Philosophical Tales* (New York: Wiley-Blackwell, 2008), 99–106.

32. *Gravity's Rainbow*, 47–48, 168–69, 97, 548, 414, 455.

33. In late November 1962 Pynchon wrote to Faith Sale that his follow-up book was coming into form, but by March 1963 that project had clearly stalled or run off the tracks. Thomas Pynchon Collection, Harry Ransom Humanities Research Center, University of Texas, Austin, box 2, folder 1 ("Correspondence"), which includes six dated and addressed letters from Pynchon to the Sales and one undated, unaddressed letter. The dated letters (most of which top a thousand words) run from October 1, 1962, when *V.* was in press, to March 27, 1964, a year after the novel's publication.

34. On the poetics of suspense in realist fiction, see Tzvetan Todorov, "The Typology of Detective Fiction," in his *The Poetics of Prose*, trans. Richard Howard (Ithaca, N.Y.: Cornell University Press, 1977), 42–52. And while we are at it, let us recognize *The Crying of Lot 49* (1966) as Pynchon's first parody of detective/suspense plotting, as many scholars have noted, just as *Vineland* (1990) and especially *Inherent Vice* (2009) demonstrate his ongoing interest in using the form.

35. *Gravity's Rainbow*, 727. Also housed in the Thomas Pynchon Collection at the Ransom Library, in box 1, folder 1, is the unfinished script he and Kirk Sale began, in 1958, while both were still at Cornell, for "Minstral Island," a raunchy, libidinous musical farce about an IBM corporation bent on ruling America.

Part 1. Novel and Decade

1. Theodore Roszak, *The Making of a Counter Culture: Reflections on the Technocratic Society and Its Youthful Opposition* (Garden City, N.Y.: Doubleday, 1969), 10–12.

2. Michael Kazin, *American Dreamers: How the Left Changed a Nation* (New York: Knopf, 2012), 209–50. See also David Chalmers, *And the Crooked Places Made Straight: The Struggle for Social Change in the 1960s* (Baltimore, Md.: Johns Hopkins University Press, 1991), 88–100.

3. Kazin, *American Dreamers*, 215.

4. Eric Meyer, "Oppositional Discourses, Unnatural Practices: *Gravity's* History and 'The 60s,'" *Pynchon Notes* 24–25 (1989): 81–104; Frederick Ashe, "Anachronism Intended: *Gravity's Rainbow* in the Sociopolitical Sixties," *Pynchon Notes* 28–29 (1991): 59–75.

5. Jeffrey Baker, "A Democratic Pynchon: Counterculture, Counterforce, and Participatory Democracy," *Pynchon Notes* 32–33 (1993): 99–131, quote on 102; and Baker, "Amerikkka über Alles: German Nationalism, American Imperialism, and the 1960s Antiwar Movement in *Gravity's Rainbow*," *Critique* 40.4 (1999): 323–41. See also Tom Schaub's useful work on Pynchon's environmentalism and references to the work of Rachel Carson and Barry Commoner in "The Environmental Pynchon: *Gravity's Rainbow* and the Ecological Context," *Pynchon Notes* 42–43 (1998): 59–72.

Chapter 1. Fromm and the Neo-Freudian Library

1. *Gravity's Rainbow*, 207, 28, 364, 555.

2. Ibid., 25.

3. Ibid., 378.

4. See Thomas Moore, *The Style of Connectedness: Gravity's Rainbow and Thomas Pynchon* (Columbia: University of Missouri Press, 1987); Ralph Schroeder, "From Puritanism to Paranoia: Trajectories of History in Weber and Pynchon," *Pynchon Notes* 26–27 (1990): 69–80; Richard Hofstadter, *The Paranoid Style in American Politics, and Other Essays* (New York: Knopf, 1965).

5. For references to the rationalization or "routinization of charisma," see *Gravity's Rainbow*, 81, 325, 464.

6. Erich Fromm, *Escape from Freedom* (1941; rpt., New York: Henry Holt, 1969), 255.

7. Ibid., 256–63.

8. Ibid., 269.

9. *Gravity's Rainbow*, 555–56.

10. Fromm, *Escape from Freedom*, 11.

11. Ibid., 15.

12. Ibid., 11, 15, 30–31, 37.

13. Ibid., 46–47.

14. Ibid., 63, 75, 84.

15. Ibid., 89, 90, 93.

16. Ibid., 188, 242, 25; John Krafft, "'And How Far-Fallen': Puritan Themes in *Gravity's Rainbow*," *Critique* 18.3 (1977): 55–73.

17. Fromm, *Escape from Freedom*, 207, 209, 219, 235; *Gravity's Rainbow*, 164.

18. *Gravity's Rainbow*, 405–6, 397, 420.

19. Ibid., 95–98, 107–8.

20. Ibid., 737.

21. Ibid.; Fromm, *Escape from Freedom*, 146–50.

Chapter 2. Marcuse: (No) Chances for Freedom in Advanced Industrial Society

1. Herbert Marcuse, "A Reply to Erich Fromm," *Dissent* 3.1 (January 1956): 81–83, quote on 82.

2. Herbert Marcuse, *Eros and Civilization: A Philosophical Inquiry into Freud* (1955; rpt., Boston: Beacon, 1966), 262, 264.

3. Marcuse, "A Reply," 83.

4. Philip Beidler, *Scriptures for a Generation: What We Were Reading in the 60s* (Athens: University of Georgia Press, 1994), 140.

5. Herbert Marcuse, *One-Dimensional Man* (Boston: Beacon, 1964), 257.

6. Molly Hite, "Reading the Value System of *Gravity's Rainbow* with Marcuse, Freud, and the Yippies," in *Approaches to Teaching Pynchon's The Crying of Lot 49 and Other Works*, ed. Thomas H. Schaub (New York: Modern Language Association of America, 2008), 41, 43; Hite, "'Fun Actually Was Becoming Quite Subversive': Herbert Marcuse, the Yippies, and the Value System of *Gravity's Rainbow*," *Contemporary Literature* 51.4 (2010): 677–702. Precursor essays to Hite's work include Joseph Slade, "Religion, Psychology, Sex and Love in *Gravity's Rainbow*," in *Approaches to Gravity's Rainbow*, ed. Charles Clerc (Columbus: Ohio State University Press, 1983), 153–98; and Nadine Attewell, "'Bouncy Little Tunes': Nostalgia, Sentimentality, and Narrative in *Gravity's Rainbow*," *Contemporary Literature* 45.1 (2004): 22–48. See also Fromm, *Escape from Freedom* (1941; rpt., New York: Henry Holt, 1969), xv; and Marcuse, *Eros and Civilization*, 45.

7. See also Luc Herman, "Antwerp and the Representation of the Holocaust in *Gravity's Rainbow*," in *Approaches to Teaching Pynchon's The Crying of Lot 49 and Other Works*, ed. Thomas H. Schaub (New York: Modern Language Association of America, 2008), 106–13; and Dale Carter, *The Final Frontier: The Rise and Fall of the American Rocket State* (London: Verso, 1988), for his analysis of the association between German and American rocket technologies.

8. See Hite, "Reading the Value System," 43; Hite, "Fun Actually," 678; and *Gravity's Rainbow*, 727.

9. *Gravity's Rainbow*, 747, 219, 671 (our ellipses); Hite, "Fun Actually," 687–89.

10. Hite, "Fun Actually," 691. Hite works here with a passage (*Gravity's Rainbow*, 720) in which Geli Tripping (and not Blicero!) offers the framing perspective, and in which Pan is the mythological figure of choice. Titans also appear elsewhere in *Gravity's Rainbow* (296, 330, 708), and they do not have a univocal meaning in the book.

11. *Gravity's Rainbow*, 749.

12. Ibid., 270.

13. Ibid., 681.

14. For the trial cover, see Clifford Mead, *Thomas Pynchon: A Bibliography of Primary and Secondary Materials* (Elmwood Park, Ill.: Dalkey Archive Press, 1989), 11; and for the first mention of the original title, see W. T. Lhamon, "The Most Irrespon-

sible Bastard," *New Republic* 168 (April 14, 1973): 27. See also *Gravity's Rainbow*, 747.

15. Hite, "Fun Actually," 691.

16. Ibid., 692.

17. Marcuse, *Eros and Civilization*, 168, 144.

18. *Gravity's Rainbow*, 737.

19. Hite, "Fun Actually," 696.

20. Ibid., 698; Kathryn Hume, *Pynchon's Mythography: An Approach to Gravity's Rainbow* (Carbondale: Southern Illinois University Press, 1987), 168–75.

21. Hite, "Fun Actually," 694–98; *Gravity's Rainbow*, 737, 622.

22. Marcuse, *Eros and Civilization*, 164, 170, 208–9.

23. Ibid., 90–91.

24. Hite, "Fun Actually," 699.

25. *Gravity's Rainbow*, 739.

26. Marcuse, *Eros and Civilization*, 145.

Chapter 3. Brown's Polymorphous Perversity and Marcuse's Repressive Tolerance

1. Herbert Marcuse, "Love Mystified: A Critique of Norman O. Brown," *Commentary* 43.2 (February 1967): 71–75; Norman O. Brown, "A Reply to Herbert Marcuse," *Commentary* 43.3 (March 1967): 83–84.

2. Lawrence Wolfley, "Repression's Rainbow: The Presence of Norman O. Brown in Pynchon's Big Novel," PMLA 92.5 (1977): 873–89, quotes on 874–76.

3. Ibid., 878 and (quoting Brown) 879.

4. *Gravity's Rainbow*, 56.

5. Ibid., 216–17; Brown quoted in Wolfley, "Repression's Rainbow," 883.

6. *Gravity's Rainbow*, 676, 684.

7. Herbert Marcuse, *One-Dimensional Man* (Boston: Beacon, 1964), 248, 247.

8. Ibid., 250.

9. Ibid., 254; and Toon Staes, "'When You Come to a Fork in the Road'—Marcuse, Intellectual Subversion and Negative Thought in *Gravity's Rainbow* and *Against the Day*," in *Against the Grain: Reading Pynchon's Counternarratives*, ed. Sascha Pöhlmann (Amsterdam: Rodopi, 2010), 97–111, quote on 99.

10. Herbert Marcuse, "Repressive Tolerance," in *A Critique of Pure Tolerance*, ed. Robert Paul Wolff, Barrington Moore Jr., and Herbert Marcuse (Boston: Beacon, 1965), 81–123, quote on 121–22.

11. Staes, "When You," 97; Marcuse, "Repressive Tolerance," 95–96, 113.

12. Luc Herman and Bart Vervaeck, "Didn't Know Any Better: Race and Unreliable Narration in 'Low-lands' by Thomas Pynchon," in *Narrative Unreliability in the Twentieth-Century First-Person Novel*, ed. Elke D'Hoker and Gunther Martens (Berlin: Walter de Gruyter, 2008), 229–46.

13. For the ad, see *Ramparts* 6.7 (February 1968): 60–61; for writers on this list, see Natalie Robbins, *Alien Ink: The FBI's War on Freedom of Expression* (New York: William Morrow, 1992), 409–12.

14. *Gravity's Rainbow*, 712.

1. *Stanley v. Georgia* 394 U.S. 557 (1969); Wesley R. Asinof, *Brief for the Appellant on the Merits, Robert E. Stanley, Appellant, v. the State of Georgia, Appellee* (October 1968).

2. *Gravity's Rainbow*, 232.

3. Charles Rembar, *The End of Obscenity: The Trials of Lady Chatterley, Tropic of Cancer, and Fanny Hill* (New York: Random House, 1968); Christopher M. Fairman, *Fuck: Word Taboo and Protecting Our First Amendment Liberties* (Naperville, Ill.: Sphinx, 2009), 69–113; Paul S. Boyer, *Purity in Print: Book Censorship in America from the Gilded Age to the Computer Age* (Madison: University of Wisconsin Press, 2002); Edward de Grazia, *Girls Lean Back Everywhere: The Law of Obscenity and the Assault on Genius* (New York: Random House, 1992).

4. Allen Ginsberg, "America," in *Howl and Other Poems* (San Francisco: City Lights, 1956), 39; Lenny Bruce, "The Fecalphiles," *Realist* 54 (November 1964): 1, 10–12. See also stand-up comedian George Carlin's "Filthy Words" monologue, included on his 1972 record album *Class Clown*, which brought a Federal Communications Commission filing against the Pacifica Radio network for broadcasting it; and finally, the test case in a landmark free speech ruling from the U.S. Supreme Court, *F.C.C. v. Pacifica Foundation* 438 U.S. 726 (1978). Carlin's seven prohibited words were fuck, motherfucker, shit, piss, cunt, cocksucker, and tits (the same words that led to Lenny Bruce's repeated arrests, though he raised the ante to nine, using ass and balls).

5. Ed Sanders, *Fug You: An Informal History of the Peace Eye Bookstore, the Fuck You Press, and Counterculture on the Lower East Side* (New York: Da Capo, 2011), 183–91.

6. See Geoffrey Rips, *Unamerican Activities: The Campaign against the Underground Press* (San Francisco: Pen American Center/City Lights, 1982), 55–138.

7. Osha Neumann, *Up Against the Wall Motherf**ker: A Memoir of the '60s, with Notes for Next Time* (New York: Seven Stories, 2008), 53, 69.

8. The *Realist* editor, Paul Krassner, recalled that in the early sixties he recognized the magazine's humor as rather toothless: "Then I began to play with satire and fact," and the writing took on a sharper political edge. See Laurence Leamer, *The Paper Revolutionaries: The Rise of the Underground Press* (New York: Simon and Schuster, 1972), 24–25. Memoirs from other underground press editors describe similar recognitions; see Sanders, *Fug You*, 36–37; and Abe Peck (editor of the *Seed*, whose 1970 circulation was over 40,000 copies), *Uncovering the Sixties: The Life and Times of the Underground Press* (New York: Pantheon, 1985).

9. Cover illustration, *Rat* (New York), February 7–13, 1970.

10. See "Underground Fuck," *San Francisco Express-Times*, December 11, 1968, 1; "Cartoon on Nixon Is Held Obscene, 3 Students Seized," *New York Times*, November 24, 1968; "Libel Trial Opens for 3 at U of H," *Hartford Courant*, December 3, 1969; "Student Convicted in Nixon Libel Case," *New York Times*, December 6, 1969; "Jack Hardy, Folk Singer and Keeper of the Tradition, Dies at 63," *New York Times*, March 12, 2012; Rips, *Unamerican Activities*, 92; John McMillian, *Smoking Type-*

writers: The Sixties Underground Press and the Rise of Alternative Media in America (New York: Oxford University Press, 2011), 127–28.

11. Terry H. Anderson, *The Movement and the Sixties: Protest in America from Greensboro to Wounded Knee* (New York: Oxford University Press, 1995), 209–27.

12. Leamer, *Paper Revolutionaries*, 125–31.

13. Rips, *Unamerican Activities*, 82; Peck, *Uncovering the Sixties*, 231.

14. Rips, *Unamerican Activities*, 71.

15. Ibid.

16. McMillian, *Smoking Typewriters*, 114–16, 126–30. See also Todd Gitlin, "The Underground Press and Its Cave-In," 19–30, as well as Rips's own account, "The Military Campaign," 139–52, both in Rips, *Unamerican Activities*.

17. Leamer, *Paper Revolutionaries*, 72–75; McMillian, *Smoking Typewriters*, 136–39.

18. Richard Nixon, "Statement about the Report of the Commission on Obscenity and Pornography," October 24, 1970, at the American Presidency Project, www .presidency.ucsb.edu/ws/index.phppid-2759 (accessed June 24, 2012).

19. "Black People," in *The Leroy Jones/Amiri Baraka Reader*, ed. William J. Harris (New York: Thunder's Mouth, 1991), 224. On the naming of UAWMF, see John Mc-Millian's interview, "Ben Morea—Garbage Guerilla," *New York Press*, June 5, 2005. On the collective's occupations and actions, see McMillian, *Smoking Typewriters*, 161, 237n61; and especially Neumann, *Up Against the Wall*.

20. Actor Peter Coyote provides a rich personal memoir of the Diggers in *Sleeping Where I Fall: A Chronicle* (Berkeley, Calif.: Counterpoint, 1998). See also Bradford D. Martin, *The Theater Is in the Street: Politics and Performance in Sixties America* (Amherst: University of Massachusetts Press, 2004), 86–124. On UAWMF actions, see Neumann, *Up Against the Wall*, 56–71; Todd Gitlin, *The Sixties: Years of Hope, Days of Rage* (New York: Bantam, 1987), 238–41; McMillian, "Ben Morea."

21. Peck, *Uncovering the Sixties*, 99–119, quotes on 103; Anderson, *The Movement and the Sixties*, 217–21; James Miller, *Democracy Is in the Streets: From Port Huron to the Siege of Chicago* (New York: Simon and Schuster, 1987); John Schultz, *The Chicago Conspiracy Trial* (1972; rev. ed., Chicago: University of Chicago Press, 2009).

22. "The Digger Papers," *Realist* 81 (August 1968): 5. See also Michael William Doyle, "Staging the Revolution: Guerilla Theater as a Countercultural Practice, 1965–1968," in *Imagine Nation: The American Counterculture of the 1960s and '70s*, ed. Peter Braunstein and Michael William Doyle (New York: Routledge, 2002), 85–86.

23. See *Black Mask* 4 (February–March 1967), 8 (October–November1967), 9 (January–February 1968), and 10 (April–May 1968), all reprinted in *Black Mask & Up Against the Wall Motherfucker: The Incomplete Works of Ron Hahne, Ben Morea, and the Black Mask Group* (Oakland, Calif.: PM Press, 2011). Similarly, former Motherfucker Osha Neumann thought that Hoffman and Rubin merely "played the revolution for laughs"; see Neumann, *Up Against the Wall*, 96.

24. *Gravity's Rainbow*, 711–17.

25. Pynchon, *Vineland* (New York: Little, Brown, 1990), 29.

26. N. Katherine Hayles, "'Who Was Saved?': Families, Snitches, and Recuperation in Pynchon's *Vineland*," *Critique* 31.2 (1990): 77.

27. Neumann, *Up Against the Wall*, 66, 73.

28. *Gravity's Rainbow*, 412.

29. "Digger Papers," 5, 7.

30. *Black Mask* 9 (January–February 1968), in *Black Mask & Up Against the Wall*, 68–69.

31. *Black Mask* 5 (April 1967), in *Black Mask & Up Against the Wall*, 33; and "Digger Papers," 5–6.

32. *I Aim at the Stars* (dir. J. Lee Thompson, Columbia Pictures, 1960); *Gravity's Rainbow*, 727.

33. *Black Mask* 1 (November 1966), in *Black Mask & Up Against the Wall*, 5; Michael J. Neufeld, *Von Braun: Dreamer of Space, Engineer of War* (New York: Vintage, 2007), 346–53; *Gravity's Rainbow*, 412–13.

34. "Dialectics of Liberation," *Realist* 81 (August 1968): 4–7; see also *Black Mask & Up Against the Wall*, 110–11.

35. Neumann, *Up Against the Wall*, 92–94.

36. William Shawcross, *Sideshow: Kissinger, Nixon, and the Destruction of Cambodia* (New York: Simon and Schuster, 1979); Michael Sherry, "The War Mentality in Triumph, 1966–1974," in his *In the Shadow of War: The United States since the 1930s* (New Haven, Conn.: Yale University Press, 1997), 283–337; Michelle Alexander, *The New Jim Crow: Mass Incarceration in the Age of Colorblindness* (New York: New Press, 2012), 41–47.

37. See "Revolution and Psychoanalysis and Revolution," *Black Mask* 9 (January–February 1968), in *Black Mask & Up Against the Wall*, 64–68; "Digger Papers," 4–5; Richard Hofstadter, *The Paranoid Style in American Politics, and Other Essays* (New York: Knopf, 1965); *Gravity's Rainbow*, 638. For an early study on the thematics of paranoia in the novel, see Mark Richard Siegel, *Pynchon: Creative Paranoia in Gravity's Rainbow* (Port Washington, N.Y.: Kennikat, 1978).

38. Vincent Bugliosi, *Helter Skelter: The True Story of the Manson Murders* (New York: Norton, 1974).

39. *Gravity's Rainbow*, 747.

40. "Dialectics of Liberation," 7.

41. *Gravity's Rainbow*, 28, 552–53.

42. Ibid., 755–56 (our ellipsis).

43. Seth Rosenfeld, *Subversives: The FBI's War on Student Radicals, and Reagan's Rise to Power* (New York: Farrar, Straus and Giroux, 2012), 70–72, 253–54.

44. News of Garden Plot first became public during the 1975 Church Committee hearings in the U.S. Congress; the committee was tasked with investigating abuses of executive authority during the Nixon administration. See Ron Ridenhour, "Garden Plot and the New Action Army," *Counterspy* 3.2 (Winter 1976): 23–58; Ron Ridenhour and Arthur Lubow, "Bringing the War Home," *New Times* (December 1975); Ronald J. Ostrow, "Army Drew Plan for Curbing Riots," *Los Angeles Times*, August 28, 1975, 1, 9. The declassified Garden Plot document is available on several online sites, such as the National Security Archive: http://nsarchive.files.wordpress.com /2010/09/garden-plot.pdf (accessed March 6, 2013).

45. Jerry Rubin and Abbie Hoffman, "Yippie Manifesto" (1968), in *Takin' It to the*

Streets: A Sixties Reader, ed. Alexander Bloom and Wini Brines (New York: Oxford University Press, 1996), 323.

46. On the "mineral consciousness" of rocks, see *Gravity's Rainbow*, 612.

47. Alan Nadel, *Containment Culture: American Narratives, Postmodernism, and the Atomic Age* (Durham, N.C.: Duke University Press, 1995).

48. On sixties environmentalist thought and practice as an aspect of movement politics, including the Yippies, see Adam Rome, "'Give Earth a Chance': The Environmental Movement and the Sixties," *Journal of American History* 90.2 (2003): 525–54; see also Anderson, *The Movement and the Sixties*, 344–50. On Pynchon's fictions in relation to that history, particularly chemist James Lovelock's 1973 Gaia theory, which understands the earth as a self-regulating system rather like an organism, see Thomas Schaub, "The Environmental Pynchon: *Gravity's Rainbow* and the Ecological Context," *Pynchon Notes* 42–43 (1998): 59–72.

49. *Gravity's Rainbow*, 740.

Chapter 5. The Law and the Liberation of Fantasy

1. On dissident satirical fiction during the Cold War, see Paul Maltby, *Dissident Postmodernism: Barthelme, Coover, Pynchon* (Philadelphia: University of Pennsylvania Press, 1991).

2. *Stanley v. Georgia* 394 U.S. 557 (1969), 561.

3. Ibid., 564–65 (our emphasis).

4. Ted Morgan, *Literary Outlaw: The Life and Times of William S. Burroughs* (New York: Norton, 2012), xiii, 557.

5. Ibid., 318–19. *Roth v. U.S.* (1957) provided the "redeeming social value" criterion for Hoffman's ruling, based on testimony from Mailer and Ginsberg, among other expert witnesses.

6. "Woolsey's Decision," appendix to *Ulysses* (New York: Random House, 1946), xi.

7. A short bibliography: Gérard Genette, *Narrative Discourse: An Essay on Method*, trans. Jane E. Lewin (1972; rpt., Ithaca, N.Y.: Cornell University Press, 1980); Dorrit Cohn, *Transparent Minds: Narrative Modes for Presenting Consciousness in Fiction* (Princeton, N.J.: Princeton University Press, 1978); Shlomith Rimmon-Kenan, *A Glance beyond Doubt: Narration, Representation, Subjectivity* (Columbus: Ohio State University Press, 1996); David Herman, ed., *The Emergence of Mind: Representations of Consciousness in Narrative Discourse in English* (Lincoln: University of Nebraska Press, 2011); Fredric Jameson, *The Political Unconscious: Narrative as a Socially Symbolic Act* (Ithaca, N.Y.: Cornell University Press, 1981); Hayden White, *The Content of the Form: Narrative Discourse and Historical Representation* (Baltimore, Md.: Johns Hopkins University Press, 1987).

8. James Joyce, *Ulysses* (New York: Random House, 1946), 358–60.

9. *Gravity's Rainbow*, 141–43.

10. Ibid., 120–24.

11. Ibid., 121.

12. Ibid., 127.

13. Ibid., 395, 461.

14. Ibid., 396.

15. Ibid., 469.

16. See Alec McHoul and David Wills, *Writing Pynchon: Strategies in Fictional Analysis* (Urbana: University of Illinois Press, 1990), 31–33, which rightly finds the narrative discourse indeterminate and resistant to closure; and Bernard Duyfhuizen's essay "'A Suspension Forever at the Hinge of Doubt': The Reader-Trap of Bianca in *Gravity's Rainbow*," *Postmodern Culture* 2.1 (1991), which goes still further—assuming the novelist's intention to mislead or entrap readers.

17. *Gravity's Rainbow*, 468–71.

18. Joyce, *Ulysses*, 516–23.

19. *Gravity's Rainbow*, 94–116.

20. On Pynchon's uses of Rilke, see Doug Haynes, "'Gravity Rushes through Him': *Volk* and Fetish in Pynchon's Rilke," *Modern Fiction Studies* 58.2 (2012): 308–33; on the *Wandervogel*, see Steven Weisenburger, *A Gravity's Rainbow Companion*, 2nd ed. (Athens: University of Georgia Press, 2006), 78.

21. Peter Kihss, "Pulitzer Jurors Dismayed on Pynchon," *New York Times*, May 8, 1974, 38.

22. *Gravity's Rainbow*, 228. There, Aaron Throwster worries, "If the old man gets moody at the wrong time the whole show can prang." Pointsman calmly assures him: "Brigadier Pudding will not go back on any of his commitments."

23. Ibid., 533.

24. Ibid., 615.

Part 2. Domination

1. *Gravity's Rainbow*, 47–49.

2. Ibid., 48–49.

3. Ibid., 51.

4. Ibid., 50–51.

5. Ibid., 53.

6. Brian McHale, "Second Person in *Gravity's Rainbow*," in his *Constructing Postmodernism* (New York: Routledge, 1992), 95–102.

7. See episode 4 of part 2 (especially 235–36) and the narrator's remarks on Pudding's death (533).

8. "'Foxes,' calls Spectro$_E$ across astral spaces, the word intended for Mr. Pointsman, who is not present." He is Spectro-sub-E because his voice is being channeled through Carroll Eventyr, Spectro having died in a v-2 strike days before. See *Gravity's Rainbow*, 138–39.

9. *Gravity's Rainbow*, 55, 399, 404, 413, 575, 583.

10. Ibid., 48, 737.

11. Ibid., 609.

12. Hannah Arendt, *The Human Condition* (Chicago: University of Chicago Press, 1958), 178–79, 176, 200.

13. See Arendt, *The Origins of Totalitarianism* (1951; rpt., New York: Schocken, 2004), especially her remarks on how the ss symbolically degraded Holocaust victims,

reducing them to "ghastly marionettes with human faces" or to Pavlov's dogs, put in "submission . . . to the most elementary reactions" (586–89), and the book's concluding chapter, "Ideology and Terror: A Novel Form of Government" (593–616).

14. See Pierre Bourdieu, *The Logic of Practice*, trans. Richard Nice (Stanford, Calif.: Stanford University Press, 1990), 127; Bourdieu, *Language and Symbolic Power*, trans. Gino Raymond and Matthew Adamson (Cambridge, Mass.: Harvard University Press, 1991), 43–66, 163–71; Bourdieu, *Masculine Domination*, trans. Richard Nice (Stanford, Calif.: Stanford University Press, 1999). See also Walter Benjamin, "Critique of Violence," in his *Reflections: Essays, Aphorisms, Autobiographical Writings*, trans. Edward Jephcott (New York: Schocken, 1978), 277–300.

15. James C. Scott, *Domination and the Arts of Resistance: Hidden Transcripts* (New Haven, Conn.: Yale University Press, 1990); Nancy Scheper-Hughes, "Introduction," in *Violence in War and Peace: An Anthology*, ed. Nancy Scheper-Hughes (New York: Wiley-Blackwell, 2003); Johann Galtung, "Cultural Violence," *Journal of Peace Research* 27.3 (1990): 291–305; Dominick LaCapra, "Toward a Critique of Violence," in his *History and Its Limits* (Ithaca, N.Y.: Cornell University Press, 2005); Judith Butler, "Violence, Mourning, Politics," in her *Precarious Life* (New York: Verso, 2004), 19–49; Slavoj Žižek, *Violence: Six Sideways Reflections* (New York: Picador, 2008), 13.

16. *Gravity's Rainbow*, 51–53, 48, 144, 16.

Chapter 6. Controlling Slothrop

1. *Gravity's Rainbow*, 10.
2. Ibid., 46.
3. Ibid., 84.
4. Ibid., 216.
5. Ibid., 84.
6. Ibid., 85.
7. Ibid., 82.
8. Ibid., 188.
9. Ibid., 272.
10. Ibid., 738.
11. Ibid., 211.
12. Ibid., 211, 227.
13. Ibid., 208.
14. Ibid., 283.
15. Ibid., 288.
16. Ibid., 75, 64.
17. Ibid., 25.
18. Ibid., 434.
19. Ibid., 490.
20. Ibid., 663.

21. See, for example, Alec McHoul and David Wills, *Writing Pynchon: Strategies in Fictional Analysis* (Urbana: University of Illinois Press, 1990), 24–45.

22. *Gravity's Rainbow*, 746.

23. Ibid., 739.

24. James W. Earl, "Freedom and Knowledge in the Zone," in *Approaches to Gravity's Rainbow*, ed. Charles Clerc (Columbus: Ohio State University Press, 1983), 229–50, quote on 231.

25. *Gravity's Rainbow*, 89; Earl, "Freedom and Knowledge," 234.

26. Alan Friedman, "Science and Technology," in *Approaches to Gravity's Rainbow*, ed. Charles Clerc (Columbus: Ohio State University Press, 1983), 69–102.

27. *Gravity's Rainbow*, 319–20.

28. Earl, "Freedom and Knowledge," 238; *Gravity's Rainbow*, 30.

29. *Gravity's Rainbow*, 391, 448.

30. Ibid., 159.

31. Ibid., 161, 164–65.

32. Ibid., 165.

33. Ibid., 249.

34. Ibid.

35. Ibid., 268.

36. Ibid., 488.

37. Carolyn Kellogg, "When Thomas Pynchon Is Just Tom: A Remarkable Collection Debuts," *Los Angeles Times*, May 5, 2011, http://latimesblogs.latimes.com/jacketcopy/2011/05/thomas-pynchon-tom-a-remarkable-collection.html (accessed August 14, 2012).

38. *Gravity's Rainbow*, 250.

39. Ibid., 250–51.

40. Ibid., 84.

41. Ibid., 83.

42. Ibid., 348.

43. Ibid., 490.

44. Ibid., 283–84.

45. Ibid., 284.

46. Ibid.

47. Ibid., 285.

48. Ibid., 738.

49. Ibid., 286.

50. Ibid.

51. Ibid., 306.

52. Ibid., 332.

53. Ibid., 581.

54. Ibid., 581–82.

55. Ibid., 587.

56. Ibid., 586.

57. Richard Hofstadter, *The Paranoid Style in American Politics, and Other Essays* (New York: Knopf, 1965).

58. *Gravity's Rainbow*, 587.

59. Ibid., 581.

60. Ibid., 580, 589.

61. Ibid., 630.

62. Ibid., 652 (our ellipsis).

63. Ibid., 654.

Chapter 7. War as a Cartel Project

1. *Gravity's Rainbow*, 250.

2. Ibid., 49.

3. Ibid., 474.

4. Ibid., 105 (the ellipsis is ours).

5. Ibid., 257.

6. Ibid., 348–49.

7. Ibid., 570.

8. Ibid., 326.

9. Ibid., 521 (the first ellipsis is ours).

10. Ibid., 81.

11. Ibid., 645 (our ellipsis).

12. Ibid., 119.

13. Ibid., 96.

14. Ibid., 102.

15. Ibid., 118.

16. Ibid., 42.

17. Ibid., 39; Ezra Pound, "Hugh Selwyn Mauberley (Life and Contacts)," in his *Personae* (New York: New Directions, 1926), 191.

18. *Gravity's Rainbow*, 126.

19. Ibid., 177.

20. Ibid., 628 (our ellipsis).

21. Ibid., 640.

22. Ibid., 128–31 (our ellipsis).

23. These terms, commonplace in German sociology of the early twentieth century, derived initially from Ferdinand Tönnies's 1887 analysis in *Gemeinschaft und Gesellschaft*, and from the work of Max Weber, Pynchon's likely source.

24. *Gravity's Rainbow*, 130–31.

25. Ibid., 133.

26. Ibid., 68–69.

27. *The Humble Advice of the Assembly of Divines, Now by Authority of Parliament Sitting at Westminster, Concerning the Confession of Faith* (London: Evan Tyler, 1647), 8.

28. Max Weber, *The Protestant Ethic and the Spirit of Capitalism*, trans. Talcott Parsons (1930; rpt., London: Routledge, 1992), 75, 58, 60, 65–66.

29. See Quentin Skinner, *The Foundations of Modern Political Thought* (New York: Cambridge University Press, 1978), 1:122–23; Edmund S. Morgan, *Inventing the People: The Rise of Popular Sovereignty in England and America* (New York: Norton, 1988).

30. George Berkeley, "Verses on the Prospect of Planting Arts and Learning in America," in his *A Miscellany: Containing Several Tracts on Various Subjects* (London, 1752), 186–87.

31. *Gravity's Rainbow*, 124.

32. Ibid., 314.

33. Ibid., 75.

34. Ibid., 645.

Chapter 8. Working for the Nazis

1. *Gravity's Rainbow*, 154–55.

2. Ibid., 162.

3. Ibid., 162–63, 465.

4. Ibid., 324.

5. Ibid., 161.

6. Ibid., 401.

7. Ibid., 405–6.

8. Ibid., 408.

9. Ibid., 410.

10. Ibid., 409, 414.

11. Ibid., 414.

12. Ibid., 417.

13. Ibid., 428.

14. Ibid., 420–21.

15. Ibid., 421.

16. Ibid., 424.

17. Ibid., 428.

18. Ibid., 430.

19. Ibid., 431.

20. Ibid., 292–93, 432, 673, 750–51.

21. Ibid., 98.

22. Ibid., 99. For analysis of the way Pynchon connects this attitude with the poetry by Rainer Maria Rilke, see Charles Hohmann, *Angel and Rocket: Pynchon's "Gravity's Rainbow" and "The Duino Elegies"* (Norderstedt: Books on Demand, 2009), a reprint of the second part of Hohmann's *Thomas Pynchon's "Gravity's Rainbow": A Study of Its Conceptual Structure and of Rilke's Influence* (New York: Peter Lang, 1986).

23. *Gravity's Rainbow*, 432.

24. Ibid.

25. Ibid. (both ellipses are ours).

26. Ibid., 433.

27. Siegfried Kracauer, *From Caligari to Hitler: A Psychological History of German Film* (Princeton, N.J.: Princeton University Press, 1947). Fromm's *Escape from Freedom* is one of Kracauer's sources (11).

28. *Gravity's Rainbow*, 578.

29. Ibid., 578–79 (our ellipses).

30. Ibid., 393–94.

31. Ibid., 397.

32. Ibid., 445.

33. Ibid., 466.

34. Ibid., 475.

35. Weisenburger, *A Gravity's Rainbow Companion*, 2nd ed. (Athens: University of Georgia Press, 2006), 264–65.

36. *Gravity's Rainbow*, 482.

37. Ibid., 487–88.

38. Ibid., 509, 670, 689.

39. Ibid., 161.

40. Ibid.

41. For a detailed genetic analysis of this chapter, see Luc Herman and John Krafft, "From the Ground Up: The Evolution of the South-West Africa Chapter in Pynchon's *V.*," *Contemporary Literature* 47.2 (2006): 261–88.

42. Thomas Pynchon, *V.* (1963; rpt., New York: Perennial, 1986), 230.

43. *Gravity's Rainbow*, 403.

44. Pynchon, *V.*, 255.

45. Ibid., 277 (our ellipsis).

46. *Gravity's Rainbow*, 408, 403–4 (our ellipsis).

47. Ibid., 404.

48. Ibid.

49. Ibid., 406, 403.

50. Ibid., 408–9.

51. Ibid., 509 (our ellipsis).

52. Ibid., 403.

53. See Victor Trimondi and Victoria Trimondi, *Hitler, Buddha, Krishna: Eine unheilige Allianz vom Dritten Reich bis heute* (Vienna: Überreuter, 2002).

54. Eugen Herrigel, *Zen in the Art of Archery: Training the Mind and Body to Become One*, trans. R. F. C. Hull (1948; rpt., London: Penguin, 2004).

55. *Gravity's Rainbow*, 403.

56. D. T. Suzuki in Herrigel, *Zen in the Art of Archery*, 6; the 1971 edition from Vintage is the likely source for *Gravity's Rainbow*.

57. All quotations in this paragraph are from *Gravity's Rainbow*, 453–54.

Chapter 9. The Logic of the Camp

1. *Gravity's Rainbow*, 3.

2. Ibid., 432.

3. Michael J. Neufeld, *Von Braun: Dreamer of Space, Engineer of War* (New York: Vintage, 2007), 333–53; *I Aim at the Stars* (dir. J. Lee Thompson, Columbia Pictures, 1960; DVD, 2002); *I Aim at the Stars: The Wernher von Braun Story* (New York: Dell, 1960); "Von Braun Film Banned," *Washington Post*, September 24, 1960; "Missile Film Picketed," *New York Times*, October 20, 1960; "Britons Protest Film," *New York Times*, November 25, 1960; "Cinema," *Time*, October 17, 1960.

4. Neufeld, *Von Braun*, 333; for details on von Braun's activities circa 1943–45, see 153–98. All quotations from *I Aim at the Stars* refer to the film, although some are also available, a few with slight variations, in the Dell text.

5. Specifically, ss records reveal that he joined on May 1, 1940, with membership number 185,068; see Neufeld, *Von Braun*, 120–22.

6. Ibid., 169–73, 176–82, 187–88.

7. Ibid., 192–95.

8. Ibid., 352.

9. Ibid., 353 (for the Teller–von Braun remark); and "Farewell Speech" of January 17, 1961, Dwight D. Eisenhower Presidential Library and Museum, Papers as President, Speech series, box 38, Final TV Talk, which is also available at http://www.eisenhower .archives.gov/research/online_documents/farewell_address.html.

10. Carolyn Kellogg, "When Thomas Pynchon Is Just Tom: A Remarkable Collection Debuts," *Los Angeles Times*, May 5, 2011, http://latimesblogs.latimes.com /jacketcopy/2011/05/thomas-pynchon-tom-a-remarkable-collection.html (accessed August 14, 2012); Adrian Wisnicki, "A Trove of New Works by Thomas Pynchon?: *Bomarc Service News* Rediscovered," *Pynchon Notes* 46–49 (2000–2001): 9–34.

11. Neil Sheehan, *A Fiery Peace in a Cold War: Bernard Schriever and the Ultimate Weapon* (New York: Random House, 2009), 413; *Bomarc Service News* 38 (September 1962): 3–5; Wisnicki, "A Trove," 19–20; Steven Weisenburger, *A Gravity's Rainbow Companion*, 2nd ed. (Athens: University of Georgia Press, 2006), 213.

12. Christopher A. Preble, *John F. Kennedy and the Missile Gap* (DeKalb: Northern Illinois University Press, 2004); James C. Dick, "The Strategic Arms Race of 1957–62: Who Opened a Missile Gap?" *Journal of Politics* 34.4 (1972): 1062–1110.

13. Qtd. in David Seed, *The Fictional Labyrinths of Thomas Pynchon* (Iowa City: University of Iowa Press, 1988), 240–41.

14. Pynchon, *V.*, 245.

15. Ibid., 267.

16. Benjamin Madley, "From Africa to Auschwitz: How German South West Africa Incubated Ideas and Methods Adopted and Developed by the Nazis in Eastern Europe," *European History Quarterly* 35.3 (2005): 429–64 (esp. 430–32).

17. Two essential historical treatments are Jens-Christian Wagner, *Produktion des Todes: Das KZ Mittelbau-Dora* (Göttingen: Wallstein, 2001); and Michael J. Neufeld, *The Rocket and the Reich: Peenemünde and the Coming of the Ballistic Missile Era* (New York: Free Press, 1995), esp. 197–238. For an interesting survey of Dora-related cultural materials, see Bruno Arich-Gerz, *Mittelbau-Dora: American and German Representations of a Nazi Concentration Camp* (Bielefeld: Transcript, 2009).

18. *Gravity's Rainbow*, 303 (our ellipsis).

19. Ibid., 110 (our emphasis).

20. Ibid., 317, 111.

21. Ibid., 289, 296.

22. Ibid., 453.

23. Ibid., 665.

24. Ibid.

25. Ibid., 666 (our ellipsis).

26. Ibid., 98–99.

27. Ibid., 549.

28. Alec McHoul and David Wills, *Writing Pynchon: Strategies in Fictional Analysis* (Urbana: University of Illinois Press, 1990), 53–61.

29. For another reading of the nationalities passage, see Sascha Pöhlmann, *Pynchon's Postnational Imagination* (Heidelberg: Winter, 2010), 276–359.

30. Hannah Arendt, *The Origins of Totalitarianism* (1951; rpt., New York: Schocken, 2004), 354.

31. *Gravity's Rainbow*, 3.

32. Ibid., 755–56 (our ellipses). On the Dora camp, see also Bruno Arich-Gerz and Luc Herman, "Darstellungen von Dora: Thomas Pynchons *Gravity's Rainbow* im Spannungsfeld von fiktionalen, historiographischen und errinerungsbasierten Repräsentationen des Konzentrationslagers Mittelbau-Dora," *Arcadia* 39.2 (2004): 390–409.

33. Stefan Mattessich, *Lines of Flight: Discursive Time and Countercultural Desire in the Work of Thomas Pynchon* (Durham, N.C.: Duke University Press, 2002), 159. Khachig Tölölyan was the first to treat the camps to any extent; see his "War as Background in *Gravity's Rainbow*," in *Approaches to Gravity's Rainbow*, ed. Charles Clerc (Columbus: Ohio State University Press, 1983). See also Arich-Gerz and Herman, "Darstellungen von Dora."

34. Giorgio Agamben, *Homo Sacer: Sovereign Power and Bare Life*, trans. Daniel Heller-Roazen (1995; rpt., Stanford, Calif.: Stanford University Press, 1998).

35. *Gravity's Rainbow*, 556.

36. See also the remarks of Der Springer, filmmaker Gerhardt von Göll, to the Argentine anarchist Squalidozzi: "I can take down your fences and your labyrinth walls. I can lead you back to the Garden you hardly remember" (ibid., 388).

37. Ibid., 290–91, 522.

38. Ibid., 289, 721 (our ellipsis).

39. Arendt, *Origins*, 569; Agamben, *Remnants of Auschwitz: The Witness and the Archive*, trans. Daniel Heller-Roazen (New York: Zone Books, 2002).

40. Agamben, *State of Exception*, trans. Kevin Attell (Chicago: University of Chicago Press, 2005), 6; *Gravity's Rainbow*, 472.

41. *Gravity's Rainbow*, 691.

42. Ibid., 340 (our ellipsis).

43. Ibid., 615.

44. Ibid., 285, 470, 615 (our ellipsis).

45. Ibid., 611–14.

46. Ibid., 80.

47. Harold Lasswell. "The Garrison State," *American Journal of Sociology* 46.4 (January 1941): 455–68, quote on 460.

48. *Gravity's Rainbow*, 349.

49. Ibid., 373, 450.

50. Arendt, *Origins*, 582, 569.

51. Ibid., 565, 587.

52. Ibid., 327.

53. Ibid., 616.

54. *Gravity's Rainbow*, 580.

55. Ralph Waldo Emerson, "The Sovereignty of Ethics," *North American Review* (May 1878), reprinted in Emerson, *Lectures and Biographical Sketches* (Boston: Houghton Mifflin, 1904), 175–206, quotes on 175, 179.

56. Qtd. in Agamben, *State of Exception*, 57.

Part 3. Freedom

1. T. S. Eliot, *The Waste Land*, ll. 54–55, in his *Selected Poems* (New York: Harcourt Brace Jovanovich, 1964), 52.

2. See *Gravity's Rainbow*, 738; A. E. Waite, *The Pictorial Key to the Tarot: Being Fragments of a Secret Tradition under the Veil of Divination* (London: Rider, 1910), 116–17, 285; Steven Weisenburger, *A Gravity's Rainbow Companion*, 2nd ed. (Athens: University of Georgia Press, 2006), 370–71, 373–75.

3. For Slothrop's tarot, see *Gravity's Rainbow*, 738.

4. Edward Sapir, *Language* (New York: Harcourt, Brace, and World, 1921), 5–6.

5. John Searle, *Speech Acts: An Essay in the Philosophy of Language* (Cambridge: Cambridge University Press, 1969), 16–18.

6. W. K. Wimsatt and M. Beardsley, "The Intentional Fallacy," *Sewanee Review* 54 (1946): 468–88.

7. W. B. Michaels and S. Knapp, "Against Theory," *Critical Inquiry* 8 (1982): 723–42.

8. For an analysis of the concept of intention vis-à-vis cognitive narratology, see David Herman, "Narrative Theory and the Intentional Stance," *Partial Answers* 6.2 (2008): 233–60. For a discussion of intention among narratologists, see David Herman et al., *Narrative Theory: Core Concepts and Critical Debates* (Columbus: Ohio State University Press, 2012).

9. A representative gathering: John W. Du Bois, "Meaning without Intention: Lessons from Divination," *International Pragmatics Association: Papers in Pragmatics* 1.2 (1987): 80–122; Harvey Whitehouse, *Arguments and Icons: Divergent Modes of Religiosity* (New York: Oxford University Press, 2000); David Brown, *Santeria Enthroned: Art, Ritual, and Innovation in Afro-Cuban Religion* (Chicago: University of Chicago Press, 2003); Martin Holbraad, "Definitive Evidence, from Cuban Gods," *Journal of the Royal Anthropological Institute* 14 (2008): 93–109; Holbraad, *Truth in Motion: The Recursive Anthropology of Cuban Divination* (Chicago: University of Chicago Press, 2012).

10. Holbraad, "Definitive Evidence," 96–97.

11. Victor Turner, *Ndembu Divination: Its Symbolism and Techniques* (Manchester, England: Manchester University Press, 1961), 17.

12. *Gravity's Rainbow*, 320.

13. Carl Schmitt, *Political Theology: Four Chapters on the Concept of Sovereignty*, trans. George Schwab (1922; rpt., Chicago: University of Chicago Press, 2005).

14. Holbraad, "Definitive Evidence," 100.

Chapter 10. Liberating Narration

1. *Gravity's Rainbow*, 29–33.

2. Ibid., 163–67.

3. Ibid., 145.

4. Ibid., 237–40.

5. Ibid., 166, 487–88.

6. Ibid., 153.

7. Ibid., 110–11.

8. Ibid., 92, 113.

9. Ibid., 53.

10. Ibid., 58.

11. Susan Sniader Lanser, *The Narrative Act: Point of View in Prose Fiction* (Princeton, N.J.: Princeton University Press, 1981), 133–48.

12. Samuli Hägg, *Narratologies of Gravity's Rainbow* (Joensuu: University of Joensuu Press, 2005), 230–35.

13. *Gravity's Rainbow*, 153.

14. Ibid., 615.

15. Ibid., 68.

16. Ibid., 167.

17. Dale Carter, *The Final Frontier: The Rise and Fall of the American Rocket State* (London: Verso, 1988), 202.

18. *Gravity's Rainbow*, 139.

19. Kurt Vonnegut, *Slaughterhouse-Five; or, The Children's Crusade* (New York: Delacorte, 1969), 63–64.

20. *Gravity's Rainbow*, 324.

21. Hayden White, *The Content of the Form: Narrative and Discourse in Historical Representation* (Baltimore, Md.: Johns Hopkins University Press, 1987), 5.

22. *Gravity's Rainbow*, 120.

23. Ibid., 147.

24. Ibid., 96.

25. Ibid., 465 (our ellipsis).

26. Ibid., 664 (our ellipsis).

27. Herman Melville, *Moby-Dick; or, The Whale* (1851; rpt., Berkeley: University of California Press, 1979), 125–26.

28. *Gravity's Rainbow*, 475–78.

29. Ibid., 753; Steven Weisenburger, *A Gravity's Rainbow Companion*, 2nd ed. (Athens: University of Georgia Press, 2006), 380.

30. Hägg, *Narratologies*, 62; see also Theodore D. Kharpertian, *A Hand to Turn the Time: The Menippean Satires of Thomas Pynchon* (Rutherford, N.J.: Associated University Presses, 1990), 138; Brian McHale, *Constructing Postmodernism* (New York: Routledge, 1992), 81.

31. Monika Fludernik, *The Fictions of Language and the Languages of Fiction: The Linguistic Representation of Speech and Consciousness* (New York: Routledge, 1993), 328–31; McHale, *Constructing Postmodernism*, 99–101.

32. Monika Fludernik, "New Wine in Old Bottles?: Voice, Focalization, and New Writing," *New Literary History* 32 (2001): 619–38; Michael L. Levine, "The Vagueness of Difference: You, the Reader, and the Dream of *Gravity's Rainbow*," *Pynchon Notes* 44–45 (1999): 117–31; Hägg, *Narratologies*, 134–44.

33. *Gravity's Rainbow*, 121, 124.

34. Ibid., 320, 414–15, 495, 664, 713.

35. Ibid., 583. In thinking through the dynamics of different narrative levels, we are also indebted to Fludernik, "New Wine in Old Bottles?"

36. *Gravity's Rainbow*, 739.

Chapter 11. Narrating Liberation

1. Steven Weisenburger, "Thomas Pynchon at Twenty-Two: A Recovered Autobiographical Sketch," *American Literature* 62.4 (1990): 692–97.

2. David Cowart, *Thomas Pynchon: The Art of Allusion* (Carbondale: Southern Illinois University Press, 1980), 86.

3. *Gravity's Rainbow*, 204.

4. Ibid., 248, 257, 253 (our ellipsis), 256.

5. Ibid., 273–74.

6. Ibid., 376, 711, 440 (our ellipsis).

7. Steven Weisenburger, *A Gravity's Rainbow Companion*, 2nd ed. (Athens: University of Georgia Press, 2006), 247–48.

8. *Gravity's Rainbow*, 440–41; Weisenburger, *Companion*, 248.

9. *Gravity's Rainbow*, 621–22, 711, 715–17.

10. Ibid., 622–23, 626, 742, 754, 745; Cowart, *Thomas Pynchon: The Art of Allusion*, 87.

11. Joseph Slade, *Thomas Pynchon* (New York: Warner, 1974), 213.

12. *Gravity's Rainbow*, 521.

13. Robert K. Merton, "Introduction," in Jacques Ellul, *The Technological Society*, trans. John Wilkinson (New York: Vintage, 1964), xxv.

14. *Gravity's Rainbow*, 520–21 (first ellipsis is ours).

15. Ibid., 520–21, 140.

16. Ibid., 539.

17. Ibid., 536–39.

18. Ibid., 544, 537–38; Teilhard de Chardin, *The Phenomenon of Man* (1955; rpt., London: Fontana, 1965).

19. *Gravity's Rainbow*, 539, 216–17.

20. Teilhard de Chardin, *Phenomenon*, 236–37.

21. Ibid.

22. On "critical mass" and the "Cosmic Bomb," see Weisenburger, *Companion*, 282–83.

23. *Gravity's Rainbow*, 11 (for the first use of "They" in this context), 715–16 (for the Krupp dinner), 540.

24. Ibid., 732, 724, 553–57.

25. Ibid., 323.

26. This chronology is set forward in episode 3 of part 3, which describes Enzian as a child who had "been walking for only a few months when his mother took him with her to join Samuel Maharero's great trek," in the closing months of 1904 (322–23). That chronology conflicts, however, with the omniscient narrator's statement,

just thirty pages later (351–52), that Enzian was conceived in December 1904 when his Russian father (Tchitcherine *père*) stopped with Admiral Rozhdestvenski's fleet "on route to the Pacific" theater of the Russo-Japanese war, where he would die "early in the evening of 27 May" 1905, a few months before Enzian's birth to his Herero mother. The two calendars simply do not align (an erratum, perhaps).

27. E. D. Morel, *Horror on the Rhine* (London: Union of Democratic Control, 1920); Weisenburger, *Companion*, 194–20. Since the most recent edition of the *Companion* was readied for publication, still more work has surfaced. See, for example, Tina M. Campt, *Other Germans: Black Germans and the Politics of Race in the Third Reich* (Ann Arbor: University of Michigan Press, 2004); Raffael Scheck, *Hitler's African Victims: The German Army Massacres of Black French Soldiers in 1940* (New York: Cambridge University Press, 2006), which is useful for general context and for a thorough bibliography; and a hard-to-find study by Dag Henrichsen and Andreas Selmeci, *Das Schwarzkommando: Thomas Pynchon und die Geschichte der Herero* (Darmstadt: Aisthesis, 1995), which is sourced to valuable primary materials in German archives and to other scholarly essays.

28. *Gravity's Rainbow*, 732.

29. Ibid., 147.

30. Ibid., 74, 276, 327.

31. Ibid., 112–13, 75, 64–65, 69.

32. See Clifton Crais and Pamela Scully, *Sara Baartman and the Hottentot Venus: A Ghost Story and a Biography* (Princeton, N.J.: Princeton University Press, 2009).

33. Luc Herman and John Krafft, "Race in Early Pynchon: Rewriting Sphere in *V.*," *Critique* 52.1 (2011): 17–29, quote on 18.

34. *Gravity's Rainbow*, 57, 727–28; "Two Year Manhunt Led to Killing," *New York Times*, September 30, 2011, 1, 12.

Chapter 12. Tyrone Slothrop's "Fuck You!"

1. *Gravity's Rainbow*, 391.

2. Ibid., 746.

3. Scott Sanders, "Pynchon's Paranoid History," in *Mindful Pleasures: Essays on Thomas Pynchon,* ed. George Levine and David Leverenz (Boston: Little, Brown, 1976), 177–92; Maureen Quilligan, *The Language of Allegory: Defining the Genre* (Ithaca, N.Y.: Cornell University Press, 1979), 274; Louis Mackey, "Paranoia, Pynchon, and Preterition," *SubStance* 30 (1981): 25–27; Harold Bloom, *Thomas Pynchon* (London: Methuen, 1982), 74–91; Katherine Hayles, *The Cosmic Web: Scientific Field Models and Literary Strategies in the 20th Century* (Ithaca, N.Y.: Cornell University Press, 1984), 187–88; Stefan Mattessich, *Lines of Flight: Discursive Time and Countercultural Desire in the Work of Thomas Pynchon* (Durham, N.C.: Duke University Press, 2002), 200; Luc Herman et al., "Pynchon, Postmodernism, and Quantification: An Empirical Content Analysis of Thomas Pynchon's *Gravity's Rainbow*," *Language and Literature* 12.1 (2003): 27–41, quote on 37–38.

4. *Gravity's Rainbow*, 203–5.

5. Ibid., 216, 255, 605.

6. Ibid., 266, 207, 208–9.

7. Ibid., 241, 272–73.

8. Ibid., 681, 688.

9. Ibid., 118, 741.

10. Ibid., 206, 516, 644; Jesse Sheidlower, *The F Word* (New York: Oxford University Press, 2009), 99–101, 154–57.

11. See *Cohen v. California*, 403 U.S. 15 (1971), 19–21; Susan Balter-Reitz, "*Cohen v. California*," in *Free Speech on Trial*, ed. Richard A. Parker (Tuscaloosa: University of Alabama Press, 2002), 160–71; *Gravity's Rainbow*, 355–56.

12. *Gravity's Rainbow*, 334, 286.

13. *Cohen v. California*, 20.

14. J. D. Salinger, *The Catcher in the Rye* (Boston: Little, Brown, 1951), 201; Bill Morgan and Nancy J. Peters, eds., *"Howl" on Trial: The Battle for Free Expression* (San Francisco: City Lights, 2006); Jonah Raskin, *Allen Ginsberg's "Howl" and the Making of the Beat Generation* (Berkeley: University of California Press, 2006); Allen Ginsberg, *Howl and Other Poems* (San Francisco: City Lights, 1956), 39.

15. See Terry H. Anderson, *The Movement and the Sixties: Protest in America from Greensboro to Wounded Knee* (New York: Oxford University Press, 1995), 101–9. On the Supreme Court and its backlogged docket of obscenity cases, see Edward de Grazia, *Girls Lean Back Everywhere: The Law of Obscenity and the Assault on Genius* (New York: Random House, 1992), 648–50.

16. John McMillian, *Smoking Typewriters: The Sixties Underground Press and the Rise of Alternative Media in America* (New York: Oxford University Press, 2011), 193; *Fuck You: A Magazine of the Arts* 8 (1963): 3; *Miller v. California*, 413 U.S. 15 (1973), 24.

17. Pynchon, "Nearer My Couch to Thee," *New York Times Book Review*, June 6, 1993, 2, 57; Walter Benjamin, *The Origin of German Tragic Drama*, trans. John Osborne (1928; rpt., New York: Verso, 2009), 150–51.

18. Gilles Deleuze, "'Bartleby'; or, The Formula," in his *Essays Critical and Clinical*, trans. Daniel W. Smith and Michael A. Greco (London: Verso, 1998); Giorgio Agamben, "Bartleby; or, On Contingency," in his *Potentialities: Collected Essays in Philosophy*, trans. Daniel Heller-Roazen (Stanford, Calif.: Stanford University Press, 1999), 243–71; Jacques Rancière, "Deleuze, Bartleby, and the Literary Formula," in his *The Flesh of Words: The Politics of Writing*, trans. Charlotte Mandell (Stanford, Calif.: Stanford University Press, 2004), 146–69. Additionally, see Michael Hardt and Antonio Negri, "Imperial Sovereignty," in their *Empire* (Cambridge, Mass.: Harvard University Press, 2000), 183–204; Jessica Whyte, "'I Would Prefer Not To': Giorgio Agamben, Bartleby, and the Potentiality of Law," *Law and Critique* 20.3 (2009): 309–24.

19. See Quang Phuc Dong [James D. McCawley], "English Sentences without Overt Grammatical Subjects," in *Studies Out in Left Field: Defamatory Essays Presented to James D. McCawley*, ed. Arnold M. Zwicky et al. (Champaign, Ill.: Linguistic Research, 1971); John Lawler, "Memorial for James D. McCawley," *Language* 79.3 (2003): 614–25.

20. On this history and the numbers, see John Hagan, *Northern Passage: American Vietnam War Resisters in Canada* (Cambridge, Mass.: Harvard University Press, 2001).

21. *Gravity's Rainbow*, 246, 370, 742.

22. On Nalline, see Steven Weisenburger, *A Gravity's Rainbow Companion*, 2nd ed. (Athens: University of Georgia Press, 2006), 28.

23. This is Judith Butler's point in a strong analysis whose goal is to reassert the claims of nonviolent resistance against imperial domination. After examining psychological and moral claims of nonviolence on us, she stakes a simple, muscular claim of her own: that, when expressed as or from a recognition of one's wounding, and when correlated with a refusal to participate in the (re)iteration of wounding in a potentially endless chain of harm, one at least has access to, and the right to utter, the "carefully crafted *Fuck You!*"; see Butler, "The Claim of Non-Violence," in her *Frames of War: When Is Life Grievable?* (New York: Verso, 2009), 180.

"Too Late" (A Conclusion)

1. Pynchon, *Vineland* (New York: Penguin, 1990), 194 (our ellipsis).

2. *Gravity's Rainbow*, 388, 612–13.

3. Ibid., 524, 701, 628.

4. Ibid., 110, 757, 744, 755, 756.

5. See, for example, Michael Wood, "Rocketing to the Apocalypse," *New York Review of Books*, March 22, 1973, 22–23; Robert K. Morris, "Jumping Off the Golden Gate Bridge" (review of *Gravity's Rainbow*), *Nation*, July 16, 1973, 53–54; Lois Parkinson Zamora, "The Entropic End: Science and Eschatology in the Works of Thomas Pynchon," *Science/Technology in the Humanities* 3.1 (1980): 35–43; Donald Weber, "West, Pynchon, Mailer, and the Jeremiad Tradition," *South Atlantic Quarterly* 83 (1984): 259–68; Joseph Dewey, "Lessons in Love and Silence: *Gravity's Rainbow* and the Apocalypse in Gödel's Universe," in his *In a Dark Time: The Apocalyptic Temper in the American Novel of the Nuclear Age* (West Lafayette, Ind.: Purdue University Press, 1990), 118–48; Theodore D. Kharpertian, *A Hand to Turn the Time: The Menippean Satires of Thomas Pynchon* (Rutherford, N.J.: Associated University Presses, 1990), 108–13; David Robson, "Frye, Derrida, Pynchon, and the Apocalyptic Space of Postmodern Fiction," in *Postmodern Apocalypse: Theory and Cultural Practice at the End*, ed. Richard Dellamore (Philadelphia: University of Pennsylvania Press, 1995), 61–78.

6. This approach to Pynchon's fiction first surfaced in Catherine R. Stimpson's essay "Pre-Apocalyptic Atavism: Thomas Pynchon's Early Fiction," in *Mindful Pleasures: Essays on Thomas Pynchon*, ed. George Levine and David Leverenz (Boston: Little, Brown, 1976), 31–48. See also David Seed, *The Fictional Labyrinths of Thomas Pynchon* (Iowa City: University of Iowa Press, 1988), 179–97; Dewey, "Lessons in Love and Silence"; Kharpertian, *A Hand to Turn the Time*.

7. *Gravity's Rainbow*, 726.

8. Ibid., 751–52.

9. Ibid., 412.

Index

25; reading sexuality of, 78; and the rocket, 31, 32, 114–16, 118, 119, 125–26; sadomasochism, 3, 170; and the serial Ilses, 31, 32, 37, 116–18, 120; technocratic nomadism of, 100

Pökler, Ilse, 143, 159, 219

Pökler, Leni, 114, 115, 121, 143, 159, 219

Political Theology (Schmitt), 157

pornography, 54

positive liberty, 14–15, 31, 54, 198; viewed by Fromm, 26–27, 28, 33, 41

Pound, Ezra, 108–10

Power Elite, The (Mills), 58

Prentice, Geoffrey "Pirate," 6, 10, 32, 143, 219; and the Counterforce, 7, 190; and creative paranoia, 66; and domination, 7, 16; fantasist-surrogate abilities, 6–7, 160, 161, 165, 166, 172; and Father Rapier, 186–87, 190; and freedom, 8, 16; and narrative authority, 172

presses, underground, 53–54, 56, 205, 207, 229n8

Prettyplace, Mitchell, 172

Protestant Ethic and the Spirit of Capitalism, The (Weber), 25

Protestantism, 25, 111–12; and Fromm, 26, 28, 29–30. *See also* Calvinism; Christianity

Psychoanalysis and Religion (Fromm), 34

Psychopathia Sexualis (von Krafft-Ebing), 51

Public Burning, The (Coover), 72, 207

Pudding, Brigadier, 47, 80, 86, 101, 102, 217; coprophagia scene, 33, 87, 102, 233n22; reading sexuality of, 78, 79, 80

Puritans and Puritanism, 24–25, 28, 96, 111, 184, 216; and individualism, 111, 112

Putney Swope, 69

Puttenham, George, 168

Pynchon, Thomas, 13, 22, 44, 135, 176; and conventional fiction, 97, 220–21; criticism of, 97; essay on sloth, 207–8;

and the publishing industry, 48; race treated by, 196; Seattle years, 133, 134–35; traveling and writing, 1962–65, 16–18, 225n33, 225n35

race, 148, 196

racism: American, 195; German, 194–95

Ramparts magazine, 50, 62, 68

Rancière, Jacques, 208

rape, 76, 78, 80, 200; and Pointsman, 90, 192; and Slothrop, 80, 96, 195

Rapier, Father, 186, 187–88, 189–90, 191, 194, 198

Rathenau, Walther, 31, 99, 102, 103, 113, 120; séance scene, 159–60, 161, 166

Reagan, Ronald, 55, 207

realism, 18, 225n34

Realist, The, 53, 54, 58, 206, 229n8

Reformation, 28, 34

refugees, 128, 140–43, 145, 147, 149

Reich, Wilhelm, 58, 62

Rembar, Charles, 52

Remnants of Auschwitz (Agamben), 145–46

repression, 47, 49–50, 56, 88, 122; viewed by Brown, 44, 45; viewed by Fromm, 216; viewed by Marcuse, 38, 47, 48–49, 81, 109, 208, 216; viewed by the Left, 46

"Repressive Tolerance" (Marcuse), 48, 61

Revolution of Everyday Life (Vaneigem), 58

Rilke, Rainer Maria, 79, 119, 125, 145, 194

rocket. *See* v-2 rocket

Rockwell, George Lincoln, 207

Rohmer, Sax, 220

Rosenfeld, Seth, 68, 207

Rossini, Gioacchino, 38, 176, 177–78, 179, 180, 181

Roszak, Theodore, 21, 24, 43, 49

Roth v. U.S., 52

Rózsavölgyi, Dr., 107

Rubin, Jerry, 58–59, 60, 69, 230n23

Vaneigem, Raoul, 58
Vietnam War, 40, 50, 57, 60, 72, 147;
  expansion of, 68; fugitives from,
  209–10; and genocide, 135; Nixon's
  promise to end, 57; protests against,
  21, 40, 50, 60, 196, 204, 206
Vineland (Pynchon), 4, 50, 72, 215,
  225n33
violence, 88, 108; symbolic, 89–90
Violence (Žižek), 90
von Braun, Maria, 129, 130, 131, 133
von Braun, Wernher, 119, 179, 219;
  epigraph, 101; film about (see I Aim
  at the Stars); missile builder and
  moon program direction for U.S., 36,
  63, 128–29; and the "too late" trope,
  217; viewed by Eisenhower, 134; war
  crimes, 38, 129–30, 131–33, 193
von Göll, Gerhardt, 97, 121, 146, 195,
  240n36
von Krafft-Ebing, Richard, 51
Vonnegut, Kurt, 13, 50, 137, 168
von Trotha, General, 124, 136, 145, 192
V-2 rocket, 13–14, 139, 189; against
  Antwerp, 214, 218; auditory paradox
  of, 2, 6; engine, 84; equality under,
  197, 198; and the freedom-domination
  dyad, 16, 181; and hysteron proteron,
  171; imaginary strike on reader, 85;
  and individual and social control, 61–
  62; and mis-knowing, 218–19; and
  the performance principle, 36; and
  Pökler, 31, 32, 114–16, 118, 119, 125–
  26; and the primacy of technology,
  181–84; Pynchon's first mention of,
  134; sexualization of, 114–15; and
  Slothrop, 2, 93, 95, 199, 202, 203;
  troping the arc of Gravity's Rainbow,
  36, 167–68; viewed by Pynchon, 18;
  and Zen teachings, 125–26

war, 220; cartelized, 108; critique of,
  in Gravity's Rainbow, 106–7; and

Emerson's balancing, 149–50; and
  technology, 185
Waste Land, The (Eliot), 10, 153, 186
Weather Underground, 55, 58, 61
Weber, Max, 26, 28, 110, 111, 236n23;
  and capitalism, 25, 30, 112;
  rationalization of charisma viewed
  by, 25, 107
Webern, Anton, 179, 181
Weissmann, Major. See Blicero,
  Dominus
White, Hayden, 169
Whitman, Walt, 110, 141
Why Are We in Vietnam? (Mailer), 174
Wiener, Norbert, 58, 62
Wilde, Alan, 11–12
Wills, David, 142
Wimpe, Verbindungsmann, 101, 106–7,
  148, 161
Wimsatt, W. K., 155
Wolfley, Lawrence, 44–46
Wood, James, 97
Wretched of the Earth, The (Fanon), 46
Wuxtry-Wuxtry, Mickey, 94, 102, 172

"Yippie Manifesto" (Rubin), 59, 70, 72
Yippies, 57–60, 67; analysis of the
  system, 63
Yoruba, 156, 157
Youth International Party. See Yippies
"Youth International Party Manifesto!,"
  68–69

Zanzel, John, 54
Zen, 125–27
Zen in the Art of Archery (Herrigel),
  125, 126
Zhlubb, Richard M., 67, 216, 217
Žižek, Slavoj, 90
Zone: in Gravity's Rainbow, 143, 144–45,
  146, 149, 150, 240n36
Zwölfkinder, 116, 117, 118, 120

4634217